Autoconf Reference Manual

A catalogue record for this book is available from the Hong Kong Public Libraries.

Published in Hong Kong by Samurai Media Limited.

Email: info@samuraimedia.org

ISBN 978-988-8381-43-2

Table of Contents

1 Introduction..................................... 1

2 The GNU Build System....................... 3
   2.1 Automake... 3
   2.2 Gnulib.. 3
   2.3 Libtool... 4
   2.4 Pointers.. 4

3 Making configure Scripts.................... 5
   3.1 Writing 'configure.ac'.................................... 6
      3.1.1 A Shell Script Compiler............................. 6
      3.1.2 The Autoconf Language............................... 7
      3.1.3 Standard 'configure.ac' Layout...................... 9
   3.2 Using autoscan to Create 'configure.ac'................. 10
   3.3 Using ifnames to List Conditionals...................... 11
   3.4 Using autoconf to Create configure..................... 11
   3.5 Using autoreconf to Update configure Scripts............ 13

4 Initialization and Output Files.............. 17
   4.1 Initializing configure.................................. 17
   4.2 Dealing with Autoconf versions......................... 18
   4.3 Notices in configure.................................... 18
   4.4 Finding configure Input................................. 19
   4.5 Outputting Files.. 20
   4.6 Performing Configuration Actions........................ 21
   4.7 Creating Configuration Files............................ 23
   4.8 Substitutions in Makefiles.............................. 23
      4.8.1 Preset Output Variables............................ 23
      4.8.2 Installation Directory Variables................... 27
      4.8.3 Changed Directory Variables........................ 30
      4.8.4 Build Directories.................................. 31
      4.8.5 Automatic Remaking................................. 32
   4.9 Configuration Header Files.............................. 33
      4.9.1 Configuration Header Templates..................... 34
      4.9.2 Using autoheader to Create 'config.h.in'........... 35
      4.9.3 Autoheader Macros.................................. 36
   4.10 Running Arbitrary Configuration Commands............... 37
   4.11 Creating Configuration Links........................... 38
   4.12 Configuring Other Packages in Subdirectories.......... 38
   4.13 Default Prefix... 39

5   Existing Tests..................................... **41**

   5.1   Common Behavior 41

      5.1.1 Standard Symbols... 41

      5.1.2 Default Includes... 41

   5.2   Alternative Programs 43

      5.2.1 Particular Program Checks............................ 43

      5.2.2 Generic Program and File Checks 46

   5.3   Files.. 49

   5.4   Library Files... 49

   5.5   Library Functions...................................... 50

      5.5.1 Portability of C Functions............................ 50

      5.5.2 Particular Function Checks............................ 53

      5.5.3 Generic Function Checks 61

   5.6   Header Files 63

      5.6.1 Portability of Headers 63

      5.6.2 Particular Header Checks............................. 65

      5.6.3 Generic Header Checks.............................. 70

   5.7   Declarations 71

      5.7.1 Particular Declaration Checks 71

      5.7.2 Generic Declaration Checks 71

   5.8   Structures 73

      5.8.1 Particular Structure Checks 73

      5.8.2 Generic Structure Checks............................ 74

   5.9   Types... 74

      5.9.1 Particular Type Checks 74

      5.9.2 Generic Type Checks................................ 77

   5.10 Compilers and Preprocessors 78

      5.10.1 Specific Compiler Characteristics 78

      5.10.2 Generic Compiler Characteristics 78

      5.10.3 C Compiler Characteristics 80

      5.10.4 C++ Compiler Characteristics 86

      5.10.5 Objective C Compiler Characteristics.................... 86

      5.10.6 Objective C++ Compiler Characteristics 87

      5.10.7 Erlang Compiler and Interpreter Characteristics 87

      5.10.8 Fortran Compiler Characteristics 88

      5.10.9 Go Compiler Characteristics........................... 96

   5.11 System Services... 96

   5.12 Posix Variants 98

   5.13 Erlang Libraries 98

6   Writing Tests 101

  6.1 Language Choice 101
  6.2 Writing Test Programs 103
      6.2.1 Guidelines for Test Programs 103
      6.2.2 Test Functions 103
      6.2.3 Generating Sources 104
  6.3 Running the Preprocessor 107
  6.4 Running the Compiler 108
  6.5 Running the Linker 108
  6.6 Checking Runtime Behavior 109
  6.7 Systemology 111
  6.8 Multiple Cases 111

7   Results of Tests 113

  7.1 Defining C Preprocessor Symbols 113
  7.2 Setting Output Variables 114
  7.3 Special Characters in Output Variables 116
  7.4 Caching Results 117
      7.4.1 Cache Variable Names 118
      7.4.2 Cache Files 119
      7.4.3 Cache Checkpointing 119
  7.5 Printing Messages 120

8   Programming in M4 123

  8.1 M4 Quotation 123
      8.1.1 Active Characters 123
      8.1.2 One Macro Call 124
      8.1.3 Quoting and Parameters 125
      8.1.4 Quotation and Nested Macros 126
      8.1.5 `changequote` is Evil 127
      8.1.6 Quadrigraphs 128
      8.1.7 Dealing with unbalanced parentheses 129
      8.1.8 Quotation Rule Of Thumb 131
  8.2 Using `autom4te` 132
      8.2.1 Invoking `autom4te` 132
      8.2.2 Customizing `autom4te` 136
  8.3 Programming in M4sugar 137
      8.3.1 Redefined M4 Macros 137
      8.3.2 Diagnostic messages from M4sugar 140
      8.3.3 Diversion support 141
      8.3.4 Conditional constructs 144
      8.3.5 Looping constructs 147
      8.3.6 Evaluation Macros 151
      8.3.7 String manipulation in M4 155
      8.3.8 Arithmetic computation in M4 158
      8.3.9 Set manipulation in M4 160
      8.3.10 Forbidden Patterns 164
  8.4 Debugging via autom4te 164

9   Programming in M4sh...................... 167
- 9.1   Common Shell Constructs............................. 167
- 9.2   Support for indirect variable names 170
- 9.3   Initialization Macros.. 173
- 9.4   File Descriptor Macros...................................... 175

10   Writing Autoconf Macros.................. 177
- 10.1   Macro Definitions... 177
- 10.2   Macro Names... 178
- 10.3   Reporting Messages... 179
- 10.4   Dependencies Between Macros 180
  - 10.4.1   Prerequisite Macros.................................. 180
  - 10.4.2   Suggested Ordering 183
  - 10.4.3   One-Shot Macros 183
- 10.5   Obsoleting Macros.. 184
- 10.6   Coding Style.. 184

11   Portable Shell Programming.............. 189
- 11.1   Shellology 190
- 11.2   Invoking the Shell 191
- 11.3   Here-Documents 192
- 11.4   File Descriptors... 193
- 11.5   Signal Handling... 196
- 11.6   File System Conventions 199
- 11.7   Shell Pattern Matching 201
- 11.8   Shell Substitutions... 201
- 11.9   Assignments... 209
- 11.10   Parentheses in Shell Scripts.............................. 210
- 11.11   Slashes in Shell Scripts 210
- 11.12   Special Shell Variables.................................... 211
- 11.13   Shell Functions... 218
- 11.14   Limitations of Shell Builtins 220
- 11.15   Limitations of Usual Tools 235

12   Portable Make Programming.............. 253
- 12.1   `$<` in Ordinary Make Rules 253
- 12.2   Failure in Make Rules...................................... 253
- 12.3   Special Characters in Make Macro Names.................. 253
- 12.4   Backslash-Newline Before Empty Lines..................... 254
- 12.5   Backslash-Newline in Make Comments 254
- 12.6   Long Lines in Makefiles 255
- 12.7   `make macro=value` and Submakes........................... 255
- 12.8   The Make Macro MAKEFLAGS 256
- 12.9   The Make Macro `SHELL`..................................... 256
- 12.10   Parallel Make.. 257
- 12.11   Comments in Make Rules................................. 259
- 12.12   Newlines in Make Rules................................... 260

12.13	Comments in Make Macros	260
12.14	Trailing whitespace in Make Macros	261
12.15	Command-line Macros and whitespace	261
12.16	The 'obj/' Subdirectory and Make	261
12.17	Exit Status of make -k	262
12.18	VPATH and Make	262
12.18.1	Variables listed in VPATH	262
12.18.2	VPATH and Double-colon Rules	262
12.18.3	$< Not Supported in Explicit Rules	262
12.18.4	Automatic Rule Rewriting	263
12.18.5	Tru64 make Creates Prerequisite Directories Magically	266
12.18.6	Make Target Lookup	266
12.19	Single Suffix Rules and Separated Dependencies	269
12.20	Timestamp Resolution and Make	269

13 Portable C and C++ Programming 271

13.1	Varieties of Unportability	271
13.2	Integer Overflow	272
13.2.1	Basics of Integer Overflow	272
13.2.2	Examples of Code Assuming Wraparound Overflow	272
13.2.3	Optimizations That Break Wraparound Arithmetic	274
13.2.4	Practical Advice for Signed Overflow Issues	275
13.2.5	Signed Integer Division and Integer Overflow	276
13.3	Preprocessor Arithmetic	276
13.4	Properties of Null Pointers	276
13.5	Buffer Overruns and Subscript Errors	276
13.6	Volatile Objects	277
13.7	Floating Point Portability	279
13.8	Exiting Portably	279

14 Manual Configuration 281

14.1	Specifying target triplets	281
14.2	Getting the Canonical System Type	282
14.3	Using the System Type	283

15 Site Configuration 285

15.1	Controlling Help Output	285
15.2	Working With External Software	285
15.3	Choosing Package Options	287
15.4	Making Your Help Strings Look Pretty	288
15.5	Controlling Checking of configure Options	289
15.6	Configuring Site Details	290
15.7	Transforming Program Names When Installing	290
15.7.1	Transformation Options	291
15.7.2	Transformation Examples	291
15.7.3	Transformation Rules	291
15.8	Setting Site Defaults	292

16   Running `configure` Scripts 295

16.1   Basic Installation 295
16.2   Compilers and Options.. 296
16.3   Compiling For Multiple Architectures 296
16.4   Installation Names... 297
16.5   Optional Features.. 297
16.6   Particular systems 298
16.7   Specifying the System Type.................................... 298
16.8   Sharing Defaults... 299
16.9   Defining Variables 299
16.10 `configure` Invocation 299

17   config.status Invocation 301

18   Obsolete Constructs 303

18.1   Obsolete 'config.status' Invocation 303
18.2   'acconfig.h'.. 304
18.3   Using autoupdate to Modernize 'configure.ac'........... 304
18.4   Obsolete Macros.. 305
18.5   Upgrading From Version 1 318
       18.5.1   Changed File Names.................................... 318
       18.5.2   Changed Makefiles 318
       18.5.3   Changed Macros....................................... 319
       18.5.4   Changed Results...................................... 319
       18.5.5   Changed Macro Writing................................ 320
18.6   Upgrading From Version 2.13 320
       18.6.1   Changed Quotation 320
       18.6.2   New Macros 321
       18.6.3   Hosts and Cross-Compilation........................... 322
       18.6.4   AC_LIBOBJ vs. LIBOBJS 324
       18.6.5   AC_*ACT*_IFELSE vs. AC_TRY_*ACT* 324

19   Generating Test Suites with Autotest..... 327

19.1   Using an Autotest Test Suite............................. 327
       19.1.1   testsuite Scripts 327
       19.1.2   Autotest Logs.. 329
19.2   Writing 'testsuite.at'... 329
19.3   Running testsuite Scripts 335
19.4   Making testsuite Scripts 337

20 Frequent Autoconf Questions, with answers 341

20.1 Distributing `configure` Scripts 341
20.2 Why Require GNU M4? 341
20.3 How Can I Bootstrap? 341
20.4 Why Not Imake? 342
20.5 How Do I #define Installation Directories? 343
20.6 What is 'autom4te.cache'? 344
20.7 Header Present But Cannot Be Compiled 344
20.8 Expanded Before Required 346
20.9 Debugging `configure` scripts 348

21 History of Autoconf 351

21.1 Genesis 351
21.2 Exodus 351
21.3 Leviticus 352
21.4 Numbers 352
21.5 Deuteronomy 353

Appendix A GNU Free Documentation License 355

Appendix B Indices 363

B.1 Environment Variable Index 363
B.2 Output Variable Index 364
B.3 Preprocessor Symbol Index 366
B.4 Cache Variable Index 368
B.5 Autoconf Macro Index 369
B.6 M4 Macro Index 373
B.7 Autotest Macro Index 376
B.8 Program and Function Index 376
B.9 Concept Index 378

1 Introduction

> A physicist, an engineer, and a computer scientist were discussing the
> nature of God. "Surely a Physicist," said the physicist, "because
> early in the Creation, God made Light; and you know, Maxwell's
> equations, the dual nature of electromagnetic waves, the relativistic
> consequences..." "An Engineer!," said the engineer, "because
> before making Light, God split the Chaos into Land and Water; it takes a
> hell of an engineer to handle that big amount of mud, and orderly
> separation of solids from liquids..." The computer scientist
> shouted: "And the Chaos, where do you think it was coming from, hmm?"

> —Anonymous

Autoconf is a tool for producing shell scripts that automatically configure software source code packages to adapt to many kinds of Posix-like systems. The configuration scripts produced by Autoconf are independent of Autoconf when they are run, so their users do not need to have Autoconf.

The configuration scripts produced by Autoconf require no manual user intervention when run; they do not normally even need an argument specifying the system type. Instead, they individually test for the presence of each feature that the software package they are for might need. (Before each check, they print a one-line message stating what they are checking for, so the user doesn't get too bored while waiting for the script to finish.) As a result, they deal well with systems that are hybrids or customized from the more common Posix variants. There is no need to maintain files that list the features supported by each release of each variant of Posix.

For each software package that Autoconf is used with, it creates a configuration script from a template file that lists the system features that the package needs or can use. After the shell code to recognize and respond to a system feature has been written, Autoconf allows it to be shared by many software packages that can use (or need) that feature. If it later turns out that the shell code needs adjustment for some reason, it needs to be changed in only one place; all of the configuration scripts can be regenerated automatically to take advantage of the updated code.

Those who do not understand Autoconf are condemned to reinvent it, poorly. The primary goal of Autoconf is making the *user's* life easier; making the *maintainer's* life easier is only a secondary goal. Put another way, the primary goal is not to make the generation of 'configure' automatic for package maintainers (although patches along that front are welcome, since package maintainers form the user base of Autoconf); rather, the goal is to make 'configure' painless, portable, and predictable for the end user of each *autoconfiscated* package. And to this degree, Autoconf is highly successful at its goal — most complaints to the Autoconf list are about difficulties in writing Autoconf input, and not in the behavior of the resulting 'configure'. Even packages that don't use Autoconf will generally provide a 'configure' script, and the most common complaint about these alternative home-grown scripts is that they fail to meet one or more of the GNU Coding Standards (see Section "Configuration" in *The GNU Coding Standards*) that users have come to expect from Autoconf-generated 'configure' scripts.

The Metaconfig package is similar in purpose to Autoconf, but the scripts it produces require manual user intervention, which is quite inconvenient when configuring large source trees. Unlike Metaconfig scripts, Autoconf scripts can support cross-compiling, if some care is taken in writing them.

Autoconf does not solve all problems related to making portable software packages—for a more complete solution, it should be used in concert with other GNU build tools like Automake and Libtool. These other tools take on jobs like the creation of a portable, recursive makefile with all of the standard targets, linking of shared libraries, and so on. See Chapter 2 [The GNU Build System], page 3, for more information.

Autoconf imposes some restrictions on the names of macros used with `#if` in C programs (see Section B.3 [Preprocessor Symbol Index], page 366).

Autoconf requires GNU M4 version 1.4.6 or later in order to generate the scripts. It uses features that some versions of M4, including GNU M4 1.3, do not have. Autoconf works better with GNU M4 version 1.4.14 or later, though this is not required.

See Section 18.5 [Autoconf 1], page 318, for information about upgrading from version 1. See Chapter 21 [History], page 351, for the story of Autoconf's development. See Chapter 20 [FAQ], page 341, for answers to some common questions about Autoconf.

See the Autoconf web page for up-to-date information, details on the mailing lists, pointers to a list of known bugs, etc.

Mail suggestions to the Autoconf mailing list. Past suggestions are archived.

Mail bug reports to the Autoconf Bugs mailing list. Past bug reports are archived.

If possible, first check that your bug is not already solved in current development versions, and that it has not been reported yet. Be sure to include all the needed information and a short 'configure.ac' that demonstrates the problem.

Autoconf's development tree is accessible via `git`; see the Autoconf Summary for details, or view the actual repository. Anonymous CVS access is also available, see 'README' for more details. Patches relative to the current `git` version can be sent for review to the Autoconf Patches mailing list, with discussion on prior patches archived; and all commits are posted in the read-only Autoconf Commit mailing list, which is also archived.

Because of its mission, the Autoconf package itself includes only a set of often-used macros that have already demonstrated their usefulness. Nevertheless, if you wish to share your macros, or find existing ones, see the Autoconf Macro Archive, which is kindly run by Peter Simons.

2 The GNU Build System

Autoconf solves an important problem—reliable discovery of system-specific build and run-time information—but this is only one piece of the puzzle for the development of portable software. To this end, the GNU project has developed a suite of integrated utilities to finish the job Autoconf started: the GNU build system, whose most important components are Autoconf, Automake, and Libtool. In this chapter, we introduce you to those tools, point you to sources of more information, and try to convince you to use the entire GNU build system for your software.

2.1 Automake

The ubiquity of `make` means that a makefile is almost the only viable way to distribute automatic build rules for software, but one quickly runs into its numerous limitations. Its lack of support for automatic dependency tracking, recursive builds in subdirectories, reliable timestamps (e.g., for network file systems), and so on, mean that developers must painfully (and often incorrectly) reinvent the wheel for each project. Portability is non-trivial, thanks to the quirks of `make` on many systems. On top of all this is the manual labor required to implement the many standard targets that users have come to expect (`make install`, `make distclean`, `make uninstall`, etc.). Since you are, of course, using Autoconf, you also have to insert repetitive code in your 'Makefile.in' to recognize @CC@, @CFLAGS@, and other substitutions provided by `configure`. Into this mess steps *Automake*.

Automake allows you to specify your build needs in a 'Makefile.am' file with a vastly simpler and more powerful syntax than that of a plain makefile, and then generates a portable 'Makefile.in' for use with Autoconf. For example, the 'Makefile.am' to build and install a simple "Hello world" program might look like:

```
bin_PROGRAMS = hello
hello_SOURCES = hello.c
```

The resulting 'Makefile.in' (~400 lines) automatically supports all the standard targets, the substitutions provided by Autoconf, automatic dependency tracking, VPATH building, and so on. `make` builds the `hello` program, and `make install` installs it in '/usr/local/bin' (or whatever prefix was given to `configure`, if not '/usr/local').

The benefits of Automake increase for larger packages (especially ones with subdirectories), but even for small programs the added convenience and portability can be substantial. And that's not all. . .

2.2 Gnulib

GNU software has a well-deserved reputation for running on many different types of systems. While our primary goal is to write software for the GNU system, many users and developers have been introduced to us through the systems that they were already using.

Gnulib is a central location for common GNU code, intended to be shared among free software packages. Its components are typically shared at the source level, rather than being a library that gets built, installed, and linked against. The idea is to copy files from Gnulib into your own source tree. There is no distribution tarball; developers should just grab source modules from the repository. The source files are available online, under various licenses, mostly GNU GPL or GNU LGPL.

Gnulib modules typically contain C source code along with Autoconf macros used to configure the source code. For example, the Gnulib `stdbool` module implements a 'stdbool.h' header that nearly conforms to C99, even on old-fashioned hosts that lack 'stdbool.h'. This module contains a source file for the replacement header, along with an Autoconf macro that arranges to use the replacement header on old-fashioned systems.

2.3 Libtool

Often, one wants to build not only programs, but libraries, so that other programs can benefit from the fruits of your labor. Ideally, one would like to produce *shared* (dynamically linked) libraries, which can be used by multiple programs without duplication on disk or in memory and can be updated independently of the linked programs. Producing shared libraries portably, however, is the stuff of nightmares—each system has its own incompatible tools, compiler flags, and magic incantations. Fortunately, GNU provides a solution: *Libtool*.

Libtool handles all the requirements of building shared libraries for you, and at this time seems to be the *only* way to do so with any portability. It also handles many other headaches, such as: the interaction of Make rules with the variable suffixes of shared libraries, linking reliably with shared libraries before they are installed by the superuser, and supplying a consistent versioning system (so that different versions of a library can be installed or upgraded without breaking binary compatibility). Although Libtool, like Autoconf, can be used without Automake, it is most simply utilized in conjunction with Automake—there, Libtool is used automatically whenever shared libraries are needed, and you need not know its syntax.

2.4 Pointers

Developers who are used to the simplicity of `make` for small projects on a single system might be daunted at the prospect of learning to use Automake and Autoconf. As your software is distributed to more and more users, however, you otherwise quickly find yourself putting lots of effort into reinventing the services that the GNU build tools provide, and making the same mistakes that they once made and overcame. (Besides, since you're already learning Autoconf, Automake is a piece of cake.)

There are a number of places that you can go to for more information on the GNU build tools.

− Web

The project home pages for Autoconf, Automake, Gnulib, and Libtool.

− Automake Manual

See Section "Automake" in *GNU Automake*, for more information on Automake.

− Books

The book *GNU Autoconf, Automake and Libtool*[1] describes the complete GNU build environment. You can also find the entire book on-line.

---

[1] *GNU Autoconf, Automake and Libtool*, by G. V. Vaughan, B. Elliston, T. Tromey, and I. L. Taylor. SAMS (originally New Riders), 2000, ISBN 1578701902.

3 Making `configure` Scripts

The configuration scripts that Autoconf produces are by convention called `configure`. When run, `configure` creates several files, replacing configuration parameters in them with appropriate values. The files that `configure` creates are:

— one or more 'Makefile' files, usually one in each subdirectory of the package (see Section 4.8 [Makefile Substitutions], page 23);

— optionally, a C header file, the name of which is configurable, containing `#define` directives (see Section 4.9 [Configuration Headers], page 33);

— a shell script called 'config.status' that, when run, recreates the files listed above (see Chapter 17 [config.status Invocation], page 301);

— an optional shell script normally called 'config.cache' (created when using 'configure --config-cache') that saves the results of running many of the tests (see Section 7.4.2 [Cache Files], page 119);

— a file called 'config.log' containing any messages produced by compilers, to help debugging if `configure` makes a mistake.

To create a `configure` script with Autoconf, you need to write an Autoconf input file 'configure.ac' (or 'configure.in') and run `autoconf` on it. If you write your own feature tests to supplement those that come with Autoconf, you might also write files called 'aclocal.m4' and 'acsite.m4'. If you use a C header file to contain `#define` directives, you might also run `autoheader`, and you can distribute the generated file 'config.h.in' with the package.

Here is a diagram showing how the files that can be used in configuration are produced. Programs that are executed are suffixed by '*'. Optional files are enclosed in square brackets ('[]'). `autoconf` and `autoheader` also read the installed Autoconf macro files (by reading 'autoconf.m4').

Files used in preparing a software package for distribution, when using just Autoconf:

```
your source files --> [autoscan*] --> [configure.scan] --> configure.ac


configure.ac --.
               |    .------> autoconf* -----> configure
[aclocal.m4] --+---+
               |    '-----> [autoheader*] --> [config.h.in]
[acsite.m4] ---'


Makefile.in
```

Additionally, if you use Automake, the following additional productions come into play:

```
[acinclude.m4] --.
                 |
[local macros] --+--> aclocal* --> aclocal.m4
                 |
configure.ac ----'
```

```
configure.ac --.
                +--> automake* --> Makefile.in
Makefile.am ---'
```

Files used in configuring a software package:

```
                          .------------> [config.cache]
configure* ------------+------------> config.log
                       |
[config.h.in] -.       v            .-> [config.h] -.
                +--> config.status* -+                +--> make*
Makefile.in ---'                     '-> Makefile ---'
```

3.1 Writing 'configure.ac'

To produce a `configure` script for a software package, create a file called 'configure.ac' that contains invocations of the Autoconf macros that test the system features your package needs or can use. Autoconf macros already exist to check for many features; see Chapter 5 [Existing Tests], page 41, for their descriptions. For most other features, you can use Autoconf template macros to produce custom checks; see Chapter 6 [Writing Tests], page 101, for information about them. For especially tricky or specialized features, 'configure.ac' might need to contain some hand-crafted shell commands; see Chapter 11 [Portable Shell Programming], page 189. The `autoscan` program can give you a good start in writing 'configure.ac' (see Section 3.2 [autoscan Invocation], page 10, for more information).

Previous versions of Autoconf promoted the name 'configure.in', which is somewhat ambiguous (the tool needed to process this file is not described by its extension), and introduces a slight confusion with 'config.h.in' and so on (for which '.in' means "to be processed by `configure`"). Using 'configure.ac' is now preferred.

3.1.1 A Shell Script Compiler

Just as for any other computer language, in order to properly program 'configure.ac' in Autoconf you must understand *what* problem the language tries to address and *how* it does so.

The problem Autoconf addresses is that the world is a mess. After all, you are using Autoconf in order to have your package compile easily on all sorts of different systems, some of them being extremely hostile. Autoconf itself bears the price for these differences: `configure` must run on all those systems, and thus `configure` must limit itself to their lowest common denominator of features.

Naturally, you might then think of shell scripts; who needs `autoconf`? A set of properly written shell functions is enough to make it easy to write `configure` scripts by hand. Sigh! Unfortunately, even in 2008, where shells without any function support are far and few between, there are pitfalls to avoid when making use of them. Also, finding a Bourne shell that accepts shell functions is not trivial, even though there is almost always one on interesting porting targets.

So, what is really needed is some kind of compiler, `autoconf`, that takes an Autoconf program, 'configure.ac', and transforms it into a portable shell script, `configure`.

How does `autoconf` perform this task?

There are two obvious possibilities: creating a brand new language or extending an existing one. The former option is attractive: all sorts of optimizations could easily be implemented in the compiler and many rigorous checks could be performed on the Autoconf program (e.g., rejecting any non-portable construct). Alternatively, you can extend an existing language, such as the `sh` (Bourne shell) language.

Autoconf does the latter: it is a layer on top of `sh`. It was therefore most convenient to implement `autoconf` as a macro expander: a program that repeatedly performs *macro expansions* on text input, replacing macro calls with macro bodies and producing a pure `sh` script in the end. Instead of implementing a dedicated Autoconf macro expander, it is natural to use an existing general-purpose macro language, such as M4, and implement the extensions as a set of M4 macros.

3.1.2 The Autoconf Language

The Autoconf language differs from many other computer languages because it treats actual code the same as plain text. Whereas in C, for instance, data and instructions have different syntactic status, in Autoconf their status is rigorously the same. Therefore, we need a means to distinguish literal strings from text to be expanded: quotation.

When calling macros that take arguments, there must not be any white space between the macro name and the open parenthesis.

```
AC_INIT ([oops], [1.0]) # incorrect
AC_INIT([hello], [1.0]) # good
```

Arguments should be enclosed within the quote characters '[' and ']', and be separated by commas. Any leading blanks or newlines in arguments are ignored, unless they are quoted. You should always quote an argument that might contain a macro name, comma, parenthesis, or a leading blank or newline. This rule applies recursively for every macro call, including macros called from other macros. For more details on quoting rules, see Chapter 8 [Programming in M4], page 123.

For instance:

```
AC_CHECK_HEADER([stdio.h],
                [AC_DEFINE([HAVE_STDIO_H], [1],
                   [Define to 1 if you have <stdio.h>.])],
                [AC_MSG_ERROR([sorry, can't do anything for you])])
```

is quoted properly. You may safely simplify its quotation to:

```
AC_CHECK_HEADER([stdio.h],
                [AC_DEFINE([HAVE_STDIO_H], 1,
                   [Define to 1 if you have <stdio.h>.])],
                [AC_MSG_ERROR([sorry, can't do anything for you])])
```

because '1' cannot contain a macro call. Here, the argument of `AC_MSG_ERROR` must be quoted; otherwise, its comma would be interpreted as an argument separator. Also, the second and third arguments of '`AC_CHECK_HEADER`' must be quoted, since they contain macro calls. The three arguments '`HAVE_STDIO_H`', '`stdio.h`', and '`Define to 1 if you have <stdio.h>.`' do not need quoting, but if you unwisely defined a macro with a name like '`Define`' or '`stdio`' then they would need quoting. Cautious Autoconf users would keep the quotes, but many Autoconf users find such precautions annoying, and would rewrite the example as follows:

```
AC_CHECK_HEADER(stdio.h,
               [AC_DEFINE(HAVE_STDIO_H, 1,
                  [Define to 1 if you have <stdio.h>.])],
               [AC_MSG_ERROR([sorry, can't do anything for you])])
```

This is safe, so long as you adopt good naming conventions and do not define macros with names like 'HAVE_STDIO_H', 'stdio', or 'h'. Though it is also safe here to omit the quotes around 'Define to 1 if you have <stdio.h>.' this is not recommended, as message strings are more likely to inadvertently contain commas.

The following example is wrong and dangerous, as it is underquoted:

```
AC_CHECK_HEADER(stdio.h,
               AC_DEFINE(HAVE_STDIO_H, 1,
                  Define to 1 if you have <stdio.h>.),
               AC_MSG_ERROR([sorry, can't do anything for you]))
```

In other cases, you may have to use text that also resembles a macro call. You must quote that text even when it is not passed as a macro argument. For example, these two approaches in 'configure.ac' (quoting just the potential problems, or quoting the entire line) will protect your script in case autoconf ever adds a macro AC_DC:

```
echo "Hard rock was here!  --[AC_DC]"
[echo "Hard rock was here!  --AC_DC"]
```

which results in this text in 'configure':

```
echo "Hard rock was here!  --AC_DC"
echo "Hard rock was here!  --AC_DC"
```

When you use the same text in a macro argument, you must therefore have an extra quotation level (since one is stripped away by the macro substitution). In general, then, it is a good idea to *use double quoting for all literal string arguments*, either around just the problematic portions, or over the entire argument:

```
AC_MSG_WARN([[AC_DC] stinks  --Iron Maiden])
AC_MSG_WARN([[AC_DC stinks  --Iron Maiden]])
```

However, the above example triggers a warning about a possibly unexpanded macro when running autoconf, because it collides with the namespace of macros reserved for the Autoconf language. To be really safe, you can use additional escaping (either a quadrigraph, or creative shell constructs) to silence that particular warning:

```
echo "Hard rock was here!  --AC""_DC"
AC_MSG_WARN([[AC@&t@_DC stinks  --Iron Maiden]])
```

You are now able to understand one of the constructs of Autoconf that has been continually misunderstood... The rule of thumb is that *whenever you expect macro expansion, expect quote expansion*; i.e., expect one level of quotes to be lost. For instance:

```
AC_COMPILE_IFELSE(AC_LANG_SOURCE([char b[10];]), [],
   [AC_MSG_ERROR([you lose])])
```

is incorrect: here, the first argument of AC_LANG_SOURCE is 'char b[10];' and is expanded once, which results in 'char b10;'; and the AC_LANG_SOURCE is also expanded prior to being passed to AC_COMPILE_IFELSE. (There was an idiom common in Autoconf's past to address this issue via the M4 changequote primitive, but do not use it!) Let's take a closer look: the author meant the first argument to be understood as a literal, and therefore it must be quoted twice; likewise, the intermediate `AC_LANG_SOURCE` macro should be quoted once so that it is only expanded after the rest of the body of `AC_COMPILE_IFELSE` is in place:

```
AC_COMPILE_IFELSE([AC_LANG_SOURCE([[char b[10];]])], [],
  [AC_MSG_ERROR([you lose])])
```

Voilà, you actually produce '`char b[10];`' this time!

On the other hand, descriptions (e.g., the last parameter of `AC_DEFINE` or `AS_HELP_STRING`) are not literals—they are subject to line breaking, for example—and should not be double quoted. Even if these descriptions are short and are not actually broken, double quoting them yields weird results.

Some macros take optional arguments, which this documentation represents as [arg] (not to be confused with the quote characters). You may just leave them empty, or use '`[]`' to make the emptiness of the argument explicit, or you may simply omit the trailing commas. The three lines below are equivalent:

```
AC_CHECK_HEADERS([stdio.h], [], [], [])
AC_CHECK_HEADERS([stdio.h],,,)
AC_CHECK_HEADERS([stdio.h])
```

It is best to put each macro call on its own line in '`configure.ac`'. Most of the macros don't add extra newlines; they rely on the newline after the macro call to terminate the commands. This approach makes the generated `configure` script a little easier to read by not inserting lots of blank lines. It is generally safe to set shell variables on the same line as a macro call, because the shell allows assignments without intervening newlines.

You can include comments in '`configure.ac`' files by starting them with the '`#`'. For example, it is helpful to begin '`configure.ac`' files with a line like this:

```
# Process this file with autoconf to produce a configure script.
```

3.1.3 Standard '`configure.ac`' Layout

The order in which '`configure.ac`' calls the Autoconf macros is not important, with a few exceptions. Every '`configure.ac`' must contain a call to `AC_INIT` before the checks, and a call to `AC_OUTPUT` at the end (see Section 4.5 [Output], page 20). Additionally, some macros rely on other macros having been called first, because they check previously set values of some variables to decide what to do. These macros are noted in the individual descriptions (see Chapter 5 [Existing Tests], page 41), and they also warn you when `configure` is created if they are called out of order.

To encourage consistency, here is a suggested order for calling the Autoconf macros. Generally speaking, the things near the end of this list are those that could depend on things earlier in it. For example, library functions could be affected by types and libraries.

```
Autoconf requirements
AC_INIT(package, version, bug-report-address)
information on the package
checks for programs
checks for libraries
checks for header files
checks for types
checks for structures
checks for compiler characteristics
checks for library functions
checks for system services
AC_CONFIG_FILES([file...])
AC_OUTPUT
```

3.2 Using autoscan to Create 'configure.ac'

The autoscan program can help you create and/or maintain a 'configure.ac' file for a software package. autoscan examines source files in the directory tree rooted at a directory given as a command line argument, or the current directory if none is given. It searches the source files for common portability problems and creates a file 'configure.scan' which is a preliminary 'configure.ac' for that package, and checks a possibly existing 'configure.ac' for completeness.

When using autoscan to create a 'configure.ac', you should manually examine 'configure.scan' before renaming it to 'configure.ac'; it probably needs some adjustments. Occasionally, autoscan outputs a macro in the wrong order relative to another macro, so that autoconf produces a warning; you need to move such macros manually. Also, if you want the package to use a configuration header file, you must add a call to AC_CONFIG_HEADERS (see Section 4.9 [Configuration Headers], page 33). You might also have to change or add some #if directives to your program in order to make it work with Autoconf (see Section 3.3 [ifnames Invocation], page 11, for information about a program that can help with that job).

When using autoscan to maintain a 'configure.ac', simply consider adding its suggestions. The file 'autoscan.log' contains detailed information on why a macro is requested.

autoscan uses several data files (installed along with Autoconf) to determine which macros to output when it finds particular symbols in a package's source files. These data files all have the same format: each line consists of a symbol, one or more blanks, and the Autoconf macro to output if that symbol is encountered. Lines starting with '#' are comments.

autoscan accepts the following options:

'--help'
'-h'   Print a summary of the command line options and exit.

'--version'
'-V'   Print the version number of Autoconf and exit.

'--verbose'
'-v'   Print the names of the files it examines and the potentially interesting symbols it finds in them. This output can be voluminous.

'`--debug`'
'`-d`'   Don't remove temporary files.

'`--include=dir`'
'`-I dir`'   Append *dir* to the include path. Multiple invocations accumulate.

'`--prepend-include=dir`'
'`-B dir`'   Prepend *dir* to the include path. Multiple invocations accumulate.

3.3 Using `ifnames` to List Conditionals

`ifnames` can help you write '`configure.ac`' for a software package. It prints the identifiers that the package already uses in C preprocessor conditionals. If a package has already been set up to have some portability, `ifnames` can thus help you figure out what its `configure` needs to check for. It may help fill in some gaps in a '`configure.ac`' generated by `autoscan` (see Section 3.2 [autoscan Invocation], page 10).

   `ifnames` scans all of the C source files named on the command line (or the standard input, if none are given) and writes to the standard output a sorted list of all the identifiers that appear in those files in `#if`, `#elif`, `#ifdef`, or `#ifndef` directives. It prints each identifier on a line, followed by a space-separated list of the files in which that identifier occurs.

`ifnames` accepts the following options:

'`--help`'
'`-h`'   Print a summary of the command line options and exit.

'`--version`'
'`-V`'   Print the version number of Autoconf and exit.

3.4 Using `autoconf` to Create `configure`

To create `configure` from '`configure.ac`', run the `autoconf` program with no arguments. `autoconf` processes '`configure.ac`' with the M4 macro processor, using the Autoconf macros. If you give `autoconf` an argument, it reads that file instead of '`configure.ac`' and writes the configuration script to the standard output instead of to `configure`. If you give `autoconf` the argument '`-`', it reads from the standard input instead of '`configure.ac`' and writes the configuration script to the standard output.

   The Autoconf macros are defined in several files. Some of the files are distributed with Autoconf; `autoconf` reads them first. Then it looks for the optional file '`acsite.m4`' in the directory that contains the distributed Autoconf macro files, and for the optional file '`aclocal.m4`' in the current directory. Those files can contain your site's or the package's own Autoconf macro definitions (see Chapter 10 [Writing Autoconf Macros], page 177, for more information). If a macro is defined in more than one of the files that `autoconf` reads, the last definition it reads overrides the earlier ones.

   `autoconf` accepts the following options:

'`--help`'
'`-h`'   Print a summary of the command line options and exit.

'`--version`'
'`-V`'   Print the version number of Autoconf and exit.

'`--verbose`'

'`-v`'   Report processing steps.

'`--debug`'

'`-d`'   Don't remove the temporary files.

'`--force`'

'`-f`'   Remake '`configure`' even if newer than its input files.

'`--include=dir`'

'`-I dir`'   Append *dir* to the include path. Multiple invocations accumulate.

'`--prepend-include=dir`'

'`-B dir`'   Prepend *dir* to the include path. Multiple invocations accumulate.

'`--output=file`'

'`-o file`'   Save output (script or trace) to *file*. The file '`-`' stands for the standard output.

'`--warnings=category`'

'`-W category`'

Report the warnings related to *category* (which can actually be a comma separated list). See Section 10.3 [Reporting Messages], page 179, macro `AC_DIAGNOSE`, for a comprehensive list of categories. Special values include:

'`all`'   report all the warnings

'`none`'   report none

'`error`'   treats warnings as errors

'`no-category`'

disable warnings falling into *category*

Warnings about '`syntax`' are enabled by default, and the environment variable `WARNINGS`, a comma separated list of categories, is honored as well. Passing '`-W category`' actually behaves as if you had passed '`--warnings syntax,$WARNINGS,category`'. To disable the defaults and `WARNINGS`, and then enable warnings about obsolete constructs, use '`-W none,obsolete`'.

Because `autoconf` uses `autom4te` behind the scenes, it displays a back trace for errors, but not for warnings; if you want them, just pass '`-W error`'. See Section 8.2.1 [autom4te Invocation], page 132, for some examples.

'`--trace=macro[:format]`'

'`-t macro[:format]`'

Do not create the `configure` script, but list the calls to *macro* according to the *format*. Multiple '`--trace`' arguments can be used to list several macros. Multiple '`--trace`' arguments for a single macro are not cumulative; instead, you should just make *format* as long as needed.

The *format* is a regular string, with newlines if desired, and several special escape codes. It defaults to '`$f:$l:$n:$%`'; see Section 8.2.1 [autom4te Invocation], page 132, for details on the *format*.

'`--initialization`'

'`-i`'   By default, '`--trace`' does not trace the initialization of the Autoconf macros
                 (typically the `AC_DEFUN` definitions). This results in a noticeable speedup, but
                 can be disabled by this option.

It is often necessary to check the content of a '`configure.ac`' file, but parsing it yourself
is extremely fragile and error-prone. It is suggested that you rely upon '`--trace`' to scan
'`configure.ac`'. For instance, to find the list of variables that are substituted, use:

```
$ autoconf -t AC_SUBST
configure.ac:2:AC_SUBST:ECHO_C
configure.ac:2:AC_SUBST:ECHO_N
configure.ac:2:AC_SUBST:ECHO_T
More traces deleted
```

The example below highlights the difference between '`$@`', '`$*`', and '`$%`'.

```
$ cat configure.ac
AC_DEFINE(This, is, [an
[example]])
$ autoconf -t 'AC_DEFINE:@: $@
*: $*
%: $%'
@: [This],[is],[an
[example]]
*: This,is,an
[example]
%: This:is:an [example]
```

The *format* gives you a lot of freedom:

```
$ autoconf -t 'AC_SUBST:$$ac_subst{"$1"} = "$f:$1";'
$ac_subst{"ECHO_C"} = "configure.ac:2";
$ac_subst{"ECHO_N"} = "configure.ac:2";
$ac_subst{"ECHO_T"} = "configure.ac:2";
More traces deleted
```

A long *separator* can be used to improve the readability of complex structures, and to ease
their parsing (for instance when no single character is suitable as a separator):

```
$ autoconf -t 'AM_MISSING_PROG:${|:::::|}*'
ACLOCAL|:::::|aclocal|:::::|$missing_dir
AUTOCONF|:::::|autoconf|:::::|$missing_dir
AUTOMAKE|:::::|automake|:::::|$missing_dir
More traces deleted
```

3.5 Using `autoreconf` to Update `configure` Scripts

Installing the various components of the GNU Build System can be tedious: running
`autopoint` for Gettext, `automake` for '`Makefile.in`' etc. in each directory. It may be
needed either because some tools such as `automake` have been updated on your system, or
because some of the sources such as '`configure.ac`' have been updated, or finally, simply
in order to install the GNU Build System in a fresh tree.

autoreconf runs autoconf, autoheader, aclocal, automake, libtoolize, and autopoint (when appropriate) repeatedly to update the GNU Build System in the specified directories and their subdirectories (see Section 4.12 [Subdirectories], page 38). By default, it only remakes those files that are older than their sources. The environment variables AUTOM4TE, AUTOCONF, AUTOHEADER, AUTOMAKE, ACLOCAL, AUTOPOINT, LIBTOOLIZE, M4, and MAKE may be used to override the invocation of the respective tools.

If you install a new version of some tool, you can make autoreconf remake *all* of the files by giving it the '--force' option.

See Section 4.8.5 [Automatic Remaking], page 32, for Make rules to automatically rebuild configure scripts when their source files change. That method handles the timestamps of configuration header templates properly, but does not pass '--autoconf-dir=*dir*' or '--localdir=*dir*'.

Gettext supplies the autopoint command to add translation infrastructure to a source package. If you use autopoint, your 'configure.ac' should invoke both AM_GNU_GETTEXT and AM_GNU_GETTEXT_VERSION(*gettext-version*). See Section "Invoking the autopoint Program" in *GNU* gettext *utilities*, for further details.

autoreconf accepts the following options:

'--help'
'-h'   Print a summary of the command line options and exit.

'--version'
'-V'   Print the version number of Autoconf and exit.

'--verbose'
'-v'   Print the name of each directory autoreconf examines and the commands it runs. If given two or more times, pass '--verbose' to subordinate tools that support it.

'--debug'
'-d'   Don't remove the temporary files.

'--force'
'-f'   Remake even 'configure' scripts and configuration headers that are newer than their input files ('configure.ac' and, if present, 'aclocal.m4').

'--install'
'-i'   Install the missing auxiliary files in the package. By default, files are copied; this can be changed with '--symlink'.

                If deemed appropriate, this option triggers calls to 'automake --add-missing', 'libtoolize', 'autopoint', etc.

'--no-recursive'
                Do not rebuild files in subdirectories to configure (see Section 4.12 [Subdirectories], page 38, macro AC_CONFIG_SUBDIRS).

'--symlink'
'-s'   When used with '--install', install symbolic links to the missing auxiliary files instead of copying them.

'`--make`'

'`-m`'   When the directories were configured, update the configuration by running '`./config.status --recheck && ./config.status`', and then run '`make`'.

'`--include=dir`'

'`-I dir`'   Append *dir* to the include path. Multiple invocations accumulate. Passed on to `aclocal`, `autoconf` and `autoheader` internally.

'`--prepend-include=dir`'

'`-B dir`'   Prepend *dir* to the include path. Multiple invocations accumulate. Passed on to `autoconf` and `autoheader` internally.

'`--warnings=category`'

'`-W category`'

Report the warnings related to *category* (which can actually be a comma separated list).

'`cross`'   related to cross compilation issues.

'`obsolete`'
            report the uses of obsolete constructs.

'`portability`'
            portability issues

'`syntax`'   dubious syntactic constructs.

'`all`'   report all the warnings

'`none`'   report none

'`error`'   treats warnings as errors

'`no-category`'
            disable warnings falling into *category*

Warnings about '`syntax`' are enabled by default, and the environment variable `WARNINGS`, a comma separated list of categories, is honored as well. Passing '`-W category`' actually behaves as if you had passed '`--warnings syntax,$WARNINGS,category`'. To disable the defaults and `WARNINGS`, and then enable warnings about obsolete constructs, use '`-W none,obsolete`'.

If you want `autoreconf` to pass flags that are not listed here on to `aclocal`, set `ACLOCAL_AMFLAGS` in your '`Makefile.am`'. Due to a limitation in the Autoconf implementation these flags currently must be set on a single line in '`Makefile.am`', without any backslash-newlines.

4 Initialization and Output Files

Autoconf-generated `configure` scripts need some information about how to initialize, such as how to find the package's source files and about the output files to produce. The following sections describe the initialization and the creation of output files.

4.1 Initializing `configure`

Every `configure` script must call `AC_INIT` before doing anything else that produces output. Calls to silent macros, such as `AC_DEFUN`, may also occur prior to `AC_INIT`, although these are generally used via '`aclocal.m4`', since that is implicitly included before the start of '`configure.ac`'. The only other required macro is `AC_OUTPUT` (see Section 4.5 [Output], page 20).

`AC_INIT` (*package*, *version*, [*bug-report*], [*tarname*], [*url*])   [Macro]
>   Process any command-line arguments and perform initialization and verification.
>
>   Set the name of the *package* and its *version*. These are typically used in '`--version`' support, including that of `configure`. The optional argument *bug-report* should be the email to which users should send bug reports. The package *tarname* differs from *package*: the latter designates the full package name (e.g., '`GNU Autoconf`'), while the former is meant for distribution tar ball names (e.g., '`autoconf`'). It defaults to *package* with '`GNU `' stripped, lower-cased, and all characters other than alphanumerics and underscores are changed to '`-`'. If provided, *url* should be the home page for the package.
>
>   The arguments of `AC_INIT` must be static, i.e., there should not be any shell computation, quotes, or newlines, but they can be computed by M4. This is because the package information strings are expanded at M4 time into several contexts, and must give the same text at shell time whether used in single-quoted strings, double-quoted strings, quoted here-documents, or unquoted here-documents. It is permissible to use `m4_esyscmd` or `m4_esyscmd_s` for computing a version string that changes with every commit to a version control system (in fact, Autoconf does just that, for all builds of the development tree made between releases).
>
>   The following M4 macros (e.g., `AC_PACKAGE_NAME`), output variables (e.g., `PACKAGE_NAME`), and preprocessor symbols (e.g., `PACKAGE_NAME`), are defined by `AC_INIT`:
>
>   `AC_PACKAGE_NAME`, `PACKAGE_NAME`
>>   Exactly *package*.
>
>   `AC_PACKAGE_TARNAME`, `PACKAGE_TARNAME`
>>   Exactly *tarname*, possibly generated from *package*.
>
>   `AC_PACKAGE_VERSION`, `PACKAGE_VERSION`
>>   Exactly *version*.
>
>   `AC_PACKAGE_STRING`, `PACKAGE_STRING`
>>   Exactly '*package version*'.
>
>   `AC_PACKAGE_BUGREPORT`, `PACKAGE_BUGREPORT`
>>   Exactly *bug-report*, if one was provided. Typically an email address, or URL to a bug management web page.

`AC_PACKAGE_URL, PACKAGE_URL`
> Exactly *url*, if one was provided. If *url* was empty, but *package* begins with 'GNU ', then this defaults to '`http://www.gnu.org/software/tarname/`', otherwise, no URL is assumed.

If your `configure` script does its own option processing, it should inspect '`$@`' or '`$*`' immediately after calling `AC_INIT`, because other Autoconf macros liberally use the `set` command to process strings, and this has the side effect of updating '`$@`' and '`$*`'. However, we suggest that you use standard macros like `AC_ARG_ENABLE` instead of attempting to implement your own option processing. See Chapter 15 [Site Configuration], page 285.

4.2 Dealing with Autoconf versions

The following optional macros can be used to help choose the minimum version of Autoconf that can successfully compile a given '`configure.ac`'.

`AC_PREREQ (version)`   [Macro]
> Ensure that a recent enough version of Autoconf is being used. If the version of Autoconf being used to create `configure` is earlier than *version*, print an error message to the standard error output and exit with failure (exit status is 63). For example:
>
>   AC_PREREQ([2.69])
>
> This macro may be used before `AC_INIT`.

`AC_AUTOCONF_VERSION`   [Macro]
> This macro was introduced in Autoconf 2.62. It identifies the version of Autoconf that is currently parsing the input file, in a format suitable for `m4_version_compare` (see [m4_version_compare], page 159); in other words, for this release of Autoconf, its value is '`2.69`'. One potential use of this macro is for writing conditional fallbacks based on when a feature was added to Autoconf, rather than using `AC_PREREQ` to require the newer version of Autoconf. However, remember that the Autoconf philosophy favors feature checks over version checks.
>
> You should not expand this macro directly; use '`m4_defn([AC_AUTOCONF_VERSION])`' instead. This is because some users might have a beta version of Autoconf installed, with arbitrary letters included in its version string. This means it is possible for the version string to contain the name of a defined macro, such that expanding `AC_AUTOCONF_VERSION` would trigger the expansion of that macro during rescanning, and change the version string to be different than what you intended to check.

4.3 Notices in `configure`

The following macros manage version numbers for `configure` scripts. Using them is optional.

`AC_COPYRIGHT (copyright-notice)`   [Macro]
> State that, in addition to the Free Software Foundation's copyright on the Autoconf macros, parts of your `configure` are covered by the *copyright-notice*.
>
> The *copyright-notice* shows up in both the head of `configure` and in '`configure --version`'.

AC_REVISION (*revision-info*)   [Macro]

Copy revision stamp *revision-info* into the `configure` script, with any dollar signs or double-quotes removed. This macro lets you put a revision stamp from 'configure.ac' into `configure` without RCS or CVS changing it when you check in `configure`. That way, you can determine easily which revision of 'configure.ac' a particular `configure` corresponds to.

For example, this line in 'configure.ac':

```
AC_REVISION([$Revision: 1.30 $])
```

produces this in `configure`:

```
#!/bin/sh
# From configure.ac Revision: 1.30
```

4.4 Finding `configure` Input

AC_CONFIG_SRCDIR (*unique-file-in-source-dir*)   [Macro]

unique-file-in-source-dir is some file that is in the package's source directory; `configure` checks for this file's existence to make sure that the directory that it is told contains the source code in fact does. Occasionally people accidentally specify the wrong directory with '--srcdir'; this is a safety check. See Section 16.10 [configure Invocation], page 299, for more information.

Packages that do manual configuration or use the `install` program might need to tell `configure` where to find some other shell scripts by calling `AC_CONFIG_AUX_DIR`, though the default places it looks are correct for most cases.

AC_CONFIG_AUX_DIR (*dir*)   [Macro]

Use the auxiliary build tools (e.g., 'install-sh', 'config.sub', 'config.guess', Cygnus `configure`, Automake and Libtool scripts, etc.) that are in directory *dir*. These are auxiliary files used in configuration. *dir* can be either absolute or relative to '*srcdir*'. The default is '*srcdir*' or '*srcdir/..*' or '*srcdir/../..*', whichever is the first that contains 'install-sh'. The other files are not checked for, so that using `AC_PROG_INSTALL` does not automatically require distributing the other auxiliary files. It checks for 'install.sh' also, but that name is obsolete because some `make` have a rule that creates 'install' from it if there is no makefile.

The auxiliary directory is commonly named 'build-aux'. If you need portability to DOS variants, do not name the auxiliary directory 'aux'. See Section 11.6 [File System Conventions], page 199.

AC_REQUIRE_AUX_FILE (*file*)   [Macro]

Declares that *file* is expected in the directory defined above. In Autoconf proper, this macro does nothing: its sole purpose is to be traced by third-party tools to produce a list of expected auxiliary files. For instance it is called by macros like `AC_PROG_INSTALL` (see Section 5.2.1 [Particular Programs], page 43) or `AC_CANONICAL_BUILD` (see Section 14.2 [Canonicalizing], page 282) to register the auxiliary files they need.

Similarly, packages that use `aclocal` should declare where local macros can be found using `AC_CONFIG_MACRO_DIR`.

AC_CONFIG_MACRO_DIR (*dir*)   [Macro]
> Specify *dir* as the location of additional local Autoconf macros. This macro is intended
> for use by future versions of commands like `autoreconf` that trace macro calls. It
> should be called directly from 'configure.ac' so that tools that install macros for
> `aclocal` can find the macros' declarations.
>
> Note that if you use `aclocal` from Automake to generate 'aclocal.m4', you must also
> set `ACLOCAL_AMFLAGS = -I dir` in your top-level 'Makefile.am'. Due to a limitation
> in the Autoconf implementation of `autoreconf`, these include directives currently
> must be set on a single line in 'Makefile.am', without any backslash-newlines.

4.5 Outputting Files

Every Autoconf script, e.g., 'configure.ac', should finish by calling `AC_OUTPUT`. That is
the macro that generates and runs 'config.status', which in turn creates the makefiles
and any other files resulting from configuration. This is the only required macro besides
`AC_INIT` (see Section 4.4 [Input], page 19).

AC_OUTPUT   [Macro]
> Generate 'config.status' and launch it. Call this macro once, at the end of
> 'configure.ac'.
>
> 'config.status' performs all the configuration actions: all the output files (see
> Section 4.7 [Configuration Files], page 23, macro `AC_CONFIG_FILES`), header files (see
> Section 4.9 [Configuration Headers], page 33, macro `AC_CONFIG_HEADERS`), commands
> (see Section 4.10 [Configuration Commands], page 37, macro `AC_CONFIG_COMMANDS`),
> links (see Section 4.11 [Configuration Links], page 38, macro `AC_CONFIG_LINKS`), sub-
> directories to configure (see Section 4.12 [Subdirectories], page 38, macro `AC_CONFIG_`
> `SUBDIRS`) are honored.
>
> The location of your `AC_OUTPUT` invocation is the exact point where configuration
> actions are taken: any code afterwards is executed by `configure` once `config.status`
> was run. If you want to bind actions to `config.status` itself (independently of
> whether `configure` is being run), see Section 4.10 [Running Arbitrary Configuration
> Commands], page 37.

Historically, the usage of `AC_OUTPUT` was somewhat different. See Section 18.4 [Obsolete
Macros], page 305, for a description of the arguments that `AC_OUTPUT` used to support.

If you run `make` in subdirectories, you should run it using the `make` variable `MAKE`. Most
versions of `make` set `MAKE` to the name of the `make` program plus any options it was given.
(But many do not include in it the values of any variables set on the command line, so those
are not passed on automatically.) Some old versions of `make` do not set this variable. The
following macro allows you to use it even with those versions.

AC_PROG_MAKE_SET   [Macro]
> If the Make command, `$MAKE` if set or else 'make', predefines `$(MAKE)`, define output
> variable `SET_MAKE` to be empty. Otherwise, define `SET_MAKE` to a macro definition
> that sets `$(MAKE)`, such as 'MAKE=make'. Calls `AC_SUBST` for `SET_MAKE`.

If you use this macro, place a line like this in each 'Makefile.in' that runs `MAKE` on
other directories:

        @SET_MAKE@

4.6 Performing Configuration Actions

'configure' is designed so that it appears to do everything itself, but there is actually a hidden slave: 'config.status'. 'configure' is in charge of examining your system, but it is 'config.status' that actually takes the proper actions based on the results of 'configure'. The most typical task of 'config.status' is to *instantiate* files.

This section describes the common behavior of the four standard instantiating macros: AC_CONFIG_FILES, AC_CONFIG_HEADERS, AC_CONFIG_COMMANDS and AC_CONFIG_LINKS. They all have this prototype:

        AC_CONFIG_ITEMS(tag..., [commands], [init-cmds])

where the arguments are:

tag...   A blank-or-newline-separated list of tags, which are typically the names of the files to instantiate.

             You are encouraged to use literals as *tags*. In particular, you should avoid

                 ... && my_foos="$my_foos fooo"
                 ... && my_foos="$my_foos foooo"
                 AC_CONFIG_ITEMS([$my_foos])

             and use this instead:

                 ... && AC_CONFIG_ITEMS([fooo])
                 ... && AC_CONFIG_ITEMS([foooo])

             The macros AC_CONFIG_FILES and AC_CONFIG_HEADERS use special *tag* values: they may have the form 'output' or 'output:inputs'. The file *output* is instantiated from its templates, *inputs* (defaulting to 'output.in').

             'AC_CONFIG_FILES([Makefile:boiler/top.mk:boiler/bot.mk])', for example, asks for the creation of the file 'Makefile' that contains the expansion of the output variables in the concatenation of 'boiler/top.mk' and 'boiler/bot.mk'.

             The special value '-' might be used to denote the standard output when used in *output*, or the standard input when used in the *inputs*. You most probably don't need to use this in 'configure.ac', but it is convenient when using the command line interface of './config.status', see Chapter 17 [config.status Invocation], page 301, for more details.

             The *inputs* may be absolute or relative file names. In the latter case they are first looked for in the build tree, and then in the source tree. Input files should be text files, and a line length below 2000 bytes should be safe.

commands
             Shell commands output literally into 'config.status', and associated with a tag that the user can use to tell 'config.status' which commands to run. The commands are run each time a *tag* request is given to 'config.status', typically each time the file '*tag*' is created.

             The variables set during the execution of configure are *not* available here: you first need to set them via the *init-cmds*. Nonetheless the following variables are precomputed:

srcdir   The name of the top source directory, assuming that the working
            directory is the top build directory. This is what the `configure`
            option '`--srcdir`' sets.

ac_top_srcdir
            The name of the top source directory, assuming that the working
            directory is the current build directory.

ac_top_build_prefix
            The name of the top build directory, assuming that the working
            directory is the current build directory. It can be empty, or else
            ends with a slash, so that you may concatenate it.

ac_srcdir
            The name of the corresponding source directory, assuming that the
            working directory is the current build directory.

tmp   The name of a temporary directory within the build tree, which
            you can use if you need to create additional temporary files. The
            directory is cleaned up when `config.status` is done or interrupted.
            Please use package-specific file name prefixes to avoid clashing with
            files that `config.status` may use internally.

The *current* directory refers to the directory (or pseudo-directory) containing
the input part of *tags*. For instance, running

```
AC_CONFIG_COMMANDS([deep/dir/out:in/in.in], [...], [...])
```

with '`--srcdir=../package`' produces the following values:

```
# Argument of --srcdir
srcdir='../package'
# Reversing deep/dir
ac_top_build_prefix='../../'
# Concatenation of $ac_top_build_prefix and srcdir
ac_top_srcdir='../../../package'
# Concatenation of $ac_top_srcdir and deep/dir
ac_srcdir='../../../package/deep/dir'
```

independently of '`in/in.in`'.

init-cmds Shell commands output *unquoted* near the beginning of '`config.status`', and
            executed each time '`config.status`' runs (regardless of the tag). Because they
            are unquoted, for example, '`$var`' is output as the value of `var`. *init-cmds* is
            typically used by '`configure`' to give '`config.status`' some variables it needs
            to run the *commands*.

            You should be extremely cautious in your variable names: all the *init-cmds*
            share the same name space and may overwrite each other in unpredictable
            ways. Sorry...

All these macros can be called multiple times, with different *tag* values, of course!

4.7 Creating Configuration Files

Be sure to read the previous section, Section 4.6 [Configuration Actions], page 21.

AC_CONFIG_FILES (*file*..., [*cmds*], [*init-cmds*])   [Macro]

> Make `AC_OUTPUT` create each '`file`' by copying an input file (by default '`file.in`'), substituting the output variable values. This macro is one of the instantiating macros; see Section 4.6 [Configuration Actions], page 21. See Section 4.8 [Makefile Substitutions], page 23, for more information on using output variables. See Section 7.2 [Setting Output Variables], page 114, for more information on creating them. This macro creates the directory that the file is in if it doesn't exist. Usually, makefiles are created this way, but other files, such as '`.gdbinit`', can be specified as well.
>
> Typical calls to `AC_CONFIG_FILES` look like this:
>
> ```
> AC_CONFIG_FILES([Makefile src/Makefile man/Makefile X/Imakefile])
> AC_CONFIG_FILES([autoconf], [chmod +x autoconf])
> ```
>
> You can override an input file name by appending to *file* a colon-separated list of input files. Examples:
>
> ```
> AC_CONFIG_FILES([Makefile:boiler/top.mk:boiler/bot.mk]
>                 [lib/Makefile:boiler/lib.mk])
> ```
>
> Doing this allows you to keep your file names acceptable to DOS variants, or to prepend and/or append boilerplate to the file.

4.8 Substitutions in Makefiles

Each subdirectory in a distribution that contains something to be compiled or installed should come with a file '`Makefile.in`', from which `configure` creates a file '`Makefile`' in that directory. To create '`Makefile`', `configure` performs a simple variable substitution, replacing occurrences of '`@variable@`' in '`Makefile.in`' with the value that `configure` has determined for that variable. Variables that are substituted into output files in this way are called *output variables*. They are ordinary shell variables that are set in `configure`. To make `configure` substitute a particular variable into the output files, the macro `AC_SUBST` must be called with that variable name as an argument. Any occurrences of '`@variable@`' for other variables are left unchanged. See Section 7.2 [Setting Output Variables], page 114, for more information on creating output variables with `AC_SUBST`.

A software package that uses a `configure` script should be distributed with a file '`Makefile.in`', but no makefile; that way, the user has to properly configure the package for the local system before compiling it.

See Section "Makefile Conventions" in *The GNU Coding Standards*, for more information on what to put in makefiles.

4.8.1 Preset Output Variables

Some output variables are preset by the Autoconf macros. Some of the Autoconf macros set additional output variables, which are mentioned in the descriptions for those macros. See Section B.2 [Output Variable Index], page 364, for a complete list of output variables. See Section 4.8.2 [Installation Directory Variables], page 27, for the list of the preset ones related to installation directories. Below are listed the other preset ones, many of which are precious variables (see Section 7.2 [Setting Output Variables], page 114, `AC_ARG_VAR`).

The preset variables which are available during 'config.status' (see Section 4.6 [Configuration Actions], page 21) may also be used during configure tests. For example, it is permissible to reference '$srcdir' when constructing a list of directories to pass via option '-I' during a compiler feature check. When used in this manner, coupled with the fact that configure is always run from the top build directory, it is sufficient to use just '$srcdir' instead of '$top_srcdir'.

CFLAGS   [Variable]

Debugging and optimization options for the C compiler. If it is not set in the environment when configure runs, the default value is set when you call AC_PROG_CC (or empty if you don't). configure uses this variable when compiling or linking programs to test for C features.

If a compiler option affects only the behavior of the preprocessor (e.g., '-Dname'), it should be put into CPPFLAGS instead. If it affects only the linker (e.g., '-Ldirectory'), it should be put into LDFLAGS instead. If it affects only the compiler proper, CFLAGS is the natural home for it. If an option affects multiple phases of the compiler, though, matters get tricky. One approach to put such options directly into CC, e.g., CC='gcc -m64'. Another is to put them into both CPPFLAGS and LDFLAGS, but not into CFLAGS.

However, remember that some 'Makefile' variables are reserved by the GNU Coding Standards for the use of the "user"—the person building the package. For instance, CFLAGS is one such variable.

Sometimes package developers are tempted to set user variables such as CFLAGS because it appears to make their job easier. However, the package itself should never set a user variable, particularly not to include switches that are required for proper compilation of the package. Since these variables are documented as being for the package builder, that person rightfully expects to be able to override any of these variables at build time. If the package developer needs to add switches without interfering with the user, the proper way to do that is to introduce an additional variable. Automake makes this easy by introducing AM_CFLAGS (see Section "Flag Variables Ordering" in *GNU Automake*), but the concept is the same even if Automake is not used.

configure_input   [Variable]

A comment saying that the file was generated automatically by configure and giving the name of the input file. AC_OUTPUT adds a comment line containing this variable to the top of every makefile it creates. For other files, you should reference this variable in a comment at the top of each input file. For example, an input shell script should begin like this:

```
#!/bin/sh
# @configure_input@
```

The presence of that line also reminds people editing the file that it needs to be processed by configure in order to be used.

CPPFLAGS   [Variable]

Preprocessor options for the C, C++, Objective C, and Objective C++ preprocessors and compilers. If it is not set in the environment when configure runs, the default value is empty. configure uses this variable when preprocessing or compiling programs to test for C, C++, Objective C, and Objective C++ features.

This variable's contents should contain options like '-I', '-D', and '-U' that affect only the behavior of the preprocessor. Please see the explanation of CFLAGS for what you can do if an option affects other phases of the compiler as well.

Currently, **configure** always links as part of a single invocation of the compiler that also preprocesses and compiles, so it uses this variable also when linking programs. However, it is unwise to depend on this behavior because the GNU Coding Standards do not require it and many packages do not use CPPFLAGS when linking programs.

See Section 7.3 [Special Chars in Variables], page 116, for limitations that CPPFLAGS might run into.

CXXFLAGS   [Variable]
Debugging and optimization options for the C++ compiler. It acts like CFLAGS, but for C++ instead of C.

DEFS   [Variable]
'-D' options to pass to the C compiler. If AC_CONFIG_HEADERS is called, **configure** replaces '@DEFS@' with '-DHAVE_CONFIG_H' instead (see Section 4.9 [Configuration Headers], page 33). This variable is not defined while **configure** is performing its tests, only when creating the output files. See Section 7.2 [Setting Output Variables], page 114, for how to check the results of previous tests.

ECHO_C   [Variable]
ECHO_N   [Variable]
ECHO_T   [Variable]
How does one suppress the trailing newline from **echo** for question-answer message pairs? These variables provide a way:

```
echo $ECHO_N "And the winner is... $ECHO_C"
sleep 100000000000
echo "${ECHO_T}dead."
```

Some old and uncommon **echo** implementations offer no means to achieve this, in which case ECHO_T is set to tab. You might not want to use it.

ERLCFLAGS   [Variable]
Debugging and optimization options for the Erlang compiler. If it is not set in the environment when **configure** runs, the default value is empty. **configure** uses this variable when compiling programs to test for Erlang features.

FCFLAGS   [Variable]
Debugging and optimization options for the Fortran compiler. If it is not set in the environment when **configure** runs, the default value is set when you call AC_PROG_FC (or empty if you don't). **configure** uses this variable when compiling or linking programs to test for Fortran features.

FFLAGS   [Variable]
Debugging and optimization options for the Fortran 77 compiler. If it is not set in the environment when **configure** runs, the default value is set when you call AC_PROG_F77 (or empty if you don't). **configure** uses this variable when compiling or linking programs to test for Fortran 77 features.

LDFLAGS   [Variable]

Options for the linker. If it is not set in the environment when `configure` runs, the default value is empty. `configure` uses this variable when linking programs to test for C, C++, Objective C, Objective C++, Fortran, and Go features.

This variable's contents should contain options like '`-s`' and '`-L`' that affect only the behavior of the linker. Please see the explanation of `CFLAGS` for what you can do if an option also affects other phases of the compiler.

Don't use this variable to pass library names ('`-l`') to the linker; use `LIBS` instead.

LIBS   [Variable]

'`-l`' options to pass to the linker. The default value is empty, but some Autoconf macros may prepend extra libraries to this variable if those libraries are found and provide necessary functions, see Section 5.4 [Libraries], page 49. `configure` uses this variable when linking programs to test for C, C++, Objective C, Objective C++, Fortran, and Go features.

OBJCFLAGS   [Variable]

Debugging and optimization options for the Objective C compiler. It acts like `CFLAGS`, but for Objective C instead of C.

OBJCXXFLAGS   [Variable]

Debugging and optimization options for the Objective C++ compiler. It acts like `CXXFLAGS`, but for Objective C++ instead of C++.

GOFLAGS   [Variable]

Debugging and optimization options for the Go compiler. It acts like `CFLAGS`, but for Go instead of C.

builddir   [Variable]

Rigorously equal to '`.`'. Added for symmetry only.

abs_builddir   [Variable]

Absolute name of `builddir`.

top_builddir   [Variable]

The relative name of the top level of the current build tree. In the top-level directory, this is the same as `builddir`.

top_build_prefix   [Variable]

The relative name of the top level of the current build tree with final slash if nonempty. This is the same as `top_builddir`, except that it contains zero or more runs of `../`, so it should not be appended with a slash for concatenation. This helps for `make` implementations that otherwise do not treat '`./file`' and '`file`' as equal in the toplevel build directory.

abs_top_builddir   [Variable]

Absolute name of `top_builddir`.

srcdir   [Variable]

The name of the directory that contains the source code for that makefile.

`abs_srcdir`   [Variable]
>   Absolute name of `srcdir`.

`top_srcdir`   [Variable]
>   The name of the top-level source code directory for the package. In the top-level
>   directory, this is the same as `srcdir`.

`abs_top_srcdir`   [Variable]
>   Absolute name of `top_srcdir`.

4.8.2 Installation Directory Variables

The following variables specify the directories for package installation, see Section "Variables
for Installation Directories" in *The GNU Coding Standards*, for more information. Each
variable corresponds to an argument of `configure`; trailing slashes are stripped so that
expressions such as '`${prefix}/lib`' expand with only one slash between directory names.
See the end of this section for details on when and how to use these variables.

`bindir`   [Variable]
>   The directory for installing executables that users run.

`datadir`   [Variable]
>   The directory for installing idiosyncratic read-only architecture-independent data.

`datarootdir`   [Variable]
>   The root of the directory tree for read-only architecture-independent data files.

`docdir`   [Variable]
>   The directory for installing documentation files (other than Info and man).

`dvidir`   [Variable]
>   The directory for installing documentation files in DVI format.

`exec_prefix`   [Variable]
>   The installation prefix for architecture-dependent files. By default it's the same as
>   `prefix`. You should avoid installing anything directly to `exec_prefix`. However, the
>   default value for directories containing architecture-dependent files should be relative
>   to `exec_prefix`.

`htmldir`   [Variable]
>   The directory for installing HTML documentation.

`includedir`   [Variable]
>   The directory for installing C header files.

`infodir`   [Variable]
>   The directory for installing documentation in Info format.

`libdir`   [Variable]
>   The directory for installing object code libraries.

`libexecdir`   [Variable]
>   The directory for installing executables that other programs run.

`localedir`   [Variable]
> The directory for installing locale-dependent but architecture-independent data, such as message catalogs. This directory usually has a subdirectory per locale.

`localstatedir`   [Variable]
> The directory for installing modifiable single-machine data.

`mandir`   [Variable]
> The top-level directory for installing documentation in man format.

`oldincludedir`   [Variable]
> The directory for installing C header files for non-GCC compilers.

`pdfdir`   [Variable]
> The directory for installing PDF documentation.

`prefix`   [Variable]
> The common installation prefix for all files. If `exec_prefix` is defined to a different value, `prefix` is used only for architecture-independent files.

`psdir`   [Variable]
> The directory for installing PostScript documentation.

`sbindir`   [Variable]
> The directory for installing executables that system administrators run.

`sharedstatedir`   [Variable]
> The directory for installing modifiable architecture-independent data.

`sysconfdir`   [Variable]
> The directory for installing read-only single-machine data.

Most of these variables have values that rely on `prefix` or `exec_prefix`. It is deliberate that the directory output variables keep them unexpanded: typically '`@datarootdir@`' is replaced by '`${prefix}/share`', not '`/usr/local/share`', and '`@datadir@`' is replaced by '`${datarootdir}`'.

This behavior is mandated by the GNU Coding Standards, so that when the user runs:

'`make`'   she can still specify a different prefix from the one specified to `configure`, in which case, if needed, the package should hard code dependencies corresponding to the make-specified prefix.

'`make install`'
               she can specify a different installation location, in which case the package *must* still depend on the location which was compiled in (i.e., never recompile when '`make install`' is run). This is an extremely important feature, as many people may decide to install all the files of a package grouped together, and then install links from the final locations to there.

In order to support these features, it is essential that `datarootdir` remains defined as '`${prefix}/share`', so that its value can be expanded based on the current value of `prefix`.

A corollary is that you should not use these variables except in makefiles. For instance, instead of trying to evaluate `datadir` in 'configure' and hard-coding it in makefiles using e.g., 'AC_DEFINE_UNQUOTED([DATADIR], ["$datadir"], [Data directory.])', you should add '-DDATADIR='$(datadir)'' to your makefile's definition of CPPFLAGS (AM_CPPFLAGS if you are also using Automake).

Similarly, you should not rely on AC_CONFIG_FILES to replace `bindir` and friends in your shell scripts and other files; instead, let `make` manage their replacement. For instance Autoconf ships templates of its shell scripts ending with '.in', and uses a makefile snippet similar to the following to build scripts like `autoheader` and `autom4te`:

```
edit = sed \
        -e 's|@bindir[@]|$(bindir)|g' \
        -e 's|@pkgdatadir[@]|$(pkgdatadir)|g' \
        -e 's|@prefix[@]|$(prefix)|g'

autoheader autom4te: Makefile
        rm -f $@ $@.tmp
        srcdir=''; \
          test -f ./$@.in || srcdir=$(srcdir)/; \
          $(edit) $${srcdir}$@.in >$@.tmp
        chmod +x $@.tmp
        chmod a-w $@.tmp
        mv $@.tmp $@

autoheader: $(srcdir)/autoheader.in
autom4te: $(srcdir)/autom4te.in
```

Some details are noteworthy:

'@bindir[@]'
>   The brackets prevent `configure` from replacing '@bindir@' in the Sed expression itself. Brackets are preferable to a backslash here, since Posix says '\@' is not portable.

'$(bindir)'
>   Don't use '@bindir@'! Use the matching makefile variable instead.

'$(pkgdatadir)'
>   The example takes advantage of the variable '$(pkgdatadir)' provided by Automake; it is equivalent to '$(datadir)/$(PACKAGE)'.

'/'
>   Don't use '/' in the Sed expressions that replace file names since most likely the variables you use, such as '$(bindir)', contain '/'. Use a shell metacharacter instead, such as '|'.

special characters
>   File names, file name components, and the value of VPATH should not contain shell metacharacters or white space. See Section 7.3 [Special Chars in Variables], page 116.

dependency on 'Makefile'
> Since edit uses values that depend on the configuration specific values (prefix, etc.) and not only on VERSION and so forth, the output depends on 'Makefile', not 'configure.ac'.

'$@'
> The main rule is generic, and uses '$@' extensively to avoid the need for multiple copies of the rule.

Separated dependencies and single suffix rules
> You can't use them! The above snippet cannot be (portably) rewritten as:

```
autoconf autoheader: Makefile
.in:
        rm -f $@ $@.tmp
        $(edit) $< >$@.tmp
        chmod +x $@.tmp
        mv $@.tmp $@
```

> See Section 12.19 [Single Suffix Rules], page 269, for details.

'$(srcdir)'
> Be sure to specify the name of the source directory, otherwise the package won't support separated builds.

For the more specific installation of Erlang libraries, the following variables are defined:

ERLANG_INSTALL_LIB_DIR   [Variable]
> The common parent directory of Erlang library installation directories. This variable is set by calling the AC_ERLANG_SUBST_INSTALL_LIB_DIR macro in 'configure.ac'.

ERLANG_INSTALL_LIB_DIR_*library*   [Variable]
> The installation directory for Erlang library *library*. This variable is set by using the 'AC_ERLANG_SUBST_INSTALL_LIB_SUBDIR' macro in 'configure.ac'.

See Section 5.13 [Erlang Libraries], page 98, for details.

4.8.3 Changed Directory Variables

In Autoconf 2.60, the set of directory variables has changed, and the defaults of some variables have been adjusted (see Section 4.8.2 [Installation Directory Variables], page 27) to changes in the GNU Coding Standards. Notably, 'datadir', 'infodir', and 'mandir' are now expressed in terms of 'datarootdir'. If you are upgrading from an earlier Autoconf version, you may need to adjust your files to ensure that the directory variables are substituted correctly (see Section 20.5 [Defining Directories], page 343), and that a definition of 'datarootdir' is in place. For example, in a 'Makefile.in', adding

```
datarootdir = @datarootdir@
```

is usually sufficient. If you use Automake to create 'Makefile.in', it will add this for you.

To help with the transition, Autoconf warns about files that seem to use datarootdir without defining it. In some cases, it then expands the value of $datarootdir in substitutions of the directory variables. The following example shows such a warning:

```
$ cat configure.ac
AC_INIT
AC_CONFIG_FILES([Makefile])
AC_OUTPUT
$ cat Makefile.in
prefix = @prefix@
datadir = @datadir@
$ autoconf
$ configure
configure: creating ./config.status
config.status: creating Makefile
config.status: WARNING:
                 Makefile.in seems to ignore the --datarootdir setting
$ cat Makefile
prefix = /usr/local
datadir = ${prefix}/share
```

Usually one can easily change the file to accommodate both older and newer Autoconf releases:

```
$ cat Makefile.in
prefix = @prefix@
datarootdir = @datarootdir@
datadir = @datadir@
$ configure
configure: creating ./config.status
config.status: creating Makefile
$ cat Makefile
prefix = /usr/local
datarootdir = ${prefix}/share
datadir = ${datarootdir}
```

In some cases, however, the checks may not be able to detect that a suitable initialization of datarootdir is in place, or they may fail to detect that such an initialization is necessary in the output file. If, after auditing your package, there are still spurious 'configure' warnings about datarootdir, you may add the line

```
AC_DEFUN([AC_DATAROOTDIR_CHECKED])
```

to your 'configure.ac' to disable the warnings. This is an exception to the usual rule that you should not define a macro whose name begins with AC_ (see Section 10.2 [Macro Names], page 178).

4.8.4 Build Directories

You can support compiling a software package for several architectures simultaneously from the same copy of the source code. The object files for each architecture are kept in their own directory.

To support doing this, make uses the VPATH variable to find the files that are in the source directory. GNU Make can do this. Most other recent make programs can do this as well, though they may have difficulties and it is often simpler to recommend GNU make

(see Section 12.18 [VPATH and Make], page 262). Older `make` programs do not support
`VPATH`; when using them, the source code must be in the same directory as the object files.

If you are using GNU Automake, the remaining details in this section are already covered
for you, based on the contents of your 'Makefile.am'. But if you are using Autoconf in
isolation, then supporting `VPATH` requires the following in your 'Makefile.in':

```
srcdir = @srcdir@
VPATH = @srcdir@
```

Do not set `VPATH` to the value of another variable (see Section 12.18.1 [Variables listed
in VPATH], page 262.

`configure` substitutes the correct value for `srcdir` when it produces 'Makefile'.

Do not use the `make` variable `$<`, which expands to the file name of the file in the source
directory (found with `VPATH`), except in implicit rules. (An implicit rule is one such as
'.c.o', which tells how to create a '.o' file from a '.c' file.) Some versions of `make` do not
set `$<` in explicit rules; they expand it to an empty value.

Instead, Make command lines should always refer to source files by prefixing them with
'`$(srcdir)/`'. For example:

```
time.info: time.texinfo
        $(MAKEINFO) '$(srcdir)/time.texinfo'
```

4.8.5 Automatic Remaking

You can put rules like the following in the top-level 'Makefile.in' for a package to automatically update the configuration information when you change the configuration files.
This example includes all of the optional files, such as 'aclocal.m4' and those related to
configuration header files. Omit from the 'Makefile.in' rules for any of these files that
your package does not use.

The '`$(srcdir)/`' prefix is included because of limitations in the `VPATH` mechanism.

The 'stamp-' files are necessary because the timestamps of 'config.h.in' and
'config.h' are not changed if remaking them does not change their contents. This feature
avoids unnecessary recompilation. You should include the file 'stamp-h.in' in your
package's distribution, so that `make` considers 'config.h.in' up to date. Don't use `touch`
(see [Limitations of Usual Tools], page 250); instead, use `echo` (using `date` would cause
needless differences, hence CVS conflicts, etc.).

```
$(srcdir)/configure: configure.ac aclocal.m4
        cd '$(srcdir)' && autoconf

# autoheader might not change config.h.in, so touch a stamp file.
$(srcdir)/config.h.in: stamp-h.in
$(srcdir)/stamp-h.in: configure.ac aclocal.m4
        cd '$(srcdir)' && autoheader
        echo timestamp > '$(srcdir)/stamp-h.in'

config.h: stamp-h
stamp-h: config.h.in config.status
        ./config.status

Makefile: Makefile.in config.status
        ./config.status

config.status: configure
        ./config.status --recheck
```

(Be careful if you copy these lines directly into your makefile, as you need to convert the indented lines to start with the tab character.)

In addition, you should use

```
AC_CONFIG_FILES([stamp-h], [echo timestamp > stamp-h])
```

so 'config.status' ensures that 'config.h' is considered up to date. See Section 4.5 [Output], page 20, for more information about `AC_OUTPUT`.

See Chapter 17 [config.status Invocation], page 301, for more examples of handling configuration-related dependencies.

4.9 Configuration Header Files

When a package contains more than a few tests that define C preprocessor symbols, the command lines to pass '-D' options to the compiler can get quite long. This causes two problems. One is that the make output is hard to visually scan for errors. More seriously, the command lines can exceed the length limits of some operating systems. As an alternative to passing '-D' options to the compiler, `configure` scripts can create a C header file containing '#define' directives. The `AC_CONFIG_HEADERS` macro selects this kind of output. Though it can be called anywhere between `AC_INIT` and `AC_OUTPUT`, it is customary to call it right after `AC_INIT`.

The package should '#include' the configuration header file before any other header files, to prevent inconsistencies in declarations (for example, if it redefines `const`).

To provide for VPATH builds, remember to pass the C compiler a '-I.' option (or '-I..'; whichever directory contains 'config.h'). Even if you use '#include "config.h"', the preprocessor searches only the directory of the currently read file, i.e., the source directory, not the build directory.

With the appropriate '-I' option, you can use '#include <config.h>'. Actually, it's a good habit to use it, because in the rare case when the source directory contains another 'config.h', the build directory should be searched first.

AC_CONFIG_HEADERS (*header* ..., [*cmds*], [*init-cmds*])   [Macro]
> This macro is one of the instantiating macros; see Section 4.6 [Configuration Actions], page 21. Make `AC_OUTPUT` create the file(s) in the blank-or-newline-separated list *header* containing C preprocessor `#define` statements, and replace '`@DEFS@`' in generated files with '`-DHAVE_CONFIG_H`' instead of the value of `DEFS`. The usual name for *header* is '`config.h`'.
>
> If *header* already exists and its contents are identical to what `AC_OUTPUT` would put in it, it is left alone. Doing this allows making some changes in the configuration without needlessly causing object files that depend on the header file to be recompiled.
>
> Usually the input file is named '`header.in`'; however, you can override the input file name by appending to *header* a colon-separated list of input files. For example, you might need to make the input file name acceptable to DOS variants:
>
> ```
> AC_CONFIG_HEADERS([config.h:config.hin])
> ```

AH_HEADER   [Macro]
> This macro is defined as the name of the first declared config header and undefined if no config headers have been declared up to this point. A third-party macro may, for example, require use of a config header without invoking AC_CONFIG_HEADERS twice, like this:
>
> ```
> AC_CONFIG_COMMANDS_PRE(
>         [m4_ifndef([AH_HEADER], [AC_CONFIG_HEADERS([config.h])])])
> ```

> See Section 4.6 [Configuration Actions], page 21, for more details on *header*.

4.9.1 Configuration Header Templates

Your distribution should contain a template file that looks as you want the final header file to look, including comments, with `#undef` statements which are used as hooks. For example, suppose your '`configure.ac`' makes these calls:

```
AC_CONFIG_HEADERS([conf.h])
AC_CHECK_HEADERS([unistd.h])
```

Then you could have code like the following in '`conf.h.in`'. The '`conf.h`' created by `configure` defines '`HAVE_UNISTD_H`' to 1, if and only if the system has '`unistd.h`'.

```
/* Define as 1 if you have unistd.h.  */
#undef HAVE_UNISTD_H
```

The format of the template file is stricter than what the C preprocessor is required to accept. A directive line should contain only whitespace, '`#undef`', and '`HAVE_UNISTD_H`'. The use of '`#define`' instead of '`#undef`', or of comments on the same line as '`#undef`', is strongly discouraged. Each hook should only be listed once. Other preprocessor lines, such as '`#ifdef`' or '`#include`', are copied verbatim from the template into the generated header.

Since it is a tedious task to keep a template header up to date, you may use `autoheader` to generate it, see Section 4.9.2 [autoheader Invocation], page 35.

During the instantiation of the header, each '`#undef`' line in the template file for each symbol defined by '`AC_DEFINE`' is changed to an appropriate '`#define`'. If the corresponding '`AC_DEFINE`' has not been executed during the `configure` run, the '`#undef`' line is commented out. (This is important, e.g., for '_POSIX_SOURCE': on many systems, it can be implicitly defined by the compiler, and undefining it in the header would then break compilation of subsequent headers.)

Currently, *all* remaining '#undef' lines in the header template are commented out, whether or not there was a corresponding 'AC_DEFINE' for the macro name; but this behavior is not guaranteed for future releases of Autoconf.

Generally speaking, since you should not use '#define', and you cannot guarantee whether a '#undef' directive in the header template will be converted to a '#define' or commented out in the generated header file, the template file cannot be used for conditional definition effects. Consequently, if you need to use the construct

```
#ifdef THIS
# define THAT
#endif
```

you must place it outside of the template. If you absolutely need to hook it to the config header itself, please put the directives to a separate file, and '#include' that file from the config header template. If you are using autoheader, you would probably use 'AH_BOTTOM' to append the '#include' directive.

4.9.2 Using autoheader to Create 'config.h.in'

The autoheader program can create a template file of C '#define' statements for configure to use. It searches for the first invocation of AC_CONFIG_HEADERS in 'configure' sources to determine the name of the template. (If the first call of AC_CONFIG_HEADERS specifies more than one input file name, autoheader uses the first one.)

It is recommended that only one input file is used. If you want to append a boilerplate code, it is preferable to use 'AH_BOTTOM([#include <conf_post.h>])'. File 'conf_post.h' is not processed during the configuration then, which make things clearer. Analogically, AH_TOP can be used to prepend a boilerplate code.

In order to do its job, autoheader needs you to document all of the symbols that you might use. Typically this is done via an AC_DEFINE or AC_DEFINE_UNQUOTED call whose first argument is a literal symbol and whose third argument describes the symbol (see Section 7.1 [Defining Symbols], page 113). Alternatively, you can use AH_TEMPLATE (see Section 4.9.3 [Autoheader Macros], page 36), or you can supply a suitable input file for a subsequent configuration header file. Symbols defined by Autoconf's builtin tests are already documented properly; you need to document only those that you define yourself.

You might wonder why autoheader is needed: after all, why would configure need to "patch" a 'config.h.in' to produce a 'config.h' instead of just creating 'config.h' from scratch? Well, when everything rocks, the answer is just that we are wasting our time maintaining autoheader: generating 'config.h' directly is all that is needed. When things go wrong, however, you'll be thankful for the existence of autoheader.

The fact that the symbols are documented is important in order to *check* that 'config.h' makes sense. The fact that there is a well-defined list of symbols that should be defined (or not) is also important for people who are porting packages to environments where configure cannot be run: they just have to *fill in the blanks*.

But let's come back to the point: the invocation of autoheader...

If you give `autoheader` an argument, it uses that file instead of 'configure.ac' and writes the header file to the standard output instead of to 'config.h.in'. If you give `autoheader` an argument of '-', it reads the standard input instead of 'configure.ac' and writes the header file to the standard output.

`autoheader` accepts the following options:

'--help'
'-h'   Print a summary of the command line options and exit.

'--version'
'-V'   Print the version number of Autoconf and exit.

'--verbose'
'-v'   Report processing steps.

'--debug'
'-d'   Don't remove the temporary files.

'--force'
'-f'   Remake the template file even if newer than its input files.

'--include=*dir*'
'-I *dir*'   Append *dir* to the include path. Multiple invocations accumulate.

'--prepend-include=*dir*'
'-B *dir*'   Prepend *dir* to the include path. Multiple invocations accumulate.

'--warnings=*category*'
'-W *category*'
                Report the warnings related to *category* (which can actually be a comma separated list). Current categories include:

                'obsolete'
                            report the uses of obsolete constructs

                'all'   report all the warnings

                'none'   report none

                'error'   treats warnings as errors

                'no-*category*'
                            disable warnings falling into *category*

4.9.3 Autoheader Macros

`autoheader` scans 'configure.ac' and figures out which C preprocessor symbols it might define. It knows how to generate templates for symbols defined by AC_CHECK_HEADERS, AC_CHECK_FUNCS etc., but if you AC_DEFINE any additional symbol, you must define a template for it. If there are missing templates, `autoheader` fails with an error message.

The template for a *symbol* is created by `autoheader` from the *description* argument to an AC_DEFINE; see Section 7.1 [Defining Symbols], page 113.

For special needs, you can use the following macros.

AH_TEMPLATE (*key, description*)   [Macro]

>   Tell `autoheader` to generate a template for *key*. This macro generates standard
>   templates just like `AC_DEFINE` when a *description* is given.

>   For example:

>    ```
>    AH_TEMPLATE([CRAY_STACKSEG_END],
>                [Define to one of _getb67, GETB67, getb67
>                 for Cray-2 and Cray-YMP systems.  This
>                 function is required for alloca.c support
>                 on those systems.])
>    ```

>   generates the following template, with the description properly justified.

>    ```
>    /* Define to one of _getb67, GETB67, getb67 for Cray-2 and
>       Cray-YMP systems.  This function is required for alloca.c
>       support on those systems.  */
>    #undef CRAY_STACKSEG_END
>    ```

AH_VERBATIM (*key, template*)   [Macro]

>   Tell `autoheader` to include the *template* as-is in the header template file. This
>   *template* is associated with the *key*, which is used to sort all the different templates
>   and guarantee their uniqueness. It should be a symbol that can be defined via `AC_DEFINE`.

AH_TOP (*text*)   [Macro]

>   Include *text* at the top of the header template file.

AH_BOTTOM (*text*)   [Macro]

>   Include *text* at the bottom of the header template file.

Please note that *text* gets included "verbatim" to the template file, not to the resulting config header, so it can easily get mangled when the template is processed. There is rarely a need for something other than

```
AH_BOTTOM([#include <custom.h>])
```

4.10 Running Arbitrary Configuration Commands

You can execute arbitrary commands before, during, and after 'config.status' is run. The three following macros accumulate the commands to run when they are called multiple times. `AC_CONFIG_COMMANDS` replaces the obsolete macro `AC_OUTPUT_COMMANDS`; see Section 18.4 [Obsolete Macros], page 305, for details.

AC_CONFIG_COMMANDS (*tag*..., [*cmds*], [*init-cmds*])   [Macro]

>   Specify additional shell commands to run at the end of 'config.status', and shell
>   commands to initialize any variables from `configure`. Associate the commands with
>   *tag*. Since typically the *cmds* create a file, *tag* should naturally be the name of
>   that file. If needed, the directory hosting *tag* is created. This macro is one of the
>   instantiating macros; see Section 4.6 [Configuration Actions], page 21.

>   Here is an unrealistic example:

```
fubar=42
AC_CONFIG_COMMANDS([fubar],
                   [echo this is extra $fubar, and so on.],
                   [fubar=$fubar])
```

Here is a better one:

```
AC_CONFIG_COMMANDS([timestamp], [date >timestamp])
```

The following two macros look similar, but in fact they are not of the same breed: they are executed directly by 'configure', so you cannot use 'config.status' to rerun them.

AC_CONFIG_COMMANDS_PRE (*cmds*)   [Macro]
Execute the *cmds* right before creating 'config.status'.

This macro presents the last opportunity to call AC_SUBST, AC_DEFINE, or AC_CONFIG_*ITEMS* macros.

AC_CONFIG_COMMANDS_POST (*cmds*)   [Macro]
Execute the *cmds* right after creating 'config.status'.

4.11 Creating Configuration Links

You may find it convenient to create links whose destinations depend upon results of tests. One can use AC_CONFIG_COMMANDS but the creation of relative symbolic links can be delicate when the package is built in a directory different from the source directory.

AC_CONFIG_LINKS (*dest:source*..., [*cmds*], [*init-cmds*])   [Macro]
Make AC_OUTPUT link each of the existing files *source* to the corresponding link name *dest*. Makes a symbolic link if possible, otherwise a hard link if possible, otherwise a copy. The *dest* and *source* names should be relative to the top level source or build directory. This macro is one of the instantiating macros; see Section 4.6 [Configuration Actions], page 21.

For example, this call:

```
AC_CONFIG_LINKS([host.h:config/$machine.h
                 object.h:config/$obj_format.h])
```

creates in the current directory 'host.h' as a link to '*srcdir*/config/$machine.h', and 'object.h' as a link to '*srcdir*/config/$obj_format.h'.

The tempting value '.' for *dest* is invalid: it makes it impossible for 'config.status' to guess the links to establish.

One can then run:

```
./config.status host.h object.h
```

to create the links.

4.12 Configuring Other Packages in Subdirectories

In most situations, calling AC_OUTPUT is sufficient to produce makefiles in subdirectories. However, configure scripts that control more than one independent package can use AC_CONFIG_SUBDIRS to run configure scripts for other packages in subdirectories.

`AC_CONFIG_SUBDIRS (dir ...)`   [Macro]

>   Make `AC_OUTPUT` run `configure` in each subdirectory *dir* in the given blank-or-newline-separated list. Each *dir* should be a literal, i.e., please do not use:

```
if test "x$package_foo_enabled" = xyes; then
  my_subdirs="$my_subdirs foo"
fi
AC_CONFIG_SUBDIRS([$my_subdirs])
```

>   because this prevents '`./configure --help=recursive`' from displaying the options of the package `foo`. Instead, you should write:

```
if test "x$package_foo_enabled" = xyes; then
  AC_CONFIG_SUBDIRS([foo])
fi
```

>   If a given *dir* is not found at `configure` run time, a warning is reported; if the subdirectory is optional, write:

```
if test -d "$srcdir/foo"; then
  AC_CONFIG_SUBDIRS([foo])
fi
```

>   If a given *dir* contains `configure.gnu`, it is run instead of `configure`. This is for packages that might use a non-Autoconf script `Configure`, which can't be called through a wrapper `configure` since it would be the same file on case-insensitive file systems. Likewise, if a *dir* contains '`configure.in`' but no `configure`, the Cygnus `configure` script found by `AC_CONFIG_AUX_DIR` is used.

>   The subdirectory `configure` scripts are given the same command line options that were given to this `configure` script, with minor changes if needed, which include:

>   — adjusting a relative name for the cache file;

>   — adjusting a relative name for the source directory;

>   — propagating the current value of `$prefix`, including if it was defaulted, and if the default values of the top level and of the subdirectory '`configure`' differ.

>   This macro also sets the output variable `subdirs` to the list of directories '`dir ...`'. Make rules can use this variable to determine which subdirectories to recurse into.

>   This macro may be called multiple times.

4.13 Default Prefix

By default, `configure` sets the prefix for files it installs to '`/usr/local`'. The user of `configure` can select a different prefix using the '`--prefix`' and '`--exec-prefix`' options. There are two ways to change the default: when creating `configure`, and when running it.

Some software packages might want to install in a directory other than '`/usr/local`' by default. To accomplish that, use the `AC_PREFIX_DEFAULT` macro.

`AC_PREFIX_DEFAULT (prefix)`   [Macro]

>   Set the default installation prefix to *prefix* instead of '`/usr/local`'.

It may be convenient for users to have `configure` guess the installation prefix from the location of a related program that they have already installed. If you wish to do that, you can call `AC_PREFIX_PROGRAM`.

AC_PREFIX_PROGRAM (*program*)   [Macro]

> If the user did not specify an installation prefix (using the '--prefix' option), guess a value for it by looking for *program* in PATH, the way the shell does. If *program* is found, set the prefix to the parent of the directory containing *program*, else default the prefix as described above ('/usr/local' or AC_PREFIX_DEFAULT). For example, if *program* is gcc and the PATH contains '/usr/local/gnu/bin/gcc', set the prefix to '/usr/local/gnu'.

5 Existing Tests

These macros test for particular system features that packages might need or want to use. If you need to test for a kind of feature that none of these macros check for, you can probably do it by calling primitive test macros with appropriate arguments (see Chapter 6 [Writing Tests], page 101).

These tests print messages telling the user which feature they're checking for, and what they find. They cache their results for future **configure** runs (see Section 7.4 [Caching Results], page 117).

Some of these macros set output variables. See Section 4.8 [Makefile Substitutions], page 23, for how to get their values. The phrase "define *name*" is used below as a shorthand to mean "define the C preprocessor symbol *name* to the value 1". See Section 7.1 [Defining Symbols], page 113, for how to get those symbol definitions into your program.

5.1 Common Behavior

Much effort has been expended to make Autoconf easy to learn. The most obvious way to reach this goal is simply to enforce standard interfaces and behaviors, avoiding exceptions as much as possible. Because of history and inertia, unfortunately, there are still too many exceptions in Autoconf; nevertheless, this section describes some of the common rules.

5.1.1 Standard Symbols

All the generic macros that `AC_DEFINE` a symbol as a result of their test transform their *argument* values to a standard alphabet. First, *argument* is converted to upper case and any asterisks ('*') are each converted to 'P'. Any remaining characters that are not alphanumeric are converted to underscores.

For instance,

```
AC_CHECK_TYPES([struct $Expensive*])
```

defines the symbol 'HAVE_STRUCT__EXPENSIVEP' if the check succeeds.

5.1.2 Default Includes

Several tests depend upon a set of header files. Since these headers are not universally available, tests actually have to provide a set of protected includes, such as:

```
#ifdef TIME_WITH_SYS_TIME
# include <sys/time.h>
# include <time.h>
#else
# ifdef HAVE_SYS_TIME_H
#  include <sys/time.h>
# else
#  include <time.h>
# endif
#endif
```

Unless you know exactly what you are doing, you should avoid using unconditional includes, and check the existence of the headers you include beforehand (see Section 5.6 [Header Files], page 63).

Most generic macros use the following macro to provide the default set of includes:

AC_INCLUDES_DEFAULT ([*include-directives*])   [Macro]
Expand to *include-directives* if defined, otherwise to:

```
#include <stdio.h>
#ifdef HAVE_SYS_TYPES_H
# include <sys/types.h>
#endif
#ifdef HAVE_SYS_STAT_H
# include <sys/stat.h>
#endif
#ifdef STDC_HEADERS
# include <stdlib.h>
# include <stddef.h>
#else
# ifdef HAVE_STDLIB_H
#  include <stdlib.h>
# endif
#endif
#ifdef HAVE_STRING_H
# if !defined STDC_HEADERS && defined HAVE_MEMORY_H
#  include <memory.h>
# endif
# include <string.h>
#endif
#ifdef HAVE_STRINGS_H
# include <strings.h>
#endif
#ifdef HAVE_INTTYPES_H
# include <inttypes.h>
#endif
#ifdef HAVE_STDINT_H
# include <stdint.h>
#endif
#ifdef HAVE_UNISTD_H
# include <unistd.h>
#endif
```

If the default includes are used, then check for the presence of these headers and their compatibility, i.e., you don't need to run **AC_HEADER_STDC**, nor check for 'stdlib.h' etc.

These headers are checked for in the same order as they are included. For instance, on some systems 'string.h' and 'strings.h' both exist, but conflict. Then **HAVE_STRING_H** is defined, not **HAVE_STRINGS_H**.

5.2 Alternative Programs

These macros check for the presence or behavior of particular programs. They are used to choose between several alternative programs and to decide what to do once one has been chosen. If there is no macro specifically defined to check for a program you need, and you don't need to check for any special properties of it, then you can use one of the general program-check macros.

5.2.1 Particular Program Checks

These macros check for particular programs—whether they exist, and in some cases whether they support certain features.

AC_PROG_AWK   [Macro]

> Check for gawk, mawk, nawk, and awk, in that order, and set output variable AWK to the first one that is found. It tries gawk first because that is reported to be the best implementation. The result can be overridden by setting the variable AWK or the cache variable ac_cv_prog_AWK.
>
> Using this macro is sufficient to avoid the pitfalls of traditional awk (see [Limitations of Usual Tools], page 235).

AC_PROG_GREP   [Macro]

> Look for the best available grep or ggrep that accepts the longest input lines possible, and that supports multiple '-e' options. Set the output variable GREP to whatever is chosen. See [Limitations of Usual Tools], page 242, for more information about portability problems with the grep command family. The result can be overridden by setting the GREP variable and is cached in the ac_cv_path_GREP variable.

AC_PROG_EGREP   [Macro]

> Check whether $GREP -E works, or else look for the best available egrep or gegrep that accepts the longest input lines possible. Set the output variable EGREP to whatever is chosen. The result can be overridden by setting the EGREP variable and is cached in the ac_cv_path_EGREP variable.

AC_PROG_FGREP   [Macro]

> Check whether $GREP -F works, or else look for the best available fgrep or gfgrep that accepts the longest input lines possible. Set the output variable FGREP to whatever is chosen. The result can be overridden by setting the FGREP variable and is cached in the ac_cv_path_FGREP variable.

AC_PROG_INSTALL   [Macro]

> Set output variable INSTALL to the name of a BSD-compatible install program, if one is found in the current PATH. Otherwise, set INSTALL to 'dir/install-sh -c', checking the directories specified to AC_CONFIG_AUX_DIR (or its default directories) to determine dir (see Section 4.5 [Output], page 20). Also set the variables INSTALL_PROGRAM and INSTALL_SCRIPT to '${INSTALL}' and INSTALL_DATA to '${INSTALL} -m 644'.
>
> '@INSTALL@' is special, as its value may vary for different configuration files.
>
> This macro screens out various instances of install known not to work. It prefers to find a C program rather than a shell script, for speed. Instead of 'install-sh',

it can also use 'install.sh', but that name is obsolete because some make programs have a rule that creates 'install' from it if there is no makefile. Further, this macro requires install to be able to install multiple files into a target directory in a single invocation.

Autoconf comes with a copy of 'install-sh' that you can use. If you use AC_PROG_INSTALL, you must include either 'install-sh' or 'install.sh' in your distribution; otherwise configure produces an error message saying it can't find them—even if the system you're on has a good install program. This check is a safety measure to prevent you from accidentally leaving that file out, which would prevent your package from installing on systems that don't have a BSD-compatible install program.

If you need to use your own installation program because it has features not found in standard install programs, there is no reason to use AC_PROG_INSTALL; just put the file name of your program into your 'Makefile.in' files.

The result of the test can be overridden by setting the variable INSTALL or the cache variable ac_cv_path_install.

AC_PROG_MKDIR_P   [Macro]
Set output variable MKDIR_P to a program that ensures that for each argument, a directory named by this argument exists, creating it and its parent directories if needed, and without race conditions when two instances of the program attempt to make the same directory at nearly the same time.

This macro uses the 'mkdir -p' command if possible. Otherwise, it falls back on invoking install-sh with the '-d' option, so your package should contain 'install-sh' as described under AC_PROG_INSTALL. An 'install-sh' file that predates Autoconf 2.60 or Automake 1.10 is vulnerable to race conditions, so if you want to support parallel installs from different packages into the same directory you need to make sure you have an up-to-date 'install-sh'. In particular, be careful about using 'autoreconf -if' if your Automake predates Automake 1.10.

This macro is related to the AS_MKDIR_P macro (see Chapter 9 [Programming in M4sh], page 167), but it sets an output variable intended for use in other files, whereas AS_MKDIR_P is intended for use in scripts like configure. Also, AS_MKDIR_P does not accept options, but MKDIR_P supports the '-m' option, e.g., a makefile might invoke $(MKDIR_P) -m 0 dir to create an inaccessible directory, and conversely a makefile should use $(MKDIR_P) -- $(FOO) if *FOO* might yield a value that begins with '-'. Finally, AS_MKDIR_P does not check for race condition vulnerability, whereas AC_PROG_MKDIR_P does.

'@MKDIR_P@' is special, as its value may vary for different configuration files.

The result of the test can be overridden by setting the variable MKDIR_P or the cache variable ac_cv_path_mkdir.

AC_PROG_LEX   [Macro]
If flex is found, set output variable LEX to 'flex' and LEXLIB to '-lfl', if that library is in a standard place. Otherwise set LEX to 'lex' and LEXLIB to '-ll', if found. If neither variant is available, set LEX to ':'; for packages that ship the generated 'file.yy.c' alongside the source 'file.l', this default allows users without a lexer

generator to still build the package even if the timestamp for 'file.1' is inadvertently changed.

Define YYTEXT_POINTER if yytext defaults to 'char *' instead of to 'char []'. Also set output variable LEX_OUTPUT_ROOT to the base of the file name that the lexer generates; usually 'lex.yy', but sometimes something else. These results vary according to whether lex or flex is being used.

You are encouraged to use Flex in your sources, since it is both more pleasant to use than plain Lex and the C source it produces is portable. In order to ensure portability, however, you must either provide a function yywrap or, if you don't use it (e.g., your scanner has no '#include'-like feature), simply include a '%noyywrap' statement in the scanner's source. Once this done, the scanner is portable (unless *you* felt free to use nonportable constructs) and does not depend on any library. In this case, and in this case only, it is suggested that you use this Autoconf snippet:

```
AC_PROG_LEX
if test "x$LEX" != xflex; then
  LEX="$SHELL $missing_dir/missing flex"
  AC_SUBST([LEX_OUTPUT_ROOT], [lex.yy])
  AC_SUBST([LEXLIB], [''])
fi
```

The shell script missing can be found in the Automake distribution.

Remember that the user may have supplied an alternate location in LEX, so if Flex is required, it is better to check that the user provided something sufficient by parsing the output of '$LEX --version' than by simply relying on test "x$LEX" = xflex.

To ensure backward compatibility, Automake's AM_PROG_LEX invokes (indirectly) this macro twice, which causes an annoying but benign "AC_PROG_LEX invoked multiple times" warning. Future versions of Automake will fix this issue; meanwhile, just ignore this message.

As part of running the test, this macro may delete any file in the configuration directory named 'lex.yy.c' or 'lexyy.c'.

The result of this test can be influenced by setting the variable LEX or the cache variable ac_cv_prog_LEX.

AC_PROG_LN_S   [Macro]

If 'ln -s' works on the current file system (the operating system and file system support symbolic links), set the output variable LN_S to 'ln -s'; otherwise, if 'ln' works, set LN_S to 'ln', and otherwise set it to 'cp -pR'.

If you make a link in a directory other than the current directory, its meaning depends on whether 'ln' or 'ln -s' is used. To safely create links using '$(LN_S)', either find out which form is used and adjust the arguments, or always invoke ln in the directory where the link is to be created.

In other words, it does not work to do:

```
$(LN_S) foo /x/bar
```

Instead, do:

```
(cd /x && $(LN_S) foo bar)
```

AC_PROG_RANLIB   [Macro]

>   Set output variable RANLIB to 'ranlib' if ranlib is found, and otherwise to ':' (do
>   nothing).

AC_PROG_SED   [Macro]

>   Set output variable SED to a Sed implementation that conforms to Posix and does
>   not have arbitrary length limits. Report an error if no acceptable Sed is found.
>   See [Limitations of Usual Tools], page 245, for more information about portability
>   problems with Sed.
>
>   The result of this test can be overridden by setting the SED variable and is cached in
>   the ac_cv_path_SED variable.

AC_PROG_YACC   [Macro]

>   If bison is found, set output variable YACC to 'bison -y'. Otherwise, if byacc is
>   found, set YACC to 'byacc'. Otherwise set YACC to 'yacc'. The result of this test can
>   be influenced by setting the variable YACC or the cache variable ac_cv_prog_YACC.

5.2.2 Generic Program and File Checks

These macros are used to find programs not covered by the "particular" test macros. If you
need to check the behavior of a program as well as find out whether it is present, you have
to write your own test for it (see Chapter 6 [Writing Tests], page 101). By default, these
macros use the environment variable PATH. If you need to check for a program that might
not be in the user's PATH, you can pass a modified path to use instead, like this:

```
AC_PATH_PROG([INETD], [inetd], [/usr/libexec/inetd],
             [$PATH$PATH_SEPARATOR/usr/libexec$PATH_SEPARATOR]dnl
[/usr/sbin$PATH_SEPARATOR/usr/etc$PATH_SEPARATOR/etc])
```

You are strongly encouraged to declare the *variable* passed to AC_CHECK_PROG etc. as
precious. See Section 7.2 [Setting Output Variables], page 114, AC_ARG_VAR, for more
details.

AC_CHECK_PROG (*variable*, *prog-to-check-for*, *value-if-found*,   [Macro]
    [*value-if-not-found*], [*path* = '$PATH'], [*reject*])

>   Check whether program *prog-to-check-for* exists in *path*. If it is found, set *variable*
>   to *value-if-found*, otherwise to *value-if-not-found*, if given. Always pass over *reject*
>   (an absolute file name) even if it is the first found in the search path; in that case,
>   set *variable* using the absolute file name of the *prog-to-check-for* found that is not
>   *reject*. If *variable* was already set, do nothing. Calls AC_SUBST for *variable*. The result
>   of this test can be overridden by setting the *variable* variable or the cache variable
>   ac_cv_prog_variable.

AC_CHECK_PROGS (*variable*, *progs-to-check-for*,   [Macro]
    [*value-if-not-found*], [*path* = '$PATH'])

>   Check for each program in the blank-separated list *progs-to-check-for* existing in the
>   *path*. If one is found, set *variable* to the name of that program. Otherwise, continue
>   checking the next program in the list. If none of the programs in the list are found,
>   set *variable* to *value-if-not-found*; if *value-if-not-found* is not specified, the value of
>   *variable* is not changed. Calls AC_SUBST for *variable*. The result of this test can

be overridden by setting the *variable* variable or the cache variable `ac_cv_prog_variable`.

AC_CHECK_TARGET_TOOL (*variable*, *prog-to-check-for*,   [Macro]
      [*value-if-not-found*], [*path* = '$PATH'])
Like `AC_CHECK_PROG`, but first looks for *prog-to-check-for* with a prefix of the target type as determined by `AC_CANONICAL_TARGET`, followed by a dash (see Section 14.2 [Canonicalizing], page 282). If the tool cannot be found with a prefix, and if the build and target types are equal, then it is also searched for without a prefix.

As noted in Section 14.1 [Specifying Target Triplets], page 281, the target is rarely specified, because most of the time it is the same as the host: it is the type of system for which any compiler tool in the package produces code. What this macro looks for is, for example, *a tool* (assembler, linker, etc.) *that the compiler driver* (`gcc` for the GNU C Compiler) *uses to produce objects, archives or executables.*

AC_CHECK_TOOL (*variable*, *prog-to-check-for*,   [Macro]
      [*value-if-not-found*], [*path* = '$PATH'])
Like `AC_CHECK_PROG`, but first looks for *prog-to-check-for* with a prefix of the host type as specified by '--host', followed by a dash. For example, if the user runs 'configure --build=x86_64-gnu --host=i386-gnu', then this call:

      AC_CHECK_TOOL([RANLIB], [ranlib], [:])

sets `RANLIB` to 'i386-gnu-ranlib' if that program exists in *path*, or otherwise to 'ranlib' if that program exists in *path*, or to ':' if neither program exists.

When cross-compiling, this macro will issue a warning if no program prefixed with the host type could be found. For more information, see Section 14.1 [Specifying Target Triplets], page 281.

AC_CHECK_TARGET_TOOLS (*variable*, *progs-to-check-for*,   [Macro]
      [*value-if-not-found*], [*path* = '$PATH'])
Like `AC_CHECK_TARGET_TOOL`, each of the tools in the list *progs-to-check-for* are checked with a prefix of the target type as determined by `AC_CANONICAL_TARGET`, followed by a dash (see Section 14.2 [Canonicalizing], page 282). If none of the tools can be found with a prefix, and if the build and target types are equal, then the first one without a prefix is used. If a tool is found, set *variable* to the name of that program. If none of the tools in the list are found, set *variable* to *value-if-not-found*; if *value-if-not-found* is not specified, the value of *variable* is not changed. Calls `AC_SUBST` for *variable*.

AC_CHECK_TOOLS (*variable*, *progs-to-check-for*,   [Macro]
      [*value-if-not-found*], [*path* = '$PATH'])
Like `AC_CHECK_TOOL`, each of the tools in the list *progs-to-check-for* are checked with a prefix of the host type as determined by `AC_CANONICAL_HOST`, followed by a dash (see Section 14.2 [Canonicalizing], page 282). If none of the tools can be found with a prefix, then the first one without a prefix is used. If a tool is found, set *variable* to the name of that program. If none of the tools in the list are found, set *variable* to *value-if-not-found*; if *value-if-not-found* is not specified, the value of *variable* is not changed. Calls `AC_SUBST` for *variable*.

When cross-compiling, this macro will issue a warning if no program prefixed with the host type could be found. For more information, see Section 14.1 [Specifying Target Triplets], page 281.

AC_PATH_PROG (*variable, prog-to-check-for,*   [Macro]
    [*value-if-not-found*], [*path* = '$PATH'])

Like `AC_CHECK_PROG`, but set *variable* to the absolute name of *prog-to-check-for* if found. The result of this test can be overridden by setting the *variable* variable. A positive result of this test is cached in the `ac_cv_path_variable` variable.

AC_PATH_PROGS (*variable, progs-to-check-for,*   [Macro]
    [*value-if-not-found*], [*path* = '$PATH'])

Like `AC_CHECK_PROGS`, but if any of *progs-to-check-for* are found, set *variable* to the absolute name of the program found. The result of this test can be overridden by setting the *variable* variable. A positive result of this test is cached in the `ac_cv_path_variable` variable.

AC_PATH_PROGS_FEATURE_CHECK (*variable, progs-to-check-for,*   [Macro]
    feature-test, [*action-if-not-found*], [*path* = '$PATH'])

This macro was introduced in Autoconf 2.62. If *variable* is not empty, then set the cache variable `ac_cv_path_variable` to its value. Otherwise, check for each program in the blank-separated list *progs-to-check-for* existing in *path*. For each program found, execute *feature-test* with `ac_path_variable` set to the absolute name of the candidate program. If no invocation of *feature-test* sets the shell variable `ac_cv_path_variable`, then *action-if-not-found* is executed. *feature-test* will be run even when `ac_cv_path_variable` is set, to provide the ability to choose a better candidate found later in *path*; to accept the current setting and bypass all further checks, *feature-test* can execute `ac_path_variable_found=:`.

Note that this macro has some subtle differences from `AC_CHECK_PROGS`. It is designed to be run inside `AC_CACHE_VAL`, therefore, it should have no side effects. In particular, *variable* is not set to the final value of `ac_cv_path_variable`, nor is `AC_SUBST` automatically run. Also, on failure, any action can be performed, whereas `AC_CHECK_PROGS` only performs *variable=value-if-not-found*.

Here is an example, similar to what Autoconf uses in its own configure script. It will search for an implementation of `m4` that supports the `indir` builtin, even if it goes by the name `gm4` or is not the first implementation on PATH.

```
AC_CACHE_CHECK([for m4 that supports indir], [ac_cv_path_M4],
  [AC_PATH_PROGS_FEATURE_CHECK([M4], [m4 gm4],
    [[m4out=`echo 'changequote([,])indir([divnum])' | $ac_path_M4`
      test "x$m4out" = x0 \
      && ac_cv_path_M4=$ac_path_M4 ac_path_M4_found=:]],
    [AC_MSG_ERROR([could not find m4 that supports indir])])])
AC_SUBST([M4], [$ac_cv_path_M4])
```

AC_PATH_TARGET_TOOL (*variable, prog-to-check-for,*   [Macro]
    [*value-if-not-found*], [*path* = '$PATH'])

Like `AC_CHECK_TARGET_TOOL`, but set *variable* to the absolute name of the program if it is found.

AC_PATH_TOOL (*variable*, *prog-to-check-for*,   [Macro]
  [*value-if-not-found*], [*path* = '$PATH'])
  Like AC_CHECK_TOOL, but set *variable* to the absolute name of the program if it is
  found.

  When cross-compiling, this macro will issue a warning if no program prefixed with the
  host type could be found. For more information, see Section 14.1 [Specifying Target
  Triplets], page 281.

5.3 Files

You might also need to check for the existence of files. Before using these macros, ask
yourself whether a runtime test might not be a better solution. Be aware that, like most
Autoconf macros, they test a feature of the host machine, and therefore, they die when
cross-compiling.

AC_CHECK_FILE (*file*, [*action-if-found*], [*action-if-not-found*])   [Macro]
  Check whether file *file* exists on the native system. If it is found, execute *action-
  if-found*, otherwise do *action-if-not-found*, if given. The result of this test is cached
  in the ac_cv_file_*file* variable, with characters not suitable for a variable name
  mapped to underscores.

AC_CHECK_FILES (*files*, [*action-if-found*], [*action-if-not-found*])   [Macro]
  Executes AC_CHECK_FILE once for each file listed in *files*. Additionally, defines
  'HAVE_*file*' (see Section 5.1.1 [Standard Symbols], page 41) for each file found. The
  results of each test are cached in the ac_cv_file_*file* variable, with characters not
  suitable for a variable name mapped to underscores.

5.4 Library Files

The following macros check for the presence of certain C, C++, Fortran, or Go library archive
files.

AC_CHECK_LIB (*library*, *function*, [*action-if-found*],   [Macro]
  [*action-if-not-found*], [*other-libraries*])
  Test whether the library *library* is available by trying to link a test program that
  calls function *function* with the library. *function* should be a function provided by
  the library. Use the base name of the library; e.g., to check for '-lmp', use 'mp' as the
  library argument.

  action-if-found is a list of shell commands to run if the link with the library succeeds;
  action-if-not-found is a list of shell commands to run if the link fails. If *action-if-
  found* is not specified, the default action prepends '-l*library*' to LIBS and defines
  'HAVE_LIB*library*' (in all capitals). This macro is intended to support building
  LIBS in a right-to-left (least-dependent to most-dependent) fashion such that library
  dependencies are satisfied as a natural side effect of consecutive tests. Linkers are
  sensitive to library ordering so the order in which LIBS is generated is important to
  reliable detection of libraries.

  If linking with *library* results in unresolved symbols that would be resolved by linking
  with additional libraries, give those libraries as the *other-libraries* argument, separated

by spaces: e.g., '-lXt -lX11'. Otherwise, this macro may fail to detect that *library* is present, because linking the test program can fail with unresolved symbols. The *other-libraries* argument should be limited to cases where it is desirable to test for one library in the presence of another that is not already in LIBS.

AC_CHECK_LIB requires some care in usage, and should be avoided in some common cases. Many standard functions like gethostbyname appear in the standard C library on some hosts, and in special libraries like nsl on other hosts. On some hosts the special libraries contain variant implementations that you may not want to use. These days it is normally better to use AC_SEARCH_LIBS([gethostbyname], [nsl]) instead of AC_CHECK_LIB([nsl], [gethostbyname]).

The result of this test is cached in the ac_cv_lib_*library*_*function* variable.

AC_SEARCH_LIBS (*function*, *search-libs*, [*action-if-found*],   [Macro]
        [*action-if-not-found*], [*other-libraries*])
Search for a library defining *function* if it's not already available. This equates to calling 'AC_LINK_IFELSE([AC_LANG_CALL([], [*function*])])' first with no libraries, then for each library listed in *search-libs*.

Prepend '-l*library*' to LIBS for the first library found to contain *function*, and run *action-if-found*. If the function is not found, run *action-if-not-found*.

If linking with *library* results in unresolved symbols that would be resolved by linking with additional libraries, give those libraries as the *other-libraries* argument, separated by spaces: e.g., '-lXt -lX11'. Otherwise, this macro fails to detect that *function* is present, because linking the test program always fails with unresolved symbols.

The result of this test is cached in the ac_cv_search_*function* variable as 'none required' if *function* is already available, as 'no' if no library containing *function* was found, otherwise as the '-l*library*' option that needs to be prepended to LIBS.

5.5 Library Functions

The following macros check for particular C library functions. If there is no macro specifically defined to check for a function you need, and you don't need to check for any special properties of it, then you can use one of the general function-check macros.

5.5.1 Portability of C Functions

Most usual functions can either be missing, or be buggy, or be limited on some architectures. This section tries to make an inventory of these portability issues. By definition, this list always requires additions. A much more complete list is maintained by the Gnulib project (see Section 2.2 [Gnulib], page 3), covering Section "Current Posix Functions" in *GNU gnulib*, Section "Legacy Functions" in *GNU gnulib*, and Section "Glibc Functions" in *GNU gnulib*. Please help us keep the gnulib list as complete as possible.

exit   On ancient hosts, exit returned int. This is because exit predates void, and there was a long tradition of it returning int.

             On current hosts, the problem more likely is that exit is not declared, due to C++ problems of some sort or another. For this reason we suggest that test programs not invoke exit, but return from main instead.

free   The C standard says a call `free (NULL)` does nothing, but some old systems don't support this (e.g., NextStep).

isinf

isnan   The C99 standard says that `isinf` and `isnan` are macros. On some systems just macros are available (e.g., HP-UX and Solaris 10), on some systems both macros and functions (e.g., glibc 2.3.2), and on some systems only functions (e.g., IRIX 6 and Solaris 9). In some cases these functions are declared in nonstandard headers like `<sunmath.h>` and defined in non-default libraries like '`-lm`' or '`-lsunmath`'.

The C99 `isinf` and `isnan` macros work correctly with `long double` arguments, but pre-C99 systems that use functions typically assume `double` arguments. On such a system, `isinf` incorrectly returns true for a finite `long double` argument that is outside the range of `double`.

The best workaround for these issues is to use gnulib modules `isinf` and `isnan` (see Section 2.2 [Gnulib], page 3). But a lighter weight solution involves code like the following.

```
#include <math.h>

#ifndef isnan
# define isnan(x) \
    (sizeof (x) == sizeof (long double) ? isnan_ld (x) \
     : sizeof (x) == sizeof (double) ? isnan_d (x) \
     : isnan_f (x))
static inline int isnan_f  (float       x) { return x != x; }
static inline int isnan_d  (double      x) { return x != x; }
static inline int isnan_ld (long double x) { return x != x; }
#endif

#ifndef isinf
# define isinf(x) \
    (sizeof (x) == sizeof (long double) ? isinf_ld (x) \
     : sizeof (x) == sizeof (double) ? isinf_d (x) \
     : isinf_f (x))
static inline int isinf_f  (float       x)
{ return !isnan (x) && isnan (x - x); }
static inline int isinf_d  (double      x)
{ return !isnan (x) && isnan (x - x); }
static inline int isinf_ld (long double x)
{ return !isnan (x) && isnan (x - x); }
#endif
```

Use `AC_C_INLINE` (see Section 5.10.3 [C Compiler], page 80) so that this code works on compilers that lack the `inline` keyword. Some optimizing compilers mishandle these definitions, but systems with that bug typically have many other floating point corner-case compliance problems anyway, so it's probably not worth worrying about.

malloc   The C standard says a call `malloc (0)` is implementation dependent. It can return either `NULL` or a new non-null pointer. The latter is more common (e.g., the GNU C Library) but is by no means universal. `AC_FUNC_MALLOC` can be used to insist on non-`NULL` (see Section 5.5.2 [Particular Functions], page 53).

putenv
: Posix prefers `setenv` to `putenv`; among other things, `putenv` is not required of all Posix implementations, but `setenv` is.

    Posix specifies that `putenv` puts the given string directly in `environ`, but some systems make a copy of it instead (e.g., glibc 2.0, or BSD). And when a copy is made, `unsetenv` might not free it, causing a memory leak (e.g., FreeBSD 4).

    On some systems `putenv ("FOO")` removes 'FOO' from the environment, but this is not standard usage and it dumps core on some systems (e.g., AIX).

    On MinGW, a call `putenv ("FOO=")` removes 'FOO' from the environment, rather than inserting it with an empty value.

realloc
: The C standard says a call `realloc (NULL, size)` is equivalent to `malloc (size)`, but some old systems don't support this (e.g., NextStep).

signal handler
: Normally `signal` takes a handler function with a return type of `void`, but some old systems required `int` instead. Any actual `int` value returned is not used; this is only a difference in the function prototype demanded.

    All systems we know of in current use return `void`. The `int` was to support K&R C, where of course `void` is not available. The obsolete macro `AC_TYPE_SIGNAL` (see [AC_TYPE_SIGNAL], page 316) can be used to establish the correct type in all cases.

    In most cases, it is more robust to use `sigaction` when it is available, rather than `signal`.

snprintf
: The C99 standard says that if the output array isn't big enough and if no other errors occur, `snprintf` and `vsnprintf` truncate the output and return the number of bytes that ought to have been produced. Some older systems return the truncated length (e.g., GNU C Library 2.0.x or IRIX 6.5), some a negative value (e.g., earlier GNU C Library versions), and some the buffer length without truncation (e.g., 32-bit Solaris 7). Also, some buggy older systems ignore the length and overrun the buffer (e.g., 64-bit Solaris 7).

sprintf
: The C standard says `sprintf` and `vsprintf` return the number of bytes written. On some ancient systems (SunOS 4 for instance) they return the buffer pointer instead, but these no longer need to be worried about.

sscanf
: On various old systems, e.g., HP-UX 9, `sscanf` requires that its input string be writable (though it doesn't actually change it). This can be a problem when using `gcc` since it normally puts constant strings in read-only memory (see Section "Incompatibilities" in *Using and Porting the GNU Compiler Collection*). Apparently in some cases even having format strings read-only can be a problem.

strerror_r
: Posix specifies that `strerror_r` returns an `int`, but many systems (e.g., GNU C Library version 2.2.4) provide a different version returning a `char *`. `AC_FUNC_STRERROR_R` can detect which is in use (see Section 5.5.2 [Particular Functions], page 53).

strnlen
: AIX 4.3 provides a broken version which produces the following results:

```
strnlen ("foobar", 0) = 0
strnlen ("foobar", 1) = 3
strnlen ("foobar", 2) = 2
strnlen ("foobar", 3) = 1
strnlen ("foobar", 4) = 0
strnlen ("foobar", 5) = 6
strnlen ("foobar", 6) = 6
strnlen ("foobar", 7) = 6
strnlen ("foobar", 8) = 6
strnlen ("foobar", 9) = 6
```

sysconf   `_SC_PAGESIZE` is standard, but some older systems (e.g., HP-UX 9) have `_SC_PAGE_SIZE` instead. This can be tested with `#ifdef`.

unlink   The Posix spec says that `unlink` causes the given file to be removed only after there are no more open file handles for it. Some non-Posix hosts have trouble with this requirement, though, and some DOS variants even corrupt the file system.

unsetenv   On MinGW, `unsetenv` is not available, but a variable 'FOO' can be removed with a call `putenv ("FOO=")`, as described under `putenv` above.

va_copy   The C99 standard provides `va_copy` for copying `va_list` variables. It may be available in older environments too, though possibly as `__va_copy` (e.g., `gcc` in strict pre-C99 mode). These can be tested with `#ifdef`. A fallback to `memcpy (&dst, &src, sizeof (va_list))` gives maximum portability.

va_list   `va_list` is not necessarily just a pointer. It can be a `struct` (e.g., `gcc` on Alpha), which means `NULL` is not portable. Or it can be an array (e.g., `gcc` in some PowerPC configurations), which means as a function parameter it can be effectively call-by-reference and library routines might modify the value back in the caller (e.g., `vsnprintf` in the GNU C Library 2.1).

Signed >>   Normally the C `>>` right shift of a signed type replicates the high bit, giving a so-called "arithmetic" shift. But care should be taken since Standard C doesn't require that behavior. On those few processors without a native arithmetic shift (for instance Cray vector systems) zero bits may be shifted in, the same as a shift of an unsigned type.

Integer /   C divides signed integers by truncating their quotient toward zero, yielding the same result as Fortran. However, before C99 the standard allowed C implementations to take the floor or ceiling of the quotient in some cases. Hardly any implementations took advantage of this freedom, though, and it's probably not worth worrying about this issue nowadays.

5.5.2 Particular Function Checks

These macros check for particular C functions—whether they exist, and in some cases how they respond when given certain arguments.

AC_FUNC_ALLOCA   [Macro]

Check how to get `alloca`. Tries to get a builtin version by checking for 'alloca.h' or the predefined C preprocessor macros `__GNUC__` and `_AIX`. If this macro finds 'alloca.h', it defines `HAVE_ALLOCA_H`.

If those attempts fail, it looks for the function in the standard C library. If any of those methods succeed, it defines `HAVE_ALLOCA`. Otherwise, it sets the output variable `ALLOCA` to '${LIBOBJDIR}alloca.o' and defines `C_ALLOCA` (so programs can periodically call 'alloca (0)' to garbage collect). This variable is separate from `LIBOBJS` so multiple programs can share the value of `ALLOCA` without needing to create an actual library, in case only some of them use the code in `LIBOBJS`. The '${LIBOBJDIR}' prefix serves the same purpose as in `LIBOBJS` (see Section 18.6.4 [AC_LIBOBJ vs LIBOBJS], page 324).

This macro does not try to get `alloca` from the System V R3 'libPW' or the System V R4 'libucb' because those libraries contain some incompatible functions that cause trouble. Some versions do not even contain `alloca` or contain a buggy version. If you still want to use their `alloca`, use `ar` to extract 'alloca.o' from them instead of compiling 'alloca.c'.

Source files that use `alloca` should start with a piece of code like the following, to declare it properly.

```
#ifdef STDC_HEADERS
# include <stdlib.h>
# include <stddef.h>
#else
# ifdef HAVE_STDLIB_H
#  include <stdlib.h>
# endif
#endif
#ifdef HAVE_ALLOCA_H
# include <alloca.h>
#elif !defined alloca
# ifdef __GNUC__
#  define alloca __builtin_alloca
# elif defined _AIX
#  define alloca __alloca
# elif defined _MSC_VER
#  include <malloc.h>
#  define alloca _alloca
# elif !defined HAVE_ALLOCA
#  ifdef __cplusplus
extern "C"
#  endif
void *alloca (size_t);
# endif
#endif
```

AC_FUNC_CHOWN   [Macro]

> If the `chown` function is available and works (in particular, it should accept '-1' for `uid` and `gid`), define `HAVE_CHOWN`. The result of this macro is cached in the `ac_cv_func_chown_works` variable.

AC_FUNC_CLOSEDIR_VOID   [Macro]

> If the `closedir` function does not return a meaningful value, define `CLOSEDIR_VOID`. Otherwise, callers ought to check its return value for an error indicator.
>
> Currently this test is implemented by running a test program. When cross compiling the pessimistic assumption that `closedir` does not return a meaningful value is made.
>
> The result of this macro is cached in the `ac_cv_func_closedir_void` variable.
>
> This macro is obsolescent, as `closedir` returns a meaningful value on current systems. New programs need not use this macro.

AC_FUNC_ERROR_AT_LINE   [Macro]

> If the `error_at_line` function is not found, require an `AC_LIBOBJ` replacement of 'error'.
>
> The result of this macro is cached in the `ac_cv_lib_error_at_line` variable.
>
> The `AC_FUNC_ERROR_AT_LINE` macro is obsolescent. New programs should use Gnulib's `error` module. See Section 2.2 [Gnulib], page 3.

AC_FUNC_FNMATCH   [Macro]

> If the `fnmatch` function conforms to Posix, define `HAVE_FNMATCH`. Detect common implementation bugs, for example, the bugs in Solaris 2.4.
>
> Unlike the other specific `AC_FUNC` macros, `AC_FUNC_FNMATCH` does not replace a broken/missing `fnmatch`. This is for historical reasons. See `AC_REPLACE_FNMATCH` below.
>
> The result of this macro is cached in the `ac_cv_func_fnmatch_works` variable.
>
> This macro is obsolescent. New programs should use Gnulib's `fnmatch-posix` module. See Section 2.2 [Gnulib], page 3.

AC_FUNC_FNMATCH_GNU   [Macro]

> Behave like `AC_REPLACE_FNMATCH` (*replace*) but also test whether `fnmatch` supports GNU extensions. Detect common implementation bugs, for example, the bugs in the GNU C Library 2.1.
>
> The result of this macro is cached in the `ac_cv_func_fnmatch_gnu` variable.
>
> This macro is obsolescent. New programs should use Gnulib's `fnmatch-gnu` module. See Section 2.2 [Gnulib], page 3.

AC_FUNC_FORK   [Macro]

> This macro checks for the `fork` and `vfork` functions. If a working `fork` is found, define `HAVE_WORKING_FORK`. This macro checks whether `fork` is just a stub by trying to run it.
>
> If 'vfork.h' is found, define `HAVE_VFORK_H`. If a working `vfork` is found, define `HAVE_WORKING_VFORK`. Otherwise, define `vfork` to be `fork` for backward compatibility with previous versions of `autoconf`. This macro checks for several known errors in implementations of `vfork` and considers the system to not have a working `vfork` if

it detects any of them. It is not considered to be an implementation error if a child's invocation of `signal` modifies the parent's signal handler, since child processes rarely change their signal handlers.

Since this macro defines `vfork` only for backward compatibility with previous versions of `autoconf` you're encouraged to define it yourself in new code:

```
#ifndef HAVE_WORKING_VFORK
# define vfork fork
#endif
```

The results of this macro are cached in the `ac_cv_func_fork_works` and `ac_cv_func_vfork_works` variables. In order to override the test, you also need to set the `ac_cv_func_fork` and `ac_cv_func_vfork` variables.

AC_FUNC_FSEEKO   [Macro]

If the `fseeko` function is available, define `HAVE_FSEEKO`. Define `_LARGEFILE_SOURCE` if necessary to make the prototype visible on some systems (e.g., glibc 2.2). Otherwise linkage problems may occur when compiling with `AC_SYS_LARGEFILE` on largefile-sensitive systems where `off_t` does not default to a 64bit entity. All systems with `fseeko` also supply `ftello`.

AC_FUNC_GETGROUPS   [Macro]

If the `getgroups` function is available and works (unlike on Ultrix 4.3, where 'getgroups (0, 0)' always fails), define `HAVE_GETGROUPS`. Set `GETGROUPS_LIBS` to any libraries needed to get that function. This macro runs `AC_TYPE_GETGROUPS`.

AC_FUNC_GETLOADAVG   [Macro]

Check how to get the system load averages. To perform its tests properly, this macro needs the file 'getloadavg.c'; therefore, be sure to set the `AC_LIBOBJ` replacement directory properly (see Section 5.5.3 [Generic Functions], page 61, `AC_CONFIG_LIBOBJ_DIR`).

If the system has the `getloadavg` function, define `HAVE_GETLOADAVG`, and set `GETLOADAVG_LIBS` to any libraries necessary to get that function. Also add `GETLOADAVG_LIBS` to `LIBS`. Otherwise, require an `AC_LIBOBJ` replacement for 'getloadavg' with source code in '*dir*/getloadavg.c', and possibly define several other C preprocessor macros and output variables:

1. Define `C_GETLOADAVG`.
2. Define `SVR4`, `DGUX`, `UMAX`, or `UMAX4_3` if on those systems.
3. If 'nlist.h' is found, define `HAVE_NLIST_H`.
4. If 'struct nlist' has an 'n_un.n_name' member, define `HAVE_STRUCT_NLIST_N_UN_N_NAME`. The obsolete symbol `NLIST_NAME_UNION` is still defined, but do not depend upon it.
5. Programs may need to be installed set-group-ID (or set-user-ID) for `getloadavg` to work. In this case, define `GETLOADAVG_PRIVILEGED`, set the output variable `NEED_SETGID` to 'true' (and otherwise to 'false'), and set `KMEM_GROUP` to the name of the group that should own the installed program.

The `AC_FUNC_GETLOADAVG` macro is obsolescent. New programs should use Gnulib's `getloadavg` module. See Section 2.2 [Gnulib], page 3.

AC_FUNC_GETMNTENT [Macro]

Check for `getmntent` in the standard C library, and then in the 'sun', 'seq', and 'gen' libraries, for UNICOS, IRIX 4, PTX, and UnixWare, respectively. Then, if `getmntent` is available, define `HAVE_GETMNTENT` and set `ac_cv_func_getmntent` to yes. Otherwise set `ac_cv_func_getmntent` to no.

The result of this macro can be overridden by setting the cache variable `ac_cv_search_getmntent`.

AC_FUNC_GETPGRP [Macro]

Define `GETPGRP_VOID` if it is an error to pass 0 to `getpgrp`; this is the Posix behavior. On older BSD systems, you must pass 0 to `getpgrp`, as it takes an argument and behaves like Posix's `getpgid`.

```
#ifdef GETPGRP_VOID
  pid = getpgrp ();
#else
  pid = getpgrp (0);
#endif
```

This macro does not check whether `getpgrp` exists at all; if you need to work in that situation, first call `AC_CHECK_FUNC` for `getpgrp`.

The result of this macro is cached in the `ac_cv_func_getpgrp_void` variable.

This macro is obsolescent, as current systems have a `getpgrp` whose signature conforms to Posix. New programs need not use this macro.

AC_FUNC_LSTAT_FOLLOWS_SLASHED_SYMLINK [Macro]

If 'link' is a symbolic link, then `lstat` should treat 'link/' the same as 'link/.'. However, many older `lstat` implementations incorrectly ignore trailing slashes.

It is safe to assume that if `lstat` incorrectly ignores trailing slashes, then other symbolic-link-aware functions like `unlink` also incorrectly ignore trailing slashes.

If `lstat` behaves properly, define `LSTAT_FOLLOWS_SLASHED_SYMLINK`, otherwise require an `AC_LIBOBJ` replacement of `lstat`.

The result of this macro is cached in the `ac_cv_func_lstat_dereferences_slashed_symlink` variable.

The `AC_FUNC_LSTAT_FOLLOWS_SLASHED_SYMLINK` macro is obsolescent. New programs should use Gnulib's `lstat` module. See Section 2.2 [Gnulib], page 3.

AC_FUNC_MALLOC [Macro]

If the `malloc` function is compatible with the GNU C library `malloc` (i.e., 'malloc (0)' returns a valid pointer), define `HAVE_MALLOC` to 1. Otherwise define `HAVE_MALLOC` to 0, ask for an `AC_LIBOBJ` replacement for 'malloc', and define `malloc` to `rpl_malloc` so that the native `malloc` is not used in the main project.

Typically, the replacement file 'malloc.c' should look like (note the '#undef malloc'):

```
#include <config.h>
#undef malloc

#include <sys/types.h>
```

```
void *malloc ();

/* Allocate an N-byte block of memory from the heap.
   If N is zero, allocate a 1-byte block.  */

void *
rpl_malloc (size_t n)
{
  if (n == 0)
    n = 1;
  return malloc (n);
}
```

The result of this macro is cached in the `ac_cv_func_malloc_0_nonnull` variable.

AC_FUNC_MBRTOWC   [Macro]

Define `HAVE_MBRTOWC` to 1 if the function `mbrtowc` and the type `mbstate_t` are properly declared.

The result of this macro is cached in the `ac_cv_func_mbrtowc` variable.

AC_FUNC_MEMCMP   [Macro]

If the `memcmp` function is not available, or does not work on 8-bit data (like the one on SunOS 4.1.3), or fails when comparing 16 bytes or more and with at least one buffer not starting on a 4-byte boundary (such as the one on NeXT x86 OpenStep), require an `AC_LIBOBJ` replacement for 'memcmp'.

The result of this macro is cached in the `ac_cv_func_memcmp_working` variable.

This macro is obsolescent, as current systems have a working `memcmp`. New programs need not use this macro.

AC_FUNC_MKTIME   [Macro]

If the `mktime` function is not available, or does not work correctly, require an `AC_LIBOBJ` replacement for 'mktime'. For the purposes of this test, `mktime` should conform to the Posix standard and should be the inverse of `localtime`.

The result of this macro is cached in the `ac_cv_func_working_mktime` variable.

The `AC_FUNC_MKTIME` macro is obsolescent. New programs should use Gnulib's `mktime` module. See Section 2.2 [Gnulib], page 3.

AC_FUNC_MMAP   [Macro]

If the `mmap` function exists and works correctly, define `HAVE_MMAP`. This checks only private fixed mapping of already-mapped memory.

The result of this macro is cached in the `ac_cv_func_mmap_fixed_mapped` variable.

AC_FUNC_OBSTACK   [Macro]

If the obstacks are found, define `HAVE_OBSTACK`, else require an `AC_LIBOBJ` replacement for 'obstack'.

The result of this macro is cached in the `ac_cv_func_obstack` variable.

AC_FUNC_REALLOC   [Macro]

> If the `realloc` function is compatible with the GNU C library `realloc` (i.e., '`realloc (NULL, 0)`' returns a valid pointer), define `HAVE_REALLOC` to 1. Otherwise define `HAVE_REALLOC` to 0, ask for an `AC_LIBOBJ` replacement for '`realloc`', and define `realloc` to `rpl_realloc` so that the native `realloc` is not used in the main project. See `AC_FUNC_MALLOC` for details.
>
> The result of this macro is cached in the `ac_cv_func_realloc_0_nonnull` variable.

AC_FUNC_SELECT_ARGTYPES   [Macro]

> Determines the correct type to be passed for each of the `select` function's arguments, and defines those types in `SELECT_TYPE_ARG1`, `SELECT_TYPE_ARG234`, and `SELECT_TYPE_ARG5` respectively. `SELECT_TYPE_ARG1` defaults to '`int`', `SELECT_TYPE_ARG234` defaults to '`int *`', and `SELECT_TYPE_ARG5` defaults to '`struct timeval *`'.
>
> This macro is obsolescent, as current systems have a `select` whose signature conforms to Posix. New programs need not use this macro.

AC_FUNC_SETPGRP   [Macro]

> If `setpgrp` takes no argument (the Posix version), define `SETPGRP_VOID`. Otherwise, it is the BSD version, which takes two process IDs as arguments. This macro does not check whether `setpgrp` exists at all; if you need to work in that situation, first call `AC_CHECK_FUNC` for `setpgrp`.
>
> The result of this macro is cached in the `ac_cv_func_setpgrp_void` variable.
>
> This macro is obsolescent, as current systems have a `setpgrp` whose signature conforms to Posix. New programs need not use this macro.

AC_FUNC_STAT   [Macro]
AC_FUNC_LSTAT   [Macro]

> Determine whether `stat` or `lstat` have the bug that it succeeds when given the zero-length file name as argument. The `stat` and `lstat` from SunOS 4.1.4 and the Hurd (as of 1998-11-01) do this.
>
> If it does, then define `HAVE_STAT_EMPTY_STRING_BUG` (or `HAVE_LSTAT_EMPTY_STRING_BUG`) and ask for an `AC_LIBOBJ` replacement of it.
>
> The results of these macros are cached in the `ac_cv_func_stat_empty_string_bug` and the `ac_cv_func_lstat_empty_string_bug` variables, respectively.
>
> These macros are obsolescent, as no current systems have the bug. New programs need not use these macros.

AC_FUNC_STRCOLL   [Macro]

> If the `strcoll` function exists and works correctly, define `HAVE_STRCOLL`. This does a bit more than '`AC_CHECK_FUNCS(strcoll)`', because some systems have incorrect definitions of `strcoll` that should not be used.
>
> The result of this macro is cached in the `ac_cv_func_strcoll_works` variable.

AC_FUNC_STRERROR_R   [Macro]

> If `strerror_r` is available, define `HAVE_STRERROR_R`, and if it is declared, define `HAVE_DECL_STRERROR_R`. If it returns a `char *` message, define `STRERROR_R_CHAR_P`; otherwise it returns an `int` error number. The Thread-Safe Functions option of

Posix requires `strerror_r` to return `int`, but many systems (including, for example, version 2.2.4 of the GNU C Library) return a `char *` value that is not necessarily equal to the buffer argument.

The result of this macro is cached in the `ac_cv_func_strerror_r_char_p` variable.

AC_FUNC_STRFTIME   [Macro]

Check for `strftime` in the 'intl' library, for SCO Unix. Then, if `strftime` is available, define `HAVE_STRFTIME`.

This macro is obsolescent, as no current systems require the 'intl' library for `strftime`. New programs need not use this macro.

AC_FUNC_STRTOD   [Macro]

If the `strtod` function does not exist or doesn't work correctly, ask for an `AC_LIBOBJ` replacement of 'strtod'. In this case, because 'strtod.c' is likely to need 'pow', set the output variable `POW_LIB` to the extra library needed.

This macro caches its result in the `ac_cv_func_strtod` variable and depends upon the result in the `ac_cv_func_pow` variable.

The `AC_FUNC_STRTOD` macro is obsolescent. New programs should use Gnulib's `strtod` module. See Section 2.2 [Gnulib], page 3.

AC_FUNC_STRTOLD   [Macro]

If the `strtold` function exists and conforms to C99, define `HAVE_STRTOLD`.

This macro caches its result in the `ac_cv_func_strtold` variable.

AC_FUNC_STRNLEN   [Macro]

If the `strnlen` function is not available, or is buggy (like the one from AIX 4.3), require an `AC_LIBOBJ` replacement for it.

This macro caches its result in the `ac_cv_func_strnlen_working` variable.

AC_FUNC_UTIME_NULL   [Macro]

If 'utime (*file*, NULL)' sets *file*'s timestamp to the present, define `HAVE_UTIME_NULL`.

This macro caches its result in the `ac_cv_func_utime_null` variable.

This macro is obsolescent, as all current systems have a `utime` that behaves this way. New programs need not use this macro.

AC_FUNC_VPRINTF   [Macro]

If `vprintf` is found, define `HAVE_VPRINTF`. Otherwise, if `_doprnt` is found, define `HAVE_DOPRNT`. (If `vprintf` is available, you may assume that `vfprintf` and `vsprintf` are also available.)

This macro is obsolescent, as all current systems have `vprintf`. New programs need not use this macro.

AC_REPLACE_FNMATCH   [Macro]

If the `fnmatch` function does not conform to Posix (see `AC_FUNC_FNMATCH`), ask for its `AC_LIBOBJ` replacement.

The files 'fnmatch.c', 'fnmatch_loop.c', and 'fnmatch_.h' in the AC_LIBOBJ replacement directory are assumed to contain a copy of the source code of GNU fnmatch.
If necessary, this source code is compiled as an AC_LIBOBJ replacement, and the
'fnmatch_.h' file is linked to 'fnmatch.h' so that it can be included in place of the
system <fnmatch.h>.

This macro caches its result in the ac_cv_func_fnmatch_works variable.

This macro is obsolescent, as it assumes the use of particular source files. New
programs should use Gnulib's fnmatch-posix module, which provides this macro
along with the source files. See Section 2.2 [Gnulib], page 3.

5.5.3 Generic Function Checks

These macros are used to find functions not covered by the "particular" test macros. If the
functions might be in libraries other than the default C library, first call AC_CHECK_LIB for
those libraries. If you need to check the behavior of a function as well as find out whether it
is present, you have to write your own test for it (see Chapter 6 [Writing Tests], page 101).

AC_CHECK_FUNC (*function*, [*action-if-found*],   [Macro]
    [*action-if-not-found*])

> If C function *function* is available, run shell commands *action-if-found*, otherwise
> *action-if-not-found*. If you just want to define a symbol if the function is available,
> consider using AC_CHECK_FUNCS instead. This macro checks for functions with C link-
> age even when AC_LANG(C++) has been called, since C is more standardized than C++.
> (see Section 6.1 [Language Choice], page 101, for more information about selecting
> the language for checks.)
>
> This macro caches its result in the ac_cv_func_*function* variable.

AC_CHECK_FUNCS (*function*..., [*action-if-found*],   [Macro]
    [*action-if-not-found*])

> For each *function* enumerated in the blank-or-newline-separated argument list, define
> HAVE_*function* (in all capitals) if it is available. If *action-if-found* is given, it is
> additional shell code to execute when one of the functions is found. You can give it
> a value of 'break' to break out of the loop on the first match. If *action-if-not-found*
> is given, it is executed when one of the functions is not found.
>
> Results are cached for each *function* as in AC_CHECK_FUNC.

AC_CHECK_FUNCS_ONCE (*function*...)   [Macro]

> For each *function* enumerated in the blank-or-newline-separated argument list, define
> HAVE_*function* (in all capitals) if it is available. This is a once-only variant of AC_
> CHECK_FUNCS. It generates the checking code at most once, so that configure is
> smaller and faster; but the checks cannot be conditionalized and are always done
> once, early during the configure run.

Autoconf follows a philosophy that was formed over the years by those who have strug-
gled for portability: isolate the portability issues in specific files, and then program as if
you were in a Posix environment. Some functions may be missing or unfixable, and your
package must be ready to replace them.

Suitable replacements for many such problem functions are available from Gnulib (see Section 2.2 [Gnulib], page 3).

AC_LIBOBJ (*function*)   [Macro]

Specify that '*function*.c' must be included in the executables to replace a missing or broken implementation of *function*.

Technically, it adds '*function*.$ac_objext' to the output variable LIBOBJS if it is not already in, and calls AC_LIBSOURCE for '*function*.c'. You should not directly change LIBOBJS, since this is not traceable.

AC_LIBSOURCE (*file*)   [Macro]

Specify that *file* might be needed to compile the project. If you need to know what files might be needed by a 'configure.ac', you should trace AC_LIBSOURCE. *file* must be a literal.

This macro is called automatically from AC_LIBOBJ, but you must call it explicitly if you pass a shell variable to AC_LIBOBJ. In that case, since shell variables cannot be traced statically, you must pass to AC_LIBSOURCE any possible files that the shell variable might cause AC_LIBOBJ to need. For example, if you want to pass a variable $foo_or_bar to AC_LIBOBJ that holds either "foo" or "bar", you should do:

```
AC_LIBSOURCE([foo.c])
AC_LIBSOURCE([bar.c])
AC_LIBOBJ([$foo_or_bar])
```

There is usually a way to avoid this, however, and you are encouraged to simply call AC_LIBOBJ with literal arguments.

Note that this macro replaces the obsolete AC_LIBOBJ_DECL, with slightly different semantics: the old macro took the function name, e.g., foo, as its argument rather than the file name.

AC_LIBSOURCES (*files*)   [Macro]

Like AC_LIBSOURCE, but accepts one or more *files* in a comma-separated M4 list. Thus, the above example might be rewritten:

```
AC_LIBSOURCES([foo.c, bar.c])
AC_LIBOBJ([$foo_or_bar])
```

AC_CONFIG_LIBOBJ_DIR (*directory*)   [Macro]

Specify that AC_LIBOBJ replacement files are to be found in *directory*, a name relative to the top level of the source tree. The replacement directory defaults to '.', the top level directory, and the most typical value is 'lib', corresponding to 'AC_CONFIG_LIBOBJ_DIR([lib])'.

configure might need to know the replacement directory for the following reasons: (i) some checks use the replacement files, (ii) some macros bypass broken system headers by installing links to the replacement headers (iii) when used in conjunction with Automake, within each makefile, *directory* is used as a relative path from $(top_srcdir) to each object named in LIBOBJS and LTLIBOBJS, etc.

It is common to merely check for the existence of a function, and ask for its AC_LIBOBJ replacement if missing. The following macro is a convenient shorthand.

AC_REPLACE_FUNCS (*function*...)   [Macro]

> Like `AC_CHECK_FUNCS`, but uses '`AC_LIBOBJ(function)`' as *action-if-not-found*.
> You can declare your replacement function by enclosing the prototype in '`#ifndef`
> `HAVE_function`'. If the system has the function, it probably declares it in a header
> file you should be including, so you shouldn't redeclare it lest your declaration
> conflict.

5.6 Header Files

The following macros check for the presence of certain C header files. If there is no macro
specifically defined to check for a header file you need, and you don't need to check for any
special properties of it, then you can use one of the general header-file check macros.

5.6.1 Portability of Headers

This section documents some collected knowledge about common headers, and the problems
they cause. By definition, this list always requires additions. A much more complete list is
maintained by the Gnulib project (see Section 2.2 [Gnulib], page 3), covering Section "Posix
Headers" in *GNU gnulib* and Section "Glibc Headers" in *GNU gnulib*. Please help us keep
the gnulib list as complete as possible.

'`limits.h`'

> C99 says that '`limits.h`' defines `LLONG_MIN`, `LLONG_MAX`, and `ULLONG_MAX`, but
> many almost-C99 environments (e.g., default GCC 4.0.2 + glibc 2.4) do not
> define them.

'`inttypes.h`' vs. '`stdint.h`'

> The C99 standard says that '`inttypes.h`' includes '`stdint.h`', so there's no
> need to include '`stdint.h`' separately in a standard environment. Some im-
> plementations have '`inttypes.h`' but not '`stdint.h`' (e.g., Solaris 7), but we
> don't know of any implementation that has '`stdint.h`' but not '`inttypes.h`'.

'`linux/irda.h`'

> It requires '`linux/types.h`' and '`sys/socket.h`'.

'`linux/random.h`'

> It requires '`linux/types.h`'.

'`net/if.h`'

> On Darwin, this file requires that '`sys/socket.h`' be included beforehand. One
> should run:
>
> ```
> AC_CHECK_HEADERS([sys/socket.h])
> AC_CHECK_HEADERS([net/if.h], [], [],
> [#include <stdio.h>
> #ifdef STDC_HEADERS
> # include <stdlib.h>
> # include <stddef.h>
> #else
> # ifdef HAVE_STDLIB_H
> #  include <stdlib.h>
> # endif
> ```

```
#endif
#ifdef HAVE_SYS_SOCKET_H
# include <sys/socket.h>
#endif
])
```

'netinet/if_ether.h'

        On Darwin, this file requires that 'stdio.h' and 'sys/socket.h' be included beforehand. One should run:

```
AC_CHECK_HEADERS([sys/socket.h])
AC_CHECK_HEADERS([netinet/if_ether.h], [], [],
[#include <stdio.h>
#ifdef STDC_HEADERS
# include <stdlib.h>
# include <stddef.h>
#else
# ifdef HAVE_STDLIB_H
#  include <stdlib.h>
# endif
#endif
#ifdef HAVE_SYS_SOCKET_H
# include <sys/socket.h>
#endif
])
```

'stdint.h'

        See above, item 'inttypes.h' vs. 'stdint.h'.

'stdlib.h'

        On many systems (e.g., Darwin), 'stdio.h' is a prerequisite.

'sys/mount.h'

        On FreeBSD 4.8 on ia32 and using gcc version 2.95.4, 'sys/params.h' is a prerequisite.

'sys/ptem.h'

        On Solaris 8, 'sys/stream.h' is a prerequisite.

'sys/socket.h'

        On Darwin, 'stdlib.h' is a prerequisite.

'sys/ucred.h'

        On Tru64 5.1, 'sys/types.h' is a prerequisite.

'X11/extensions/scrnsaver.h'

        Using XFree86, this header requires 'X11/Xlib.h', which is probably so required that you might not even consider looking for it.

```
AC_CHECK_HEADERS([X11/extensions/scrnsaver.h], [], [],
[[#include <X11/Xlib.h>
]])
```

5.6.2 Particular Header Checks

These macros check for particular system header files—whether they exist, and in some cases whether they declare certain symbols.

AC_CHECK_HEADER_STDBOOL   [Macro]

> Check whether 'stdbool.h' exists and conforms to C99, and cache the result in the ac_cv_header_stdbool_h variable. If the type _Bool is defined, define HAVE__BOOL to 1.
>
> This macro is intended for use by Gnulib (see Section 2.2 [Gnulib], page 3) and other packages that supply a substitute 'stdbool.h' on platforms lacking a conforming one. The AC_HEADER_STDBOOL macro is better for code that explicitly checks for 'stdbool.h'.

AC_HEADER_ASSERT   [Macro]

> Check whether to enable assertions in the style of 'assert.h'. Assertions are enabled by default, but the user can override this by invoking configure with the '--disable-assert' option.

AC_HEADER_DIRENT   [Macro]

> Check for the following header files. For the first one that is found and defines 'DIR', define the listed C preprocessor macro:
>
> | 'dirent.h' | HAVE_DIRENT_H |
> |--------------|-----------------|
> | 'sys/ndir.h' | HAVE_SYS_NDIR_H |
> | 'sys/dir.h' | HAVE_SYS_DIR_H |
> | 'ndir.h' | HAVE_NDIR_H |
>
> The directory-library declarations in your source code should look something like the following:
>
> ```
> #include <sys/types.h>
> #ifdef HAVE_DIRENT_H
> # include <dirent.h>
> # define NAMLEN(dirent) strlen ((dirent)->d_name)
> #else
> # define dirent direct
> # define NAMLEN(dirent) ((dirent)->d_namlen)
> # ifdef HAVE_SYS_NDIR_H
> #  include <sys/ndir.h>
> # endif
> # ifdef HAVE_SYS_DIR_H
> #  include <sys/dir.h>
> # endif
> # ifdef HAVE_NDIR_H
> #  include <ndir.h>
> # endif
> #endif
> ```
>
> Using the above declarations, the program would declare variables to be of type struct dirent, not struct direct, and would access the length of a directory entry name by passing a pointer to a struct dirent to the NAMLEN macro.

This macro also checks for the SCO Xenix 'dir' and 'x' libraries.

This macro is obsolescent, as all current systems with directory libraries have <dirent.h>. New programs need not use this macro.

Also see AC_STRUCT_DIRENT_D_INO and AC_STRUCT_DIRENT_D_TYPE (see Section 5.8.1 [Particular Structures], page 73).

AC_HEADER_MAJOR   [Macro]

If 'sys/types.h' does not define major, minor, and makedev, but 'sys/mkdev.h' does, define MAJOR_IN_MKDEV; otherwise, if 'sys/sysmacros.h' does, define MAJOR_IN_SYSMACROS.

AC_HEADER_RESOLV   [Macro]

Checks for header 'resolv.h', checking for prerequisites first. To properly use 'resolv.h', your code should contain something like the following:

```
#ifdef HAVE_SYS_TYPES_H
#  include <sys/types.h>
#endif
#ifdef HAVE_NETINET_IN_H
#  include <netinet/in.h>   /* inet_ functions / structs */
#endif
#ifdef HAVE_ARPA_NAMESER_H
#  include <arpa/nameser.h> /* DNS HEADER struct */
#endif
#ifdef HAVE_NETDB_H
#  include <netdb.h>
#endif
#include <resolv.h>
```

AC_HEADER_STAT   [Macro]

If the macros S_ISDIR, S_ISREG, etc. defined in 'sys/stat.h' do not work properly (returning false positives), define STAT_MACROS_BROKEN. This is the case on Tektronix UTekV, Amdahl UTS and Motorola System V/88.

This macro is obsolescent, as no current systems have the bug. New programs need not use this macro.

AC_HEADER_STDBOOL   [Macro]

If 'stdbool.h' exists and conforms to C99, define HAVE_STDBOOL_H to 1; if the type _Bool is defined, define HAVE__BOOL to 1. To fulfill the C99 requirements, your program could contain the following code:

```
#ifdef HAVE_STDBOOL_H
# include <stdbool.h>
#else
# ifndef HAVE__BOOL
#  ifdef __cplusplus
typedef bool _Bool;
#  else
#   define _Bool signed char
#  endif
# endif
# define bool _Bool
# define false 0
# define true 1
# define __bool_true_false_are_defined 1
#endif
```

Alternatively you can use the 'stdbool' package of Gnulib (see Section 2.2 [Gnulib], page 3). It simplifies your code so that it can say just `#include <stdbool.h>`, and it adds support for less-common platforms.

This macro caches its result in the `ac_cv_header_stdbool_h` variable.

This macro differs from `AC_CHECK_HEADER_STDBOOL` only in that it defines `HAVE_STDBOOL_H` whereas `AC_CHECK_HEADER_STDBOOL` does not.

AC_HEADER_STDC   [Macro]
Define `STDC_HEADERS` if the system has C header files conforming to ANSI C89 (ISO C90). Specifically, this macro checks for 'stdlib.h', 'stdarg.h', 'string.h', and 'float.h'; if the system has those, it probably has the rest of the C89 header files. This macro also checks whether 'string.h' declares `memchr` (and thus presumably the other `mem` functions), whether 'stdlib.h' declare `free` (and thus presumably `malloc` and other related functions), and whether the 'ctype.h' macros work on characters with the high bit set, as the C standard requires.

If you use this macro, your code can refer to `STDC_HEADERS` to determine whether the system has conforming header files (and probably C library functions).

This macro caches its result in the `ac_cv_header_stdc` variable.

This macro is obsolescent, as current systems have conforming header files. New programs need not use this macro.

Nowadays 'string.h' is part of the C standard and declares functions like `strcpy`, and 'strings.h' is standardized by Posix and declares BSD functions like `bcopy`; but historically, string functions were a major sticking point in this area. If you still want to worry about portability to ancient systems without standard headers, there is so much variation that it is probably easier to declare the functions you use than to figure out exactly what the system header files declare. Some ancient systems contained a mix of functions from the C standard and from BSD; some were mostly standard but lacked 'memmove'; some defined the BSD functions as macros in 'string.h' or 'strings.h'; some had only the BSD functions but 'string.h'; some declared the memory functions in 'memory.h', some in 'string.h'; etc. It is probably sufficient to check for one string function and one memory function; if the library had the standard

versions of those then it probably had most of the others. If you put the following in
'configure.ac':

```
# This example is obsolescent.
# Nowadays you can omit these macro calls.
AC_HEADER_STDC
AC_CHECK_FUNCS([strchr memcpy])
```

then, in your code, you can use declarations like this:

```
/* This example is obsolescent.
   Nowadays you can just #include <string.h>.  */
#ifdef STDC_HEADERS
# include <string.h>
#else
# ifndef HAVE_STRCHR
#  define strchr index
#  define strrchr rindex
# endif
char *strchr (), *strrchr ();
# ifndef HAVE_MEMCPY
#  define memcpy(d, s, n) bcopy ((s), (d), (n))
#  define memmove(d, s, n) bcopy ((s), (d), (n))
# endif
#endif
```

If you use a function like `memchr`, `memset`, `strtok`, or `strspn`, which have no BSD
equivalent, then macros don't suffice to port to ancient hosts; you must provide an implementation of each function. An easy way to incorporate your implementations only
when needed (since the ones in system C libraries may be hand optimized) is to, taking
`memchr` for example, put it in 'memchr.c' and use 'AC_REPLACE_FUNCS([memchr])'.

AC_HEADER_SYS_WAIT   [Macro]
  If 'sys/wait.h' exists and is compatible with Posix, define `HAVE_SYS_WAIT_H`. Incompatibility can occur if 'sys/wait.h' does not exist, or if it uses the old BSD `union`
  `wait` instead of `int` to store a status value. If 'sys/wait.h' is not Posix compatible,
  then instead of including it, define the Posix macros with their usual interpretations.
  Here is an example:

```
#include <sys/types.h>
#ifdef HAVE_SYS_WAIT_H
# include <sys/wait.h>
#endif
#ifndef WEXITSTATUS
# define WEXITSTATUS(stat_val) ((unsigned int) (stat_val) >> 8)
#endif
#ifndef WIFEXITED
# define WIFEXITED(stat_val) (((stat_val) & 255) == 0)
#endif
```

  This macro caches its result in the `ac_cv_header_sys_wait_h` variable.

This macro is obsolescent, as current systems are compatible with Posix. New programs need not use this macro.

`_POSIX_VERSION` is defined when 'unistd.h' is included on Posix systems. If there is no 'unistd.h', it is definitely not a Posix system. However, some non-Posix systems do have 'unistd.h'.

The way to check whether the system supports Posix is:

```
#ifdef HAVE_UNISTD_H
# include <sys/types.h>
# include <unistd.h>
#endif

#ifdef _POSIX_VERSION
/* Code for Posix systems.  */
#endif
```

`AC_HEADER_TIME`   [Macro]

If a program may include both 'time.h' and 'sys/time.h', define `TIME_WITH_SYS_TIME`. On some ancient systems, 'sys/time.h' included 'time.h', but 'time.h' was not protected against multiple inclusion, so programs could not explicitly include both files. This macro is useful in programs that use, for example, `struct timeval` as well as `struct tm`. It is best used in conjunction with `HAVE_SYS_TIME_H`, which can be checked for using `AC_CHECK_HEADERS([sys/time.h])`.

```
#ifdef TIME_WITH_SYS_TIME
# include <sys/time.h>
# include <time.h>
#else
# ifdef HAVE_SYS_TIME_H
#  include <sys/time.h>
# else
#  include <time.h>
# endif
#endif
```

This macro caches its result in the `ac_cv_header_time` variable.

This macro is obsolescent, as current systems can include both files when they exist. New programs need not use this macro.

`AC_HEADER_TIOCGWINSZ`   [Macro]

If the use of `TIOCGWINSZ` requires '<sys/ioctl.h>', then define `GWINSZ_IN_SYS_IOCTL`. Otherwise `TIOCGWINSZ` can be found in '<termios.h>'.

Use:

```
#ifdef HAVE_TERMIOS_H
# include <termios.h>
#endif

#ifdef GWINSZ_IN_SYS_IOCTL
# include <sys/ioctl.h>
#endif
```

5.6.3 Generic Header Checks

These macros are used to find system header files not covered by the "particular" test macros. If you need to check the contents of a header as well as find out whether it is present, you have to write your own test for it (see Chapter 6 [Writing Tests], page 101).

AC_CHECK_HEADER (*header-file*, [*action-if-found*],   [Macro]
         [*action-if-not-found*], [*includes*])

If the system header file *header-file* is compilable, execute shell commands *action-if-found*, otherwise execute *action-if-not-found*. If you just want to define a symbol if the header file is available, consider using **AC_CHECK_HEADERS** instead.

includes is decoded to determine the appropriate include directives. If omitted or empty, '**configure**' will check for both header existence (with the preprocessor) and usability (with the compiler), using **AC_INCLUDES_DEFAULT** for the compile test. If there is a discrepancy between the results, a warning is issued to the user, and the compiler results are favored (see Section 20.7 [Present But Cannot Be Compiled], page 344). In general, favoring the compiler results means that a header will be treated as not found even though the file exists, because you did not provide enough prerequisites.

Providing a non-empty *includes* argument allows the code to provide any prerequisites prior to including the header under test; it is common to use the argument **AC_INCLUDES_DEFAULT** (see Section 5.1.2 [Default Includes], page 41). With an explicit fourth argument, no preprocessor test is needed. As a special case, an *includes* of exactly '**-**' triggers the older preprocessor check, which merely determines existence of the file in the preprocessor search path; this should only be used as a last resort (it is safer to determine the actual prerequisites and perform a compiler check, or else use **AC_PREPROC_IFELSE** to make it obvious that only a preprocessor check is desired).

This macro caches its result in the **ac_cv_header_*header-file*** variable, with characters not suitable for a variable name mapped to underscores.

AC_CHECK_HEADERS (*header-file*..., [*action-if-found*],   [Macro]
         [*action-if-not-found*], [*includes*])

For each given system header file *header-file* in the blank-separated argument list that exists, define **HAVE_*header-file*** (in all capitals). If *action-if-found* is given, it is additional shell code to execute when one of the header files is found. You can give it a value of '**break**' to break out of the loop on the first match. If *action-if-not-found* is given, it is executed when one of the header files is not found.

includes is interpreted as in **AC_CHECK_HEADER**, in order to choose the set of preprocessor directives supplied before the header under test.

This macro caches its result in the `ac_cv_header_header-file` variable, with characters not suitable for a variable name mapped to underscores.

Previous versions of Autoconf merely checked whether the header was accepted by the preprocessor. This was changed because the old test was inappropriate for typical uses. Headers are typically used to compile, not merely to preprocess, and the old behavior sometimes accepted headers that clashed at compile-time (see Section 20.7 [Present But Cannot Be Compiled], page 344). If you need to check whether a header is preprocessable, you can use `AC_PREPROC_IFELSE` (see Section 6.3 [Running the Preprocessor], page 107).

Actually requiring a header to compile improves the robustness of the test, but it also requires that you make sure that headers that must be included before the *header-file* be part of the *includes*, (see Section 5.1.2 [Default Includes], page 41). If looking for 'bar.h', which requires that 'foo.h' be included before if it exists, we suggest the following scheme:

```
AC_CHECK_HEADERS([foo.h])
AC_CHECK_HEADERS([bar.h], [], [],
[#ifdef HAVE_FOO_H
# include <foo.h>
#endif
])
```

The following variant generates smaller, faster `configure` files if you do not need the full power of `AC_CHECK_HEADERS`.

AC_CHECK_HEADERS_ONCE (*header-file*...) [Macro]
> For each given system header file *header-file* in the blank-separated argument list that exists, define HAVE_*header-file* (in all capitals). This is a once-only variant of `AC_CHECK_HEADERS`. It generates the checking code at most once, so that `configure` is smaller and faster; but the checks cannot be conditionalized and are always done once, early during the `configure` run. Thus, this macro is only safe for checking headers that do not have prerequisites beyond what `AC_INCLUDES_DEFAULT` provides.

5.7 Declarations

The following macros check for the declaration of variables and functions. If there is no macro specifically defined to check for a symbol you need, then you can use the general macros (see Section 5.7.2 [Generic Declarations], page 71) or, for more complex tests, you may use `AC_COMPILE_IFELSE` (see Section 6.4 [Running the Compiler], page 108).

5.7.1 Particular Declaration Checks

There are no specific macros for declarations.

5.7.2 Generic Declaration Checks

These macros are used to find declarations not covered by the "particular" test macros.

AC_CHECK_DECL (*symbol*, [*action-if-found*], [*action-if-not-found*], [Macro]
> **[*includes* = 'AC_INCLUDES_DEFAULT'])**
> If *symbol* (a function, variable, or constant) is not declared in *includes* and a declaration is needed, run the shell commands *action-if-not-found*, otherwise *action-if-found*.

includes is a series of include directives, defaulting to `AC_INCLUDES_DEFAULT` (see Section 5.1.2 [Default Includes], page 41), which are used prior to the declaration under test.

This macro actually tests whether *symbol* is defined as a macro or can be used as an r-value, not whether it is really declared, because it is much safer to avoid introducing extra declarations when they are not needed. In order to facilitate use of C++ and overloaded function declarations, it is possible to specify function argument types in parentheses for types which can be zero-initialized:

```
AC_CHECK_DECL([basename(char *)])
```

This macro caches its result in the `ac_cv_have_decl_symbol` variable, with characters not suitable for a variable name mapped to underscores.

AC_CHECK_DECLS (*symbols*, [*action-if-found*],   [Macro]
    [*action-if-not-found*], [*includes* = '`AC_INCLUDES_DEFAULT`'])
For each of the *symbols* (*comma*-separated list with optional function argument types for C++ overloads), define `HAVE_DECL_symbol` (in all capitals) to '1' if *symbol* is declared, otherwise to '0'. If *action-if-not-found* is given, it is additional shell code to execute when one of the function declarations is needed, otherwise *action-if-found* is executed.

includes is a series of include directives, defaulting to `AC_INCLUDES_DEFAULT` (see Section 5.1.2 [Default Includes], page 41), which are used prior to the declarations under test.

This macro uses an M4 list as first argument:

```
AC_CHECK_DECLS([strdup])
AC_CHECK_DECLS([strlen])
AC_CHECK_DECLS([malloc, realloc, calloc, free])
AC_CHECK_DECLS([j0], [], [], [[#include <math.h>]])
AC_CHECK_DECLS([[basename(char *)], [dirname(char *)]])
```

Unlike the other '`AC_CHECK_*S`' macros, when a *symbol* is not declared, `HAVE_DECL_symbol` is defined to '0' instead of leaving `HAVE_DECL_symbol` undeclared. When you are *sure* that the check was performed, use `HAVE_DECL_symbol` in #if:

```
#if !HAVE_DECL_SYMBOL
extern char *symbol;
#endif
```

If the test may have not been performed, however, because it is safer *not* to declare a symbol than to use a declaration that conflicts with the system's one, you should use:

```
#if defined HAVE_DECL_MALLOC && !HAVE_DECL_MALLOC
void *malloc (size_t *s);
#endif
```

You fall into the second category only in extreme situations: either your files may be used without being configured, or they are used during the configuration. In most cases the traditional approach is enough.

This macro caches its results in `ac_cv_have_decl_symbol` variables, with characters not suitable for a variable name mapped to underscores.

AC_CHECK_DECLS_ONCE (*symbols*) [Macro]

> For each of the *symbols* (*comma*-separated list), define HAVE_DECL_*symbol* (in all capitals) to '1' if *symbol* is declared in the default include files, otherwise to '0'. This is a once-only variant of AC_CHECK_DECLS. It generates the checking code at most once, so that configure is smaller and faster; but the checks cannot be conditionalized and are always done once, early during the configure run.

5.8 Structures

The following macros check for the presence of certain members in C structures. If there is no macro specifically defined to check for a member you need, then you can use the general structure-member macros (see Section 5.8.2 [Generic Structures], page 74) or, for more complex tests, you may use AC_COMPILE_IFELSE (see Section 6.4 [Running the Compiler], page 108).

5.8.1 Particular Structure Checks

The following macros check for certain structures or structure members.

AC_STRUCT_DIRENT_D_INO [Macro]

> Perform all the actions of AC_HEADER_DIRENT (see Section 5.6.2 [Particular Headers], page 65). Then, if struct dirent contains a d_ino member, define HAVE_STRUCT_DIRENT_D_INO.
>
> HAVE_STRUCT_DIRENT_D_INO indicates only the presence of d_ino, not whether its contents are always reliable. Traditionally, a zero d_ino indicated a deleted directory entry, though current systems hide this detail from the user and never return zero d_ino values. Many current systems report an incorrect d_ino for a directory entry that is a mount point.

AC_STRUCT_DIRENT_D_TYPE [Macro]

> Perform all the actions of AC_HEADER_DIRENT (see Section 5.6.2 [Particular Headers], page 65). Then, if struct dirent contains a d_type member, define HAVE_STRUCT_DIRENT_D_TYPE.

AC_STRUCT_ST_BLOCKS [Macro]

> If struct stat contains an st_blocks member, define HAVE_STRUCT_STAT_ST_BLOCKS. Otherwise, require an AC_LIBOBJ replacement of 'fileblocks'. The former name, HAVE_ST_BLOCKS is to be avoided, as its support will cease in the future.
>
> This macro caches its result in the ac_cv_member_struct_stat_st_blocks variable.

AC_STRUCT_TM [Macro]

> If 'time.h' does not define struct tm, define TM_IN_SYS_TIME, which means that including 'sys/time.h' had better define struct tm.
>
> This macro is obsolescent, as 'time.h' defines struct tm in current systems. New programs need not use this macro.

AC_STRUCT_TIMEZONE [Macro]

> Figure out how to get the current timezone. If struct tm has a tm_zone member, define HAVE_STRUCT_TM_TM_ZONE (and the obsoleted HAVE_TM_ZONE). Otherwise, if

the external array `tzname` is found, define `HAVE_TZNAME`; if it is declared, define `HAVE_DECL_TZNAME`.

5.8.2 Generic Structure Checks

These macros are used to find structure members not covered by the "particular" test macros.

AC_CHECK_MEMBER (*aggregate.member*, [*action-if-found*],   [Macro]
        [*action-if-not-found*], [*includes* = 'AC_INCLUDES_DEFAULT*'])
> Check whether *member* is a member of the aggregate *aggregate*. If no *includes* are specified, the default includes are used (see Section 5.1.2 [Default Includes], page 41).
>
> ```
> AC_CHECK_MEMBER([struct passwd.pw_gecos], [],
>                 [AC_MSG_ERROR([we need 'passwd.pw_gecos'])],
>                 [[#include <pwd.h>]])
> ```
>
> You can use this macro for submembers:
>
> ```
> AC_CHECK_MEMBER(struct top.middle.bot)
> ```
>
> This macro caches its result in the `ac_cv_member_`*aggregate*`_`*member* variable, with characters not suitable for a variable name mapped to underscores.

AC_CHECK_MEMBERS (*members*, [*action-if-found*],   [Macro]
        [*action-if-not-found*], [*includes* = 'AC_INCLUDES_DEFAULT*'])
> Check for the existence of each '*aggregate*.*member*' of *members* using the previous macro. When *member* belongs to *aggregate*, define `HAVE_`*aggregate*`_`*member* (in all capitals, with spaces and dots replaced by underscores). If *action-if-found* is given, it is executed for each of the found members. If *action-if-not-found* is given, it is executed for each of the members that could not be found.
>
> *includes* is a series of include directives, defaulting to `AC_INCLUDES_DEFAULT` (see Section 5.1.2 [Default Includes], page 41), which are used prior to the members under test.
>
> This macro uses M4 lists:
>
> ```
> AC_CHECK_MEMBERS([struct stat.st_rdev, struct stat.st_blksize])
> ```

5.9 Types

The following macros check for C types, either builtin or typedefs. If there is no macro specifically defined to check for a type you need, and you don't need to check for any special properties of it, then you can use a general type-check macro.

5.9.1 Particular Type Checks

These macros check for particular C types in 'sys/types.h', 'stdlib.h', 'stdint.h', 'inttypes.h' and others, if they exist.

The Gnulib `stdint` module is an alternate way to define many of these symbols; it is useful if you prefer your code to assume a C99-or-better environment. See Section 2.2 [Gnulib], page 3.

AC_TYPE_GETGROUPS   [Macro]

Define `GETGROUPS_T` to be whichever of `gid_t` or `int` is the base type of the array argument to `getgroups`.

This macro caches the base type in the `ac_cv_type_getgroups` variable.

AC_TYPE_INT8_T   [Macro]

If 'stdint.h' or 'inttypes.h' does not define the type `int8_t`, define `int8_t` to a signed integer type that is exactly 8 bits wide and that uses two's complement representation, if such a type exists. If you are worried about porting to hosts that lack such a type, you can use the results of this macro in C89-or-later code as follows:

```
#if HAVE_STDINT_H
# include <stdint.h>
#endif
#if defined INT8_MAX || defined int8_t
 code using int8_t
#else
 complicated alternative using >8-bit 'signed char'
#endif
```

This macro caches the type in the `ac_cv_c_int8_t` variable.

AC_TYPE_INT16_T   [Macro]

This is like `AC_TYPE_INT8_T`, except for 16-bit integers.

AC_TYPE_INT32_T   [Macro]

This is like `AC_TYPE_INT8_T`, except for 32-bit integers.

AC_TYPE_INT64_T   [Macro]

This is like `AC_TYPE_INT8_T`, except for 64-bit integers.

AC_TYPE_INTMAX_T   [Macro]

If 'stdint.h' or 'inttypes.h' defines the type `intmax_t`, define `HAVE_INTMAX_T`. Otherwise, define `intmax_t` to the widest signed integer type.

AC_TYPE_INTPTR_T   [Macro]

If 'stdint.h' or 'inttypes.h' defines the type `intptr_t`, define `HAVE_INTPTR_T`. Otherwise, define `intptr_t` to a signed integer type wide enough to hold a pointer, if such a type exists.

AC_TYPE_LONG_DOUBLE   [Macro]

If the C compiler supports a working `long double` type, define `HAVE_LONG_DOUBLE`. The `long double` type might have the same range and precision as `double`.

This macro caches its result in the `ac_cv_type_long_double` variable.

This macro is obsolescent, as current C compilers support `long double`. New programs need not use this macro.

AC_TYPE_LONG_DOUBLE_WIDER   [Macro]

If the C compiler supports a working `long double` type with more range or precision than the `double` type, define `HAVE_LONG_DOUBLE_WIDER`.

This macro caches its result in the `ac_cv_type_long_double_wider` variable.

AC_TYPE_LONG_LONG_INT   [Macro]

> If the C compiler supports a working `long long int` type, define `HAVE_LONG_LONG_INT`. However, this test does not test `long long int` values in preprocessor `#if` expressions, because too many compilers mishandle such expressions. See Section 13.3 [Preprocessor Arithmetic], page 276.
>
> This macro caches its result in the `ac_cv_type_long_long_int` variable.

AC_TYPE_MBSTATE_T   [Macro]

> Define `HAVE_MBSTATE_T` if `<wchar.h>` declares the `mbstate_t` type. Also, define `mbstate_t` to be a type if `<wchar.h>` does not declare it.
>
> This macro caches its result in the `ac_cv_type_mbstate_t` variable.

AC_TYPE_MODE_T   [Macro]

> Define `mode_t` to a suitable type, if standard headers do not define it.
>
> This macro caches its result in the `ac_cv_type_mode_t` variable.

AC_TYPE_OFF_T   [Macro]

> Define `off_t` to a suitable type, if standard headers do not define it.
>
> This macro caches its result in the `ac_cv_type_off_t` variable.

AC_TYPE_PID_T   [Macro]

> Define `pid_t` to a suitable type, if standard headers do not define it.
>
> This macro caches its result in the `ac_cv_type_pid_t` variable.

AC_TYPE_SIZE_T   [Macro]

> Define `size_t` to a suitable type, if standard headers do not define it.
>
> This macro caches its result in the `ac_cv_type_size_t` variable.

AC_TYPE_SSIZE_T   [Macro]

> Define `ssize_t` to a suitable type, if standard headers do not define it.
>
> This macro caches its result in the `ac_cv_type_ssize_t` variable.

AC_TYPE_UID_T   [Macro]

> Define `uid_t` and `gid_t` to suitable types, if standard headers do not define them.
>
> This macro caches its result in the `ac_cv_type_uid_t` variable.

AC_TYPE_UINT8_T   [Macro]

> If 'stdint.h' or 'inttypes.h' does not define the type `uint8_t`, define `uint8_t` to an unsigned integer type that is exactly 8 bits wide, if such a type exists. This is like `AC_TYPE_INT8_T`, except for unsigned integers.

AC_TYPE_UINT16_T   [Macro]

> This is like `AC_TYPE_UINT8_T`, except for 16-bit integers.

AC_TYPE_UINT32_T   [Macro]

> This is like `AC_TYPE_UINT8_T`, except for 32-bit integers.

AC_TYPE_UINT64_T   [Macro]

> This is like `AC_TYPE_UINT8_T`, except for 64-bit integers.

AC_TYPE_UINTMAX_T   [Macro]

> If 'stdint.h' or 'inttypes.h' defines the type uintmax_t, define HAVE_UINTMAX_T. Otherwise, define uintmax_t to the widest unsigned integer type.

AC_TYPE_UINTPTR_T   [Macro]

> If 'stdint.h' or 'inttypes.h' defines the type uintptr_t, define HAVE_UINTPTR_T. Otherwise, define uintptr_t to an unsigned integer type wide enough to hold a pointer, if such a type exists.

AC_TYPE_UNSIGNED_LONG_LONG_INT   [Macro]

> If the C compiler supports a working unsigned long long int type, define HAVE_UNSIGNED_LONG_LONG_INT. However, this test does not test unsigned long long int values in preprocessor #if expressions, because too many compilers mishandle such expressions. See Section 13.3 [Preprocessor Arithmetic], page 276.
>
> This macro caches its result in the ac_cv_type_unsigned_long_long_int variable.

5.9.2 Generic Type Checks

These macros are used to check for types not covered by the "particular" test macros.

AC_CHECK_TYPE (type, [action-if-found], [action-if-not-found],   [Macro]
[includes = 'AC_INCLUDES_DEFAULT'])

> Check whether type is defined. It may be a compiler builtin type or defined by the includes. includes is a series of include directives, defaulting to AC_INCLUDES_DEFAULT (see Section 5.1.2 [Default Includes], page 41), which are used prior to the type under test.
>
> In C, type must be a type-name, so that the expression 'sizeof (type)' is valid (but 'sizeof ((type))' is not). The same test is applied when compiling for C++, which means that in C++ type should be a type-id and should not be an anonymous 'struct' or 'union'.
>
> This macro caches its result in the ac_cv_type_type variable, with '*' mapped to 'p' and other characters not suitable for a variable name mapped to underscores.

AC_CHECK_TYPES (types, [action-if-found], [action-if-not-found],   [Macro]
[includes = 'AC_INCLUDES_DEFAULT'])

> For each type of the types that is defined, define HAVE_type (in all capitals). Each type must follow the rules of AC_CHECK_TYPE. If no includes are specified, the default includes are used (see Section 5.1.2 [Default Includes], page 41). If action-if-found is given, it is additional shell code to execute when one of the types is found. If action-if-not-found is given, it is executed when one of the types is not found.
>
> This macro uses M4 lists:
>
> ```
> AC_CHECK_TYPES([ptrdiff_t])
> AC_CHECK_TYPES([unsigned long long int, uintmax_t])
> AC_CHECK_TYPES([float_t], [], [], [[#include <math.h>]])
> ```

Autoconf, up to 2.13, used to provide to another version of AC_CHECK_TYPE, broken by design. In order to keep backward compatibility, a simple heuristic, quite safe but not totally, is implemented. In case of doubt, read the documentation of the former AC_CHECK_TYPE, see Section 18.4 [Obsolete Macros], page 305.

5.10 Compilers and Preprocessors

All the tests for compilers (`AC_PROG_CC`, `AC_PROG_CXX`, `AC_PROG_F77`) define the output variable `EXEEXT` based on the output of the compiler, typically to the empty string if Posix and '`.exe`' if a DOS variant.

They also define the output variable `OBJEXT` based on the output of the compiler, after '`.c`' files have been excluded, typically to '`o`' if Posix, '`obj`' if a DOS variant.

If the compiler being used does not produce executables, the tests fail. If the executables can't be run, and cross-compilation is not enabled, they fail too. See Chapter 14 [Manual Configuration], page 281, for more on support for cross compiling.

5.10.1 Specific Compiler Characteristics

Some compilers exhibit different behaviors.

Static/Dynamic Expressions

Autoconf relies on a trick to extract one bit of information from the C compiler: using negative array sizes. For instance the following excerpt of a C source demonstrates how to test whether '`int`' objects are 4 bytes wide:

```
static int test_array[sizeof (int) == 4 ? 1 : -1];
```

To our knowledge, there is a single compiler that does not support this trick: the HP C compilers (the real ones, not only the "bundled") on HP-UX 11.00. They incorrectly reject the above program with the diagnostic "Variable-length arrays cannot have static storage." This bug comes from HP compilers' mishandling of `sizeof (int)`, not from the `? 1 : -1`, and Autoconf works around this problem by casting `sizeof (int)` to `long int` before comparing it.

5.10.2 Generic Compiler Characteristics

`AC_CHECK_SIZEOF` (*type-or-expr*, [*unused*], [*includes* =   [Macro]
          '`AC_INCLUDES_DEFAULT`'])

Define `SIZEOF_`*type-or-expr* (see Section 5.1.1 [Standard Symbols], page 41) to be the size in bytes of *type-or-expr*, which may be either a type or an expression returning a value that has a size. If the expression '`sizeof (type-or-expr)`' is invalid, the result is 0. *includes* is a series of include directives, defaulting to `AC_INCLUDES_DEFAULT` (see Section 5.1.2 [Default Includes], page 41), which are used prior to the expression under test.

This macro now works even when cross-compiling. The *unused* argument was used when cross-compiling.

For example, the call

```
AC_CHECK_SIZEOF([int *])
```

defines `SIZEOF_INT_P` to be 8 on DEC Alpha AXP systems.

This macro caches its result in the `ac_cv_sizeof_`*type-or-expr* variable, with '`*`' mapped to '`p`' and other characters not suitable for a variable name mapped to underscores.

AC_CHECK_ALIGNOF (*type*, [*includes* = 'AC_INCLUDES_DEFAULT'])   [Macro]

> Define ALIGNOF_*type* (see Section 5.1.1 [Standard Symbols], page 41) to be the alignment in bytes of *type*. '*type* y;' must be valid as a structure member declaration. If '*type*' is unknown, the result is 0. If no *includes* are specified, the default includes are used (see Section 5.1.2 [Default Includes], page 41).
>
> This macro caches its result in the ac_cv_alignof_*type-or-expr* variable, with '*' mapped to 'p' and other characters not suitable for a variable name mapped to underscores.

AC_COMPUTE_INT (*var*, *expression*, [*includes* =   [Macro]
     'AC_INCLUDES_DEFAULT'], [*action-if-fails*])

> Store into the shell variable *var* the value of the integer *expression*. The value should fit in an initializer in a C variable of type signed long. To support cross compilation (in which case, the macro only works on hosts that use twos-complement arithmetic), it should be possible to evaluate the expression at compile-time. If no *includes* are specified, the default includes are used (see Section 5.1.2 [Default Includes], page 41).
>
> Execute *action-if-fails* if the value cannot be determined correctly.

AC_LANG_WERROR   [Macro]

> Normally Autoconf ignores warnings generated by the compiler, linker, and preprocessor. If this macro is used, warnings count as fatal errors for the current language. This macro is useful when the results of configuration are used where warnings are unacceptable; for instance, if parts of a program are built with the GCC '-Werror' option. If the whole program is built using '-Werror' it is often simpler to put '-Werror' in the compiler flags (CFLAGS, etc.).

AC_OPENMP   [Macro]

> OpenMP specifies extensions of C, C++, and Fortran that simplify optimization of shared memory parallelism, which is a common problem on multicore CPUs.
>
> If the current language is C, the macro AC_OPENMP sets the variable OPENMP_CFLAGS to the C compiler flags needed for supporting OpenMP. OPENMP_CFLAGS is set to empty if the compiler already supports OpenMP, if it has no way to activate OpenMP support, or if the user rejects OpenMP support by invoking 'configure' with the '--disable-openmp' option.
>
> OPENMP_CFLAGS needs to be used when compiling programs, when preprocessing program source, and when linking programs. Therefore you need to add $(OPENMP_CFLAGS) to the CFLAGS of C programs that use OpenMP. If you preprocess OpenMP-specific C code, you also need to add $(OPENMP_CFLAGS) to CPPFLAGS. The presence of OpenMP support is revealed at compile time by the preprocessor macro _OPENMP.
>
> Linking a program with OPENMP_CFLAGS typically adds one more shared library to the program's dependencies, so its use is recommended only on programs that actually require OpenMP.
>
> If the current language is C++, AC_OPENMP sets the variable OPENMP_CXXFLAGS, suitably for the C++ compiler. The same remarks hold as for C.
>
> If the current language is Fortran 77 or Fortran, AC_OPENMP sets the variable OPENMP_FFLAGS or OPENMP_FCFLAGS, respectively. Similar remarks as for C hold, except that

`CPPFLAGS` is not used for Fortran, and no preprocessor macro signals OpenMP support.

For portability, it is best to avoid spaces between '#' and '`pragma omp`'. That is, write '`#pragma omp`', not '`# pragma omp`'. The Sun WorkShop 6.2 C compiler chokes on the latter.

This macro caches its result in the `ac_cv_prog_c_openmp`, `ac_cv_prog_cxx_openmp`, `ac_cv_prog_f77_openmp`, or `ac_cv_prog_fc_openmp` variable, depending on the current language.

5.10.3 C Compiler Characteristics

The following macros provide ways to find and exercise a C Compiler. There are a few constructs that ought to be avoided, but do not deserve being checked for, since they can easily be worked around.

Don't use lines containing solitary backslashes

They tickle a bug in the HP-UX C compiler (checked on HP-UX 10.20, 11.00, and 11i). When given the following source:

```
#ifdef __STDC__
/\
* A comment with backslash-newlines in it.   %{ %} *\
\
/
char str[] = "\\
" A string with backslash-newlines in it %{ %} \\
"";
char apostrophe = '\\
\
'\
';
#endif
```

the compiler incorrectly fails with the diagnostics "Non-terminating comment at end of file" and "Missing '`#endif`' at end of file." Removing the lines with solitary backslashes solves the problem.

Don't compile several files at once if output matters to you

Some compilers, such as HP's, report names of files being compiled when given more than one file operand. For instance:

```
$ cc a.c b.c
a.c:
b.c:
```

This can cause problems if you observe the output of the compiler to detect failures. Invoking '`cc -c a.c && cc -c b.c && cc -o c a.o b.o`' solves the issue.

Don't rely on `#error` failing

The IRIX C compiler does not fail when #error is preprocessed; it simply emits a diagnostic and continues, exiting successfully. So, instead of an error directive like `#error "Unsupported word size"` it is more portable to use an invalid directive like `#Unsupported word size` in Autoconf tests. In ordinary source code, `#error` is OK, since installers with inadequate compilers like IRIX can simply examine these compilers' diagnostic output.

Don't rely on correct `#line` support

On Solaris, `c89` (at least Sun C 5.3 through 5.8) diagnoses `#line` directives whose line numbers are greater than 32767. Nothing in Posix makes this invalid. That is why Autoconf stopped issuing `#line` directives.

AC_PROG_CC (*[compiler-search-list]*)   [Macro]

Determine a C compiler to use. If `CC` is not already set in the environment, check for `gcc` and `cc`, then for other C compilers. Set output variable `CC` to the name of the compiler found.

This macro may, however, be invoked with an optional first argument which, if specified, must be a blank-separated list of C compilers to search for. This just gives the user an opportunity to specify an alternative search list for the C compiler. For example, if you didn't like the default order, then you could invoke `AC_PROG_CC` like this:

```
AC_PROG_CC([gcc cl cc])
```

If the C compiler does not handle function prototypes correctly by default, try to add an option to output variable `CC` to make it so. This macro tries various options that select standard-conformance modes on various systems.

After calling this macro you can check whether the C compiler has been set to accept ANSI C89 (ISO C90); if not, the shell variable `ac_cv_prog_cc_c89` is set to 'no'. See also `AC_C_PROTOTYPES` below.

If using the GNU C compiler, set shell variable `GCC` to '`yes`'. If output variable `CFLAGS` was not already set, set it to '`-g -O2`' for the GNU C compiler ('`-O2`' on systems where `GCC` does not accept '`-g`'), or '`-g`' for other compilers. If your package does not like this default, then it is acceptable to insert the line '`: ${CFLAGS=""}`' after `AC_INIT` and before `AC_PROG_CC` to select an empty default instead.

Many Autoconf macros use a compiler, and thus call '`AC_REQUIRE([AC_PROG_CC])`' to ensure that the compiler has been determined before the body of the outermost `AC_DEFUN` macro. Although `AC_PROG_CC` is safe to directly expand multiple times, it performs certain checks (such as the proper value of `EXEEXT`) only on the first invocation. Therefore, care must be used when invoking this macro from within another macro rather than at the top level (see Section 20.8 [Expanded Before Required], page 346).

AC_PROG_CC_C_O   [Macro]

If the C compiler does not accept the '`-c`' and '`-o`' options simultaneously, define `NO_MINUS_C_MINUS_O`. This macro actually tests both the compiler found by `AC_PROG_CC`, and, if different, the first `cc` in the path. The test fails if one fails. This macro was created for GNU Make to choose the default C compilation rule.

For the compiler *compiler*, this macro caches its result in the `ac_cv_prog_cc_compiler_c_o` variable.

AC_PROG_CPP   [Macro]

Set output variable CPP to a command that runs the C preprocessor. If '$CC -E' doesn't work, '/lib/cpp' is used. It is only portable to run CPP on files with a '.c' extension.

Some preprocessors don't indicate missing include files by the error status. For such preprocessors an internal variable is set that causes other macros to check the standard error from the preprocessor and consider the test failed if any warnings have been reported. For most preprocessors, though, warnings do not cause include-file tests to fail unless AC_PROG_CPP_WERROR is also specified.

AC_PROG_CPP_WERROR   [Macro]

This acts like AC_PROG_CPP, except it treats warnings from the preprocessor as errors even if the preprocessor exit status indicates success. This is useful for avoiding headers that generate mandatory warnings, such as deprecation notices.

The following macros check for C compiler or machine architecture features. To check for characteristics not listed here, use AC_COMPILE_IFELSE (see Section 6.4 [Running the Compiler], page 108) or AC_RUN_IFELSE (see Section 6.6 [Runtime], page 109).

AC_PROG_CC_STDC   [Macro]

If the C compiler cannot compile ISO Standard C (currently C99), try to add an option to output variable CC to make it work. If the compiler does not support C99, fall back to supporting ANSI C89 (ISO C90).

After calling this macro you can check whether the C compiler has been set to accept Standard C; if not, the shell variable ac_cv_prog_cc_stdc is set to 'no'.

AC_PROG_CC_C89   [Macro]

If the C compiler is not in ANSI C89 (ISO C90) mode by default, try to add an option to output variable CC to make it so. This macro tries various options that select ANSI C89 on some system or another, preferring extended functionality modes over strict conformance modes. It considers the compiler to be in ANSI C89 mode if it handles function prototypes correctly.

After calling this macro you can check whether the C compiler has been set to accept ANSI C89; if not, the shell variable ac_cv_prog_cc_c89 is set to 'no'.

This macro is called automatically by AC_PROG_CC.

AC_PROG_CC_C99   [Macro]

If the C compiler is not in C99 mode by default, try to add an option to output variable CC to make it so. This macro tries various options that select C99 on some system or another, preferring extended functionality modes over strict conformance modes. It considers the compiler to be in C99 mode if it handles _Bool, // comments, flexible array members, inline, signed and unsigned long long int, mixed code and declarations, named initialization of structs, restrict, va_copy, varargs macros, variable declarations in for loops, and variable length arrays.

After calling this macro you can check whether the C compiler has been set to accept C99; if not, the shell variable ac_cv_prog_cc_c99 is set to 'no'.

AC_C_BACKSLASH_A   [Macro]

> Define 'HAVE_C_BACKSLASH_A' to 1 if the C compiler understands '\a'.
>
> This macro is obsolescent, as current C compilers understand '\a'. New programs need not use this macro.

AC_C_BIGENDIAN ([*action-if-true*], [*action-if-false*],   [Macro]
        [*action-if-unknown*], [*action-if-universal*])

> If words are stored with the most significant byte first (like Motorola and SPARC CPUs), execute *action-if-true*. If words are stored with the least significant byte first (like Intel and VAX CPUs), execute *action-if-false*.
>
> This macro runs a test-case if endianness cannot be determined from the system header files. When cross-compiling, the test-case is not run but grep'ed for some magic values. *action-if-unknown* is executed if the latter case fails to determine the byte sex of the host system.
>
> In some cases a single run of a compiler can generate code for multiple architectures. This can happen, for example, when generating Mac OS X universal binary files, which work on both PowerPC and Intel architectures. In this case, the different variants might be for different architectures whose endiannesses differ. If configure detects this, it executes *action-if-universal* instead of *action-if-unknown*.
>
> The default for *action-if-true* is to define 'WORDS_BIGENDIAN'. The default for *action-if-false* is to do nothing. The default for *action-if-unknown* is to abort configure and tell the installer how to bypass this test. And finally, the default for *action-if-universal* is to ensure that 'WORDS_BIGENDIAN' is defined if and only if a universal build is detected and the current code is big-endian; this default works only if autoheader is used (see Section 4.9.2 [autoheader Invocation], page 35).
>
> If you use this macro without specifying *action-if-universal*, you should also use AC_CONFIG_HEADERS; otherwise 'WORDS_BIGENDIAN' may be set incorrectly for Mac OS X universal binary files.

AC_C_CONST   [Macro]

> If the C compiler does not fully support the const keyword, define const to be empty. Some C compilers that do not define __STDC__ do support const; some compilers that define __STDC__ do not completely support const. Programs can simply use const as if every C compiler supported it; for those that don't, the makefile or configuration header file defines it as empty.
>
> Occasionally installers use a C++ compiler to compile C code, typically because they lack a C compiler. This causes problems with const, because C and C++ treat const differently. For example:
>
>   const int foo;
>
> is valid in C but not in C++. These differences unfortunately cannot be papered over by defining const to be empty.
>
> If autoconf detects this situation, it leaves const alone, as this generally yields better results in practice. However, using a C++ compiler to compile C code is not recommended or supported, and installers who run into trouble in this area should get a C compiler like GCC to compile their C code.

This macro caches its result in the `ac_cv_c_const` variable.

This macro is obsolescent, as current C compilers support `const`. New programs need not use this macro.

AC_C_RESTRICT   [Macro]

If the C compiler recognizes a variant spelling for the `restrict` keyword (`__restrict`, `__restrict__`, or `_Restrict`), then define `restrict` to that; this is more likely to do the right thing with compilers that support language variants where plain `restrict` is not a keyword. Otherwise, if the C compiler recognizes the `restrict` keyword, don't do anything. Otherwise, define `restrict` to be empty. Thus, programs may simply use `restrict` as if every C compiler supported it; for those that do not, the makefile or configuration header defines it away.

Although support in C++ for the `restrict` keyword is not required, several C++ compilers do accept the keyword. This macro works for them, too.

This macro caches 'no' in the `ac_cv_c_restrict` variable if `restrict` is not supported, and a supported spelling otherwise.

AC_C_VOLATILE   [Macro]

If the C compiler does not understand the keyword `volatile`, define `volatile` to be empty. Programs can simply use `volatile` as if every C compiler supported it; for those that do not, the makefile or configuration header defines it as empty.

If the correctness of your program depends on the semantics of `volatile`, simply defining it to be empty does, in a sense, break your code. However, given that the compiler does not support `volatile`, you are at its mercy anyway. At least your program compiles, when it wouldn't before. See Section 13.6 [Volatile Objects], page 277, for more about `volatile`.

In general, the `volatile` keyword is a standard C feature, so you might expect that `volatile` is available only when `__STDC__` is defined. However, Ultrix 4.3's native compiler does support volatile, but does not define `__STDC__`.

This macro is obsolescent, as current C compilers support `volatile`. New programs need not use this macro.

AC_C_INLINE   [Macro]

If the C compiler supports the keyword `inline`, do nothing. Otherwise define `inline` to `__inline__` or `__inline` if it accepts one of those, otherwise define `inline` to be empty.

AC_C_CHAR_UNSIGNED   [Macro]

If the C type `char` is unsigned, define `__CHAR_UNSIGNED__`, unless the C compiler predefines it.

These days, using this macro is not necessary. The same information can be determined by this portable alternative, thus avoiding the use of preprocessor macros in the namespace reserved for the implementation.

```
#include <limits.h>
#if CHAR_MIN == 0
# define CHAR_UNSIGNED 1
#endif
```

AC_C_STRINGIZE   [Macro]

If the C preprocessor supports the stringizing operator, define `HAVE_STRINGIZE`. The stringizing operator is '#' and is found in macros such as this:

```
#define x(y) #y
```

This macro is obsolescent, as current C compilers support the stringizing operator. New programs need not use this macro.

AC_C_FLEXIBLE_ARRAY_MEMBER   [Macro]

If the C compiler supports flexible array members, define `FLEXIBLE_ARRAY_MEMBER` to nothing; otherwise define it to 1. That way, a declaration like this:

```
struct s
  {
    size_t n_vals;
    double val[FLEXIBLE_ARRAY_MEMBER];
  };
```

will let applications use the "struct hack" even with compilers that do not support flexible array members. To allocate and use such an object, you can use code like this:

```
size_t i;
size_t n = compute_value_count ();
struct s *p =
    malloc (offsetof (struct s, val)
            + n * sizeof (double));
p->n_vals = n;
for (i = 0; i < n; i++)
  p->val[i] = compute_value (i);
```

AC_C_VARARRAYS   [Macro]

If the C compiler supports variable-length arrays, define `HAVE_C_VARARRAYS`. A variable-length array is an array of automatic storage duration whose length is determined at run time, when the array is declared.

AC_C_TYPEOF   [Macro]

If the C compiler supports GCC's `typeof` syntax either directly or through a different spelling of the keyword (e.g., `__typeof__`), define `HAVE_TYPEOF`. If the support is available only through a different spelling, define `typeof` to that spelling.

AC_C_PROTOTYPES   [Macro]

If function prototypes are understood by the compiler (as determined by `AC_PROG_CC`), define `PROTOTYPES` and `__PROTOTYPES`. Defining `__PROTOTYPES` is for the benefit of header files that cannot use macros that infringe on user name space.

This macro is obsolescent, as current C compilers support prototypes. New programs need not use this macro.

AC_PROG_GCC_TRADITIONAL   [Macro]

Add '`-traditional`' to output variable `CC` if using the GNU C compiler and `ioctl` does not work properly without '`-traditional`'. That usually happens when the fixed header files have not been installed on an old system.

This macro is obsolescent, since current versions of the GNU C compiler fix the header files automatically when installed.

5.10.4 C++ Compiler Characteristics

AC_PROG_CXX ([*compiler-search-list*])   [Macro]

Determine a C++ compiler to use. Check whether the environment variable CXX or CCC (in that order) is set; if so, then set output variable CXX to its value.

Otherwise, if the macro is invoked without an argument, then search for a C++ compiler under the likely names (first g++ and c++ then other names). If none of those checks succeed, then as a last resort set CXX to g++.

This macro may, however, be invoked with an optional first argument which, if specified, must be a blank-separated list of C++ compilers to search for. This just gives the user an opportunity to specify an alternative search list for the C++ compiler. For example, if you didn't like the default order, then you could invoke AC_PROG_CXX like this:

        AC_PROG_CXX([gcc cl KCC CC cxx cc++ xlC aCC c++ g++])

If using the GNU C++ compiler, set shell variable GXX to 'yes'. If output variable CXXFLAGS was not already set, set it to '-g -O2' for the GNU C++ compiler ('-O2' on systems where G++ does not accept '-g'), or '-g' for other compilers. If your package does not like this default, then it is acceptable to insert the line ': ${CXXFLAGS=""}' after AC_INIT and before AC_PROG_CXX to select an empty default instead.

AC_PROG_CXXCPP   [Macro]

Set output variable CXXCPP to a command that runs the C++ preprocessor. If '$CXX -E' doesn't work, '/lib/cpp' is used. It is portable to run CXXCPP only on files with a '.c', '.C', '.cc', or '.cpp' extension.

Some preprocessors don't indicate missing include files by the error status. For such preprocessors an internal variable is set that causes other macros to check the standard error from the preprocessor and consider the test failed if any warnings have been reported. However, it is not known whether such broken preprocessors exist for C++.

AC_PROG_CXX_C_O   [Macro]

Test whether the C++ compiler accepts the options '-c' and '-o' simultaneously, and define CXX_NO_MINUS_C_MINUS_O, if it does not.

5.10.5 Objective C Compiler Characteristics

AC_PROG_OBJC ([*compiler-search-list*])   [Macro]

Determine an Objective C compiler to use. If OBJC is not already set in the environment, check for Objective C compilers. Set output variable OBJC to the name of the compiler found.

This macro may, however, be invoked with an optional first argument which, if specified, must be a blank-separated list of Objective C compilers to search for. This just gives the user an opportunity to specify an alternative search list for the Objective C compiler. For example, if you didn't like the default order, then you could invoke AC_PROG_OBJC like this:

```
AC_PROG_OBJC([gcc objcc objc])
```

If using the GNU Objective C compiler, set shell variable GOBJC to 'yes'. If output variable OBJCFLAGS was not already set, set it to '-g -O2' for the GNU Objective C compiler ('-O2' on systems where gcc does not accept '-g'), or '-g' for other compilers.

AC_PROG_OBJCPP   [Macro]
   Set output variable OBJCPP to a command that runs the Objective C preprocessor. If '$OBJC -E' doesn't work, '/lib/cpp' is used.

5.10.6 Objective C++ Compiler Characteristics

AC_PROG_OBJCXX ([*compiler-search-list*])   [Macro]
   Determine an Objective C++ compiler to use. If OBJCXX is not already set in the environment, check for Objective C++ compilers. Set output variable OBJCXX to the name of the compiler found.

   This macro may, however, be invoked with an optional first argument which, if specified, must be a blank-separated list of Objective C++ compilers to search for. This just gives the user an opportunity to specify an alternative search list for the Objective C++ compiler. For example, if you didn't like the default order, then you could invoke AC_PROG_OBJCXX like this:

```
AC_PROG_OBJCXX([gcc g++ objcc++ objcxx])
```

   If using the GNU Objective C++ compiler, set shell variable GOBJCXX to 'yes'. If output variable OBJCXXFLAGS was not already set, set it to '-g -O2' for the GNU Objective C++ compiler ('-O2' on systems where gcc does not accept '-g'), or '-g' for other compilers.

AC_PROG_OBJCXXCPP   [Macro]
   Set output variable OBJCXXCPP to a command that runs the Objective C++ preprocessor. If '$OBJCXX -E' doesn't work, '/lib/cpp' is used.

5.10.7 Erlang Compiler and Interpreter Characteristics

Autoconf defines the following macros for determining paths to the essential Erlang/OTP programs:

AC_ERLANG_PATH_ERLC ([*value-if-not-found*], [*path* = '$PATH'])   [Macro]
   Determine an Erlang compiler to use. If ERLC is not already set in the environment, check for erlc. Set output variable ERLC to the complete path of the compiler command found. In addition, if ERLCFLAGS is not set in the environment, set it to an empty value.

   The two optional arguments have the same meaning as the two last arguments of macro AC_PATH_PROG for looking for the erlc program. For example, to look for erlc only in the '/usr/lib/erlang/bin' directory:

```
AC_ERLANG_PATH_ERLC([not found], [/usr/lib/erlang/bin])
```

AC_ERLANG_NEED_ERLC ([*path* = '$PATH'])   [Macro]
   A simplified variant of the AC_ERLANG_PATH_ERLC macro, that prints an error message and exits the configure script if the erlc program is not found.

AC_ERLANG_PATH_ERL ([*value-if-not-found*], [*path* = '$PATH'])   [Macro]
> Determine an Erlang interpreter to use. If ERL is not already set in the environment, check for erl. Set output variable ERL to the complete path of the interpreter command found.
>
> The two optional arguments have the same meaning as the two last arguments of macro AC_PATH_PROG for looking for the erl program. For example, to look for erl only in the '/usr/lib/erlang/bin' directory:
>
> > AC_ERLANG_PATH_ERL([not found], [/usr/lib/erlang/bin])

AC_ERLANG_NEED_ERL ([*path* = '$PATH'])   [Macro]
> A simplified variant of the AC_ERLANG_PATH_ERL macro, that prints an error message and exits the configure script if the erl program is not found.

5.10.8 Fortran Compiler Characteristics

The Autoconf Fortran support is divided into two categories: legacy Fortran 77 macros (F77), and modern Fortran macros (FC). The former are intended for traditional Fortran 77 code, and have output variables like F77, FFLAGS, and FLIBS. The latter are for newer programs that can (or must) compile under the newer Fortran standards, and have output variables like FC, FCFLAGS, and FCLIBS.

Except for the macros AC_FC_SRCEXT, AC_FC_FREEFORM, AC_FC_FIXEDFORM, and AC_FC_LINE_LENGTH (see below), the FC and F77 macros behave almost identically, and so they are documented together in this section.

AC_PROG_F77 ([*compiler-search-list*])   [Macro]
> Determine a Fortran 77 compiler to use. If F77 is not already set in the environment, then check for g77 and f77, and then some other names. Set the output variable F77 to the name of the compiler found.
>
> This macro may, however, be invoked with an optional first argument which, if specified, must be a blank-separated list of Fortran 77 compilers to search for. This just gives the user an opportunity to specify an alternative search list for the Fortran 77 compiler. For example, if you didn't like the default order, then you could invoke AC_PROG_F77 like this:
>
> > AC_PROG_F77([f132 f77 fort77 xlf g77 f90 xlf90])
>
> If using g77 (the GNU Fortran 77 compiler), then set the shell variable G77 to 'yes'. If the output variable FFLAGS was not already set in the environment, then set it to '-g -O2' for g77 (or '-O2' where g77 does not accept '-g'). Otherwise, set FFLAGS to '-g' for all other Fortran 77 compilers.
>
> The result of the GNU test is cached in the ac_cv_f77_compiler_gnu variable, acceptance of '-g' in the ac_cv_prog_f77_g variable.

AC_PROG_FC ([*compiler-search-list*], [*dialect*])   [Macro]
> Determine a Fortran compiler to use. If FC is not already set in the environment, then dialect is a hint to indicate what Fortran dialect to search for; the default is to search for the newest available dialect. Set the output variable FC to the name of the compiler found.

By default, newer dialects are preferred over older dialects, but if `dialect` is specified then older dialects are preferred starting with the specified dialect. `dialect` can currently be one of Fortran 77, Fortran 90, or Fortran 95. However, this is only a hint of which compiler *name* to prefer (e.g., `f90` or `f95`), and no attempt is made to guarantee that a particular language standard is actually supported. Thus, it is preferable that you avoid the `dialect` option, and use AC_PROG_FC only for code compatible with the latest Fortran standard.

This macro may, alternatively, be invoked with an optional first argument which, if specified, must be a blank-separated list of Fortran compilers to search for, just as in `AC_PROG_F77`.

If using `gfortran` or `g77` (the GNU Fortran compilers), then set the shell variable `GFC` to 'yes'. If the output variable `FCFLAGS` was not already set in the environment, then set it to '-g -02' for GNU g77 (or '-02' where g77 does not accept '-g'). Otherwise, set `FCFLAGS` to '-g' for all other Fortran compilers.

The result of the GNU test is cached in the `ac_cv_fc_compiler_gnu` variable, acceptance of '-g' in the `ac_cv_prog_fc_g` variable.

AC_PROG_F77_C_O   [Macro]
AC_PROG_FC_C_O   [Macro]
Test whether the Fortran compiler accepts the options '-c' and '-o' simultaneously, and define F77_NO_MINUS_C_MINUS_O or FC_NO_MINUS_C_MINUS_O, respectively, if it does not.

The result of the test is cached in the `ac_cv_prog_f77_c_o` or `ac_cv_prog_fc_c_o` variable, respectively.

The following macros check for Fortran compiler characteristics. To check for characteristics not listed here, use `AC_COMPILE_IFELSE` (see Section 6.4 [Running the Compiler], page 108) or `AC_RUN_IFELSE` (see Section 6.6 [Runtime], page 109), making sure to first set the current language to Fortran 77 or Fortran via `AC_LANG([Fortran 77])` or `AC_LANG(Fortran)` (see Section 6.1 [Language Choice], page 101).

AC_F77_LIBRARY_LDFLAGS   [Macro]
AC_FC_LIBRARY_LDFLAGS   [Macro]
Determine the linker flags (e.g., '-L' and '-l') for the *Fortran intrinsic and runtime libraries* that are required to successfully link a Fortran program or shared library. The output variable `FLIBS` or `FCLIBS` is set to these flags (which should be included after `LIBS` when linking).

This macro is intended to be used in those situations when it is necessary to mix, e.g., C++ and Fortran source code in a single program or shared library (see Section "Mixing Fortran 77 With C and C++" in *GNU Automake*).

For example, if object files from a C++ and Fortran compiler must be linked together, then the C++ compiler/linker must be used for linking (since special C++-ish things need to happen at link time like calling global constructors, instantiating templates, enabling exception support, etc.).

However, the Fortran intrinsic and runtime libraries must be linked in as well, but the C++ compiler/linker doesn't know by default how to add these Fortran 77 libraries. Hence, this macro was created to determine these Fortran libraries.

The macros `AC_F77_DUMMY_MAIN` and `AC_FC_DUMMY_MAIN` or `AC_F77_MAIN` and `AC_FC_MAIN` are probably also necessary to link C/C++ with Fortran; see below. Further, it is highly recommended that you use `AC_CONFIG_HEADERS` (see Section 4.9 [Configuration Headers], page 33) because the complex defines that the function wrapper macros create may not work with C/C++ compiler drivers.

These macros internally compute the flag needed to verbose linking output and cache it in `ac_cv_prog_f77_v` or `ac_cv_prog_fc_v` variables, respectively. The computed linker flags are cached in `ac_cv_f77_libs` or `ac_cv_fc_libs`, respectively.

`AC_F77_DUMMY_MAIN` ([*action-if-found*], [*action-if-not-found* = '   [Macro]
        `AC_MSG_FAILURE`'])
`AC_FC_DUMMY_MAIN` ([*action-if-found*], [*action-if-not-found* = '   [Macro]
        `AC_MSG_FAILURE`'])
With many compilers, the Fortran libraries detected by `AC_F77_LIBRARY_LDFLAGS` or `AC_FC_LIBRARY_LDFLAGS` provide their own `main` entry function that initializes things like Fortran I/O, and which then calls a user-provided entry function named (say) `MAIN__` to run the user's program. The `AC_F77_DUMMY_MAIN` and `AC_FC_DUMMY_MAIN` or `AC_F77_MAIN` and `AC_FC_MAIN` macros figure out how to deal with this interaction.

When using Fortran for purely numerical functions (no I/O, etc.) often one prefers to provide one's own `main` and skip the Fortran library initializations. In this case, however, one may still need to provide a dummy `MAIN__` routine in order to prevent linking errors on some systems. `AC_F77_DUMMY_MAIN` or `AC_FC_DUMMY_MAIN` detects whether any such routine is *required* for linking, and what its name is; the shell variable `F77_DUMMY_MAIN` or `FC_DUMMY_MAIN` holds this name, `unknown` when no solution was found, and `none` when no such dummy main is needed.

By default, *action-if-found* defines `F77_DUMMY_MAIN` or `FC_DUMMY_MAIN` to the name of this routine (e.g., `MAIN__`) *if* it is required. *action-if-not-found* defaults to exiting with an error.

In order to link with Fortran routines, the user's C/C++ program should then include the following code to define the dummy main if it is needed:

```
#ifdef F77_DUMMY_MAIN
#  ifdef __cplusplus
     extern "C"
#  endif
   int F77_DUMMY_MAIN () { return 1; }
#endif
```

(Replace `F77` with `FC` for Fortran instead of Fortran 77.)

Note that this macro is called automatically from `AC_F77_WRAPPERS` or `AC_FC_WRAPPERS`; there is generally no need to call it explicitly unless one wants to change the default actions.

The result of this macro is cached in the `ac_cv_f77_dummy_main` or `ac_cv_fc_dummy_main` variable, respectively.

AC_F77_MAIN   [Macro]
AC_FC_MAIN   [Macro]

As discussed above, many Fortran libraries allow you to provide an entry point called (say) MAIN__ instead of the usual main, which is then called by a main function in the Fortran libraries that initializes things like Fortran I/O. The AC_F77_MAIN and AC_FC_MAIN macros detect whether it is *possible* to utilize such an alternate main function, and defines F77_MAIN and FC_MAIN to the name of the function. (If no alternate main function name is found, F77_MAIN and FC_MAIN are simply defined to main.)

Thus, when calling Fortran routines from C that perform things like I/O, one should use this macro and declare the "main" function like so:

```
#ifdef __cplusplus
  extern "C"
#endif
int F77_MAIN (int argc, char *argv[]);
```

(Again, replace F77 with FC for Fortran instead of Fortran 77.)

The result of this macro is cached in the ac_cv_f77_main or ac_cv_fc_main variable, respectively.

AC_F77_WRAPPERS   [Macro]
AC_FC_WRAPPERS   [Macro]

Defines C macros F77_FUNC (name, NAME), FC_FUNC (name, NAME), F77_FUNC_ (name, NAME), and FC_FUNC_(name, NAME) to properly mangle the names of C/C++ identifiers, and identifiers with underscores, respectively, so that they match the name-mangling scheme used by the Fortran compiler.

Fortran is case-insensitive, and in order to achieve this the Fortran compiler converts all identifiers into a canonical case and format. To call a Fortran subroutine from C or to write a C function that is callable from Fortran, the C program must explicitly use identifiers in the format expected by the Fortran compiler. In order to do this, one simply wraps all C identifiers in one of the macros provided by AC_F77_WRAPPERS or AC_FC_WRAPPERS. For example, suppose you have the following Fortran 77 subroutine:

```
subroutine foobar (x, y)
double precision x, y
y = 3.14159 * x
return
end
```

You would then declare its prototype in C or C++ as:

```
#define FOOBAR_F77 F77_FUNC (foobar, FOOBAR)
#ifdef __cplusplus
extern "C"  /* prevent C++ name mangling */
#endif
void FOOBAR_F77 (double *x, double *y);
```

Note that we pass both the lowercase and uppercase versions of the function name to F77_FUNC so that it can select the right one. Note also that all parameters to Fortran

77 routines are passed as pointers (see Section "Mixing Fortran 77 With C and C++" in *GNU Automake*).

(Replace `F77` with `FC` for Fortran instead of Fortran 77.)

Although Autoconf tries to be intelligent about detecting the name-mangling scheme of the Fortran compiler, there may be Fortran compilers that it doesn't support yet. In this case, the above code generates a compile-time error, but some other behavior (e.g., disabling Fortran-related features) can be induced by checking whether `F77_FUNC` or `FC_FUNC` is defined.

Now, to call that routine from a C program, we would do something like:

```
{
        double x = 2.7183, y;
        FOOBAR_F77 (&x, &y);
}
```

If the Fortran identifier contains an underscore (e.g., `foo_bar`), you should use `F77_FUNC_` or `FC_FUNC_` instead of `F77_FUNC` or `FC_FUNC` (with the same arguments). This is because some Fortran compilers mangle names differently if they contain an underscore.

The name mangling scheme is encoded in the `ac_cv_f77_mangling` or `ac_cv_fc_mangling` cache variable, respectively, and also used for the `AC_F77_FUNC` and `AC_FC_FUNC` macros described below.

AC_F77_FUNC (*name*, [*shellvar*])   [Macro]
AC_FC_FUNC (*name*, [*shellvar*])   [Macro]
> Given an identifier *name*, set the shell variable *shellvar* to hold the mangled version *name* according to the rules of the Fortran linker (see also `AC_F77_WRAPPERS` or `AC_FC_WRAPPERS`). *shellvar* is optional; if it is not supplied, the shell variable is simply *name*. The purpose of this macro is to give the caller a way to access the name-mangling information other than through the C preprocessor as above, for example, to call Fortran routines from some language other than C/C++.

AC_FC_SRCEXT (*ext*, [*action-if-success*], [*action-if-failure* =   [Macro]
    '`AC_MSG_FAILURE`'])
AC_FC_PP_SRCEXT (*ext*, [*action-if-success*], [*action-if-failure* =   [Macro]
    '`AC_MSG_FAILURE`'])
> By default, the `FC` macros perform their tests using a '`.f`' extension for source-code files. Some compilers, however, only enable newer language features for appropriately named files, e.g., Fortran 90 features only for '`.f90`' files, or preprocessing only with '`.F`' files or maybe other upper-case extensions. On the other hand, some other compilers expect all source files to end in '`.f`' and require special flags to support other file name extensions. The `AC_FC_SRCEXT` and `AC_FC_PP_SRCEXT` macros deal with these issues.

> The `AC_FC_SRCEXT` macro tries to get the `FC` compiler to accept files ending with the extension '`.ext`' (i.e., *ext* does *not* contain the dot). If any special compiler flags are needed for this, it stores them in the output variable `FCFLAGS_ext`. This extension and these flags are then used for all subsequent `FC` tests (until `AC_FC_SRCEXT` or `AC_FC_PP_SRCEXT` is called another time).

For example, you would use `AC_FC_SRCEXT(f90)` to employ the '.f90' extension in future tests, and it would set the `FCFLAGS_f90` output variable with any extra flags that are needed to compile such files.

Similarly, the `AC_FC_PP_SRCEXT` macro tries to get the `FC` compiler to preprocess and compile files with the extension '.ext'. When both `fpp` and `cpp` style preprocessing are provided, the former is preferred, as the latter may treat continuation lines, // tokens, and white space differently from what some Fortran dialects expect. Conversely, if you do not want files to be preprocessed, use only lower-case characters in the file name extension. Like with `AC_FC_SRCEXT(f90)`, any needed flags are stored in the `FCFLAGS_ext` variable.

The `FCFLAGS_ext` flags can *not* be simply absorbed into `FCFLAGS`, for two reasons based on the limitations of some compilers. First, only one `FCFLAGS_ext` can be used at a time, so files with different extensions must be compiled separately. Second, `FCFLAGS_ext` must appear *immediately* before the source-code file name when compiling. So, continuing the example above, you might compile a 'foo.f90' file in your makefile with the command:

```
foo.o: foo.f90
        $(FC) -c $(FCFLAGS) $(FCFLAGS_f90) '$(srcdir)/foo.f90'
```

If `AC_FC_SRCEXT` or `AC_FC_PP_SRCEXT` succeeds in compiling files with the *ext* extension, it calls *action-if-success* (defaults to nothing). If it fails, and cannot find a way to make the `FC` compiler accept such files, it calls *action-if-failure* (defaults to exiting with an error message).

The `AC_FC_SRCEXT` and `AC_FC_PP_SRCEXT` macros cache their results in `ac_cv_fc_srcext_ext` and `ac_cv_fc_pp_srcext_ext` variables, respectively.

`AC_FC_PP_DEFINE` ([*action-if-success*], [*action-if-failure* = '   [Macro]
    `AC_MSG_FAILURE`'])

Find a flag to specify defines for preprocessed Fortran. Not all Fortran compilers use '-D'. Substitute `FC_DEFINE` with the result and call *action-if-success* (defaults to nothing) if successful, and *action-if-failure* (defaults to failing with an error message) if not.

This macro calls `AC_FC_PP_SRCEXT([F])` in order to learn how to preprocess a 'conftest.F' file, but restores a previously used Fortran source file extension afterwards again.

The result of this test is cached in the `ac_cv_fc_pp_define` variable.

`AC_FC_FREEFORM` ([*action-if-success*], [*action-if-failure* = '   [Macro]
    `AC_MSG_FAILURE`'])

Try to ensure that the Fortran compiler (`$FC`) allows free-format source code (as opposed to the older fixed-format style from Fortran 77). If necessary, it may add some additional flags to `FCFLAGS`.

This macro is most important if you are using the default '.f' extension, since many compilers interpret this extension as indicating fixed-format source unless an additional flag is supplied. If you specify a different extension with `AC_FC_SRCEXT`, such as '.f90', then `AC_FC_FREEFORM` ordinarily succeeds without modifying `FCFLAGS`. For extensions which the compiler does not know about, the flag set by the `AC_FC_SRCEXT` macro might let the compiler assume Fortran 77 by default, however.

If `AC_FC_FREEFORM` succeeds in compiling free-form source, it calls *action-if-success* (defaults to nothing). If it fails, it calls *action-if-failure* (defaults to exiting with an error message).

The result of this test, or 'none' or 'unknown', is cached in the `ac_cv_fc_freeform` variable.

`AC_FC_FIXEDFORM` ([*action-if-success*], [*action-if-failure* = '   [Macro]
     `AC_MSG_FAILURE`'])

Try to ensure that the Fortran compiler (`$FC`) allows the old fixed-format source code (as opposed to free-format style). If necessary, it may add some additional flags to `FCFLAGS`.

This macro is needed for some compilers alias names like `xlf95` which assume free-form source code by default, and in case you want to use fixed-form source with an extension like '.f90' which many compilers interpret as free-form by default. If you specify a different extension with `AC_FC_SRCEXT`, such as '.f', then `AC_FC_FIXEDFORM` ordinarily succeeds without modifying `FCFLAGS`.

If `AC_FC_FIXEDFORM` succeeds in compiling fixed-form source, it calls *action-if-success* (defaults to nothing). If it fails, it calls *action-if-failure* (defaults to exiting with an error message).

The result of this test, or 'none' or 'unknown', is cached in the `ac_cv_fc_fixedform` variable.

`AC_FC_LINE_LENGTH` ([*length*], [*action-if-success*],   [Macro]
     [*action-if-failure* = '`AC_MSG_FAILURE`'])

Try to ensure that the Fortran compiler (`$FC`) accepts long source code lines. The *length* argument may be given as 80, 132, or unlimited, and defaults to 132. Note that line lengths above 254 columns are not portable, and some compilers do not accept more than 132 columns at least for fixed format source. If necessary, it may add some additional flags to `FCFLAGS`.

If `AC_FC_LINE_LENGTH` succeeds in compiling fixed-form source, it calls *action-if-success* (defaults to nothing). If it fails, it calls *action-if-failure* (defaults to exiting with an error message).

The result of this test, or 'none' or 'unknown', is cached in the `ac_cv_fc_line_length` variable.

`AC_FC_CHECK_BOUNDS` ([*action-if-success*], [*action-if-failure* =   [Macro]
     '`AC_MSG_FAILURE`'])

The `AC_FC_CHECK_BOUNDS` macro tries to enable array bounds checking in the Fortran compiler. If successful, the *action-if-success* is called and any needed flags are added to `FCFLAGS`. Otherwise, *action-if-failure* is called, which defaults to failing with an error message. The macro currently requires Fortran 90 or a newer dialect.

The result of the macro is cached in the `ac_cv_fc_check_bounds` variable.

AC_F77_IMPLICIT_NONE ([*action-if-success*], [*action-if-failure*   [Macro]
    = 'AC_MSG_FAILURE'])
AC_FC_IMPLICIT_NONE ([*action-if-success*], [*action-if-failure* =   [Macro]
    'AC_MSG_FAILURE'])

Try to disallow implicit declarations in the Fortran compiler. If successful, *action-if-success* is called and any needed flags are added to FFLAGS or FCFLAGS, respectively. Otherwise, *action-if-failure* is called, which defaults to failing with an error message.

The result of these macros are cached in the ac_cv_f77_implicit_none and ac_cv_fc_implicit_none variables, respectively.

AC_FC_MODULE_EXTENSION   [Macro]

Find the Fortran 90 module file name extension. Most Fortran 90 compilers store module information in files separate from the object files. The module files are usually named after the name of the module rather than the source file name, with characters possibly turned to upper case, plus an extension, often '.mod'.

Not all compilers use module files at all, or by default. The Cray Fortran compiler requires '-e m' in order to store and search module information in '.mod' files rather than in object files. Likewise, the Fujitsu Fortran compilers uses the '-Am' option to indicate how module information is stored.

The AC_FC_MODULE_EXTENSION macro computes the module extension without the leading dot, and stores that in the FC_MODEXT variable. If the compiler does not produce module files, or the extension cannot be determined, FC_MODEXT is empty. Typically, the result of this macro may be used in cleanup make rules as follows:

```
clean-modules:
        -test -z "$(FC_MODEXT)" || rm -f *.$(FC_MODEXT)
```

The extension, or 'unknown', is cached in the ac_cv_fc_module_ext variable.

AC_FC_MODULE_FLAG ([*action-if-success*], [*action-if-failure* =   [Macro]
    'AC_MSG_FAILURE'])

Find the compiler flag to include Fortran 90 module information from another directory, and store that in the FC_MODINC variable. Call *action-if-success* (defaults to nothing) if successful, and set FC_MODINC to empty and call *action-if-failure* (defaults to exiting with an error message) if not.

Most Fortran 90 compilers provide a way to specify module directories. Some have separate flags for the directory to write module files to, and directories to search them in, whereas others only allow writing to the current directory or to the first directory specified in the include path. Further, with some compilers, the module search path and the preprocessor search path can only be modified with the same flag. Thus, for portability, write module files to the current directory only and list that as first directory in the search path.

There may be no whitespace between FC_MODINC and the following directory name, but FC_MODINC may contain trailing white space. For example, if you use Automake and would like to search '../lib' for module files, you can use the following:

```
AM_FCFLAGS = $(FC_MODINC). $(FC_MODINC)../lib
```

Inside configure tests, you can use:

```
if test -n "$FC_MODINC"; then
  FCFLAGS="$FCFLAGS $FC_MODINC. $FC_MODINC../lib"
fi
```

The flag is cached in the `ac_cv_fc_module_flag` variable. The substituted value of `FC_MODINC` may refer to the `ac_empty` dummy placeholder empty variable, to avoid losing the significant trailing whitespace in a 'Makefile'.

AC_FC_MODULE_OUTPUT_FLAG ([*action-if-success*],   [Macro]
    [*action-if-failure* = 'AC_MSG_FAILURE'])

Find the compiler flag to write Fortran 90 module information to another directory, and store that in the `FC_MODOUT` variable. Call *action-if-success* (defaults to nothing) if successful, and set `FC_MODOUT` to empty and call *action-if-failure* (defaults to exiting with an error message) if not.

Not all Fortran 90 compilers write module files, and of those that do, not all allow writing to a directory other than the current one, nor do all have separate flags for writing and reading; see the description of `AC_FC_MODULE_FLAG` above. If you need to be able to write to another directory, for maximum portability use `FC_MODOUT` before any `FC_MODINC` and include both the current directory and the one you write to in the search path:

```
AM_FCFLAGS = $(FC_MODOUT)../mod $(FC_MODINC)../mod $(FC_MODINC). ...
```

The flag is cached in the `ac_cv_fc_module_output_flag` variable. The substituted value of `FC_MODOUT` may refer to the `ac_empty` dummy placeholder empty variable, to avoid losing the significant trailing whitespace in a 'Makefile'.

5.10.9 Go Compiler Characteristics

Autoconf provides basic support for the Go programming language when using the `gccgo` compiler (there is currently no support for the 6g and 8g compilers).

AC_PROG_GO ([*compiler-search-list*])   [Macro]

Find the Go compiler to use. Check whether the environment variable `GOC` is set; if so, then set output variable `GOC` to its value.

Otherwise, if the macro is invoked without an argument, then search for a Go compiler named `gccgo`. If it is not found, then as a last resort set `GOC` to `gccgo`.

This macro may be invoked with an optional first argument which, if specified, must be a blank-separated list of Go compilers to search for.

If output variable `GOFLAGS` was not already set, set it to '`-g -O2`'. If your package does not like this default, `GOFLAGS` may be set before `AC_PROG_GO`.

5.11 System Services

The following macros check for operating system services or capabilities.

AC_PATH_X   [Macro]

Try to locate the X Window System include files and libraries. If the user gave the command line options '`--x-includes=dir`' and '`--x-libraries=dir`', use those directories.

If either or both were not given, get the missing values by running `xmkmf` (or an executable pointed to by the `XMKMF` environment variable) on a trivial 'Imakefile' and examining the makefile that it produces. Setting `XMKMF` to 'false' disables this method.

If this method fails to find the X Window System, `configure` looks for the files in several directories where they often reside. If either method is successful, set the shell variables `x_includes` and `x_libraries` to their locations, unless they are in directories the compiler searches by default.

If both methods fail, or the user gave the command line option '--without-x', set the shell variable `no_x` to 'yes'; otherwise set it to the empty string.

`AC_PATH_XTRA`   [Macro]

An enhanced version of `AC_PATH_X`. It adds the C compiler flags that X needs to output variable `X_CFLAGS`, and the X linker flags to `X_LIBS`. Define `X_DISPLAY_MISSING` if X is not available.

This macro also checks for special libraries that some systems need in order to compile X programs. It adds any that the system needs to output variable `X_EXTRA_LIBS`. And it checks for special X11R6 libraries that need to be linked with before '-lX11', and adds any found to the output variable `X_PRE_LIBS`.

`AC_SYS_INTERPRETER`   [Macro]

Check whether the system supports starting scripts with a line of the form '#!/bin/sh' to select the interpreter to use for the script. After running this macro, shell code in 'configure.ac' can check the shell variable `interpval`; it is set to 'yes' if the system supports '#!', 'no' if not.

`AC_SYS_LARGEFILE`   [Macro]

Arrange for 64-bit file offsets, known as large-file support. On some hosts, one must use special compiler options to build programs that can access large files. Append any such options to the output variable `CC`. Define `_FILE_OFFSET_BITS` and `_LARGE_FILES` if necessary.

Large-file support can be disabled by configuring with the '--disable-largefile' option.

If you use this macro, check that your program works even when `off_t` is wider than `long int`, since this is common when large-file support is enabled. For example, it is not correct to print an arbitrary `off_t` value X with `printf ("%ld", (long int) X)`.

The LFS introduced the `fseeko` and `ftello` functions to replace their C counterparts `fseek` and `ftell` that do not use `off_t`. Take care to use `AC_FUNC_FSEEKO` to make their prototypes available when using them and large-file support is enabled.

`AC_SYS_LONG_FILE_NAMES`   [Macro]

If the system supports file names longer than 14 characters, define `HAVE_LONG_FILE_NAMES`.

`AC_SYS_POSIX_TERMIOS`   [Macro]

Check to see if the Posix termios headers and functions are available on the system. If so, set the shell variable `ac_cv_sys_posix_termios` to 'yes'. If not, set the variable to 'no'.

5.12 Posix Variants

The following macro makes it possible to use features of Posix that are extensions to C, as well as platform extensions not defined by Posix.

AC_USE_SYSTEM_EXTENSIONS   [Macro]

> This macro was introduced in Autoconf 2.60. If possible, enable extensions to C or Posix on hosts that normally disable the extensions, typically due to standards-conformance namespace issues. This should be called before any macros that run the C compiler. The following preprocessor macros are defined where appropriate:
>
> **_GNU_SOURCE**
> > Enable extensions on GNU/Linux.
>
> **__EXTENSIONS__**
> > Enable general extensions on Solaris.
>
> **_POSIX_PTHREAD_SEMANTICS**
> > Enable threading extensions on Solaris.
>
> **_TANDEM_SOURCE**
> > Enable extensions for the HP NonStop platform.
>
> **_ALL_SOURCE**
> > Enable extensions for AIX 3, and for Interix.
>
> **_POSIX_SOURCE**
> > Enable Posix functions for Minix.
>
> **_POSIX_1_SOURCE**
> > Enable additional Posix functions for Minix.
>
> **_MINIX**   Identify Minix platform. This particular preprocessor macro is obsolescent, and may be removed in a future release of Autoconf.

5.13 Erlang Libraries

The following macros check for an installation of Erlang/OTP, and for the presence of certain Erlang libraries. All those macros require the configuration of an Erlang interpreter and an Erlang compiler (see Section 5.10.7 [Erlang Compiler and Interpreter], page 87).

AC_ERLANG_SUBST_ERTS_VER   [Macro]

> Set the output variable `ERLANG_ERTS_VER` to the version of the Erlang runtime system (as returned by Erlang's `erlang:system_info(version)` function). The result of this test is cached if caching is enabled when running `configure`. The `ERLANG_ERTS_VER` variable is not intended to be used for testing for features of specific ERTS versions, but to be used for substituting the ERTS version in Erlang/OTP release resource files (`.rel` files), as shown below.

AC_ERLANG_SUBST_ROOT_DIR   [Macro]

> Set the output variable `ERLANG_ROOT_DIR` to the path to the base directory in which Erlang/OTP is installed (as returned by Erlang's `code:root_dir/0` function). The result of this test is cached if caching is enabled when running `configure`.

AC_ERLANG_SUBST_LIB_DIR   [Macro]

Set the output variable `ERLANG_LIB_DIR` to the path of the library directory of Erlang/OTP (as returned by Erlang's `code:lib_dir/0` function), which subdirectories each contain an installed Erlang/OTP library. The result of this test is cached if caching is enabled when running `configure`.

AC_ERLANG_CHECK_LIB (*library*, [*action-if-found*],   [Macro]
      [*action-if-not-found*])

Test whether the Erlang/OTP library *library* is installed by calling Erlang's `code:lib_dir/1` function. The result of this test is cached if caching is enabled when running `configure`. *action-if-found* is a list of shell commands to run if the library is installed; *action-if-not-found* is a list of shell commands to run if it is not. Additionally, if the library is installed, the output variable 'ERLANG_LIB_DIR_*library*' is set to the path to the library installation directory, and the output variable 'ERLANG_LIB_VER_*library*' is set to the version number that is part of the subdirectory name, if it is in the standard form (*library-version*). If the directory name does not have a version part, 'ERLANG_LIB_VER_*library*' is set to the empty string. If the library is not installed, 'ERLANG_LIB_DIR_*library*' and 'ERLANG_LIB_VER_*library*' are set to `"not found"`. For example, to check if library `stdlib` is installed:

```
AC_ERLANG_CHECK_LIB([stdlib],
  [echo "stdlib version \"$ERLANG_LIB_VER_stdlib\""
   echo "is installed in \"$ERLANG_LIB_DIR_stdlib\""],
  [AC_MSG_ERROR([stdlib was not found!])])
```

The 'ERLANG_LIB_VER_*library*' variables (set by `AC_ERLANG_CHECK_LIB`) and the `ERLANG_ERTS_VER` variable (set by `AC_ERLANG_SUBST_ERTS_VER`) are not intended to be used for testing for features of specific versions of libraries or of the Erlang runtime system. Those variables are intended to be substituted in Erlang release resource files (`.rel` files). For instance, to generate a 'example.rel' file for an application depending on the `stdlib` library, 'configure.ac' could contain:

```
AC_ERLANG_SUBST_ERTS_VER
AC_ERLANG_CHECK_LIB([stdlib],
  [],
  [AC_MSG_ERROR([stdlib was not found!])])
AC_CONFIG_FILES([example.rel])
```

The 'example.rel.in' file used to generate 'example.rel' should contain:

```
{release,
    {"@PACKAGE@", "@VERSION@"},
    {erts, "@ERLANG_ERTS_VER@"},
    [{stdlib, "@ERLANG_LIB_VER_stdlib@"},
     {@PACKAGE@, "@VERSION@"}]}.
```

In addition to the above macros, which test installed Erlang libraries, the following macros determine the paths to the directories into which newly built Erlang libraries are to be installed:

AC_ERLANG_SUBST_INSTALL_LIB_DIR   [Macro]

> Set the ERLANG_INSTALL_LIB_DIR output variable to the directory into which
> every built Erlang library should be installed in a separate subdirectory. If this
> variable is not set in the environment when configure runs, its default value is
> ${libdir}/erlang/lib.

AC_ERLANG_SUBST_INSTALL_LIB_SUBDIR (*library*, *version*)   [Macro]

> Set the 'ERLANG_INSTALL_LIB_DIR_*library*' output variable to the directory into
> which the built Erlang library *library* version *version* should be installed. If this
> variable is not set in the environment when configure runs, its default value is
> '$ERLANG_INSTALL_LIB_DIR/*library-version*', the value of the ERLANG_INSTALL_
> LIB_DIR variable being set by the AC_ERLANG_SUBST_INSTALL_LIB_DIR macro.

6 Writing Tests

If the existing feature tests don't do something you need, you have to write new ones. These macros are the building blocks. They provide ways for other macros to check whether various kinds of features are available and report the results.

This chapter contains some suggestions and some of the reasons why the existing tests are written the way they are. You can also learn a lot about how to write Autoconf tests by looking at the existing ones. If something goes wrong in one or more of the Autoconf tests, this information can help you understand the assumptions behind them, which might help you figure out how to best solve the problem.

These macros check the output of the compiler system of the current language (see Section 6.1 [Language Choice], page 101). They do not cache the results of their tests for future use (see Section 7.4 [Caching Results], page 117), because they don't know enough about the information they are checking for to generate a cache variable name. They also do not print any messages, for the same reason. The checks for particular kinds of features call these macros and do cache their results and print messages about what they're checking for.

When you write a feature test that could be applicable to more than one software package, the best thing to do is encapsulate it in a new macro. See Chapter 10 [Writing Autoconf Macros], page 177, for how to do that.

6.1 Language Choice

Autoconf-generated `configure` scripts check for the C compiler and its features by default. Packages that use other programming languages (maybe more than one, e.g., C and C++) need to test features of the compilers for the respective languages. The following macros determine which programming language is used in the subsequent tests in 'configure.ac'.

AC_LANG (*language*)   [Macro]
> Do compilation tests using the compiler, preprocessor, and file extensions for the specified *language*.
>
> Supported languages are:
>
> 'C'   Do compilation tests using CC and CPP and use extension '.c' for test programs. Use compilation flags: CPPFLAGS with CPP, and both CPPFLAGS and CFLAGS with CC.
>
> 'C++'   Do compilation tests using CXX and CXXCPP and use extension '.C' for test programs. Use compilation flags: CPPFLAGS with CXXCPP, and both CPPFLAGS and CXXFLAGS with CXX.
>
> 'Fortran 77'
>   Do compilation tests using F77 and use extension '.f' for test programs. Use compilation flags: FFLAGS.
>
> 'Fortran' Do compilation tests using FC and use extension '.f' (or whatever has been set by AC_FC_SRCEXT) for test programs. Use compilation flags: FCFLAGS.

'Erlang'   Compile and execute tests using ERLC and ERL and use extension '.erl'
              for test Erlang modules. Use compilation flags: ERLCFLAGS.

'Objective C'
              Do compilation tests using OBJC and OBJCPP and use extension '.m' for
              test programs. Use compilation flags: CPPFLAGS with OBJCPP, and both
              CPPFLAGS and OBJCFLAGS with OBJC.

'Objective C++'
              Do compilation tests using OBJCXX and OBJCXXCPP and use extension '.mm'
              for test programs. Use compilation flags: CPPFLAGS with OBJCXXCPP, and
              both CPPFLAGS and OBJCXXFLAGS with OBJCXX.

'Go'   Do compilation tests using GOC and use extension '.go' for test programs.
              Use compilation flags GOFLAGS.

AC_LANG_PUSH (*language*)   [Macro]
              Remember the current language (as set by AC_LANG) on a stack, and then select the
              language. Use this macro and AC_LANG_POP in macros that need to temporarily switch
              to a particular language.

AC_LANG_POP ([*language*])   [Macro]
              Select the language that is saved on the top of the stack, as set by AC_LANG_PUSH,
              and remove it from the stack.

              If given, *language* specifies the language we just *quit*. It is a good idea to specify it
              when it's known (which should be the case...), since Autoconf detects inconsistencies.

```
AC_LANG_PUSH([Fortran 77])
# Perform some tests on Fortran 77.
# ...
AC_LANG_POP([Fortran 77])
```

AC_LANG_ASSERT (*language*)   [Macro]
              Check statically that the current language is *language*. You should use this in your
              language specific macros to avoid that they be called with an inappropriate language.

              This macro runs only at autoconf time, and incurs no cost at configure time. Sadly
              enough and because Autoconf is a two layer language[1], the macros AC_LANG_PUSH
              and AC_LANG_POP cannot be "optimizing", therefore as much as possible you ought to
              avoid using them to wrap your code, rather, require from the user to run the macro
              with a correct current language, and check it with AC_LANG_ASSERT. And anyway,
              that may help the user understand she is running a Fortran macro while expecting a
              result about her Fortran 77 compiler...

AC_REQUIRE_CPP   [Macro]
              Ensure that whichever preprocessor would currently be used for tests has been found.
              Calls AC_REQUIRE (see Section 10.4.1 [Prerequisite Macros], page 180) with an ar-
              gument of either AC_PROG_CPP or AC_PROG_CXXCPP, depending on which language is
              current.

---

[1] Because M4 is not aware of Sh code, especially conditionals, some optimizations that look nice statically
    may produce incorrect results at runtime.

6.2 Writing Test Programs

Autoconf tests follow a common scheme: feed some program with some input, and most of the time, feed a compiler with some source file. This section is dedicated to these source samples.

6.2.1 Guidelines for Test Programs

The most important rule to follow when writing testing samples is:

Look for realism.

This motto means that testing samples must be written with the same strictness as real programs are written. In particular, you should avoid "shortcuts" and simplifications.

Don't just play with the preprocessor if you want to prepare a compilation. For instance, using `cpp` to check whether a header is functional might let your `configure` accept a header which causes some *compiler* error. Do not hesitate to check a header with other headers included before, especially required headers.

Make sure the symbols you use are properly defined, i.e., refrain from simply declaring a function yourself instead of including the proper header.

Test programs should not write to standard output. They should exit with status 0 if the test succeeds, and with status 1 otherwise, so that success can be distinguished easily from a core dump or other failure; segmentation violations and other failures produce a nonzero exit status. Unless you arrange for `exit` to be declared, test programs should `return`, not `exit`, from `main`, because on many systems `exit` is not declared by default.

Test programs can use `#if` or `#ifdef` to check the values of preprocessor macros defined by tests that have already run. For example, if you call `AC_HEADER_STDBOOL`, then later on in 'configure.ac' you can have a test program that includes 'stdbool.h' conditionally:

```
#ifdef HAVE_STDBOOL_H
# include <stdbool.h>
#endif
```

Both `#if HAVE_STDBOOL_H` and `#ifdef HAVE_STDBOOL_H` will work with any standard C compiler. Some developers prefer `#if` because it is easier to read, while others prefer `#ifdef` because it avoids diagnostics with picky compilers like GCC with the '-Wundef' option.

If a test program needs to use or create a data file, give it a name that starts with 'conftest', such as 'conftest.data'. The `configure` script cleans up by running 'rm -f -r conftest*' after running test programs and if the script is interrupted.

6.2.2 Test Functions

These days it's safe to assume support for function prototypes (introduced in C89).

Functions that test programs declare should also be conditionalized for C++, which requires 'extern "C"' prototypes. Make sure to not include any header files containing clashing prototypes.

```
#ifdef __cplusplus
extern "C"
#endif
void *valloc (size_t);
```

If a test program calls a function with invalid parameters (just to see whether it exists), organize the program to ensure that it never invokes that function. You can do this by calling it in another function that is never invoked. You can't do it by putting it after a call to `exit`, because GCC version 2 knows that `exit` never returns and optimizes out any code that follows it in the same block.

If you include any header files, be sure to call the functions relevant to them with the correct number of arguments, even if they are just 0, to avoid compilation errors due to prototypes. GCC version 2 has internal prototypes for several functions that it automatically inlines; for example, `memcpy`. To avoid errors when checking for them, either pass them the correct number of arguments or redeclare them with a different return type (such as `char`).

6.2.3 Generating Sources

Autoconf provides a set of macros that can be used to generate test source files. They are written to be language generic, i.e., they actually depend on the current language (see Section 6.1 [Language Choice], page 101) to "format" the output properly.

AC_LANG_CONFTEST (*source*)   [Macro]
>   Save the *source* text in the current test source file: '`conftest.extension`' where the *extension* depends on the current language. As of Autoconf 2.63b, the source file also contains the results of all of the `AC_DEFINE` performed so far.
>
>   Note that the *source* is evaluated exactly once, like regular Autoconf macro arguments, and therefore (i) you may pass a macro invocation, (ii) if not, be sure to double quote if needed.
>
>   This macro issues a warning during `autoconf` processing if *source* does not include an expansion of the macro `AC_LANG_DEFINES_PROVIDED` (note that both `AC_LANG_SOURCE` and `AC_LANG_PROGRAM` call this macro, and thus avoid the warning).
>
>   This macro is seldom called directly, but is used under the hood by more common macros such as `AC_COMPILE_IFELSE` and `AC_RUN_IFELSE`.

AC_LANG_DEFINES_PROVIDED   [Macro]
>   This macro is called as a witness that the file '`conftest.extension`' appropriate for the current language is complete, including all previously determined results from `AC_DEFINE`. This macro is seldom called directly, but exists if you have a compelling reason to write a conftest file without using `AC_LANG_SOURCE`, yet still want to avoid a syntax warning from `AC_LANG_CONFTEST`.

AC_LANG_SOURCE (*source*)   [Macro]
>   Expands into the *source*, with the definition of all the `AC_DEFINE` performed so far. This macro includes an expansion of `AC_LANG_DEFINES_PROVIDED`.
>
>   In many cases, you may find it more convenient to use the wrapper `AC_LANG_PROGRAM`.

For instance, executing (observe the double quotation!):

```
AC_INIT([Hello], [1.0], [bug-hello@example.org], [],
        [http://www.example.org/])
AC_DEFINE([HELLO_WORLD], ["Hello, World\n"],
  [Greetings string.])
AC_LANG([C])
```

```
AC_LANG_CONFTEST(
    [AC_LANG_SOURCE([[const char hw[] = "Hello, World\n";]])])
gcc -E -dD conftest.c
```

on a system with `gcc` installed, results in:

```
...
# 1 "conftest.c"

#define PACKAGE_NAME "Hello"
#define PACKAGE_TARNAME "hello"
#define PACKAGE_VERSION "1.0"
#define PACKAGE_STRING "Hello 1.0"
#define PACKAGE_BUGREPORT "bug-hello@example.org"
#define PACKAGE_URL "http://www.example.org/"
#define HELLO_WORLD "Hello, World\n"

const char hw[] = "Hello, World\n";
```

When the test language is Fortran, Erlang, or Go, the `AC_DEFINE` definitions are not automatically translated into constants in the source code by this macro.

AC_LANG_PROGRAM (*prologue*, *body*)   [Macro]

Expands into a source file which consists of the *prologue*, and then *body* as body of the main function (e.g., `main` in C). Since it uses `AC_LANG_SOURCE`, the features of the latter are available.

For instance:

```
AC_INIT([Hello], [1.0], [bug-hello@example.org], [],
        [http://www.example.org/])
AC_DEFINE([HELLO_WORLD], ["Hello, World\n"],
  [Greetings string.])
AC_LANG_CONFTEST(
[AC_LANG_PROGRAM([[const char hw[] = "Hello, World\n";]],
                  [[fputs (hw, stdout);]])])
gcc -E -dD conftest.c
```

on a system with `gcc` installed, results in:

```
...
# 1 "conftest.c"

#define PACKAGE_NAME "Hello"
#define PACKAGE_TARNAME "hello"
#define PACKAGE_VERSION "1.0"
#define PACKAGE_STRING "Hello 1.0"
#define PACKAGE_BUGREPORT "bug-hello@example.org"
#define PACKAGE_URL "http://www.example.org/"
#define HELLO_WORLD "Hello, World\n"

const char hw[] = "Hello, World\n";
```

```
int
main ()
{
fputs (hw, stdout);
  ;
  return 0;
}
```

In Erlang tests, the created source file is that of an Erlang module called `conftest`
('`conftest.erl`'). This module defines and exports at least one `start/0` function, which
is called to perform the test. The *prologue* is optional code that is inserted between the
module header and the `start/0` function definition. *body* is the body of the `start/0`
function without the final period (see Section 6.6 [Runtime], page 109, about constraints
on this function's behavior).

For instance:

```
AC_INIT([Hello], [1.0], [bug-hello@example.org])
AC_LANG(Erlang)
AC_LANG_CONFTEST(
[AC_LANG_PROGRAM([[-define(HELLO_WORLD, "Hello, world!").]],
                [[io:format("~s~n", [?HELLO_WORLD])]])])
cat conftest.erl
```

results in:

```
-module(conftest).
-export([start/0]).
-define(HELLO_WORLD, "Hello, world!").
start() ->
io:format("~s~n", [?HELLO_WORLD])
.
```

AC_LANG_CALL (*prologue*, *function*)   [Macro]

    Expands into a source file which consists of the *prologue*, and then a call to the
function as body of the main function (e.g., `main` in C). Since it uses `AC_LANG_`
`PROGRAM`, the feature of the latter are available.

    This function will probably be replaced in the future by a version which would enable
specifying the arguments. The use of this macro is not encouraged, as it violates
strongly the typing system.

    This macro cannot be used for Erlang tests.

AC_LANG_FUNC_LINK_TRY (*function*)   [Macro]

    Expands into a source file which uses the *function* in the body of the main func-
tion (e.g., `main` in C). Since it uses `AC_LANG_PROGRAM`, the features of the latter are
available.

    As `AC_LANG_CALL`, this macro is documented only for completeness. It is considered
to be severely broken, and in the future will be removed in favor of actual function
calls (with properly typed arguments).

    This macro cannot be used for Erlang tests.

6.3 Running the Preprocessor

Sometimes one might need to run the preprocessor on some source file. *Usually it is a bad idea*, as you typically need to *compile* your project, not merely run the preprocessor on it; therefore you certainly want to run the compiler, not the preprocessor. Resist the temptation of following the easiest path.

Nevertheless, if you need to run the preprocessor, then use `AC_PREPROC_IFELSE`.

The macros described in this section cannot be used for tests in Erlang, Fortran, or Go, since those languages require no preprocessor.

AC_PREPROC_IFELSE (*input*, [*action-if-true*], [*action-if-false*])   [Macro]
>   Run the preprocessor of the current language (see Section 6.1 [Language Choice], page 101) on the *input*, run the shell commands *action-if-true* on success, *action-if-false* otherwise. The *input* can be made by `AC_LANG_PROGRAM` and friends.
>
>   This macro uses `CPPFLAGS`, but not `CFLAGS`, because '-g', '-O', etc. are not valid options to many C preprocessors.
>
>   It is customary to report unexpected failures with `AC_MSG_FAILURE`. If needed, *action-if-true* can further access the preprocessed output in the file 'conftest.i'.

For instance:

```
AC_INIT([Hello], [1.0], [bug-hello@example.org])
AC_DEFINE([HELLO_WORLD], ["Hello, World\n"],
  [Greetings string.])
AC_PREPROC_IFELSE(
    [AC_LANG_PROGRAM([[const char hw[] = "Hello, World\n";]],
                     [[fputs (hw, stdout);]])],
    [AC_MSG_RESULT([OK])],
    [AC_MSG_FAILURE([unexpected preprocessor failure])])
```

results in:

```
checking for gcc... gcc
checking for C compiler default output file name... a.out
checking whether the C compiler works... yes
checking whether we are cross compiling... no
checking for suffix of executables...
checking for suffix of object files... o
checking whether we are using the GNU C compiler... yes
checking whether gcc accepts -g... yes
checking for gcc option to accept ISO C89... none needed
checking how to run the C preprocessor... gcc -E
OK
```

The macro `AC_TRY_CPP` (see Section 18.4 [Obsolete Macros], page 305) used to play the role of `AC_PREPROC_IFELSE`, but double quotes its argument, making it impossible to use it to elaborate sources. You are encouraged to get rid of your old use of the macro `AC_TRY_CPP` in favor of `AC_PREPROC_IFELSE`, but, in the first place, are you sure you need to run the *preprocessor* and not the compiler?

AC_EGREP_HEADER (*pattern, header-file, action-if-found,*   [Macro]
     [*action-if-not-found*])

> If the output of running the preprocessor on the system header file *header-file* matches
> the extended regular expression *pattern*, execute shell commands *action-if-found*, oth-
> erwise execute *action-if-not-found*.

AC_EGREP_CPP (*pattern, program,* [*action-if-found*],   [Macro]
     [*action-if-not-found*])

> *program* is the text of a C or C++ program, on which shell variable, back quote, and
> backslash substitutions are performed. If the output of running the preprocessor on
> *program* matches the extended regular expression *pattern*, execute shell commands
> *action-if-found*, otherwise execute *action-if-not-found*.

6.4 Running the Compiler

To check for a syntax feature of the current language's (see Section 6.1 [Language Choice],
page 101) compiler, such as whether it recognizes a certain keyword, or simply to try some
library feature, use AC_COMPILE_IFELSE to try to compile a small program that uses that
feature.

AC_COMPILE_IFELSE (*input,* [*action-if-true*], [*action-if-false*])   [Macro]

> Run the compiler and compilation flags of the current language (see Section 6.1 [Lan-
> guage Choice], page 101) on the *input*, run the shell commands *action-if-true* on
> success, *action-if-false* otherwise. The *input* can be made by AC_LANG_PROGRAM and
> friends.
>
> It is customary to report unexpected failures with AC_MSG_FAILURE. This macro does
> not try to link; use AC_LINK_IFELSE if you need to do that (see Section 6.5 [Running
> the Linker], page 108). If needed, *action-if-true* can further access the just-compiled
> object file 'conftest.$OBJEXT'.
>
> This macro uses AC_REQUIRE for the compiler associated with the current language,
> which means that if the compiler has not yet been determined, the compiler determi-
> nation will be made prior to the body of the outermost AC_DEFUN macro that triggered
> this macro to expand (see Section 20.8 [Expanded Before Required], page 346).

For tests in Erlang, the *input* must be the source code of a module named conftest. AC_
COMPILE_IFELSE generates a 'conftest.beam' file that can be interpreted by the Erlang
virtual machine (ERL). It is recommended to use AC_LANG_PROGRAM to specify the test
program, to ensure that the Erlang module has the right name.

6.5 Running the Linker

To check for a library, a function, or a global variable, Autoconf configure scripts try to
compile and link a small program that uses it. This is unlike Metaconfig, which by default
uses nm or ar on the C library to try to figure out which functions are available. Trying
to link with the function is usually a more reliable approach because it avoids dealing with
the variations in the options and output formats of nm and ar and in the location of the
standard libraries. It also allows configuring for cross-compilation or checking a function's
runtime behavior if needed. On the other hand, it can be slower than scanning the libraries
once, but accuracy is more important than speed.

AC_LINK_IFELSE is used to compile test programs to test for functions and global variables. It is also used by AC_CHECK_LIB to check for libraries (see Section 5.4 [Libraries], page 49), by adding the library being checked for to LIBS temporarily and trying to link a small program.

AC_LINK_IFELSE (*input*, [*action-if-true*], [*action-if-false*])   [Macro]
> Run the compiler (and compilation flags) and the linker of the current language (see Section 6.1 [Language Choice], page 101) on the *input*, run the shell commands *action-if-true* on success, *action-if-false* otherwise. The *input* can be made by AC_LANG_PROGRAM and friends. If needed, *action-if-true* can further access the just-linked program file 'conftest$EXEEXT'.
>
> LDFLAGS and LIBS are used for linking, in addition to the current compilation flags.
>
> It is customary to report unexpected failures with AC_MSG_FAILURE. This macro does not try to execute the program; use AC_RUN_IFELSE if you need to do that (see Section 6.6 [Runtime], page 109).

The AC_LINK_IFELSE macro cannot be used for Erlang tests, since Erlang programs are interpreted and do not require linking.

6.6 Checking Runtime Behavior

Sometimes you need to find out how a system performs at runtime, such as whether a given function has a certain capability or bug. If you can, make such checks when your program runs instead of when it is configured. You can check for things like the machine's endianness when your program initializes itself.

If you really need to test for a runtime behavior while configuring, you can write a test program to determine the result, and compile and run it using AC_RUN_IFELSE. Avoid running test programs if possible, because this prevents people from configuring your package for cross-compiling.

AC_RUN_IFELSE (*input*, [*action-if-true*], [*action-if-false*],   [Macro]
          [*action-if-cross-compiling* = 'AC_MSG_FAILURE'])
> Run the compiler (and compilation flags) and the linker of the current language (see Section 6.1 [Language Choice], page 101) on the *input*, then execute the resulting program. If the program returns an exit status of 0 when executed, run shell commands *action-if-true*. Otherwise, run shell commands *action-if-false*.
>
> The *input* can be made by AC_LANG_PROGRAM and friends. LDFLAGS and LIBS are used for linking, in addition to the compilation flags of the current language (see Section 6.1 [Language Choice], page 101). Additionally, *action-if-true* can run ./conftest$EXEEXT for further testing.
>
> In the *action-if-false* section, the failing exit status is available in the shell variable '$?'. This exit status might be that of a failed compilation, or it might be that of a failed program execution.
>
> If cross-compilation mode is enabled (this is the case if either the compiler being used does not produce executables that run on the system where configure is being run, or if the options --build and --host were both specified and their values are

different), then the test program is not run. If the optional shell commands *action-if-cross-compiling* are given, those commands are run instead; typically these commands provide pessimistic defaults that allow cross-compilation to work even if the guess was wrong. If the fourth argument is empty or omitted, but cross-compilation is detected, then `configure` prints an error message and exits. If you want your package to be useful in a cross-compilation scenario, you *should* provide a non-empty *action-if-cross-compiling* clause, as well as wrap the `AC_RUN_IFELSE` compilation inside an `AC_CACHE_CHECK` (see Section 7.4 [Caching Results], page 117) which allows the user to override the pessimistic default if needed.

It is customary to report unexpected failures with `AC_MSG_FAILURE`.

`autoconf` prints a warning message when creating `configure` each time it encounters a call to `AC_RUN_IFELSE` with no *action-if-cross-compiling* argument given. If you are not concerned about users configuring your package for cross-compilation, you may ignore the warning. A few of the macros distributed with Autoconf produce this warning message; but if this is a problem for you, please report it as a bug, along with an appropriate pessimistic guess to use instead.

To configure for cross-compiling you can also choose a value for those parameters based on the canonical system name (see Chapter 14 [Manual Configuration], page 281). Alternatively, set up a test results cache file with the correct values for the host system (see Section 7.4 [Caching Results], page 117).

To provide a default for calls of `AC_RUN_IFELSE` that are embedded in other macros, including a few of the ones that come with Autoconf, you can test whether the shell variable `cross_compiling` is set to 'yes', and then use an alternate method to get the results instead of calling the macros.

It is also permissible to temporarily assign to `cross_compiling` in order to force tests to behave as though they are in a cross-compilation environment, particularly since this provides a way to test your *action-if-cross-compiling* even when you are not using a cross-compiler.

```
# We temporarily set cross-compile mode to force AC_COMPUTE_INT
# to use the slow link-only method
save_cross_compiling=$cross_compiling
cross_compiling=yes
AC_COMPUTE_INT([...])
cross_compiling=$save_cross_compiling
```

A C or C++ runtime test should be portable. See Chapter 13 [Portable C and C++], page 271.

Erlang tests must exit themselves the Erlang VM by calling the `halt/1` function: the given status code is used to determine the success of the test (status is 0) or its failure (status is different than 0), as explained above. It must be noted that data output through the standard output (e.g., using `io:format/2`) may be truncated when halting the VM. Therefore, if a test must output configuration information, it is recommended to create and to output data into the temporary file named 'conftest.out', using the functions of module `file`. The `conftest.out` file is automatically deleted by the `AC_RUN_IFELSE` macro. For instance, a simplified implementation of Autoconf's `AC_ERLANG_SUBST_LIB_DIR` macro is:

```
AC_INIT([LibdirTest], [1.0], [bug-libdirtest@example.org])
AC_ERLANG_NEED_ERL
AC_LANG(Erlang)
AC_RUN_IFELSE(
  [AC_LANG_PROGRAM([], [dnl
    file:write_file("conftest.out", code:lib_dir()),
    halt(0)])],
  [echo "code:lib_dir() returned: `cat conftest.out`"],
  [AC_MSG_FAILURE([test Erlang program execution failed])])
```

6.7 Systemology

This section aims at presenting some systems and pointers to documentation. It may help you addressing particular problems reported by users.

Posix-conforming systems are derived from the Unix operating system.

The Rosetta Stone for Unix contains a table correlating the features of various Posix-conforming systems. Unix History is a simplified diagram of how many Unix systems were derived from each other.

The Heirloom Project provides some variants of traditional implementations of Unix utilities.

Darwin   Darwin is also known as Mac OS X. Beware that the file system *can* be case-preserving, but case insensitive. This can cause nasty problems, since for instance the installation attempt for a package having an 'INSTALL' file can result in 'make install' report that nothing was to be done!

That's all dependent on whether the file system is a UFS (case sensitive) or HFS+ (case preserving). By default Apple wants you to install the OS on HFS+. Unfortunately, there are some pieces of software which really need to be built on UFS. We may want to rebuild Darwin to have both UFS and HFS+ available (and put the /local/build tree on the UFS).

QNX 4.25   QNX is a realtime operating system running on Intel architecture meant to be scalable from the small embedded systems to the hundred processor super-computer. It claims to be Posix certified. More information is available on the QNX home page.

Tru64   Documentation of several versions of Tru64 is available in different formats.

Unix version 7
            Officially this was called the "Seventh Edition" of "the UNIX time-sharing system" but we use the more-common name "Unix version 7". Documentation is available in the Unix Seventh Edition Manual. Previous versions of Unix are called "Unix version 6", etc., but they were not as widely used.

6.8 Multiple Cases

Some operations are accomplished in several possible ways, depending on the OS variant. Checking for them essentially requires a "case statement". Autoconf does not directly provide one; however, it is easy to simulate by using a shell variable to keep track of whether a way to perform the operation has been found yet.

Here is an example that uses the shell variable `fstype` to keep track of whether the remaining cases need to be checked. Note that since the value of `fstype` is under our control, we don't have to use the longer 'test "x$fstype" = xno'.

```
AC_MSG_CHECKING([how to get file system type])
fstype=no
# The order of these tests is important.
AC_COMPILE_IFELSE([AC_LANG_PROGRAM([[#include <sys/statvfs.h>
#include <sys/fstyp.h>]])],
                  [AC_DEFINE([FSTYPE_STATVFS], [1],
                     [Define if statvfs exists.])
                   fstype=SVR4])
if test $fstype = no; then
  AC_COMPILE_IFELSE([AC_LANG_PROGRAM([[#include <sys/statfs.h>
#include <sys/fstyp.h>]])],
                  [AC_DEFINE([FSTYPE_USG_STATFS], [1],
                     [Define if USG statfs.])
                   fstype=SVR3])
fi
if test $fstype = no; then
  AC_COMPILE_IFELSE([AC_LANG_PROGRAM([[#include <sys/statfs.h>
#include <sys/vmount.h>]])],
                  [AC_DEFINE([FSTYPE_AIX_STATFS], [1],
                     [Define if AIX statfs.])
                   fstype=AIX])
fi
# (more cases omitted here)
AC_MSG_RESULT([$fstype])
```

7 Results of Tests

Once `configure` has determined whether a feature exists, what can it do to record that information? There are four sorts of things it can do: define a C preprocessor symbol, set a variable in the output files, save the result in a cache file for future `configure` runs, and print a message letting the user know the result of the test.

7.1 Defining C Preprocessor Symbols

A common action to take in response to a feature test is to define a C preprocessor symbol indicating the results of the test. That is done by calling `AC_DEFINE` or `AC_DEFINE_UNQUOTED`.

By default, `AC_OUTPUT` places the symbols defined by these macros into the output variable `DEFS`, which contains an option '`-Dsymbol=value`' for each symbol defined. Unlike in Autoconf version 1, there is no variable `DEFS` defined while `configure` is running. To check whether Autoconf macros have already defined a certain C preprocessor symbol, test the value of the appropriate cache variable, as in this example:

```
AC_CHECK_FUNC([vprintf], [AC_DEFINE([HAVE_VPRINTF], [1],
                          [Define if vprintf exists.])])
if test "x$ac_cv_func_vprintf" != xyes; then
  AC_CHECK_FUNC([_doprnt], [AC_DEFINE([HAVE_DOPRNT], [1],
                            [Define if _doprnt exists.])])
fi
```

If `AC_CONFIG_HEADERS` has been called, then instead of creating `DEFS`, `AC_OUTPUT` creates a header file by substituting the correct values into `#define` statements in a template file. See Section 4.9 [Configuration Headers], page 33, for more information about this kind of output.

`AC_DEFINE` (*variable*, *value*, [*description*])   [Macro]
`AC_DEFINE` (*variable*)   [Macro]

    Define *variable* to *value* (verbatim), by defining a C preprocessor macro for *variable*. *variable* should be a C identifier, optionally suffixed by a parenthesized argument list to define a C preprocessor macro with arguments. The macro argument list, if present, should be a comma-separated list of C identifiers, possibly terminated by an ellipsis '`...`' if C99 syntax is employed. *variable* should not contain comments, white space, trigraphs, backslash-newlines, universal character names, or non-ASCII characters.

    value may contain backslash-escaped newlines, which will be preserved if you use `AC_CONFIG_HEADERS` but flattened if passed via `@DEFS@` (with no effect on the compilation, since the preprocessor sees only one line in the first place). *value* should not contain raw newlines. If you are not using `AC_CONFIG_HEADERS`, *value* should not contain any '`#`' characters, as `make` tends to eat them. To use a shell variable, use `AC_DEFINE_UNQUOTED` instead.

    description is only useful if you are using `AC_CONFIG_HEADERS`. In this case, *description* is put into the generated '`config.h.in`' as the comment before the macro define. The following example defines the C preprocessor variable `EQUATION` to be the string constant '`"$a > $b"`':

```
AC_DEFINE([EQUATION], ["$a > $b"],
    [Equation string.])
```

If neither *value* nor *description* are given, then *value* defaults to 1 instead of to the empty string. This is for backwards compatibility with older versions of Autoconf, but this usage is obsolescent and may be withdrawn in future versions of Autoconf.

If the *variable* is a literal string, it is passed to `m4_pattern_allow` (see Section 8.3.10 [Forbidden Patterns], page 164).

If multiple `AC_DEFINE` statements are executed for the same *variable* name (not counting any parenthesized argument list), the last one wins.

AC_DEFINE_UNQUOTED (*variable*, *value*, [*description*])   [Macro]
AC_DEFINE_UNQUOTED (*variable*)   [Macro]

Like `AC_DEFINE`, but three shell expansions are performed—once—on *variable* and *value*: variable expansion ('$'), command substitution ('`'), and backslash escaping ('\'), as if in an unquoted here-document. Single and double quote characters in the value have no special meaning. Use this macro instead of `AC_DEFINE` when *variable* or *value* is a shell variable. Examples:

```
AC_DEFINE_UNQUOTED([config_machfile], ["$machfile"],
    [Configuration machine file.])
AC_DEFINE_UNQUOTED([GETGROUPS_T], [$ac_cv_type_getgroups],
    [getgroups return type.])
AC_DEFINE_UNQUOTED([$ac_tr_hdr], [1],
    [Translated header name.])
```

Due to a syntactical bizarreness of the Bourne shell, do not use semicolons to separate `AC_DEFINE` or `AC_DEFINE_UNQUOTED` calls from other macro calls or shell code; that can cause syntax errors in the resulting `configure` script. Use either blanks or newlines. That is, do this:

```
AC_CHECK_HEADER([elf.h],
    [AC_DEFINE([SVR4], [1], [System V Release 4]) LIBS="-lelf $LIBS"])
```

or this:

```
AC_CHECK_HEADER([elf.h],
    [AC_DEFINE([SVR4], [1], [System V Release 4])
     LIBS="-lelf $LIBS"])
```

instead of this:

```
AC_CHECK_HEADER([elf.h],
    [AC_DEFINE([SVR4], [1], [System V Release 4]); LIBS="-lelf $LIBS"])
```

7.2 Setting Output Variables

Another way to record the results of tests is to set *output variables*, which are shell variables whose values are substituted into files that `configure` outputs. The two macros below create new output variables. See Section 4.8.1 [Preset Output Variables], page 23, for a list of output variables that are always available.

AC_SUBST (*variable*, [*value*])   [Macro]

Create an output variable from a shell variable. Make `AC_OUTPUT` substitute the variable *variable* into output files (typically one or more makefiles). This means that `AC_OUTPUT` replaces instances of '`@variable@`' in input files with the value that the shell variable *variable* has when `AC_OUTPUT` is called. The value can contain any non-NUL character, including newline. If you are using Automake 1.11 or newer, for newlines in values you might want to consider using `AM_SUBST_NOTMAKE` to prevent `automake` from adding a line `variable = @variable@` to the '`Makefile.in`' files (see Section "Automake" in *Other things Automake recognizes*).

Variable occurrences should not overlap: e.g., an input file should not contain '`@var1@var2@`' if *var1* and *var2* are variable names. The substituted value is not rescanned for more output variables; occurrences of '`@variable@`' in the value are inserted literally into the output file. (The algorithm uses the special marker `|#_!!_#|` internally, so neither the substituted value nor the output file may contain `|#_!!_#|`.)

If *value* is given, in addition assign it to *variable*.

The string *variable* is passed to `m4_pattern_allow` (see Section 8.3.10 [Forbidden Patterns], page 164).

AC_SUBST_FILE (*variable*)   [Macro]

Another way to create an output variable from a shell variable. Make `AC_OUTPUT` insert (without substitutions) the contents of the file named by shell variable *variable* into output files. This means that `AC_OUTPUT` replaces instances of '`@variable@`' in output files (such as '`Makefile.in`') with the contents of the file that the shell variable *variable* names when `AC_OUTPUT` is called. Set the variable to '`/dev/null`' for cases that do not have a file to insert. This substitution occurs only when the '`@variable@`' is on a line by itself, optionally surrounded by spaces and tabs. The substitution replaces the whole line, including the spaces, tabs, and the terminating newline.

This macro is useful for inserting makefile fragments containing special dependencies or other `make` directives for particular host or target types into makefiles. For example, '`configure.ac`' could contain:

```
AC_SUBST_FILE([host_frag])
host_frag=$srcdir/conf/sun4.mh
```

and then a '`Makefile.in`' could contain:

```
@host_frag@
```

The string *variable* is passed to `m4_pattern_allow` (see Section 8.3.10 [Forbidden Patterns], page 164).

Running `configure` in varying environments can be extremely dangerous. If for instance the user runs '`CC=bizarre-cc ./configure`', then the cache, '`config.h`', and many other output files depend upon `bizarre-cc` being the C compiler. If for some reason the user runs `./configure` again, or if it is run via '`./config.status --recheck`', (See Section 4.8.5 [Automatic Remaking], page 32, and see Chapter 17 [config.status Invocation], page 301), then the configuration can be inconsistent, composed of results depending upon two different compilers.

Environment variables that affect this situation, such as 'CC' above, are called *precious variables*, and can be declared as such by `AC_ARG_VAR`.

`AC_ARG_VAR` (`variable, description`)   [Macro]

Declare *variable* is a precious variable, and include its *description* in the variable section of './configure --help'.

Being precious means that

— *variable* is substituted via `AC_SUBST`.

— The value of *variable* when `configure` was launched is saved in the cache, including if it was not specified on the command line but via the environment. Indeed, while `configure` can notice the definition of CC in './configure CC=bizarre-cc', it is impossible to notice it in 'CC=bizarre-cc ./configure', which, unfortunately, is what most users do.

We emphasize that it is the *initial* value of *variable* which is saved, not that found during the execution of `configure`. Indeed, specifying './configure FOO=foo' and letting './configure' guess that FOO is foo can be two different things.

— *variable* is checked for consistency between two `configure` runs. For instance:

```
$ ./configure --silent --config-cache
$ CC=cc ./configure --silent --config-cache
configure: error: 'CC' was not set in the previous run
configure: error: changes in the environment can compromise \
the build
configure: error: run 'make distclean' and/or \
'rm config.cache' and start over
```

and similarly if the variable is unset, or if its content is changed. If the content has white space changes only, then the error is degraded to a warning only, but the old value is reused.

— *variable* is kept during automatic reconfiguration (see Chapter 17 [config.status Invocation], page 301) as if it had been passed as a command line argument, including when no cache is used:

```
$ CC=/usr/bin/cc ./configure var=raboof --silent
$ ./config.status --recheck
running CONFIG_SHELL=/bin/sh /bin/sh ./configure var=raboof \
CC=/usr/bin/cc  --no-create --no-recursion
```

7.3 Special Characters in Output Variables

Many output variables are intended to be evaluated both by `make` and by the shell. Some characters are expanded differently in these two contexts, so to avoid confusion these variables' values should not contain any of the following characters:

```
" # $ & ' ( ) * ; < > ? [ \ ^ ` |
```

Also, these variables' values should neither contain newlines, nor start with '~', nor contain white space or ':' immediately followed by '~'. The values can contain nonempty sequences of white space characters like tabs and spaces, but each such sequence might arbitrarily be replaced by a single space during substitution.

These restrictions apply both to the values that `configure` computes, and to the values set directly by the user. For example, the following invocations of `configure` are problematic, since they attempt to use special characters within CPPFLAGS and white space within $(srcdir):

```
CPPFLAGS='-DOUCH="&\"#$*?"' '../My Source/ouch-1.0/configure'

'../My Source/ouch-1.0/configure' CPPFLAGS='-DOUCH="&\"#$*?"'
```

7.4 Caching Results

To avoid checking for the same features repeatedly in various `configure` scripts (or in repeated runs of one script), `configure` can optionally save the results of many checks in a *cache file* (see Section 7.4.2 [Cache Files], page 119). If a `configure` script runs with caching enabled and finds a cache file, it reads the results of previous runs from the cache and avoids rerunning those checks. As a result, `configure` can then run much faster than if it had to perform all of the checks every time.

`AC_CACHE_VAL` (*cache-id, commands-to-set-it*)   [Macro]

   Ensure that the results of the check identified by *cache-id* are available. If the results of the check were in the cache file that was read, and `configure` was not given the '`--quiet`' or '`--silent`' option, print a message saying that the result was cached; otherwise, run the shell commands *commands-to-set-it*. If the shell commands are run to determine the value, the value is saved in the cache file just before `configure` creates its output files. See Section 7.4.1 [Cache Variable Names], page 118, for how to choose the name of the *cache-id* variable.

   The *commands-to-set-it must have no side effects* except for setting the variable *cache-id*, see below.

`AC_CACHE_CHECK` (*message, cache-id, commands-to-set-it*)   [Macro]

   A wrapper for `AC_CACHE_VAL` that takes care of printing the messages. This macro provides a convenient shorthand for the most common way to use these macros. It calls `AC_MSG_CHECKING` for *message*, then `AC_CACHE_VAL` with the *cache-id* and *commands* arguments, and `AC_MSG_RESULT` with *cache-id*.

   The *commands-to-set-it must have no side effects* except for setting the variable *cache-id*, see below.

It is common to find buggy macros using `AC_CACHE_VAL` or `AC_CACHE_CHECK`, because people are tempted to call `AC_DEFINE` in the *commands-to-set-it*. Instead, the code that *follows* the call to `AC_CACHE_VAL` should call `AC_DEFINE`, by examining the value of the cache variable. For instance, the following macro is broken:

```
AC_DEFUN([AC_SHELL_TRUE],
[AC_CACHE_CHECK([whether true(1) works], [my_cv_shell_true_works],
               [my_cv_shell_true_works=no
                (true) 2>/dev/null && my_cv_shell_true_works=yes
                if test "x$my_cv_shell_true_works" = xyes; then
                  AC_DEFINE([TRUE_WORKS], [1],
                            [Define if 'true(1)' works properly.])
                fi])
])
```

This fails if the cache is enabled: the second time this macro is run, TRUE_WORKS *will not be defined*. The proper implementation is:

```
AC_DEFUN([AC_SHELL_TRUE],
[AC_CACHE_CHECK([whether true(1) works], [my_cv_shell_true_works],
               [my_cv_shell_true_works=no
                (true) 2>/dev/null && my_cv_shell_true_works=yes])
 if test "x$my_cv_shell_true_works" = xyes; then
   AC_DEFINE([TRUE_WORKS], [1],
             [Define if 'true(1)' works properly.])
 fi
])
```

Also, *commands-to-set-it* should not print any messages, for example with AC_MSG_CHECKING; do that before calling AC_CACHE_VAL, so the messages are printed regardless of whether the results of the check are retrieved from the cache or determined by running the shell commands.

7.4.1 Cache Variable Names

The names of cache variables should have the following format:

*package-prefix*_cv_*value-type*_*specific-value*_[*additional-options*]

for example, 'ac_cv_header_stat_broken' or 'ac_cv_prog_gcc_traditional'. The parts of the variable name are:

package-prefix
> An abbreviation for your package or organization; the same prefix you begin local Autoconf macros with, except lowercase by convention. For cache values used by the distributed Autoconf macros, this value is 'ac'.

_cv_
> Indicates that this shell variable is a cache value. This string *must* be present in the variable name, including the leading underscore.

value-type
> A convention for classifying cache values, to produce a rational naming system. The values used in Autoconf are listed in Section 10.2 [Macro Names], page 178.

specific-value
> Which member of the class of cache values this test applies to. For example, which function ('alloca'), program ('gcc'), or output variable ('INSTALL').

additional-options

> Any particular behavior of the specific member that this test applies to. For example, 'broken' or 'set'. This part of the name may be omitted if it does not apply.

The values assigned to cache variables may not contain newlines. Usually, their values are Boolean ('yes' or 'no') or the names of files or functions; so this is not an important restriction. Section B.4 [Cache Variable Index], page 368 for an index of cache variables with documented semantics.

7.4.2 Cache Files

A cache file is a shell script that caches the results of configure tests run on one system so they can be shared between configure scripts and configure runs. It is not useful on other systems. If its contents are invalid for some reason, the user may delete or edit it, or override documented cache variables on the configure command line.

By default, configure uses no cache file, to avoid problems caused by accidental use of stale cache files.

To enable caching, configure accepts '--config-cache' (or '-C') to cache results in the file 'config.cache'. Alternatively, '--cache-file=*file*' specifies that *file* be the cache file. The cache file is created if it does not exist already. When configure calls configure scripts in subdirectories, it uses the '--cache-file' argument so that they share the same cache. See Section 4.12 [Subdirectories], page 38, for information on configuring subdirectories with the AC_CONFIG_SUBDIRS macro.

'config.status' only pays attention to the cache file if it is given the '--recheck' option, which makes it rerun configure.

It is wrong to try to distribute cache files for particular system types. There is too much room for error in doing that, and too much administrative overhead in maintaining them. For any features that can't be guessed automatically, use the standard method of the canonical system type and linking files (see Chapter 14 [Manual Configuration], page 281).

The site initialization script can specify a site-wide cache file to use, instead of the usual per-program cache. In this case, the cache file gradually accumulates information whenever someone runs a new configure script. (Running configure merges the new cache results with the existing cache file.) This may cause problems, however, if the system configuration (e.g., the installed libraries or compilers) changes and the stale cache file is not deleted.

If configure is interrupted at the right time when it updates a cache file outside of the build directory where the configure script is run, it may leave behind a temporary file named after the cache file with digits following it. You may safely delete such a file.

7.4.3 Cache Checkpointing

If your configure script, or a macro called from 'configure.ac', happens to abort the configure process, it may be useful to checkpoint the cache a few times at key points using AC_CACHE_SAVE. Doing so reduces the amount of time it takes to rerun the configure script with (hopefully) the error that caused the previous abort corrected.

AC_CACHE_LOAD   [Macro]

> Loads values from existing cache file, or creates a new cache file if a cache file is not found. Called automatically from AC_INIT.

AC_CACHE_SAVE   [Macro]
> Flushes all cached values to the cache file. Called automatically from AC_OUTPUT, but
> it can be quite useful to call AC_CACHE_SAVE at key points in 'configure.ac'.

For instance:

```
... AC_INIT, etc. ...
# Checks for programs.
AC_PROG_CC
AC_PROG_AWK
... more program checks ...
AC_CACHE_SAVE

# Checks for libraries.
AC_CHECK_LIB([nsl], [gethostbyname])
AC_CHECK_LIB([socket], [connect])
... more lib checks ...
AC_CACHE_SAVE

# Might abort...
AM_PATH_GTK([1.0.2], [], [AC_MSG_ERROR([GTK not in path])])
AM_PATH_GTKMM([0.9.5], [], [AC_MSG_ERROR([GTK not in path])])
... AC_OUTPUT, etc. ...
```

7.5 Printing Messages

configure scripts need to give users running them several kinds of information. The following macros print messages in ways appropriate for each kind. The arguments to all of them get enclosed in shell double quotes, so the shell performs variable and back-quote substitution on them.

These macros are all wrappers around the echo shell command. They direct output to the appropriate file descriptor (see Section 9.4 [File Descriptor Macros], page 175). configure scripts should rarely need to run echo directly to print messages for the user. Using these macros makes it easy to change how and when each kind of message is printed; such changes need only be made to the macro definitions and all the callers change automatically.

To diagnose static issues, i.e., when autoconf is run, see Section 8.3.2 [Diagnostic Macros], page 140.

AC_MSG_CHECKING (*feature-description*)   [Macro]
> Notify the user that configure is checking for a particular feature. This macro
> prints a message that starts with 'checking ' and ends with '...' and no newline.
> It must be followed by a call to AC_MSG_RESULT to print the result of the check and
> the newline. The *feature-description* should be something like 'whether the Fortran
> compiler accepts C++ comments' or 'for c89'.

> This macro prints nothing if configure is run with the '--quiet' or '--silent'
> option.

AC_MSG_RESULT (*result-description*) [Macro]

> Notify the user of the results of a check. *result-description* is almost always the value of the cache variable for the check, typically 'yes', 'no', or a file name. This macro should follow a call to AC_MSG_CHECKING, and the *result-description* should be the completion of the message printed by the call to AC_MSG_CHECKING.
>
> This macro prints nothing if configure is run with the '--quiet' or '--silent' option.

AC_MSG_NOTICE (*message*) [Macro]

> Deliver the *message* to the user. It is useful mainly to print a general description of the overall purpose of a group of feature checks, e.g.,
>
>   AC_MSG_NOTICE([checking if stack overflow is detectable])
>
> This macro prints nothing if configure is run with the '--quiet' or '--silent' option.

AC_MSG_ERROR (*error-description*, [*exit-status* = '$?/1']) [Macro]

> Notify the user of an error that prevents configure from completing. This macro prints an error message to the standard error output and exits configure with *exit-status* ('$?' by default, except that '0' is converted to '1'). *error-description* should be something like 'invalid value $HOME for \$HOME'.
>
> The *error-description* should start with a lower-case letter, and "cannot" is preferred to "can't".

AC_MSG_FAILURE (*error-description*, [*exit-status*]) [Macro]

> This AC_MSG_ERROR wrapper notifies the user of an error that prevents configure from completing *and* that additional details are provided in 'config.log'. This is typically used when abnormal results are found during a compilation.

AC_MSG_WARN (*problem-description*) [Macro]

> Notify the configure user of a possible problem. This macro prints the message to the standard error output; configure continues running afterward, so macros that call AC_MSG_WARN should provide a default (back-up) behavior for the situations they warn about. *problem-description* should be something like 'ln -s seems to make hard links'.

8 Programming in M4

Autoconf is written on top of two layers: *M4sugar*, which provides convenient macros for pure M4 programming, and *M4sh*, which provides macros dedicated to shell script generation.

As of this version of Autoconf, these two layers still contain experimental macros, whose interface might change in the future. As a matter of fact, *anything that is not documented must not be used.*

8.1 M4 Quotation

The most common problem with existing macros is an improper quotation. This section, which users of Autoconf can skip, but which macro writers *must* read, first justifies the quotation scheme that was chosen for Autoconf and then ends with a rule of thumb. Understanding the former helps one to follow the latter.

8.1.1 Active Characters

To fully understand where proper quotation is important, you first need to know what the special characters are in Autoconf: '#' introduces a comment inside which no macro expansion is performed, ',' separates arguments, '[' and ']' are the quotes themselves[1], '(' and ')' (which M4 tries to match by pairs), and finally '$' inside a macro definition.

In order to understand the delicate case of macro calls, we first have to present some obvious failures. Below they are "obvious-ified", but when you find them in real life, they are usually in disguise.

Comments, introduced by a hash and running up to the newline, are opaque tokens to the top level: active characters are turned off, and there is no macro expansion:

```
# define([def], ine)
⇒# define([def], ine)
```

Each time there can be a macro expansion, there is a quotation expansion, i.e., one level of quotes is stripped:

```
int tab[10];
⇒int tab10;
[int tab[10];]
⇒int tab[10];
```

Without this in mind, the reader might try hopelessly to use her macro **array**:

```
define([array], [int tab[10];])
array
⇒int tab10;
[array]
⇒array
```

How can you correctly output the intended results[2]?

---

[1] By itself, M4 uses '`' and '`'; it is the M4sugar layer that sets up the preferred quotes of '[' and ']'.

[2] Using **defn**.

8.1.2 One Macro Call

Let's proceed on the interaction between active characters and macros with this small macro, which just returns its first argument:

```
define([car], [$1])
```

The two pairs of quotes above are not part of the arguments of define; rather, they are understood by the top level when it tries to find the arguments of define. Therefore, assuming car is not already defined, it is equivalent to write:

```
define(car, $1)
```

But, while it is acceptable for a 'configure.ac' to avoid unnecessary quotes, it is bad practice for Autoconf macros which must both be more robust and also advocate perfect style.

At the top level, there are only two possibilities: either you quote or you don't:

```
car(foo, bar, baz)
⇒foo
[car(foo, bar, baz)]
⇒car(foo, bar, baz)
```

Let's pay attention to the special characters:

```
car(#)
```
error EOF in argument list

The closing parenthesis is hidden in the comment; with a hypothetical quoting, the top level understood it this way:

```
car([#)]
```

Proper quotation, of course, fixes the problem:

```
car([#])
⇒#
```

Here are more examples:

```
car(foo, bar)
⇒foo
car([foo, bar])
⇒foo, bar
car((foo, bar))
⇒(foo, bar)
car([(foo], [bar)])
⇒(foo
define([a], [b])
⇒
car(a)
⇒b
car([a])
⇒b
car([[a]])
⇒a
car([[[a]]])
⇒[a]
```

8.1.3 Quoting and Parameters

When M4 encounters '$' within a macro definition, followed immediately by a character it recognizes ('0'...'9', '#', '@', or '*'), it will perform M4 parameter expansion. This happens regardless of how many layers of quotes the parameter expansion is nested within, or even if it occurs in text that will be rescanned as a comment.

```
define([none], [$1])
⇒
define([one], [[$1]])
⇒
define([two], [[[$1]]])
⇒
define([comment], [# $1])
⇒
define([active], [ACTIVE])
⇒
none([active])
⇒ACTIVE
one([active])
⇒active
two([active])
⇒[active]
comment([active])
⇒# active
```

On the other hand, since autoconf generates shell code, you often want to output shell variable expansion, rather than performing M4 parameter expansion. To do this, you must use M4 quoting to separate the '$' from the next character in the definition of your macro. If the macro definition occurs in single-quoted text, then insert another level of quoting; if the usage is already inside a double-quoted string, then split it into concatenated strings.

```
define([single], [a single-quoted $[]1 definition])
⇒
define([double], [[a double-quoted $][1 definition]])
⇒
single
⇒a single-quoted $1 definition
double
⇒a double-quoted $1 definition
```

Posix states that M4 implementations are free to provide implementation extensions when '${' is encountered in a macro definition. Autoconf reserves the longer sequence '${{' for use with planned extensions that will be available in the future GNU M4 2.0, but guarantees that all other instances of '${' will be output literally. Therefore, this idiom can also be used to output shell code parameter references:

```
define([first], [${1}])first
⇒${1}
```

Posix also states that '$11' should expand to the first parameter concatenated with a literal '1', although some versions of GNU M4 expand the eleventh parameter instead. For portability, you should only use single-digit M4 parameter expansion.

With this in mind, we can explore the cases where macros invoke macros...

8.1.4 Quotation and Nested Macros

The examples below use the following macros:

```
define([car], [$1])
define([active], [ACT, IVE])
define([array], [int tab[10]])
```

Each additional embedded macro call introduces other possible interesting quotations:

```
car(active)
⇒ACT
car([active])
⇒ACT, IVE
car([[active]])
⇒active
```

In the first case, the top level looks for the arguments of `car`, and finds 'active'. Because M4 evaluates its arguments before applying the macro, 'active' is expanded, which results in:

```
car(ACT, IVE)
⇒ACT
```

In the second case, the top level gives 'active' as first and only argument of `car`, which results in:

```
active
⇒ACT, IVE
```

i.e., the argument is evaluated *after* the macro that invokes it. In the third case, `car` receives '[active]', which results in:

```
[active]
⇒active
```

exactly as we already saw above.

The example above, applied to a more realistic example, gives:

```
car(int tab[10];)
⇒int tab10;
car([int tab[10];])
⇒int tab10;
car([[int tab[10];]])
⇒int tab[10];
```

Huh? The first case is easily understood, but why is the second wrong, and the third right? To understand that, you must know that after M4 expands a macro, the resulting text is immediately subjected to macro expansion and quote removal. This means that the quote removal occurs twice—first before the argument is passed to the `car` macro, and second after the `car` macro expands to the first argument.

As the author of the Autoconf macro car, you then consider it to be incorrect that your users have to double-quote the arguments of car, so you "fix" your macro. Let's call it qar for quoted car:

```
define([qar], [[$1]])
```

and check that qar is properly fixed:

```
qar([int tab[10];])
⇒int tab[10];
```

Ahhh! That's much better.

But note what you've done: now that the result of qar is always a literal string, the only time a user can use nested macros is if she relies on an *unquoted* macro call:

```
qar(active)
⇒ACT
qar([active])
⇒active
```

leaving no way for her to reproduce what she used to do with car:

```
car([active])
⇒ACT, IVE
```

Worse yet: she wants to use a macro that produces a set of cpp macros:

```
define([my_includes], [#include <stdio.h>])
car([my_includes])
⇒#include <stdio.h>
qar(my_includes)
```
⎡error⎤ EOF in argument list

This macro, qar, because it double quotes its arguments, forces its users to leave their macro calls unquoted, which is dangerous. Commas and other active symbols are interpreted by M4 before they are given to the macro, often not in the way the users expect. Also, because qar behaves differently from the other macros, it's an exception that should be avoided in Autoconf.

8.1.5 changequote is Evil

The temptation is often high to bypass proper quotation, in particular when it's late at night. Then, many experienced Autoconf hackers finally surrender to the dark side of the force and use the ultimate weapon: changequote.

The M4 builtin changequote belongs to a set of primitives that allow one to adjust the syntax of the language to adjust it to one's needs. For instance, by default M4 uses '`' and '´' as quotes, but in the context of shell programming (and actually of most programming languages), that's about the worst choice one can make: because of strings and back-quoted expressions in shell code (such as '`this´' and "`that`"), and because of literal characters in usual programming languages (as in ''0''), there are many unbalanced '`' and '´'. Proper M4 quotation then becomes a nightmare, if not impossible. In order to make M4 useful in such a context, its designers have equipped it with changequote, which makes it possible to choose another pair of quotes. M4sugar, M4sh, Autoconf, and Autotest all have chosen to use '[' and ']'. Not especially because they are unlikely characters, but *because they are characters unlikely to be unbalanced.*

There are other magic primitives, such as **changecom** to specify what syntactic forms are comments (it is common to see 'changecom(<!--, -->)' when M4 is used to produce HTML pages), **changeword** and **changesyntax** to change other syntactic details (such as the character to denote the nth argument, '**$**' by default, the parentheses around arguments, etc.).

These primitives are really meant to make M4 more useful for specific domains: they should be considered like command line options: '**--quotes**', '**--comments**', '**--words**', and '**--syntax**'. Nevertheless, they are implemented as M4 builtins, as it makes M4 libraries self contained (no need for additional options).

There lies the problem...

The problem is that it is then tempting to use them in the middle of an M4 script, as opposed to its initialization. This, if not carefully thought out, can lead to disastrous effects: *you are changing the language in the middle of the execution*. Changing and restoring the syntax is often not enough: if you happened to invoke macros in between, these macros are lost, as the current syntax is probably not the one they were implemented with.

8.1.6 Quadrigraphs

When writing an Autoconf macro you may occasionally need to generate special characters that are difficult to express with the standard Autoconf quoting rules. For example, you may need to output the regular expression '[^[]', which matches any character other than '['. This expression contains unbalanced brackets so it cannot be put easily into an M4 macro.

Additionally, there are a few m4sugar macros (such as **m4_split** and **m4_expand**) which internally use special markers in addition to the regular quoting characters. If the arguments to these macros contain the literal strings '-=<{(' or ')}>=-', the macros might behave incorrectly.

You can work around these problems by using one of the following *quadrigraphs*:

'@<:@'   '['

'@:>@'   ']'

'@S|@'   '$'

'@%:@'   '#'

'@{:@'   '('

'@:}@'   ')'

'@&t@'   Expands to nothing.

Quadrigraphs are replaced at a late stage of the translation process, after m4 is run, so they do not get in the way of M4 quoting. For example, the string '^@<:@', independently of its quotation, appears as '^[' in the output.

The empty quadrigraph can be used:

– to mark trailing spaces explicitly

   Trailing spaces are smashed by **autom4te**. This is a feature.

— to produce quadrigraphs and other strings reserved by m4sugar

For instance '@<@&t@:@' produces '@<:@'. For a more contrived example:

```
m4_define([a], [A])m4_define([b], [B])m4_define([c], [C])dnl
m4_split([a )}>=- b -=<{( c])
⇒[a], [], [B], [], [c]
m4_split([a )}@&t@>=- b -=<@&t@{( c])
⇒[a], [)}>=-], [b], [-=<{(], [c]
```

— to escape *occurrences* of forbidden patterns

For instance you might want to mention AC_FOO in a comment, while still being sure that autom4te still catches unexpanded 'AC_*'. Then write 'AC@&t@_FOO'.

The name '@&t@' was suggested by Paul Eggert:

I should give some credit to the '@&t@' pun. The '&' is my own invention, but the 't' came from the source code of the ALGOL68C compiler, written by Steve Bourne (of Bourne shell fame), and which used 'mt' to denote the empty string. In C, it would have looked like something like:

```
char const mt[] = "";
```

but of course the source code was written in Algol 68.

I don't know where he got 'mt' from: it could have been his own invention, and I suppose it could have been a common pun around the Cambridge University computer lab at the time.

8.1.7 Dealing with unbalanced parentheses

One of the pitfalls of portable shell programming is that case statements require unbalanced parentheses (see [Limitations of Shell Builtins], page 221). With syntax highlighting editors, the presence of unbalanced ')' can interfere with editors that perform syntax highlighting of macro contents based on finding the matching '('. Another concern is how much editing must be done when transferring code snippets between shell scripts and macro definitions. But most importantly, the presence of unbalanced parentheses can introduce expansion bugs.

For an example, here is an underquoted attempt to use the macro my_case, which happens to expand to a portable case statement:

```
AC_DEFUN([my_case],
[case $file_name in
  *.c) echo "C source code";;
esac])
AS_IF(:, my_case)
```

In the above example, the AS_IF call underquotes its arguments. As a result, the unbalanced ')' generated by the premature expansion of my_case results in expanding AS_IF with a truncated parameter, and the expansion is syntactically invalid:

```
if :; then
  case $file_name in
  *.c
fi echo "C source code";;
  esac)
```

If nothing else, this should emphasize the importance of the quoting arguments to macro calls. On the other hand, there are several variations for defining `my_case` to be more robust, even when used without proper quoting, each with some benefits and some drawbacks.

Creative literal shell comment

```
AC_DEFUN([my_case],
[case $file_name in #(
  *.c) echo "C source code";;
esac])
```

This version provides balanced parentheses to several editors, and can be copied and pasted into a terminal as is. Unfortunately, it is still unbalanced as an Autoconf argument, since '#(' is an M4 comment that masks the normal properties of '('.

Quadrigraph shell comment

```
AC_DEFUN([my_case],
[case $file_name in @%:@(
  *.c) echo "C source code";;
esac])
```

This version provides balanced parentheses to even more editors, and can be used as a balanced Autoconf argument. Unfortunately, it requires some editing before it can be copied and pasted into a terminal, and the use of the quadrigraph '@%:@' for '#' reduces readability.

Quoting just the parenthesis

```
AC_DEFUN([my_case],
[case $file_name in
  *.c[)] echo "C source code";;
esac])
```

This version quotes the ')', so that it can be used as a balanced Autoconf argument. As written, this is not balanced to an editor, but it can be coupled with '[#(]' to meet that need, too. However, it still requires some edits before it can be copied and pasted into a terminal.

Double-quoting the entire statement

```
AC_DEFUN([my_case],
[[case $file_name in #(
  *.c) echo "C source code";;
esac]])
```

Since the entire macro is double-quoted, there is no problem with using this as an Autoconf argument; and since the double-quoting is over the entire statement, this code can be easily copied and pasted into a terminal. However, the double quoting prevents the expansion of any macros inside the case statement, which may cause its own set of problems.

Using `AS_CASE`

```
AC_DEFUN([my_case],
[AS_CASE([$file_name],
  [*.c], [echo "C source code"])])
```

This version avoids the balancing issue altogether, by relying on `AS_CASE` (see Section 9.1 [Common Shell Constructs], page 167); it also allows for the expansion of `AC_REQUIRE` to occur prior to the entire case statement, rather than within a branch of the case statement that might not be taken. However, the abstraction comes with a penalty that it is no longer a quick copy, paste, and edit to get back to shell code.

8.1.8 Quotation Rule Of Thumb

To conclude, the quotation rule of thumb is:

One pair of quotes per pair of parentheses.

Never over-quote, never under-quote, in particular in the definition of macros. In the few places where the macros need to use brackets (usually in C program text or regular expressions), properly quote *the arguments*!

It is common to read Autoconf programs with snippets like:

```
AC_TRY_LINK(
changequote(<<, >>)dnl
<<#include <time.h>
#ifndef tzname /* For SGI.  */
extern char *tzname[]; /* RS6000 and others reject char **tzname.  */
#endif>>,
changequote([, ])dnl
[atoi (*tzname);], ac_cv_var_tzname=yes, ac_cv_var_tzname=no)
```

which is incredibly useless since `AC_TRY_LINK` is *already* double quoting, so you just need:

```
AC_TRY_LINK(
[#include <time.h>
#ifndef tzname /* For SGI.  */
extern char *tzname[]; /* RS6000 and others reject char **tzname.  */
#endif],
             [atoi (*tzname);],
             [ac_cv_var_tzname=yes],
             [ac_cv_var_tzname=no])
```

The M4-fluent reader might note that these two examples are rigorously equivalent, since M4 swallows both the 'changequote(<<, >>)' and '<<' '>>' when it *collects* the arguments: these quotes are not part of the arguments!

Simplified, the example above is just doing this:

```
changequote(<<, >>)dnl
<<[]>>
changequote([, ])dnl
```

instead of simply:

```
[[]]
```

With macros that do not double quote their arguments (which is the rule), double-quote the (risky) literals:

```
AC_LINK_IFELSE([AC_LANG_PROGRAM(
[[#include <time.h>
#ifndef tzname /* For SGI.  */
```

```
extern char *tzname[]; /* RS6000 and others reject char **tzname. */
#endif]],
                                    [atoi (*tzname);])],
                [ac_cv_var_tzname=yes],
                [ac_cv_var_tzname=no])
```

Please note that the macro `AC_TRY_LINK` is obsolete, so you really should be using `AC_LINK_IFELSE` instead.

See Section 8.1.6 [Quadrigraphs], page 128, for what to do if you run into a hopeless case where quoting does not suffice.

When you create a `configure` script using newly written macros, examine it carefully to check whether you need to add more quotes in your macros. If one or more words have disappeared in the M4 output, you need more quotes. When in doubt, quote.

However, it's also possible to put on too many layers of quotes. If this happens, the resulting `configure` script may contain unexpanded macros. The `autoconf` program checks for this problem by looking for the string 'AC_' in 'configure'. However, this heuristic does not work in general: for example, it does not catch overquoting in `AC_DEFINE` descriptions.

8.2 Using autom4te

The Autoconf suite, including M4sugar, M4sh, and Autotest, in addition to Autoconf per se, heavily rely on M4. All these different uses revealed common needs factored into a layer over M4: `autom4te`[3].

`autom4te` is a preprocessor that is like m4. It supports M4 extensions designed for use in tools like Autoconf.

8.2.1 Invoking autom4te

The command line arguments are modeled after M4's:

     autom4te *options files*

where the *files* are directly passed to `m4`. By default, GNU M4 is found during configuration, but the environment variable `M4` can be set to tell `autom4te` where to look. In addition to the regular expansion, it handles the replacement of the quadrigraphs (see Section 8.1.6 [Quadrigraphs], page 128), and of '`__oline__`', the current line in the output. It supports an extended syntax for the *files*:

'`file.m4f`'
                This file is an M4 frozen file. Note that *all the previous files are ignored*. See the option '`--melt`' for the rationale.

'`file?`'   If found in the library path, the *file* is included for expansion, otherwise it is ignored instead of triggering a failure.

Of course, it supports the Autoconf common subset of options:

'`--help`'
'`-h`'   Print a summary of the command line options and exit.

---

[3]   Yet another great name from Lars J. Aas.

'--version'

'-V'   Print the version number of Autoconf and exit.

'--verbose'

'-v'   Report processing steps.

'--debug'

'-d'   Don't remove the temporary files and be even more verbose.

'--include=*dir*'

'-I *dir*' Also look for input files in *dir*. Multiple invocations accumulate.

'--output=*file*'

'-o *file*' Save output (script or trace) to *file*. The file '-' stands for the standard output.

As an extension of `m4`, it includes the following options:

'--warnings=*category*'

'-W *category*'

> Report the warnings related to *category* (which can actually be a comma separated list). See Section 10.3 [Reporting Messages], page 179, macro `AC_DIAGNOSE`, for a comprehensive list of categories. Special values include:

> 'all'   report all the warnings

> 'none'   report none

> 'error'   treats warnings as errors

> 'no-*category*'
>> disable warnings falling into *category*

> Warnings about 'syntax' are enabled by default, and the environment variable `WARNINGS`, a comma separated list of categories, is honored. 'autom4te -W *category*' actually behaves as if you had run:

>> `autom4te --warnings=syntax,$WARNINGS,category`

> For example, if you want to disable defaults and `WARNINGS` of `autom4te`, but enable the warnings about obsolete constructs, you would use '-W none,obsolete'.

> `autom4te` displays a back trace for errors, but not for warnings; if you want them, just pass '-W error'.

'--melt'

'-M'   Do not use frozen files. Any argument *file*.m4f is replaced by *file*.m4. This helps tracing the macros which are executed only when the files are frozen, typically `m4_define`. For instance, running:

>> `autom4te --melt 1.m4 2.m4f 3.m4 4.m4f input.m4`

> is roughly equivalent to running:

>> `m4 1.m4 2.m4 3.m4 4.m4 input.m4`

> while

```
autom4te 1.m4 2.m4f 3.m4 4.m4f input.m4
```

is equivalent to:

```
m4 --reload-state=4.m4f input.m4
```

'--freeze'
'-F'   Produce a frozen state file. `autom4te` freezing is stricter than M4's: it must
                produce no warnings, and no output other than empty lines (a line with white
                space is *not* empty) and comments (starting with '#'). Unlike `m4`'s similarly-
                named option, this option takes no argument:

```
autom4te 1.m4 2.m4 3.m4 --freeze --output=3.m4f
```

                corresponds to

```
m4 1.m4 2.m4 3.m4 --freeze-state=3.m4f
```

'--mode=*octal-mode*'
'-m *octal-mode*'
                Set the mode of the non-traces output to *octal-mode*; by default '0666'.

As another additional feature over `m4`, `autom4te` caches its results. GNU M4 is able to
produce a regular output and traces at the same time. Traces are heavily used in the GNU
Build System: `autoheader` uses them to build 'config.h.in', `autoreconf` to determine
what GNU Build System components are used, `automake` to "parse" 'configure.ac' etc.
To avoid recomputation, traces are cached while performing regular expansion, and conversely. This cache is (actually, the caches are) stored in the directory 'autom4te.cache'.
It can safely be removed at any moment (especially if for some reason `autom4te` considers
it trashed).

'--cache=*directory*'
'-C *directory*'
                Specify the name of the directory where the result should be cached. Passing
                an empty value disables caching. Be sure to pass a relative file name, as for the
                time being, global caches are not supported.

'--no-cache'
                Don't cache the results.

'--force'
'-f'   If a cache is used, consider it obsolete (but update it anyway).

Because traces are so important to the GNU Build System, `autom4te` provides high level
tracing features as compared to M4, and helps exploiting the cache:

'--trace=*macro*[:*format*]'
'-t *macro*[:*format*]'
                Trace the invocations of *macro* according to the *format*. Multiple '--trace'
                arguments can be used to list several macros. Multiple '--trace' arguments
                for a single macro are not cumulative; instead, you should just make *format* as
                long as needed.

The *format* is a regular string, with newlines if desired, and several special escape codes. It defaults to '`$f:$l:$n:$%`'. It can use the following special escapes:

'`$$`'   The character '`$`'.

'`$f`'   The file name from which *macro* is called.

'`$l`'   The line number from which *macro* is called.

'`$d`'   The depth of the *macro* call. This is an M4 technical detail that you probably don't want to know about.

'`$n`'   The name of the *macro*.

'`$num`'   The *num*th argument of the call to *macro*.

'`$@`'
'`$sep@`'
'`${separator}@`'
                All the arguments passed to *macro*, separated by the character *sep* or the string *separator* ('`,`' by default). Each argument is quoted, i.e., enclosed in a pair of square brackets.

'`$*`'
'`$sep*`'
'`${separator}*`'
                As above, but the arguments are not quoted.

'`$%`'
'`$sep%`'
'`${separator}%`'
                As above, but the arguments are not quoted, all new line characters in the arguments are smashed, and the default separator is '`:`'.

                The escape '`$%`' produces single-line trace outputs (unless you put newlines in the '`separator`'), while '`$@`' and '`$*`' do not.

        See Section 3.4 [autoconf Invocation], page 11, for examples of trace uses.

'`--preselect=macro`'
'`-p macro`'
                Cache the traces of *macro*, but do not enable traces. This is especially important to save CPU cycles in the future. For instance, when invoked, `autoconf` preselects all the macros that `autoheader`, `automake`, `autoreconf`, etc., trace, so that running `m4` is not needed to trace them: the cache suffices. This results in a huge speed-up.

        Finally, `autom4te` introduces the concept of *Autom4te libraries*. They consists in a powerful yet extremely simple feature: sets of combined command line arguments:

'`--language=language`'
'`-l language`'
                Use the *language* Autom4te library. Current languages include:

M4sugar   create M4sugar output.

M4sh   create M4sh executable shell scripts.

Autotest   create Autotest executable test suites.

Autoconf-without-aclocal-m4
            create Autoconf executable configure scripts without reading
            'aclocal.m4'.

Autoconf   create Autoconf executable configure scripts. This language inher-
            its all the characteristics of Autoconf-without-aclocal-m4 and
            additionally reads 'aclocal.m4'.

'--prepend-include=dir'
'-B dir'   Prepend directory dir to the search path. This is used to include the language-
            specific files before any third-party macros.

As an example, if Autoconf is installed in its default location, '/usr/local', the command 'autom4te -l m4sugar foo.m4' is strictly equivalent to the command:

```
autom4te --prepend-include /usr/local/share/autoconf \
    m4sugar/m4sugar.m4f --warnings syntax foo.m4
```

Recursive expansion applies here: the command 'autom4te -l m4sh foo.m4' is the same as
'autom4te --language M4sugar m4sugar/m4sh.m4f foo.m4', i.e.:

```
autom4te --prepend-include /usr/local/share/autoconf \
    m4sugar/m4sugar.m4f m4sugar/m4sh.m4f --mode 777 foo.m4
```

The definition of the languages is stored in 'autom4te.cfg'.

8.2.2 Customizing autom4te

One can customize autom4te via '~/.autom4te.cfg' (i.e., as found in the user home
directory), and './.autom4te.cfg' (i.e., as found in the directory from which autom4te
is run). The order is first reading 'autom4te.cfg', then '~/.autom4te.cfg', then
'./.autom4te.cfg', and finally the command line arguments.

In these text files, comments are introduced with #, and empty lines are ignored. Cus-
tomization is performed on a per-language basis, wrapped in between a 'begin-language:
"language"', 'end-language: "language"' pair.

Customizing a language stands for appending options (see Section 8.2.1 [autom4te In-
vocation], page 132) to the current definition of the language. Options, and more generally
arguments, are introduced by 'args: arguments'. You may use the traditional shell syntax
to quote the arguments.

As an example, to disable Autoconf caches ('autom4te.cache') globally, include the
following lines in '~/.autom4te.cfg':

```
## ------------------ ##
## User Preferences.  ##
## ------------------ ##


begin-language: "Autoconf-without-aclocal-m4"
args: --no-cache
end-language: "Autoconf-without-aclocal-m4"
```

8.3 Programming in M4sugar

M4 by itself provides only a small, but sufficient, set of all-purpose macros. M4sugar introduces additional generic macros. Its name was coined by Lars J. Aas: "Readability And Greater Understanding Stands 4 M4sugar".

M4sugar reserves the macro namespace '^_m4_' for internal use, and the macro namespace '^m4_' for M4sugar macros. You should not define your own macros into these namespaces.

8.3.1 Redefined M4 Macros

With a few exceptions, all the M4 native macros are moved in the 'm4_' pseudo-namespace, e.g., M4sugar renames `define` as `m4_define` etc.

The list of macros unchanged from M4, except for their name, is:

- m4_builtin
- m4_changecom
- m4_changequote
- m4_debugfile
- m4_debugmode
- m4_decr
- m4_define
- m4_divnum
- m4_errprint
- m4_esyscmd
- m4_eval
- m4_format
- m4_ifdef
- m4_incr
- m4_index
- m4_indir
- m4_len
- m4_pushdef
- m4_shift
- m4_substr
- m4_syscmd
- m4_sysval
- m4_traceoff
- m4_traceon
- m4_translit

Some M4 macros are redefined, and are slightly incompatible with their native equivalent.

`__file__`   [Macro]

`__line__`   [Macro]

All M4 macros starting with '`__`' retain their original name: for example, no `m4__file__` is defined.

`__oline__`   [Macro]

This is not technically a macro, but a feature of Autom4te. The sequence `__oline__` can be used similarly to the other m4sugar location macros, but rather than expanding to the location of the input file, it is translated to the line number where it appears in the output file after all other M4 expansions.

`dnl`   [Macro]

This macro kept its original name: no `m4_dnl` is defined.

`m4_bpatsubst (`*string*`, `*regexp*`, [`*replacement*`])`   [Macro]

This macro corresponds to `patsubst`. The name `m4_patsubst` is kept for future versions of M4sugar, once GNU M4 2.0 is released and supports extended regular expression syntax.

`m4_bregexp (`*string*`, `*regexp*`, [`*replacement*`])`   [Macro]

This macro corresponds to `regexp`. The name `m4_regexp` is kept for future versions of M4sugar, once GNU M4 2.0 is released and supports extended regular expression syntax.

`m4_copy (`*source*`, `*dest*`)`   [Macro]

`m4_copy_force (`*source*`, `*dest*`)`   [Macro]

`m4_rename (`*source*`, `*dest*`)`   [Macro]

`m4_rename_force (`*source*`, `*dest*`)`   [Macro]

These macros aren't directly builtins, but are closely related to `m4_pushdef` and `m4_defn`. `m4_copy` and `m4_rename` ensure that *dest* is undefined, while `m4_copy_force` and `m4_rename_force` overwrite any existing definition. All four macros then proceed to copy the entire pushdef stack of definitions of *source* over to *dest*. `m4_copy` and `m4_copy_force` preserve the source (including in the special case where *source* is undefined), while `m4_rename` and `m4_rename_force` undefine the original macro name (making it an error to rename an undefined *source*).

Note that attempting to invoke a renamed macro might not work, since the macro may have a dependence on helper macros accessed via composition of '`$0`' but that were not also renamed; likewise, other macros may have a hard-coded dependence on *source* and could break if *source* has been deleted. On the other hand, it is always safe to rename a macro to temporarily move it out of the way, then rename it back later to restore original semantics.

`m4_defn (`*macro*`...)`   [Macro]

This macro fails if *macro* is not defined, even when using older versions of M4 that did not warn. See `m4_undefine`. Unfortunately, in order to support these older versions of M4, there are some situations involving unbalanced quotes where concatenating multiple macros together will work in newer M4 but not in m4sugar; use quadrigraphs to work around this.

m4_divert (*diversion*)   [Macro]

M4sugar relies heavily on diversions, so rather than behaving as a primitive, m4_divert behaves like:

>   m4_divert_pop()m4_divert_push([*diversion*])

See Section 8.3.3 [Diversion support], page 141, for more details about the use of the diversion stack. In particular, this implies that *diversion* should be a named diversion rather than a raw number. But be aware that it is seldom necessary to explicitly change the diversion stack, and that when done incorrectly, it can lead to syntactically invalid scripts.

m4_dumpdef (*name*...)   [Macro]
m4_dumpdefs (*name*...)   [Macro]

m4_dumpdef is like the M4 builtin, except that this version requires at least one argument, output always goes to standard error rather than the current debug file, no sorting is done on multiple arguments, and an error is issued if any *name* is undefined. m4_dumpdefs is a convenience macro that calls m4_dumpdef for all of the m4_pushdef stack of definitions, starting with the current, and silently does nothing if *name* is undefined.

Unfortunately, due to a limitation in M4 1.4.x, any macro defined as a builtin is output as the empty string. This behavior is rectified by using M4 1.6 or newer. However, this behavior difference means that m4_dumpdef should only be used while developing m4sugar macros, and never in the final published form of a macro.

m4_esyscmd_s (*command*)   [Macro]

Like m4_esyscmd, this macro expands to the result of running *command* in a shell. The difference is that any trailing newlines are removed, so that the output behaves more like shell command substitution.

m4_exit (*exit-status*)   [Macro]

This macro corresponds to m4exit.

m4_if (*comment*)   [Macro]
m4_if (*string-1*, *string-2*, *equal*, [*not-equal*])   [Macro]
m4_if (*string-1*, *string-2*, *equal-1*, *string-3*, *string-4*, *equal-2*,   [Macro]
..., [*not-equal*])

This macro corresponds to ifelse. *string-1* and *string-2* are compared literally, so usually one of the two arguments is passed unquoted. See Section 8.3.4 [Conditional constructs], page 144, for more conditional idioms.

m4_include (*file*)   [Macro]
m4_sinclude (*file*)   [Macro]

Like the M4 builtins, but warn against multiple inclusions of *file*.

m4_mkstemp (*template*)   [Macro]
m4_maketemp (*template*)   [Macro]

Posix requires maketemp to replace the trailing 'X' characters in *template* with the process id, without regards to the existence of a file by that name, but this a security hole. When this was pointed out to the Posix folks, they agreed to invent a new macro `mkstemp` that always creates a uniquely named file, but not all versions of GNU M4 support the new macro. In M4sugar, `m4_maketemp` and `m4_mkstemp` are synonyms for each other, and both have the secure semantics regardless of which macro the underlying M4 provides.

m4_popdef (*macro...*)   [Macro]

This macro fails if *macro* is not defined, even when using older versions of M4 that did not warn. See `m4_undefine`.

m4_undefine (*macro...*)   [Macro]

This macro fails if *macro* is not defined, even when using older versions of M4 that did not warn. Use

```
m4_ifdef([macro], [m4_undefine([macro])])
```

if you are not sure whether *macro* is defined.

m4_undivert (*diversion...*)   [Macro]

Unlike the M4 builtin, at least one *diversion* must be specified. Also, since the M4sugar diversion stack prefers named diversions, the use of `m4_undivert` to include files is risky. See Section 8.3.3 [Diversion support], page 141, for more details about the use of the diversion stack. But be aware that it is seldom necessary to explicitly change the diversion stack, and that when done incorrectly, it can lead to syntactically invalid scripts.

m4_wrap (*text*)   [Macro]
m4_wrap_lifo (*text*)   [Macro]

These macros correspond to `m4wrap`. Posix requires arguments of multiple wrap calls to be reprocessed at EOF in the same order as the original calls (first-in, first-out). GNU M4 versions through 1.4.10, however, reprocess them in reverse order (last-in, first-out). Both orders are useful, therefore, you can rely on `m4_wrap` to provide FIFO semantics and `m4_wrap_lifo` for LIFO semantics, regardless of the underlying GNU M4 version.

Unlike the GNU M4 builtin, these macros only recognize one argument, and avoid token pasting between consecutive invocations. On the other hand, nested calls to `m4_wrap` from within wrapped text work just as in the builtin.

8.3.2 Diagnostic messages from M4sugar

When macros statically diagnose abnormal situations, benign or fatal, they should report them using these macros. For issuing dynamic issues, i.e., when `configure` is run, see Section 7.5 [Printing Messages], page 120.

m4_assert (*expression*, [*exit-status* = '1'])   [Macro]

Assert that the arithmetic *expression* evaluates to non-zero. Otherwise, issue a fatal error, and exit `autom4te` with *exit-status*.

m4_errprintn (*message*)   [Macro]

Similar to the builtin `m4_errprint`, except that a newline is guaranteed after *message*.

m4_fatal (*message*)   [Macro]

Report a severe error *message* prefixed with the current location, and have `autom4te` die.

`m4_location`   [Macro]
> Useful as a prefix in a message line. Short for:
>
> > `__file__:__line__`

`m4_warn (category, message)`   [Macro]
> Report *message* as a warning (or as an error if requested by the user) if warnings of
> the *category* are turned on. If the message is emitted, it is prefixed with the current
> location, and followed by a call trace of all macros defined via `AC_DEFUN` used to
> get to the current expansion. You are encouraged to use standard categories, which
> currently include:
>
> 'all'   messages that don't fall into one of the following categories. Use of an
>   empty *category* is equivalent.
>
> 'cross'   related to cross compilation issues.
>
> 'obsolete'
>   use of an obsolete construct.
>
> 'syntax'   dubious syntactic constructs, incorrectly ordered macro calls.

8.3.3 Diversion support

M4sugar makes heavy use of diversions under the hood, because it is often the case that
text that must appear early in the output is not discovered until late in the input. Additionally, some of the topological sorting algorithms used in resolving macro dependencies use
diversions. However, most macros should not need to change diversions directly, but rather
rely on higher-level M4sugar macros to manage diversions transparently. If you change diversions improperly, you risk generating a syntactically invalid script, because an incorrect
diversion will violate assumptions made by many macros about whether prerequisite text
has been previously output. In short, if you manually change the diversion, you should not
expect any macros provided by the Autoconf package to work until you have restored the
diversion stack back to its original state.

   In the rare case that it is necessary to write a macro that explicitly outputs text to a
different diversion, it is important to be aware of an M4 limitation regarding diversions: text
only goes to a diversion if it is not part of argument collection. Therefore, any macro that
changes the current diversion cannot be used as an unquoted argument to another macro,
but must be expanded at the top level. The macro `m4_expand` will diagnose any attempt to
change diversions, since it is generally useful only as an argument to another macro. The
following example shows what happens when diversion manipulation is attempted within
macro arguments:

```
m4_do([normal text]
m4_divert_push([KILL])unwanted[]m4_divert_pop([KILL])
[m4_divert_push([KILL])discarded[]m4_divert_pop([KILL])])dnl
⇒normal text
⇒unwanted
```

Notice that the unquoted text `unwanted` is output, even though it was processed while the
current diversion was KILL, because it was collected as part of the argument to `m4_do`.
However, the text `discarded` disappeared as desired, because the diversion changes were
single-quoted, and were not expanded until the top-level rescan of the output of `m4_do`.

To make diversion management easier, M4sugar uses the concept of named diversions. Rather than using diversion numbers directly, it is nicer to associate a name with each diversion. The diversion number associated with a particular diversion name is an implementation detail, and a syntax warning is issued if a diversion number is used instead of a name. In general, you should not output text to a named diversion until after calling the appropriate initialization routine for your language (`m4_init`, `AS_INIT`, `AT_INIT`, ...), although there are some exceptions documented below.

M4sugar defines two named diversions.

KILL   Text written to this diversion is discarded. This is the default diversion once M4sugar is initialized.

GROW   This diversion is used behind the scenes by topological sorting macros, such as `AC_REQUIRE`.

M4sh adds several more named diversions.

BINSH   This diversion is reserved for the '`#!`' interpreter line.

HEADER-REVISION
            This diversion holds text from `AC_REVISION`.

HEADER-COMMENT
            This diversion holds comments about the purpose of a file.

HEADER-COPYRIGHT
            This diversion is managed by `AC_COPYRIGHT`.

M4SH-SANITIZE
            This diversion contains M4sh sanitization code, used to ensure M4sh is executing in a reasonable shell environment.

M4SH-INIT
            This diversion contains M4sh initialization code, initializing variables that are required by other M4sh macros.

BODY   This diversion contains the body of the shell code, and is the default diversion once M4sh is initialized.

Autotest inherits diversions from M4sh, and changes the default diversion from BODY back to KILL. It also adds several more named diversions, with the following subset designed for developer use.

PREPARE_TESTS
            This diversion contains initialization sequences which are executed after '`atconfig`' and '`atlocal`', and after all command line arguments have been parsed, but prior to running any tests. It can be used to set up state that is required across all tests. This diversion will work even before `AT_INIT`.

Autoconf inherits diversions from M4sh, and adds the following named diversions which developers can utilize.

DEFAULTS   This diversion contains shell variable assignments to set defaults that must be in place before arguments are parsed. This diversion is placed early enough in '`configure`' that it is unsafe to expand any autoconf macros into this diversion.

HELP_ENABLE

> If AC_PRESERVE_HELP_ORDER was used, then text placed in this diversion will be included as part of a quoted here-doc providing all of the '--help' output of 'configure' related to options created by AC_ARG_WITH and AC_ARG_ENABLE.

INIT_PREPARE

> This diversion occurs after all command line options have been parsed, but prior to the main body of the 'configure' script. This diversion is the last chance to insert shell code such as variable assignments or shell function declarations that will used by the expansion of other macros.

For now, the remaining named diversions of Autoconf, Autoheader, and Autotest are not documented. In other words, intentionally outputting text into an undocumented diversion is subject to breakage in a future release of Autoconf.

m4_cleardivert (*diversion*...)   [Macro]

> Permanently discard any text that has been diverted into *diversion*.

m4_divert_once (*diversion*, [*content*])   [Macro]

> Similar to m4_divert_text, except that *content* is only output to *diversion* if this is the first time that m4_divert_once has been called with its particular arguments.

m4_divert_pop ([*diversion*])   [Macro]

> If provided, check that the current diversion is indeed *diversion*. Then change to the diversion located earlier on the stack, giving an error if an attempt is made to pop beyond the initial m4sugar diversion of KILL.

m4_divert_push (*diversion*)   [Macro]

> Remember the former diversion on the diversion stack, and output subsequent text into *diversion*. M4sugar maintains a diversion stack, and issues an error if there is not a matching pop for every push.

m4_divert_text (*diversion*, [*content*])   [Macro]

> Output *content* and a newline into *diversion*, without affecting the current diversion. Shorthand for:
>
> ```
> m4_divert_push([diversion])content
> m4_divert_pop([diversion])dnl
> ```
>
> One use of m4_divert_text is to develop two related macros, where macro 'MY_A' does the work, but adjusts what work is performed based on whether the optional macro 'MY_B' has also been expanded. Of course, it is possible to use AC_BEFORE within MY_A to require that 'MY_B' occurs first, if it occurs at all. But this imposes an ordering restriction on the user; it would be nicer if macros 'MY_A' and 'MY_B' can be invoked in either order. The trick is to let 'MY_B' leave a breadcrumb in an early diversion, which 'MY_A' can then use to determine whether 'MY_B' has been expanded.
>
> ```
> AC_DEFUN([MY_A],
> [# various actions
> if test -n "$b_was_used"; then
>   # extra action
> fi])
> ```

```
AC_DEFUN([MY_B],
[AC_REQUIRE([MY_A])dnl
m4_divert_text([INIT_PREPARE], [b_was_used=true])])
```

m4_init   [Macro]

> Initialize the M4sugar environment, setting up the default named diversion to be KILL.

8.3.4 Conditional constructs

The following macros provide additional conditional constructs as convenience wrappers around m4_if.

m4_bmatch (*string*, *regex-1*, *value-1*, [*regex-2*], [*value-2*], ...,   [Macro]
    [*default*])

> The string *string* is repeatedly compared against a series of *regex* arguments; if a match is found, the expansion is the corresponding *value*, otherwise, the macro moves on to the next *regex*. If no *regex* match, then the result is the optional *default*, or nothing.

m4_bpatsubsts (*string*, *regex-1*, *subst-1*, [*regex-2*], [*subst-2*], ...)   [Macro]
> The string *string* is altered by *regex-1* and *subst-1*, as if by:

> > m4_bpatsubst([[*string*]], [*regex*], [*subst*])

> The result of the substitution is then passed through the next set of *regex* and *subst*, and so forth. An empty *subst* implies deletion of any matched portions in the current string. Note that this macro over-quotes *string*; this behavior is intentional, so that the result of each step of the recursion remains as a quoted string. However, it means that anchors ('^' and '$' in the *regex* will line up with the extra quotations, and not the characters of the original string. The overquoting is removed after the final substitution.

m4_case (*string*, *value-1*, *if-value-1*, [*value-2*], [*if-value-2*], ...,   [Macro]
    [*default*])

> Test *string* against multiple *value* possibilities, resulting in the first *if-value* for a match, or in the optional *default*. This is shorthand for:

> > m4_if([*string*], [*value-1*], [*if-value-1*],
> >   [*string*], [*value-2*], [*if-value-2*], ...,
> >   [*default*])

m4_cond (*test-1*, *value-1*, *if-value-1*, [*test-2*], [*value-2*],   [Macro]
    [*if-value-2*], ..., [*default*])

> This macro was introduced in Autoconf 2.62. Similar to m4_if, except that each *test* is expanded only when it is encountered. This is useful for short-circuiting expensive tests; while m4_if requires all its strings to be expanded up front before doing comparisons, m4_cond only expands a *test* when all earlier tests have failed.

> For an example, these two sequences give the same result, but in the case where '$1' does not contain a backslash, the m4_cond version only expands m4_index once, instead of five times, for faster computation if this is a common case for '$1'. Notice that every third argument is unquoted for m4_if, and quoted for m4_cond:

```
    m4_if(m4_index([$1], [\]), [-1], [$2],
        m4_eval(m4_index([$1], [\\]) >= 0), [1], [$2],
        m4_eval(m4_index([$1], [\$]) >= 0), [1], [$2],
        m4_eval(m4_index([$1], [\`]) >= 0), [1], [$3],
        m4_eval(m4_index([$1], [\"]) >= 0), [1], [$3],
        [$2])
    m4_cond([m4_index([$1], [\])], [-1], [$2],
        [m4_eval(m4_index([$1], [\\]) >= 0)], [1], [$2],
        [m4_eval(m4_index([$1], [\$]) >= 0)], [1], [$2],
        [m4_eval(m4_index([$1], [\`]) >= 0)], [1], [$3],
        [m4_eval(m4_index([$1], [\"]) >= 0)], [1], [$3],
        [$2])
```

m4_default (*expr-1*, *expr-2*)   [Macro]
m4_default_quoted (*expr-1*, *expr-2*)   [Macro]
m4_default_nblank (*expr-1*, [*expr-2*])   [Macro]
m4_default_nblank_quoted (*expr-1*, [*expr-2*])   [Macro]

If *expr-1* contains text, use it. Otherwise, select *expr-2*. m4_default expands the result, while m4_default_quoted does not. Useful for providing a fixed default if the expression that results in *expr-1* would otherwise be empty. The difference between m4_default and m4_default_nblank is whether an argument consisting of just blanks (space, tab, newline) is significant. When using the expanding versions, note that an argument may contain text but still expand to an empty string.

```
    m4_define([active], [ACTIVE])dnl
    m4_define([empty], [])dnl
    m4_define([demo1], [m4_default([$1], [$2])])dnl
    m4_define([demo2], [m4_default_quoted([$1], [$2])])dnl
    m4_define([demo3], [m4_default_nblank([$1], [$2])])dnl
    m4_define([demo4], [m4_default_nblank_quoted([$1], [$2])])dnl
    demo1([active], [default])
    ⇒ACTIVE
    demo1([], [active])
    ⇒ACTIVE
    demo1([empty], [text])
    ⇒
    -demo1([ ], [active])-
    ⇒- -
    demo2([active], [default])
    ⇒active
    demo2([], [active])
    ⇒active
    demo2([empty], [text])
    ⇒empty
    -demo2([ ], [active])-
    ⇒- -
    demo3([active], [default])
    ⇒ACTIVE
```

```
demo3([], [active])
⇒ACTIVE
demo3([empty], [text])
⇒
-demo3([ ], [active])-
⇒-ACTIVE-
demo4([active], [default])
⇒active
demo4([], [active])
⇒active
demo4([empty], [text])
⇒empty
-demo4([ ], [active])-
⇒-active-
```

m4_define_default (*macro*, [*default-definition*])   [Macro]

> If *macro* does not already have a definition, then define it to *default-definition*.

m4_ifblank (*cond*, [*if-blank*], [*if-text*])   [Macro]
m4_ifnblank (*cond*, [*if-text*], [*if-blank*])   [Macro]

> If *cond* is empty or consists only of blanks (space, tab, newline), then expand *if-blank*; otherwise, expand *if-text*. Two variants exist, in order to make it easier to select the correct logical sense when using only two parameters. Note that this is more efficient than the equivalent behavior of:
>
> ```
> m4_ifval(m4_normalize([cond]), if-text, if-blank)
> ```

m4_ifndef (*macro*, *if-not-defined*, [*if-defined*])   [Macro]

> This is shorthand for:
>
> ```
> m4_ifdef([macro], [if-defined], [if-not-defined])
> ```

m4_ifset (*macro*, [*if-true*], [*if-false*])   [Macro]

> If *macro* is undefined, or is defined as the empty string, expand to *if-false*. Otherwise, expands to *if-true*. Similar to:
>
> ```
> m4_ifval(m4_defn([macro]), [if-true], [if-false])
> ```
>
> except that it is not an error if *macro* is undefined.

m4_ifval (*cond*, [*if-true*], [*if-false*])   [Macro]

> Expands to *if-true* if *cond* is not empty, otherwise to *if-false*. This is shorthand for:
>
> ```
> m4_if([cond], [], [if-false], [if-true])
> ```

m4_ifvaln (*cond*, [*if-true*], [*if-false*])   [Macro]

> Similar to m4_ifval, except guarantee that a newline is present after any non-empty expansion. Often followed by dnl.

m4_n (*text*)   [Macro]

> Expand to *text*, and add a newline if *text* is not empty. Often followed by dnl.

8.3.5 Looping constructs

The following macros are useful in implementing recursive algorithms in M4, including
loop operations. An M4 list is formed by quoting a list of quoted elements; generally the
lists are comma-separated, although `m4_foreach_w` is whitespace-separated. For example,
the list '[[a], [b,c]]' contains two elements: '[a]' and '[b,c]'. It is common to see
lists with unquoted elements when those elements are not likely to be macro names, as in
'[fputc_unlocked, fgetc_unlocked]'.

Although not generally recommended, it is possible for quoted lists to have side effects;
all side effects are expanded only once, and prior to visiting any list element. On the other
hand, the fact that unquoted macros are expanded exactly once means that macros without
side effects can be used to generate lists. For example,

```
m4_foreach([i], [[1], [2], [3]m4_errprintn([hi])], [i])
```
⊣error⊢ hi
⇒123
```
m4_define([list], [[1], [2], [3]])
```
⇒
```
m4_foreach([i], [list], [i])
```
⇒123

m4_argn (*n*, [*arg*]...)   [Macro]

    Extracts argument *n* (larger than 0) from the remaining arguments. If there are too
    few arguments, the empty string is used. For any *n* besides 1, this is more efficient
    than the similar 'm4_car(m4_shiftn([n], [], [arg...]))'.

m4_car (*arg*...)   [Macro]

    Expands to the quoted first *arg*. Can be used with `m4_cdr` to recursively iterate
    through a list. Generally, when using quoted lists of quoted elements, `m4_car` should
    be called without any extra quotes.

m4_cdr (*arg*...)   [Macro]

    Expands to a quoted list of all but the first *arg*, or the empty string if there was only
    one argument. Generally, when using quoted lists of quoted elements, `m4_cdr` should
    be called without any extra quotes.

    For example, this is a simple implementation of `m4_map`; note how each iteration checks
    for the end of recursion, then merely applies the first argument to the first element of
    the list, then repeats with the rest of the list. (The actual implementation in M4sugar
    is a bit more involved, to gain some speed and share code with `m4_map_sep`, and also
    to avoid expanding side effects in '$2' twice).

```
m4_define([m4_map], [m4_ifval([$2],
  [m4_apply([$1], m4_car($2))[]$0([$1], m4_cdr($2))])])dnl
m4_map([ m4_eval], [[[1]], [[1+1]], [[10],[16]]])
```
⇒ 1 2 a

m4_for (*var*, *first*, *last*, [*step*], *expression*)   [Macro]

    Loop over the numeric values between *first* and *last* including bounds by increments of
    step. For each iteration, expand *expression* with the numeric value assigned to *var*. If
    step is omitted, it defaults to '1' or '-1' depending on the order of the limits. If given,

step has to match this order. The number of iterations is determined independently from definition of *var*; iteration cannot be short-circuited or lengthened by modifying *var* from within *expression*.

m4_foreach (*var*, *list*, *expression*)   [Macro]

Loop over the comma-separated M4 list *list*, assigning each value to *var*, and expand *expression*. The following example outputs two lines:

```
m4_foreach([myvar], [[foo], [bar, baz]],
           [echo myvar
])dnl
⇒echo foo
⇒echo bar, baz
```

Note that for some forms of *expression*, it may be faster to use `m4_map_args`.

m4_foreach_w (*var*, *list*, *expression*)   [Macro]

Loop over the white-space-separated list *list*, assigning each value to *var*, and expand *expression*. If *var* is only referenced once in *expression*, it is more efficient to use `m4_map_args_w`.

The deprecated macro `AC_FOREACH` is an alias of `m4_foreach_w`.

m4_map (*macro*, *list*)   [Macro]
m4_mapall (*macro*, *list*)   [Macro]
m4_map_sep (*macro*, *separator*, *list*)   [Macro]
m4_mapall_sep (*macro*, *separator*, *list*)   [Macro]

Loop over the comma separated quoted list of argument descriptions in *list*, and invoke *macro* with the arguments. An argument description is in turn a comma-separated quoted list of quoted elements, suitable for `m4_apply`. The macros `m4_map` and `m4_map_sep` ignore empty argument descriptions, while `m4_mapall` and `m4_mapall_sep` invoke *macro* with no arguments. The macros `m4_map_sep` and `m4_mapall_sep` additionally expand *separator* between invocations of *macro*.

Note that *separator* is expanded, unlike in `m4_join`. When separating output with commas, this means that the map result can be used as a series of arguments, by using a single-quoted comma as *separator*, or as a single string, by using a double-quoted comma.

```
m4_map([m4_count], [])
⇒
m4_map([ m4_count], [[],
                     [[1]],
                     [[1], [2]]])
⇒ 1 2
m4_mapall([ m4_count], [[],
                        [[1]],
                        [[1], [2]]])
⇒ 0 1 2
m4_map_sep([m4_eval], [,], [[[1+2]],
                            [[10], [16]]])
⇒3,a
```

```
        m4_map_sep([m4_echo], [,], [[[a]], [[b]]])
        ⇒a,b
        m4_count(m4_map_sep([m4_echo], [,], [[[a]], [[b]]]))
        ⇒2
        m4_map_sep([m4_echo], [[,]], [[[a]], [[b]]])
        ⇒a,b
        m4_count(m4_map_sep([m4_echo], [[,]], [[[a]], [[b]]]))
        ⇒1
```

m4_map_args (*macro*, *arg*...)   [Macro]

Repeatedly invoke *macro* with each successive *arg* as its only argument. In the following example, three solutions are presented with the same expansion; the solution using m4_map_args is the most efficient.

```
        m4_define([active], [ACTIVE])dnl
        m4_foreach([var], [[plain], [active]], [ m4_echo(m4_defn([var]))])
        ⇒ plain active
        m4_map([ m4_echo], [[[plain]], [[active]]])
        ⇒ plain active
        m4_map_args([ m4_echo], [plain], [active])
        ⇒ plain active
```

In cases where it is useful to operate on additional parameters besides the list elements, the macro m4_curry can be used in *macro* to supply the argument currying necessary to generate the desired argument list. In the following example, list_add_n is more efficient than list_add_x. On the other hand, using m4_map_args_sep can be even more efficient.

```
        m4_define([list], [[1], [2], [3]])dnl
        m4_define([add], [m4_eval((([$1]) + ([$2])))])dnl
        dnl list_add_n(N, ARG...)
        dnl Output a list consisting of each ARG added to N
        m4_define([list_add_n],
        [m4_shift(m4_map_args([,m4_curry([add], [$1])], m4_shift($@)))])dnl
        list_add_n([1], list)
        ⇒2,3,4
        list_add_n([2], list)
        ⇒3,4,5
        m4_define([list_add_x],
        [m4_shift(m4_foreach([var], m4_dquote(m4_shift($@)),
          [,add([$1],m4_defn([var]))]))])dnl
        list_add_x([1], list)
        ⇒2,3,4
```

m4_map_args_pair (*macro*, [*macro-end* = 'macro'], *arg*...)   [Macro]

For every pair of arguments *arg*, invoke *macro* with two arguments. If there is an odd number of arguments, invoke *macro-end*, which defaults to *macro*, with the remaining argument.

```
        m4_map_args_pair([, m4_reverse], [], [1], [2], [3])
        ⇒, 2, 1, 3
```

```
m4_map_args_pair([, m4_reverse], [, m4_dquote], [1], [2], [3])
⇒, 2, 1, [3]
m4_map_args_pair([, m4_reverse], [, m4_dquote], [1], [2], [3], [4])
⇒, 2, 1, 4, 3
```

m4_map_args_sep (*[pre]*, *[post]*, *[sep]*, *arg*...)   [Macro]

Expand the sequence *pre*[*arg*]*post* for each argument, additionally expanding *sep* between arguments. One common use of this macro is constructing a macro call, where the opening and closing parentheses are split between *pre* and *post*; in particular, `m4_map_args([macro], [arg])` is equivalent to `m4_map_args_sep([macro(), ()], [], [arg])`. This macro provides the most efficient means for iterating over an arbitrary list of arguments, particularly when repeatedly constructing a macro call with more arguments than *arg*.

m4_map_args_w (*string*, *[pre]*, *[post]*, *[sep]*)   [Macro]

Expand the sequence *pre*[*word*]*post* for each word in the whitespace-separated *string*, additionally expanding *sep* between words. This macro provides the most efficient means for iterating over a whitespace-separated string. In particular, `m4_map_args_w([string], [action(), ()])` is more efficient than `m4_foreach_w([var], [string], [action(m4_defn([var]))])`.

m4_shiftn (*count*, ...)   [Macro]
m4_shift2 (...)   [Macro]
m4_shift3 (...)   [Macro]

`m4_shiftn` performs *count* iterations of `m4_shift`, along with validation that enough arguments were passed in to match the shift count, and that the count is positive. `m4_shift2` and `m4_shift3` are specializations of `m4_shiftn`, introduced in Autoconf 2.62, and are more efficient for two and three shifts, respectively.

m4_stack_foreach (*macro*, *action*)   [Macro]
m4_stack_foreach_lifo (*macro*, *action*)   [Macro]

For each of the `m4_pushdef` definitions of *macro*, expand *action* with the single argument of a definition of *macro*. `m4_stack_foreach` starts with the oldest definition, while `m4_stack_foreach_lifo` starts with the current definition. *action* should not push or pop definitions of *macro*, nor is there any guarantee that the current definition of *macro* matches the argument that was passed to *action*. The macro `m4_curry` can be used if *action* needs more than one argument, although in that case it is more efficient to use *m4_stack_foreach_sep*.

Due to technical limitations, there are a few low-level m4sugar functions, such as `m4_pushdef`, that cannot be used as the *macro* argument.

```
m4_pushdef([a], [1])m4_pushdef([a], [2])dnl
m4_stack_foreach([a], [ m4_incr])
⇒ 2 3
m4_stack_foreach_lifo([a], [ m4_curry([m4_substr], [abcd])])
⇒ cd bcd
```

m4_stack_foreach_sep (*macro*, [*pre*], [*post*], [*sep*])   [Macro]
m4_stack_foreach_sep_lifo (*macro*, [*pre*], [*post*], [*sep*])   [Macro]
>   Expand the sequence *pre*[definition]*post* for each m4_pushdef definition of
>   *macro*, additionally expanding *sep* between definitions. m4_stack_foreach_sep
>   visits the oldest definition first, while m4_stack_foreach_sep_lifo visits the
>   current definition first. This macro provides the most efficient means for iterating
>   over a pushdef stack. In particular, m4_stack_foreach([macro], [action]) is
>   short for m4_stack_foreach_sep([macro], [action(], [)]).

8.3.6 Evaluation Macros

The following macros give some control over the order of the evaluation by adding or
removing levels of quotes.

m4_apply (*macro*, *list*)   [Macro]
>   Apply the elements of the quoted, comma-separated *list* as the arguments to *macro*.
>   If *list* is empty, invoke *macro* without arguments. Note the difference between m4_
>   indir, which expects its first argument to be a macro name but can use names that
>   are otherwise invalid, and m4_apply, where *macro* can contain other text, but must
>   end in a valid macro name.
>
> ```
>        m4_apply([m4_count], [])
>        ⇒0
>        m4_apply([m4_count], [[]])
>        ⇒1
>        m4_apply([m4_count], [[1], [2]])
>        ⇒2
>        m4_apply([m4_join], [[|], [1], [2]])
>        ⇒1|2
> ```

m4_count (*arg*, ...)   [Macro]
>   This macro returns the decimal count of the number of arguments it was passed.

m4_curry (*macro*, *arg*...)   [Macro]
>   This macro performs argument currying. The expansion of this macro is another
>   macro name that expects exactly one argument; that argument is then appended to
>   the *arg* list, and then *macro* is expanded with the resulting argument list.
>
> ```
>        m4_curry([m4_curry], [m4_reverse], [1])([2])([3])
>        ⇒3, 2, 1
> ```

Unfortunately, due to a limitation in M4 1.4.x, it is not possible to pass the definition
of a builtin macro as the argument to the output of m4_curry; the empty string is
used instead of the builtin token. This behavior is rectified by using M4 1.6 or newer.

m4_do (*arg*, ...)   [Macro]
>   This macro loops over its arguments and expands each *arg* in sequence. Its main
>   use is for readability; it allows the use of indentation and fewer dnl to result in
>   the same expansion. This macro guarantees that no expansion will be concatenated
>   with subsequent text; to achieve full concatenation, use m4_unquote(m4_join([],
>   *arg*...)).

```
m4_define([ab],[1])m4_define([bc],[2])m4_define([abc],[3])dnl
m4_do([a],[b])c
⇒abc
m4_unquote(m4_join([],[a],[b]))c
⇒3
m4_define([a],[A])m4_define([b],[B])m4_define([c],[C])dnl
m4_define([AB],[4])m4_define([BC],[5])m4_define([ABC],[6])dnl
m4_do([a],[b])c
⇒ABC
m4_unquote(m4_join([],[a],[b]))c
⇒3
```

m4_dquote (*arg*, ...)   [Macro]
> Return the arguments as a quoted list of quoted arguments. Conveniently, if there is just one *arg*, this effectively adds a level of quoting.

m4_dquote_elt (*arg*, ...)   [Macro]
> Return the arguments as a series of double-quoted arguments. Whereas `m4_dquote` returns a single argument, `m4_dquote_elt` returns as many arguments as it was passed.

m4_echo (*arg*, ...)   [Macro]
> Return the arguments, with the same level of quoting. Other than discarding whitespace after unquoted commas, this macro is a no-op.

m4_expand (*arg*)   [Macro]
> Return the expansion of *arg* as a quoted string. Whereas `m4_quote` is designed to collect expanded text into a single argument, `m4_expand` is designed to perform one level of expansion on quoted text. One distinction is in the treatment of whitespace following a comma in the original *arg*. Any time multiple arguments are collected into one with `m4_quote`, the M4 argument collection rules discard the whitespace. However, with `m4_expand`, whitespace is preserved, even after the expansion of macros contained in *arg*. Additionally, `m4_expand` is able to expand text that would involve an unterminated comment, whereas expanding that same text as the argument to `m4_quote` runs into difficulty in finding the end of the argument. Since manipulating diversions during argument collection is inherently unsafe, `m4_expand` issues an error if *arg* attempts to change the current diversion (see Section 8.3.3 [Diversion support], page 141).

```
m4_define([active], [ACT, IVE])dnl
m4_define([active2], [[ACT, IVE]])dnl
m4_quote(active, active)
⇒ACT,IVE,ACT,IVE
m4_expand([active, active])
⇒ACT, IVE, ACT, IVE
m4_quote(active2, active2)
⇒ACT, IVE,ACT, IVE
m4_expand([active2, active2])
⇒ACT, IVE, ACT, IVE
m4_expand([# m4_echo])
```

```
⇒# m4_echo
m4_quote(# m4_echo)
)
⇒# m4_echo)
⇒
```

Note that m4_expand cannot handle an *arg* that expands to literal unbalanced quotes, but that quadrigraphs can be used when unbalanced output is necessary. Likewise, unbalanced parentheses should be supplied with double quoting or a quadrigraph.

```
m4_define([pattern], [[!@<:@]])dnl
m4_define([bar], [BAR])dnl
m4_expand([case $foo in
  m4_defn([pattern])@:}@ bar ;;
  *[)] blah ;;
esac])
⇒case $foo in
⇒  [![]) BAR ;;
⇒  *) blah ;;
⇒esac
```

m4_ignore (...)   [Macro]
This macro was introduced in Autoconf 2.62. Expands to nothing, ignoring all of its arguments. By itself, this isn't very useful. However, it can be used to conditionally ignore an arbitrary number of arguments, by deciding which macro name to apply to a list of arguments.

```
dnl foo outputs a message only if [debug] is defined.
m4_define([foo],
[m4_ifdef([debug],[AC_MSG_NOTICE],[m4_ignore])([debug message])])
```

Note that for earlier versions of Autoconf, the macro __gnu__ can serve the same purpose, although it is less readable.

m4_make_list (arg, ...)   [Macro]
This macro exists to aid debugging of M4sugar algorithms. Its net effect is similar to m4_dquote—it produces a quoted list of quoted arguments, for each *arg*. The difference is that this version uses a comma-newline separator instead of just comma, to improve readability of the list; with the result that it is less efficient than m4_dquote.

```
m4_define([zero],[0])m4_define([one],[1])m4_define([two],[2])dnl
m4_dquote(zero, [one], [[two]])
⇒[0],[one],[[two]]
m4_make_list(zero, [one], [[two]])
⇒[0],
⇒[one],
⇒[[two]]
m4_foreach([number], m4_dquote(zero, [one], [[two]]), [ number])
⇒ 0 1 two
m4_foreach([number], m4_make_list(zero, [one], [[two]]), [ number])
⇒ 0 1 two
```

m4_quote (*arg*, ...)   [Macro]

> Return the arguments as a single entity, i.e., wrap them into a pair of quotes. This effectively collapses multiple arguments into one, although it loses whitespace after unquoted commas in the process.

m4_reverse (*arg*, ...)   [Macro]

> Outputs each argument with the same level of quoting, but in reverse order, and with space following each comma for readability.

> ```
> m4_define([active], [ACT,IVE])
> ⇒
> m4_reverse(active, [active])
> ⇒active, IVE, ACT
> ```

m4_unquote (*arg*, ...)   [Macro]

> This macro was introduced in Autoconf 2.62. Expand each argument, separated by commas. For a single *arg*, this effectively removes a layer of quoting, and m4_unquote([*arg*]) is more efficient than the equivalent m4_do([*arg*]). For multiple arguments, this results in an unquoted list of expansions. This is commonly used with m4_split, in order to convert a single quoted list into a series of quoted elements.

The following example aims at emphasizing the difference between several scenarios: not using these macros, using m4_defn, using m4_quote, using m4_dquote, and using m4_expand.

```
$ cat example.m4
dnl Overquote, so that quotes are visible.
m4_define([show], [$[]1 = [$1], $[]@ = [$@]])
m4_define([a], [A])
m4_define([mkargs], [1, 2[,] 3])
m4_define([arg1], [[$1]])
m4_divert([0])dnl
show(a, b)
show([a, b])
show(m4_quote(a, b))
show(m4_dquote(a, b))
show(m4_expand([a, b]))

arg1(mkargs)
arg1([mkargs])
arg1(m4_defn([mkargs]))
arg1(m4_quote(mkargs))
arg1(m4_dquote(mkargs))
arg1(m4_expand([mkargs]))
$ autom4te -l m4sugar example.m4
$1 = A, $@ = [A],[b]
$1 = a, b, $@ = [a, b]
$1 = A,b, $@ = [A,b]
$1 = [A],[b], $@ = [[A],[b]]
```

```
$1 = A, b, $@ = [A, b]

1
mkargs
1, 2[,] 3
1,2, 3
[1],[2, 3]
1, 2, 3
```

8.3.7 String manipulation in M4

The following macros may be used to manipulate strings in M4. Many of the macros in this section intentionally result in quoted strings as output, rather than subjecting the arguments to further expansions. As a result, if you are manipulating text that contains active M4 characters, the arguments are passed with single quoting rather than double.

m4_append (*macro-name*, *string*, [*separator*])   [Macro]
m4_append_uniq (*macro-name*, *string*, [*separator*] [*if-uniq*],   [Macro]
    [*if-duplicate*])

> Redefine *macro-name* to its former contents with *separator* and *string* added at the end. If *macro-name* was undefined before (but not if it was defined but empty), then no *separator* is added. As of Autoconf 2.62, neither *string* nor *separator* are expanded during this macro; instead, they are expanded when *macro-name* is invoked.
>
> m4_append can be used to grow strings, and m4_append_uniq to grow strings without duplicating substrings. Additionally, m4_append_uniq takes two optional parameters as of Autoconf 2.62; *if-uniq* is expanded if *string* was appended, and *if-duplicate* is expanded if *string* was already present. Also, m4_append_uniq warns if *separator* is not empty, but occurs within *string*, since that can lead to duplicates.
>
> Note that m4_append can scale linearly in the length of the final string, depending on the quality of the underlying M4 implementation, while m4_append_uniq has an inherent quadratic scaling factor. If an algorithm can tolerate duplicates in the final string, use the former for speed. If duplicates must be avoided, consider using m4_set_add instead (see Section 8.3.9 [Set manipulation Macros], page 160).
>
> ```
> m4_define([active], [ACTIVE])dnl
> m4_append([sentence], [This is an])dnl
> m4_append([sentence], [ active ])dnl
> m4_append([sentence], [symbol.])dnl
> sentence
> ⇒This is an ACTIVE symbol.
> m4_undefine([active])dnl
> ⇒This is an active symbol.
> m4_append_uniq([list], [one], [, ], [new], [existing])
> ⇒new
> m4_append_uniq([list], [one], [, ], [new], [existing])
> ⇒existing
> m4_append_uniq([list], [two], [, ], [new], [existing])
> ⇒new
> ```

```
m4_append_uniq([list], [three], [, ], [new], [existing])
⇒new
m4_append_uniq([list], [two], [, ], [new], [existing])
⇒existing
list
⇒one, two, three
m4_dquote(list)
⇒[one],[two],[three]
m4_append([list2], [one], [[, ]])dnl
m4_append_uniq([list2], [two], [[, ]])dnl
m4_append([list2], [three], [[, ]])dnl
list2
⇒one, two, three
m4_dquote(list2)
⇒[one, two, three]
```

m4_append_uniq_w (*macro-name*, *strings*)   [Macro]

> This macro was introduced in Autoconf 2.62. It is similar to `m4_append_uniq`, but treats *strings* as a whitespace separated list of words to append, and only appends unique words. *macro-name* is updated with a single space between new words.
>
> ```
> m4_append_uniq_w([numbers], [1 1 2])dnl
> m4_append_uniq_w([numbers], [ 2 3 ])dnl
> numbers
> ⇒1 2 3
> ```

m4_chomp (*string*)   [Macro]
m4_chomp_all (*string*)   [Macro]

> Output *string* in quotes, but without a trailing newline. The macro `m4_chomp` is slightly faster, and removes at most one newline; the macro `m4_chomp_all` removes all consecutive trailing newlines. Unlike `m4_flatten`, embedded newlines are left intact, and backslash does not influence the result.

m4_combine ([*separator*], *prefix-list*, [*infix*], *suffix-1*,   [Macro]
> [*suffix-2*], ...)

> This macro produces a quoted string containing the pairwise combination of every element of the quoted, comma-separated *prefix-list*, and every element from the *suffix* arguments. Each pairwise combination is joined with *infix* in the middle, and successive pairs are joined by *separator*. No expansion occurs on any of the arguments. No output occurs if either the *prefix* or *suffix* list is empty, but the lists can contain empty elements.
>
> ```
> m4_define([a], [oops])dnl
> m4_combine([, ], [[a], [b], [c]], [-], [1], [2], [3])
> ⇒a-1, a-2, a-3, b-1, b-2, b-3, c-1, c-2, c-3
> m4_combine([, ], [[a], [b]], [-])
> ⇒
> m4_combine([, ], [[a], [b]], [-], [])
> ⇒a-, b-
> ```
```
```

```
m4_combine([, ], [], [-], [1], [2])
⇒
m4_combine([, ], [[]], [-], [1], [2])
⇒-1, -2
```

m4_escape (*string*) [Macro]

Convert all instances of '[', ']', '#', and '$' within *string* into their respective quadrigraphs. The result is still a quoted string.

m4_flatten (*string*) [Macro]

Flatten *string* into a single line. Delete all backslash-newline pairs, and replace all remaining newlines with a space. The result is still a quoted string.

m4_join ([*separator*], *args*...) [Macro]
m4_joinall ([*separator*], *args*...) [Macro]

Concatenate each *arg*, separated by *separator*. joinall uses every argument, while join omits empty arguments so that there are no back-to-back separators in the output. The result is a quoted string.

```
m4_define([active], [ACTIVE])dnl
m4_join([|], [one], [], [active], [two])
⇒one|active|two
m4_joinall([|], [one], [], [active], [two])
⇒one||active|two
```

Note that if all you intend to do is join *args* with commas between them, to form a quoted list suitable for m4_foreach, it is more efficient to use m4_dquote.

m4_newline ([*text*]) [Macro]

This macro was introduced in Autoconf 2.62, and expands to a newline, followed by any *text*. It is primarily useful for maintaining macro formatting, and ensuring that M4 does not discard leading whitespace during argument collection.

m4_normalize (*string*) [Macro]

Remove leading and trailing spaces and tabs, sequences of backslash-then-newline, and replace multiple spaces, tabs, and newlines with a single space. This is a combination of m4_flatten and m4_strip. To determine if *string* consists only of bytes that would be removed by m4_normalize, you can use m4_ifblank.

m4_re_escape (*string*) [Macro]

Backslash-escape all characters in *string* that are active in regexps.

m4_split (*string*, [*regexp* = '[\t]+']) [Macro]

Split *string* into an M4 list of elements quoted by '[' and ']', while keeping white space at the beginning and at the end. If *regexp* is given, use it instead of '[\t]+' for splitting. If *string* is empty, the result is an empty list.

m4_strip (*string*) [Macro]

Strip whitespace from *string*. Sequences of spaces and tabs are reduced to a single space, then leading and trailing spaces are removed. The result is still a quoted string. Note that this does not interfere with newlines; if you want newlines stripped as well, consider m4_flatten, or do it all at once with m4_normalize. To quickly test if *string* has only whitespace, use m4_ifblank.

m4_text_box (*message*, [*frame* = '-'])   [Macro]
> Add a text box around *message*, using *frame* as the border character above and
> below the message. The *frame* argument must be a single byte, and does not support
> quadrigraphs. The frame correctly accounts for the subsequent expansion of *message*.
> For example:
>
> ```
> m4_define([macro], [abc])dnl
> m4_text_box([macro])
> ⇒## --- ##
> ⇒## abc ##
> ⇒## --- ##
> ```
>
> The *message* must contain balanced quotes and parentheses, although quadrigraphs
> can be used to work around this.

m4_text_wrap (*string*, [*prefix*], [*prefix1* = '*prefix*'], [*width* = '79'])   [Macro]
> Break *string* into a series of whitespace-separated words, then output those words
> separated by spaces, and wrapping lines any time the output would exceed *width*
> columns. If given, *prefix1* begins the first line, and *prefix* begins all wrapped lines.
> If *prefix1* is longer than *prefix*, then the first line consists of just *prefix1*. If *prefix* is
> longer than *prefix1*, padding is inserted so that the first word of *string* begins at the
> same indentation as all wrapped lines. Note that using literal tab characters in any
> of the arguments will interfere with the calculation of width. No expansions occur on
> *prefix*, *prefix1*, or the words of *string*, although quadrigraphs are recognized.
>
> For some examples:
>
> ```
> m4_text_wrap([Short string */], [   ], [/* ], [20])
> ⇒/* Short string */
> m4_text_wrap([Much longer string */], [   ], [/* ], [20])
> ⇒/* Much longer
> ⇒   string */
> m4_text_wrap([Short doc.], [              ], [  --short ], [30])
> ⇒  --short Short doc.
> m4_text_wrap([Short doc.], [              ], [  --too-wide ], [30])
> ⇒  --too-wide
> ⇒              Short doc.
> m4_text_wrap([Super long documentation.], [      ],
>              [  --too-wide ], 30)
> ⇒  --too-wide
> ⇒      Super long
> ⇒      documentation.
> ```

m4_tolower (*string*)   [Macro]
m4_toupper (*string*)   [Macro]
> Return *string* with letters converted to upper or lower case, respectively.

8.3.8 Arithmetic computation in M4

The following macros facilitate integer arithmetic operations. Where a parameter is documented as taking an arithmetic expression, you can use anything that can be parsed by `m4_eval`.

m4_cmp (*expr-1*, *expr-2*)   [Macro]

> Compare the arithmetic expressions *expr-1* and *expr-2*, and expand to '-1' if *expr-1* is smaller, '0' if they are equal, and '1' if *expr-1* is larger.

m4_list_cmp (*list-1*, *list-2*)   [Macro]

> Compare the two M4 lists consisting of comma-separated arithmetic expressions, left to right. Expand to '-1' for the first element pairing where the value from *list-1* is smaller, '1' where the value from *list-2* is smaller, or '0' if both lists have the same values. If one list is shorter than the other, the remaining elements of the longer list are compared against zero.

```
m4_list_cmp([1, 0],       [1])
⇒0
m4_list_cmp([1, [1 * 0]], [1, 0])
⇒0
m4_list_cmp([1, 2],       [1, 0])
⇒1
m4_list_cmp([1, [1+1], 3],[1, 2])
⇒1
m4_list_cmp([1, 2, -3],   [1, 2])
⇒-1
m4_list_cmp([1, 0],       [1, 2])
⇒-1
m4_list_cmp([1],          [1, 2])
⇒-1
```

m4_max (*arg*, ...)   [Macro]

> This macro was introduced in Autoconf 2.62. Expand to the decimal value of the maximum arithmetic expression among all the arguments.

m4_min (*arg*, ...)   [Macro]

> This macro was introduced in Autoconf 2.62. Expand to the decimal value of the minimum arithmetic expression among all the arguments.

m4_sign (*expr*)   [Macro]

> Expand to '-1' if the arithmetic expression *expr* is negative, '1' if it is positive, and '0' if it is zero.

m4_version_compare (*version-1*, *version-2*)   [Macro]

> This macro was introduced in Autoconf 2.53, but had a number of usability limitations that were not lifted until Autoconf 2.62. Compare the version strings *version-1* and *version-2*, and expand to '-1' if *version-1* is smaller, '0' if they are the same, or '1' *version-2* is smaller. Version strings must be a list of elements separated by '.', ',' or '-', where each element is a number along with optional case-insensitive letters designating beta releases. The comparison stops at the leftmost element that contains a difference, although a 0 element compares equal to a missing element.
>
> It is permissible to include commit identifiers in *version*, such as an abbreviated SHA1 of the commit, provided there is still a monotonically increasing prefix to allow for accurate version-based comparisons. For example, this paragraph was written when

the development snapshot of autoconf claimed to be at version '2.61a-248-dc51', or 248 commits after the 2.61a release, with an abbreviated commit identification of 'dc51'.

```
m4_version_compare([1.1], [2.0])
⇒-1
m4_version_compare([2.0b], [2.0a])
⇒1
m4_version_compare([1.1.1], [1.1.1a])
⇒-1
m4_version_compare([1.2], [1.1.1a])
⇒1
m4_version_compare([1.0], [1])
⇒0
m4_version_compare([1.1pre], [1.1PRE])
⇒0
m4_version_compare([1.1a], [1,10])
⇒-1
m4_version_compare([2.61a], [2.61a-248-dc51])
⇒-1
m4_version_compare([2.61b], [2.61a-248-dc51])
⇒1
```

m4_version_prereq (*version*, [*if-new-enough*], [*if-old* =   [Macro]
    'm4_fatal'])

Compares *version* against the version of Autoconf currently running. If the running version is at *version* or newer, expand *if-new-enough*, but if *version* is larger than the version currently executing, expand *if-old*, which defaults to printing an error message and exiting m4sugar with status 63. When given only one argument, this behaves like **AC_PREREQ** (see Section 4.2 [Versioning], page 18). Remember that the autoconf philosophy favors feature checks over version checks.

8.3.9 Set manipulation in M4

Sometimes, it is necessary to track a set of data, where the order does not matter and where there are no duplicates in the set. The following macros facilitate set manipulations. Each set is an opaque object, which can only be accessed via these basic operations. The underlying implementation guarantees linear scaling for set creation, which is more efficient than using the quadratic **m4_append_uniq**. Both set names and values can be arbitrary strings, except for unbalanced quotes. This implementation ties up memory for removed elements until the next operation that must traverse all the elements of a set; and although that may slow down some operations until the memory for removed elements is pruned, it still guarantees linear performance.

m4_set_add (*set*, *value*, [*if-uniq*], [*if-dup*])   [Macro]
Adds the string *value* as a member of set *set*. Expand *if-uniq* if the element was added, or *if-dup* if it was previously in the set. Operates in amortized constant time, so that set creation scales linearly.

m4_set_add_all (*set, value*...)   [Macro]
> Adds each *value* to the set *set*. This is slightly more efficient than repeatedly invoking
> `m4_set_add`.

m4_set_contains (*set, value*, [*if-present*], [*if-absent*])   [Macro]
> Expands *if-present* if the string *value* is a member of *set*, otherwise *if-absent*.
>
> ```
>       m4_set_contains([a], [1], [yes], [no])
>       ⇒no
>       m4_set_add([a], [1], [added], [dup])
>       ⇒added
>       m4_set_add([a], [1], [added], [dup])
>       ⇒dup
>       m4_set_contains([a], [1], [yes], [no])
>       ⇒yes
>       m4_set_remove([a], [1], [removed], [missing])
>       ⇒removed
>       m4_set_contains([a], [1], [yes], [no])
>       ⇒no
>       m4_set_remove([a], [1], [removed], [missing])
>       ⇒missing
> ```

m4_set_contents (*set*, [*sep*])   [Macro]
m4_set_dump (*set*, [*sep*])   [Macro]
> Expands to a single string consisting of all the members of the set *set*, each separated
> by *sep*, which is not expanded. `m4_set_contents` leaves the elements in *set* but re-
> claims any memory occupied by removed elements, while `m4_set_dump` is a faster one-
> shot action that also deletes the set. No provision is made for disambiguating members
> that contain a non-empty *sep* as a substring; use `m4_set_empty` to distinguish between
> an empty set and the set containing only the empty string. The order of the output
> is unspecified; in the current implementation, part of the speed of `m4_set_dump` re-
> sults from using a different output order than `m4_set_contents`. These macros scale
> linearly in the size of the set before memory pruning, and `m4_set_contents([set]`,
> `[sep])` is faster than `m4_joinall([sep]m4_set_listc([set]))`.
>
> ```
>       m4_set_add_all([a], [1], [2], [3])
>       ⇒
>       m4_set_contents([a], [-])
>       ⇒1-2-3
>       m4_joinall([-]m4_set_listc([a]))
>       ⇒1-2-3
>       m4_set_dump([a], [-])
>       ⇒3-2-1
>       m4_set_contents([a])
>       ⇒
>       m4_set_add([a], [])
>       ⇒
>       m4_set_contents([a], [-])
>       ⇒
> ```

m4_set_delete (*set*)   [Macro]
>   Delete all elements and memory associated with *set*. This is linear in the set size, and
>   faster than removing one element at a time.

m4_set_difference (*seta*, *setb*)   [Macro]
m4_set_intersection (*seta*, *setb*)   [Macro]
m4_set_union (*seta*, *setb*)   [Macro]
>   Compute the relation between *seta* and *setb*, and output the result as a list of quoted
>   arguments without duplicates and with a leading comma. Set difference selects the
>   elements in *seta* but not *setb*, intersection selects only elements in both sets, and
>   union selects elements in either set. These actions are linear in the sum of the set
>   sizes. The leading comma is necessary to distinguish between no elements and the
>   empty string as the only element.
>
> ```
>       m4_set_add_all([a], [1], [2], [3])
>       ⇒
>       m4_set_add_all([b], [3], [], [4])
>       ⇒
>       m4_set_difference([a], [b])
>       ⇒,1,2
>       m4_set_difference([b], [a])
>       ⇒,,4
>       m4_set_intersection([a], [b])
>       ⇒,3
>       m4_set_union([a], [b])
>       ⇒,1,2,3,,4
> ```

m4_set_empty (*set*, [*if-empty*], [*if-elements*])   [Macro]
>   Expand *if-empty* if the set *set* has no elements, otherwise expand *if-elements*. This
>   macro operates in constant time. Using this macro can help disambiguate output
>   from `m4_set_contents` or `m4_set_list`.

m4_set_foreach (*set*, *variable*, *action*)   [Macro]
>   For each element in the set *set*, expand *action* with the macro *variable* defined as
>   the set element. Behavior is unspecified if *action* recursively lists the contents of
>   *set* (although listing other sets is acceptable), or if it modifies the set in any way
>   other than removing the element currently contained in *variable*. This macro is faster
>   than the corresponding `m4_foreach([variable], m4_indir([m4_dquote]m4_set_`
>   `listc([set])), [action])`, although `m4_set_map` might be faster still.
>
> ```
>       m4_set_add_all([a]m4_for([i], [1], [5], [], [,i]))
>       ⇒
>       m4_set_contents([a])
>       ⇒12345
>       m4_set_foreach([a], [i],
>         [m4_if(m4_eval(i&1), [0], [m4_set_remove([a], i, [i])])])
>       ⇒24
>       m4_set_contents([a])
>       ⇒135
> ```

m4_set_list (*set*) [Macro]

m4_set_listc (*set*) [Macro]

Produce a list of arguments, where each argument is a quoted element from the set *set*. The variant `m4_set_listc` is unambiguous, by adding a leading comma if there are any set elements, whereas the variant `m4_set_list` cannot distinguish between an empty set and a set containing only the empty string. These can be directly used in macros that take multiple arguments, such as `m4_join` or `m4_set_add_all`, or wrapped by `m4_dquote` for macros that take a quoted list, such as `m4_map` or `m4_foreach`. Any memory occupied by removed elements is reclaimed during these macros.

```
m4_set_add_all([a], [1], [2], [3])
⇒
m4_set_list([a])
⇒1,2,3
m4_set_list([b])
⇒
m4_set_listc([b])
⇒
m4_count(m4_set_list([b]))
⇒1
m4_set_empty([b], [0], [m4_count(m4_set_list([b]))])
⇒0
m4_set_add([b], [])
⇒
m4_set_list([b])
⇒
m4_set_listc([b])
⇒,
m4_count(m4_set_list([b]))
⇒1
m4_set_empty([b], [0], [m4_count(m4_set_list([b]))])
⇒1
```

m4_set_map (*set*, *action*) [Macro]

For each element in the set *set*, expand *action* with a single argument of the set element. Behavior is unspecified if *action* recursively lists the contents of *set* (although listing other sets is acceptable), or if it modifies the set in any way other than removing the element passed as an argument. This macro is faster than either corresponding counterpart of `m4_map_args([action]m4_set_listc([set]))` or `m4_set_foreach([set], [var], [action(m4_defn([var]))])`. It is possible to use `m4_curry` if more than one argument is needed for *action*, although it is more efficient to use `m4_set_map_sep` in that case.

m4_set_map_sep (*set*, [*pre*], [*post*], [*sep*]) [Macro]

For each element in the set *set*, expand *pre*`[element]`*post*, additionally expanding *sep* between elements. Behavior is unspecified if the expansion recursively lists the contents of *set* (although listing other sets is acceptable), or if it modifies the set in any way other than removing the element visited by the expansion. This macro provides the most efficient means for non-destructively visiting the elements of a set; in particular, `m4_set_map([set], [action])` is equivalent to `m4_set_map_sep([set], [action(], [)])`.

m4_set_remove (*set*, *value*, [*if-present*], [*if-absent*])   [Macro]

If *value* is an element in the set *set*, then remove it and expand *if-present*. Otherwise expand *if-absent*. This macro operates in constant time so that multiple removals will scale linearly rather than quadratically; but when used outside of `m4_set_foreach` or `m4_set_map`, it leaves memory occupied until the set is later compacted by `m4_set_contents` or `m4_set_list`. Several other set operations are then less efficient between the time of element removal and subsequent memory compaction, but still maintain their guaranteed scaling performance.

m4_set_size (*set*)   [Macro]

Expand to the size of the set *set*. This implementation operates in constant time, and is thus more efficient than `m4_eval(m4_count(m4_set_listc([set])) - 1)`.

8.3.10 Forbidden Patterns

M4sugar provides a means to define suspicious patterns, patterns describing tokens which should not be found in the output. For instance, if an Autoconf 'configure' script includes tokens such as 'AC_DEFINE', or 'dnl', then most probably something went wrong (typically a macro was not evaluated because of overquotation).

M4sugar forbids all the tokens matching '^_?m4_' and '^dnl$'. Additional layers, such as M4sh and Autoconf, add additional forbidden patterns to the list.

m4_pattern_forbid (*pattern*)   [Macro]

Declare that no token matching *pattern* must be found in the output. Comments are not checked; this can be a problem if, for instance, you have some macro left unexpanded after an '#include'. No consensus is currently found in the Autoconf community, as some people consider it should be valid to name macros in comments (which doesn't make sense to the authors of this documentation: input, such as macros, should be documented by 'dnl' comments; reserving '#'-comments to document the output).

Of course, you might encounter exceptions to these generic rules, for instance you might have to refer to '$m4_flags'.

m4_pattern_allow (*pattern*)   [Macro]

Any token matching *pattern* is allowed, including if it matches an `m4_pattern_forbid` pattern.

8.4 Debugging via autom4te

At times, it is desirable to see what was happening inside m4, to see why output was not matching expectations. However, post-processing done by `autom4te` means that directly using the m4 builtin `m4_traceon` is likely to interfere with operation. Also, frequent diversion changes and the concept of forbidden tokens make it difficult to use `m4_defn` to generate inline comments in the final output.

There are a couple of tools to help with this. One is the use of the '--trace' option provided by autom4te (as well as each of the programs that wrap autom4te, such as autoconf),
in order to inspect when a macro is called and with which arguments. For example, when
this paragraph was written, the autoconf version could be found by:

```
$ autoconf --trace=AC_INIT
configure.ac:23:AC_INIT:GNU Autoconf:2.63b.95-3963:bug-autoconf@gnu.org
$ autoconf --trace='AC_INIT:version is $2'
version is 2.63b.95-3963
```

Another trick is to print out the expansion of various m4 expressions to standard error
or to an independent file, with no further m4 expansion, and without interfering with
diversion changes or the post-processing done to standard output. m4_errprintn shows a
given expression on standard error. For example, if you want to see the expansion of an
autoconf primitive or of one of your autoconf macros, you can do it like this:

```
$ cat <<\EOF > configure.ac
AC_INIT
m4_errprintn([The definition of AC_DEFINE_UNQUOTED:])
m4_errprintn(m4_defn([AC_DEFINE_UNQUOTED]))
AC_OUTPUT
EOF
$ autoconf
error The definition of AC_DEFINE_UNQUOTED:
error _AC_DEFINE_Q([], $@)
```

9 Programming in M4sh

M4sh, pronounced "mash", is aiming at producing portable Bourne shell scripts. This name was coined by Lars J. Aas, who notes that, according to the Webster's Revised Unabridged Dictionary (1913):

> Mash \Mash\, n. [Akin to G. meisch, maisch, meische, maische, mash, wash, and prob. to AS. miscian to mix. See "Mix".]
>
> 1. A mass of mixed ingredients reduced to a soft pulpy state by beating or pressure. . .
>
> 2. A mixture of meal or bran and water fed to animals.
>
> 3. A mess; trouble. [Obs.] –Beau. & Fl.

M4sh reserves the M4 macro namespace '`^_AS_`' for internal use, and the namespace '`^AS_`' for M4sh macros. It also reserves the shell and environment variable namespace '`^as_`', and the here-document delimiter namespace '`^_AS[A-Z]`' in the output file. You should not define your own macros or output shell code that conflicts with these namespaces.

9.1 Common Shell Constructs

M4sh provides portable alternatives for some common shell constructs that unfortunately are not portable in practice.

AS_BOX (*text*, [*char* = '`-`'])   [Macro]
> Expand into shell code that will output *text* surrounded by a box with *char* in the top and bottom border. *text* should not contain a newline, but may contain shell expansions valid for unquoted here-documents. *char* defaults to '`-`', but can be any character except '`/`', '`'`', '`"`', '`\`', '`&`', or '` ` `'. This is useful for outputting a comment box into log files to separate distinct phases of script operation.

AS_CASE (*word*, [*pattern1*], [*if-matched1*], . . ., [*default*])   [Macro]
> Expand into a shell '`case`' statement, where *word* is matched against one or more patterns. *if-matched* is run if the corresponding pattern matched *word*, else *default* is run. Avoids several portability issues (see [Limitations of Shell Builtins], page 221).

AS_DIRNAME (*file-name*)   [Macro]
> Output the directory portion of *file-name*. For example, if `$file` is '`/one/two/three`', the command `dir=`AS_DIRNAME(["$file"])`` sets `dir` to '`/one/two`'.

> This interface may be improved in the future to avoid forks and losing trailing newlines.

AS_ECHO (*word*)   [Macro]
> Emits *word* to the standard output, followed by a newline. *word* must be a single shell word (typically a quoted string). The bytes of *word* are output as-is, even if it starts with "`-`" or contains "`\`". Redirections can be placed outside the macro invocation. This is much more portable than using `echo` (see [Limitations of Shell Builtins], page 223).

AS_ECHO_N (*word*)   [Macro]

Emits *word* to the standard output, without a following newline. *word* must be a single shell word (typically a quoted string) and, for portability, should not include more than one newline. The bytes of *word* are output as-is, even if it starts with "-" or contains "\". Redirections can be placed outside the macro invocation.

AS_ESCAPE (*string*, [*chars* = "\"$'])   [Macro]

Expands to *string*, with any characters in *chars* escaped with a backslash ('\'). *chars* should be at most four bytes long, and only contain characters from the set "\"$'; however, characters may be safely listed more than once in *chars* for the sake of syntax highlighting editors. The current implementation expands *string* after adding escapes; if *string* contains macro calls that in turn expand to text needing shell quoting, you can use `AS_ESCAPE(m4_dquote(m4_expand([string])))`.

The default for *chars* ('\"$'') is the set of characters needing escapes when *string* will be used literally within double quotes. One common variant is the set of characters to protect when *string* will be used literally within back-ticks or an unquoted here-document ('\$''). Another common variant is '"""', which can be used to form a double-quoted string containing the same expansions that would have occurred if *string* were expanded in an unquoted here-document; however, when using this variant, care must be taken that *string* does not use double quotes within complex variable expansions (such as '${foo-`echo "hi"`}') that would be broken with improper escapes.

This macro is often used with `AS_ECHO`. For an example, observe the output generated by the shell code generated from this snippet:

```
foo=bar
AS_ECHO(["AS_ESCAPE(["$foo" = ])AS_ESCAPE(["$foo"], [""])"])
⇒"$foo" = "bar"
m4_define([macro], [a, [\b]])
AS_ECHO(["AS_ESCAPE([[macro]])"])
⇒macro
AS_ECHO(["AS_ESCAPE([macro])"])
⇒a, b
AS_ECHO(["AS_ESCAPE(m4_dquote(m4_expand([macro])))"])
⇒a, \b
```

To escape a string that will be placed within single quotes, use:

```
m4_bpatsubst([[string]], ['], ['\\''])
```

AS_EXECUTABLE_P (*file*)   [Macro]

Emit code to probe whether *file* is a regular file with executable permissions (and not a directory with search permissions). The caller is responsible for quoting *file*.

AS_EXIT ([*status* = '$?'])   [Macro]

Emit code to exit the shell with *status*, defaulting to '$?'. This macro works around shells that see the exit status of the command prior to **exit** inside a 'trap 0' handler (see [Limitations of Shell Builtins], page 233).

AS_IF (*test1*, [*run-if-true1*], ..., [*run-if-false*])   [Macro]

Run shell code *test1*. If *test1* exits with a zero status then run shell code *run-if-true1*, else examine further tests. If no test exits with a zero status, run shell code *run-if-false*, with simplifications if either *run-if-true1* or *run-if-false* is empty. For example,

```
AS_IF([test "x$foo" = xyes], [HANDLE_FOO([yes])],
      [test "x$foo" != xno], [HANDLE_FOO([maybe])],
      [echo foo not specified])
```

ensures any required macros of `HANDLE_FOO` are expanded before the first test.

AS_MKDIR_P (*file-name*)   [Macro]

Make the directory *file-name*, including intervening directories as necessary. This is equivalent to 'mkdir -p -- *file-name*', except that it is portable to older versions of `mkdir` that lack support for the '-p' option or for the '--' delimiter (see [Limitations of Usual Tools], page 243). Also, `AS_MKDIR_P` succeeds if *file-name* is a symbolic link to an existing directory, even though Posix is unclear whether 'mkdir -p' should succeed in that case. If creation of *file-name* fails, exit the script.

Also see the `AC_PROG_MKDIR_P` macro (see Section 5.2.1 [Particular Programs], page 43).

AS_SET_STATUS (*status*)   [Macro]

Emit shell code to set the value of '$?' to *status*, as efficiently as possible. However, this is not guaranteed to abort a shell running with `set -e` (see [Limitations of Shell Builtins], page 228). This should also be used at the end of a complex shell function instead of 'return' (see Section 11.13 [Shell Functions], page 218) to avoid a DJGPP shell bug.

AS_TR_CPP (*expression*)   [Macro]

Transform *expression* into a valid right-hand side for a C `#define`. For example:

```
# This outputs "#define HAVE_CHAR_P 1".
# Notice the m4 quoting around #, to prevent an m4 comment
type="char *"
echo "[#]define AS_TR_CPP([HAVE_$type]) 1"
```

AS_TR_SH (*expression*)   [Macro]

Transform *expression* into shell code that generates a valid shell variable name. The result is literal when possible at m4 time, but must be used with `eval` if *expression* causes shell indirections. For example:

```
# This outputs "Have it!".
header="sys/some file.h"
eval AS_TR_SH([HAVE_$header])=yes
if test "x$HAVE_sys_some_file_h" = xyes; then echo "Have it!"; fi
```

AS_SET_CATFILE (*var*, *dir*, *file*)   [Macro]

Set the polymorphic shell variable *var* to *dir*/*file*, but optimizing the common cases (*dir* or *file* is '.', *file* is absolute, etc.).

AS_UNSET (*var*)   [Macro]

> Unsets the shell variable *var*, working around bugs in older shells (see [Limitations of Shell Builtins], page 234). *var* can be a literal or indirect variable name.

AS_VERSION_COMPARE (*version-1*, *version-2*, [*action-if-less*],   [Macro]
        [*action-if-equal*], [*action-if-greater*])

> Compare two strings *version-1* and *version-2*, possibly containing shell variables, as version strings, and expand *action-if-less*, *action-if-equal*, or *action-if-greater* depending upon the result. The algorithm to compare is similar to the one used by strverscmp in glibc (see Section "String/Array Comparison" in *The GNU C Library*).

9.2 Support for indirect variable names

Often, it is convenient to write a macro that will emit shell code operating on a shell variable. The simplest case is when the variable name is known. But a more powerful idiom is writing shell code that can work through an indirection, where another variable or command substitution produces the name of the variable to actually manipulate. M4sh supports the notion of polymorphic shell variables, making it easy to write a macro that can deal with either literal or indirect variable names and output shell code appropriate for both use cases. Behavior is undefined if expansion of an indirect variable does not result in a literal variable name.

AS_LITERAL_IF (*expression*, [*if-literal*], [*if-not*], [*if-simple-ref*   [Macro]
        = '*if-not*'])
AS_LITERAL_WORD_IF (*expression*, [*if-literal*], [*if-not*],   [Macro]
        [*if-simple-ref* = '*if-not*'])

> If the expansion of *expression* is definitely a shell literal, expand *if-literal*. If the expansion of *expression* looks like it might contain shell indirections (such as `$var` or `'expr'`), then *if-not* is expanded. Sometimes, it is possible to output optimized code if *expression* consists only of shell variable expansions (such as `${var}`), in which case *if-simple-ref* can be provided; but defaulting to *if-not* should always be safe. **AS_LITERAL_WORD_IF** only expands *if-literal* if *expression* looks like a single shell word, containing no whitespace; while **AS_LITERAL_IF** allows whitespace in *expression*.
>
> In order to reduce the time spent recognizing whether an *expression* qualifies as a literal or a simple indirection, the implementation is somewhat conservative: *expression* must be a single shell word (possibly after stripping whitespace), consisting only of bytes that would have the same meaning whether unquoted or enclosed in double quotes (for example, 'a.b' results in *if-literal*, even though it is not a valid shell variable name; while both '`'a'`' and '`[$]`' result in *if-not*, because they behave differently than '`"'a'"`' and '`"[$]"`'). This macro can be used in contexts for recognizing portable file names (such as in the implementation of **AC_LIBSOURCE**), or coupled with some transliterations for forming valid variable names (such as in the implementation of **AS_TR_SH**, which uses an additional **m4_translit** to convert '.' to '_').
>
> This example shows how to read the contents of the shell variable **bar**, exercising all three arguments to **AS_LITERAL_IF**. It results in a script that will output the line 'hello' three times.

```
AC_DEFUN([MY_ACTION],
```

```
    [AS_LITERAL_IF([$1],
      [echo "$$1"],
      [AS_VAR_COPY([var], [$1])
       echo "$var"],
      [eval 'echo "$'"$1"\"")])])
    foo=bar bar=hello
    MY_ACTION([bar])
    MY_ACTION(['echo bar'])
    MY_ACTION([$foo])
```

AS_VAR_APPEND (*var*, *text*)   [Macro]

Emit shell code to append the shell expansion of *text* to the end of the current contents of the polymorphic shell variable *var*, taking advantage of shells that provide the '+=' extension for more efficient scaling.

For situations where the final contents of *var* are relatively short (less than 256 bytes), it is more efficient to use the simpler code sequence of *var*=$\{*var*\}*text* (or its polymorphic equivalent of AS_VAR_COPY([t], [var]) and AS_VAR_SET([var], ["$t"*text*])). But in the case when the script will be repeatedly appending text into var, issues of scaling start to become apparent. A naive implementation requires execution time linear to the length of the current contents of *var* as well as the length of *text* for a single append, for an overall quadratic scaling with multiple appends. This macro takes advantage of shells which provide the extension *var*+=*text*, which can provide amortized constant time for a single append, for an overall linear scaling with multiple appends. Note that unlike AS_VAR_SET, this macro requires that *text* be quoted properly to avoid field splitting and file name expansion.

AS_VAR_ARITH (*var*, *expression*)   [Macro]

Emit shell code to compute the arithmetic expansion of *expression*, assigning the result as the contents of the polymorphic shell variable *var*. The code takes advantage of shells that provide '$(())' for fewer forks, but uses expr as a fallback. Therefore, the syntax for a valid *expression* is rather limited: all operators must occur as separate shell arguments and with proper quoting, there is no portable equality operator, all variables containing numeric values must be expanded prior to the computation, all numeric values must be provided in decimal without leading zeroes, and the first shell argument should not be a negative number. In the following example, this snippet will print '(2+3)*4 == 20'.

```
    bar=3
    AS_VAR_ARITH([foo], [\( 2 + $bar \) \* 4])
    echo "(2+$bar)*4 == $foo"
```

AS_VAR_COPY (*dest*, *source*)   [Macro]

Emit shell code to assign the contents of the polymorphic shell variable *source* to the polymorphic shell variable *dest*. For example, executing this M4sh snippet will output 'bar hi':

```
    foo=bar bar=hi
    AS_VAR_COPY([a], [foo])
    AS_VAR_COPY([b], [$foo])
```

```
echo "$a $b"
```

When it is necessary to access the contents of an indirect variable inside a shell double-quoted context, the recommended idiom is to first copy the contents into a temporary literal shell variable.

```
for header in stdint_h inttypes_h ; do
  AS_VAR_COPY([var], [ac_cv_header_$header])
    echo "$header detected: $var"
done
```

AS_VAR_IF (*var*, [*word*], [*if-equal*], [*if-not-equal*])   [Macro]
Output a shell conditional statement. If the contents of the polymorphic shell variable *var* match the string *word*, execute *if-equal*; otherwise execute *if-not-equal*. *word* must be a single shell word (typically a quoted string). Avoids shell bugs if an interrupt signal arrives while a command substitution in *var* is being expanded.

AS_VAR_PUSHDEF (*m4-name*, *value*)   [Macro]
AS_VAR_POPDEF (*m4-name*)   [Macro]
A common M4sh idiom involves composing shell variable names from an m4 argument (for example, writing a macro that uses a cache variable). *value* can be an arbitrary string, which will be transliterated into a valid shell name by **AS_TR_SH**. In order to access the composed variable name based on *value*, it is easier to declare a temporary m4 macro *m4-name* with **AS_VAR_PUSHDEF**, then use that macro as the argument to subsequent **AS_VAR** macros as a polymorphic variable name, and finally free the temporary macro with **AS_VAR_POPDEF**. These macros are often followed with **dnl**, to avoid excess newlines in the output.

Here is an involved example, that shows the power of writing macros that can handle composed shell variable names:

```
m4_define([MY_CHECK_HEADER],
[AS_VAR_PUSHDEF([my_Header], [ac_cv_header_$1])dnl
AS_VAR_IF([my_Header], [yes], [echo "header $1 detected"])dnl
AS_VAR_POPDEF([my_Header])dnl
])
MY_CHECK_HEADER([stdint.h])
for header in inttypes.h stdlib.h ; do
  MY_CHECK_HEADER([$header])
done
```

In the above example, **MY_CHECK_HEADER** can operate on polymorphic variable names. In the first invocation, the m4 argument is **stdint.h**, which transliterates into a literal **stdint_h**. As a result, the temporary macro **my_Header** expands to the literal shell name 'ac_cv_header_stdint_h'. In the second invocation, the m4 argument to **MY_CHECK_HEADER** is $header, and the temporary macro **my_Header** expands to the indirect shell name '$as_my_Header'. During the shell execution of the for loop, when '$header' contains 'inttypes.h', then '$as_my_Header' contains 'ac_cv_header_inttypes_h'. If this script is then run on a platform where all three headers have been previously detected, the output of the script will include:

```
header stdint.h detected
header inttypes.h detected
header stdlib.h detected
```

AS_VAR_SET (*var*, [*value*]) [Macro]

Emit shell code to assign the contents of the polymorphic shell variable *var* to the shell expansion of *value*. *value* is not subject to field splitting or file name expansion, so if command substitution is used, it may be done with ''""'' rather than using an intermediate variable (see Section 11.8 [Shell Substitutions], page 201). However, *value* does undergo rescanning for additional macro names; behavior is unspecified if late expansion results in any shell meta-characters.

AS_VAR_SET_IF (*var*, [*if-set*], [*if-undef*]) [Macro]

Emit a shell conditional statement, which executes *if-set* if the polymorphic shell variable **var** is set to any value, and *if-undef* otherwise.

AS_VAR_TEST_SET (*var*) [Macro]

Emit a shell statement that results in a successful exit status only if the polymorphic shell variable **var** is set.

9.3 Initialization Macros

AS_BOURNE_COMPATIBLE [Macro]

Set up the shell to be more compatible with the Bourne shell as standardized by Posix, if possible. This may involve setting environment variables, or setting options, or similar implementation-specific actions. This macro is deprecated, since **AS_INIT** already invokes it.

AS_INIT [Macro]

Initialize the M4sh environment. This macro calls **m4_init**, then outputs the **#!/bin/sh** line, a notice about where the output was generated from, and code to sanitize the environment for the rest of the script. Among other initializations, this sets **SHELL** to the shell chosen to run the script (see [CONFIG_SHELL], page 302), and **LC_ALL** to ensure the C locale. Finally, it changes the current diversion to **BODY**. **AS_INIT** is called automatically by **AC_INIT** and **AT_INIT**, so shell code in 'configure', 'config.status', and 'testsuite' all benefit from a sanitized shell environment.

AS_INIT_GENERATED (*file*, [*comment*]) [Macro]

Emit shell code to start the creation of a subsidiary shell script in *file*, including changing *file* to be executable. This macro populates the child script with information learned from the parent (thus, the emitted code is equivalent in effect, but more efficient, than the code output by **AS_INIT**, **AS_BOURNE_COMPATIBLE**, and **AS_SHELL_SANITIZE**). If present, *comment* is output near the beginning of the child, prior to the shell initialization code, and is subject to parameter expansion, command substitution, and backslash quote removal. The parent script should check the exit status after this macro, in case *file* could not be properly created (for example, if the disk was full). If successfully created, the parent script can then proceed to append additional M4sh constructs into the child script.

Note that the child script starts life without a log file open, so if the parent script uses logging (see [AS_MESSAGE_LOG_FD], page 175), you must temporarily disable any attempts to use the log file until after emitting code to open a log within the child. On the other hand, if the parent script has **AS_MESSAGE_FD** redirected somewhere besides

'1', then the child script already has code that copies stdout to that descriptor. Currently, the suggested idiom for writing a M4sh shell script from within another script is:

```
AS_INIT_GENERATED([file], [[# My child script.
]]) || { AS_ECHO(["Failed to create child script"]); AS_EXIT; }
m4_pushdef([AS_MESSAGE_LOG_FD])dnl
cat >> "file" <<\__EOF__
# Code to initialize AS_MESSAGE_LOG_FD
m4_popdef([AS_MESSAGE_LOG_FD])dnl
# Additional code
__EOF__
```

This, however, may change in the future as the M4sh interface is stabilized further.

Also, be aware that use of LINENO within the child script may report line numbers relative to their location in the parent script, even when using AS_LINENO_PREPARE, if the parent script was unable to locate a shell with working LINENO support.

AS_LINENO_PREPARE [Macro]

Find a shell that supports the special variable LINENO, which contains the number of the currently executing line. This macro is automatically invoked by AC_INIT in configure scripts.

AS_ME_PREPARE [Macro]

Set up variable as_me to be the basename of the currently executing script. This macro is automatically invoked by AC_INIT in configure scripts.

AS_TMPDIR (*prefix*, [*dir* = '${TMPDIR:=/tmp}']) [Macro]

Create, as safely as possible, a temporary sub-directory within *dir* with a name starting with *prefix*. *prefix* should be 2-4 characters, to make it slightly easier to identify the owner of the directory. If *dir* is omitted, then the value of TMPDIR will be used (defaulting to '/tmp'). On success, the name of the newly created directory is stored in the shell variable tmp. On error, the script is aborted.

Typically, this macro is coupled with some exit traps to delete the created directory and its contents on exit or interrupt. However, there is a slight window between when the directory is created and when the name is actually known to the shell, so an interrupt at the right moment might leave the temporary directory behind. Hence it is important to use a *prefix* that makes it easier to determine if a leftover temporary directory from an interrupted script is safe to delete.

The use of the output variable '$tmp' rather than something in the 'as_' namespace is historical; it has the unfortunate consequence that reusing this otherwise common name for any other purpose inside your script has the potential to break any cleanup traps designed to remove the temporary directory.

AS_SHELL_SANITIZE [Macro]

Initialize the shell suitably for configure scripts. This has the effect of AS_BOURNE_COMPATIBLE, and sets some other environment variables for predictable results from configuration tests. For example, it sets LC_ALL to change to the default C locale. See Section 11.12 [Special Shell Variables], page 211. This macro is deprecated, since AS_INIT already invokes it.

9.4 File Descriptor Macros

The following macros define file descriptors used to output messages (or input values) from
'configure' scripts. For example:

```
echo "$wombats found" >&AS_MESSAGE_LOG_FD
echo 'Enter desired kangaroo count:' >&AS_MESSAGE_FD
read kangaroos <&AS_ORIGINAL_STDIN_FD`
```

However doing so is seldom needed, because Autoconf provides higher level macros as
described below.

AS_MESSAGE_FD   [Macro]

> The file descriptor for 'checking for...' messages and results. By default, AS_INIT
> sets this to '1' for standalone M4sh clients. However, AC_INIT shuffles things around
> to another file descriptor, in order to allow the '-q' option of configure to choose
> whether messages should go to the script's standard output or be discarded.
>
> If you want to display some messages, consider using one of the printing macros (see
> Section 7.5 [Printing Messages], page 120) instead. Copies of messages output via
> these macros are also recorded in 'config.log'.

AS_MESSAGE_LOG_FD   [Macro]

> This must either be empty, or expand to a file descriptor for log messages. By
> default, AS_INIT sets this macro to the empty string for standalone M4sh clients, thus
> disabling logging. However, AC_INIT shuffles things around so that both configure
> and config.status use 'config.log' for log messages. Macros that run tools, like
> AC_COMPILE_IFELSE (see Section 6.4 [Running the Compiler], page 108), redirect all
> output to this descriptor. You may want to do so if you develop such a low-level
> macro.

AS_ORIGINAL_STDIN_FD   [Macro]

> This must expand to a file descriptor for the original standard input. By default, AS_
> INIT sets this macro to '0' for standalone M4sh clients. However, AC_INIT shuffles
> things around for safety.
>
> When configure runs, it may accidentally execute an interactive command that has
> the same name as the non-interactive meant to be used or checked. If the standard
> input was the terminal, such interactive programs would cause configure to stop,
> pending some user input. Therefore configure redirects its standard input from
> '/dev/null' during its initialization. This is not normally a problem, since configure
> normally does not need user input.
>
> In the extreme case where your 'configure' script really needs to obtain some values
> from the original standard input, you can read them explicitly from AS_ORIGINAL_
> STDIN_FD.

10 Writing Autoconf Macros

When you write a feature test that could be applicable to more than one software package, the best thing to do is encapsulate it in a new macro. Here are some instructions and guidelines for writing Autoconf macros.

10.1 Macro Definitions

AC_DEFUN (*name*, [*body*])   [Macro]
> Autoconf macros are defined using the AC_DEFUN macro, which is similar to the M4 builtin m4_define macro; this creates a macro named *name* and with *body* as its expansion. In addition to defining a macro, AC_DEFUN adds to it some code that is used to constrain the order in which macros are called, while avoiding redundant output (see Section 10.4.1 [Prerequisite Macros], page 180).

An Autoconf macro definition looks like this:

    AC_DEFUN(macro-name, macro-body)

You can refer to any arguments passed to the macro as '$1', '$2', etc. See Section "How to define new macros" in *GNU M4*, for more complete information on writing M4 macros.

Most macros fall in one of two general categories. The first category includes macros which take arguments, in order to generate output parameterized by those arguments. Macros in this category are designed to be directly expanded, often multiple times, and should not be used as the argument to AC_REQUIRE. The other category includes macros which are shorthand for a fixed block of text, and therefore do not take arguments. For this category of macros, directly expanding the macro multiple times results in redundant output, so it is more common to use the macro as the argument to AC_REQUIRE, or to declare the macro with AC_DEFUN_ONCE (see Section 10.4.3 [One-Shot Macros], page 183).

Be sure to properly quote both the *macro-body and* the *macro-name* to avoid any problems if the macro happens to have been previously defined.

Each macro should have a header comment that gives its prototype, and a brief description. When arguments have default values, display them in the prototype. For example:

    # AC_MSG_ERROR(ERROR, [EXIT-STATUS = 1])
    # -------------------------------------
    m4_define([AC_MSG_ERROR],
      [{ AS_MESSAGE([error: $1], [2])
        exit m4_default([$2], [1]); }])

Comments about the macro should be left in the header comment. Most other comments make their way into 'configure', so just keep using '#' to introduce comments.

If you have some special comments about pure M4 code, comments that make no sense in 'configure' and in the header comment, then use the builtin dnl: it causes M4 to discard the text through the next newline.

Keep in mind that dnl is rarely needed to introduce comments; dnl is more useful to get rid of the newlines following macros that produce no output, such as AC_REQUIRE.

Public third-party macros need to use AC_DEFUN, and not m4_define, in order to be found by aclocal (see Section "Extending aclocal" in *GNU Automake*). Additionally, if it is ever determined that a macro should be made obsolete, it is easy to convert from `AC_DEFUN` to `AU_DEFUN` in order to have **autoupdate** assist the user in choosing a better alternative, but there is no corresponding way to make **m4_define** issue an upgrade notice (see [AU_DEFUN], page 184).

There is another subtle, but important, difference between using **m4_define** and `AC_DEFUN`: only the former is unaffected by `AC_REQUIRE`. When writing a file, it is always safe to replace a block of text with a **m4_define** macro that will expand to the same text. But replacing a block of text with an `AC_DEFUN` macro with the same content does not necessarily give the same results, because it changes the location where any embedded but unsatisfied `AC_REQUIRE` invocations within the block will be expanded. For an example of this, see Section 20.8 [Expanded Before Required], page 346.

10.2 Macro Names

All of the public Autoconf macros have all-uppercase names in the namespace '`^AC_`' to prevent them from accidentally conflicting with other text; Autoconf also reserves the namespace '`^_AC_`' for internal macros. All shell variables that they use for internal purposes have mostly-lowercase names starting with '`ac_`'. Autoconf also uses here-document delimiters in the namespace '`^_AC[A-Z]`'. During **configure**, files produced by Autoconf make heavy use of the file system namespace '`^conf`'.

Since Autoconf is built on top of M4sugar (see Section 8.3 [Programming in M4sugar], page 137) and M4sh (see Chapter 9 [Programming in M4sh], page 167), you must also be aware of those namespaces ('`^_?\(m4\|AS\)_`'). And since '`configure.ac`' is also designed to be scanned by Autoheader, Autoscan, Autoupdate, and Automake, you should be aware of the '`^_?A[HNUM]_`' namespaces. In general, you *should not use* the namespace of a package that does not own the macro or shell code you are writing.

To ensure that your macros don't conflict with present or future Autoconf macros, you should prefix your own macro names and any shell variables they use with some other sequence. Possibilities include your initials, or an abbreviation for the name of your organization or software package. Historically, people have not always followed the rule of using a namespace appropriate for their package, and this has made it difficult for determining the origin of a macro (and where to report bugs about that macro), as well as difficult for the true namespace owner to add new macros without interference from pre-existing uses of third-party macros. Perhaps the best example of this confusion is the `AM_GNU_GETTEXT` macro, which belongs, not to Automake, but to Gettext.

Most of the Autoconf macros' names follow a structured naming convention that indicates the kind of feature check by the name. The macro names consist of several words, separated by underscores, going from most general to most specific. The names of their cache variables use the same convention (see Section 7.4.1 [Cache Variable Names], page 118, for more information on them).

The first word of the name after the namespace initials (such as '`AC_`') usually tells the category of the feature being tested. Here are the categories used in Autoconf for specific test macros, the kind of macro that you are more likely to write. They are also used for cache variables, in all-lowercase. Use them where applicable; where they're not, invent your own categories.

C   C language builtin features.

DECL	Declarations of C variables in header files.
FUNC	Functions in libraries.
GROUP	Posix group owners of files.
HEADER	Header files.
LIB	C libraries.
PROG	The base names of programs.
MEMBER	Members of aggregates.
SYS	Operating system features.
TYPE	C builtin or declared types.
VAR	C variables in libraries.

After the category comes the name of the particular feature being tested. Any further words in the macro name indicate particular aspects of the feature. For example, `AC_PROG_CC_STDC` checks whether the C compiler supports ISO Standard C.

An internal macro should have a name that starts with an underscore; Autoconf internals should therefore start with '`_AC_`'. Additionally, a macro that is an internal subroutine of another macro should have a name that starts with an underscore and the name of that other macro, followed by one or more words saying what the internal macro does. For example, `AC_PATH_X` has internal macros `_AC_PATH_X_XMKMF` and `_AC_PATH_X_DIRECT`.

10.3 Reporting Messages

When macros statically diagnose abnormal situations, benign or fatal, it is possible to make **autoconf** detect the problem, and refuse to create '`configure`' in the case of an error. The macros in this section are considered obsolescent, and new code should use M4sugar macros for this purpose, see Section 8.3.2 [Diagnostic Macros], page 140.

On the other hand, it is possible to want to detect errors when **configure** is run, which are dependent on the environment of the user rather than the maintainer. For dynamic diagnostics, see Section 7.5 [Printing Messages], page 120.

AC_DIAGNOSE (*category*, *message*)   [Macro]
  Report *message* as a warning (or as an error if requested by the user) if warnings of the *category* are turned on. This macro is obsolescent; you are encouraged to use:

      m4_warn([*category*], [*message*])

  instead. See [m4_warn], page 141, for more details, including valid *category* names.

AC_WARNING (*message*)   [Macro]
  Report *message* as a syntax warning. This macro is obsolescent; you are encouraged to use:

      m4_warn([syntax], [*message*])

  instead. See [m4_warn], page 141, for more details, as well as better finer-grained categories of warnings (not all problems have to do with syntax).

`AC_FATAL (message)`   [Macro]

    Report a severe error *message*, and have **autoconf** die. This macro is obsolescent; you are encouraged to use:

        `m4_fatal([message])`

    instead. See [m4_fatal], page 140, for more details.

    When the user runs 'autoconf -W error', warnings from `m4_warn` (including those issued through `AC_DIAGNOSE` and `AC_WARNING`) are reported as errors, see Section 3.4 [autoconf Invocation], page 11.

10.4 Dependencies Between Macros

Some Autoconf macros depend on other macros having been called first in order to work correctly. Autoconf provides a way to ensure that certain macros are called if needed and a way to warn the user if macros are called in an order that might cause incorrect operation.

10.4.1 Prerequisite Macros

A macro that you write might need to use values that have previously been computed by other macros. For example, `AC_DECL_YYTEXT` examines the output of **flex** or **lex**, so it depends on `AC_PROG_LEX` having been called first to set the shell variable `LEX`.

    Rather than forcing the user of the macros to keep track of the dependencies between them, you can use the `AC_REQUIRE` macro to do it automatically. `AC_REQUIRE` can ensure that a macro is only called if it is needed, and only called once.

`AC_REQUIRE (macro-name)`   [Macro]

    If the M4 macro *macro-name* has not already been called, call it (without any arguments). Make sure to quote *macro-name* with square brackets. *macro-name* must have been defined using `AC_DEFUN` or else contain a call to `AC_PROVIDE` to indicate that it has been called.

    `AC_REQUIRE` must be used inside a macro defined by `AC_DEFUN`; it must not be called from the top level. Also, it does not make sense to require a macro that takes parameters.

    `AC_REQUIRE` is often misunderstood. It really implements dependencies between macros in the sense that if one macro depends upon another, the latter is expanded *before* the body of the former. To be more precise, the required macro is expanded before the outermost defined macro in the current expansion stack. In particular, 'AC_REQUIRE([FOO])' is not replaced with the body of FOO. For instance, this definition of macros:

```
AC_DEFUN([TRAVOLTA],
[test "$body_temperature_in_celsius" -gt "38" &&
  dance_floor=occupied])
AC_DEFUN([NEWTON_JOHN],
[test "x$hair_style" = xcurly &&
  dance_floor=occupied])
```

```
AC_DEFUN([RESERVE_DANCE_FLOOR],
[if date | grep '^Sat.*pm' >/dev/null 2>&1; then
  AC_REQUIRE([TRAVOLTA])
  AC_REQUIRE([NEWTON_JOHN])
fi])
```

with this 'configure.ac'

```
AC_INIT([Dance Manager], [1.0], [bug-dance@example.org])
RESERVE_DANCE_FLOOR
if test "x$dance_floor" = xoccupied; then
  AC_MSG_ERROR([cannot pick up here, let's move])
fi
```

does not leave you with a better chance to meet a kindred soul at other times than Saturday night since it expands into:

```
test "$body_temperature_in_Celsius" -gt "38" &&
  dance_floor=occupied
test "x$hair_style" = xcurly &&
  dance_floor=occupied
fi
if date | grep '^Sat.*pm' >/dev/null 2>&1; then


fi
```

This behavior was chosen on purpose: (i) it prevents messages in required macros from interrupting the messages in the requiring macros; (ii) it avoids bad surprises when shell conditionals are used, as in:

```
if ...; then
  AC_REQUIRE([SOME_CHECK])
fi
...
SOME_CHECK
```

However, this implementation can lead to another class of problems. Consider the case where an outer macro first expands, then indirectly requires, an inner macro:

```
AC_DEFUN([TESTA], [[echo in A
if test -n "$SEEN_A" ; then echo duplicate ; fi
SEEN_A=:]])
AC_DEFUN([TESTB], [AC_REQUIRE([TESTA])[echo in B
if test -z "$SEEN_A" ; then echo bug ; fi]])
AC_DEFUN([TESTC], [AC_REQUIRE([TESTB])[echo in C]])
AC_DEFUN([OUTER], [[echo in OUTER]
TESTA
TESTC])
OUTER
```

Prior to Autoconf 2.64, the implementation of AC_REQUIRE recognized that TESTB needed to be hoisted prior to the expansion of OUTER, but because TESTA had already been directly expanded, it failed to hoist `TESTA`. Therefore, the expansion of `TESTB` occurs prior to its prerequisites, leading to the following output:

```
in B
bug
in OUTER
in A
in C
```

Newer Autoconf is smart enough to recognize this situation, and hoists `TESTA` even though it has already been expanded, but issues a syntax warning in the process. This is because the hoisted expansion of `TESTA` defeats the purpose of using `AC_REQUIRE` to avoid redundant code, and causes its own set of problems if the hoisted macro is not idempotent:

```
in A
in B
in OUTER
in A
duplicate
in C
```

The bug is not in Autoconf, but in the macro definitions. If you ever pass a particular macro name to `AC_REQUIRE`, then you are implying that the macro only needs to be expanded once. But to enforce this, either the macro must be declared with `AC_DEFUN_ONCE` (although this only helps in Autoconf 2.64 or newer), or all uses of that macro should be through `AC_REQUIRE`; directly expanding the macro defeats the point of using `AC_REQUIRE` to eliminate redundant expansion. In the example, this rule of thumb was violated because `TESTB` requires `TESTA` while `OUTER` directly expands it. One way of fixing the bug is to factor `TESTA` into two macros, the portion designed for direct and repeated use (here, named `TESTA`), and the portion designed for one-shot output and used only inside `AC_REQUIRE` (here, named `TESTA_PREREQ`). Then, by fixing all clients to use the correct calling convention according to their needs:

```
AC_DEFUN([TESTA], [AC_REQUIRE([TESTA_PREREQ])[echo in A]])
AC_DEFUN([TESTA_PREREQ], [[echo in A_PREREQ
if test -n "$SEEN_A" ; then echo duplicate ; fi
SEEN_A=:]])
AC_DEFUN([TESTB], [AC_REQUIRE([TESTA_PREREQ])[echo in B
if test -z "$SEEN_A" ; then echo bug ; fi]])
AC_DEFUN([TESTC], [AC_REQUIRE([TESTB])[echo in C]])
AC_DEFUN([OUTER], [[echo in OUTER]
TESTA
TESTC]])
OUTER
```

the resulting output will then obey all dependency rules and avoid any syntax warnings, whether the script is built with old or new Autoconf versions:

```
in A_PREREQ
in B
in OUTER
in A
```

`in C`

The helper macros `AS_IF` and `AS_CASE` may be used to enforce expansion of required macros outside of shell conditional constructs. You are furthermore encouraged, although not required, to put all `AC_REQUIRE` calls at the beginning of a macro. You can use `dnl` to avoid the empty lines they leave.

10.4.2 Suggested Ordering

Some macros should be run before another macro if both are called, but neither *requires* that the other be called. For example, a macro that changes the behavior of the C compiler should be called before any macros that run the C compiler. Many of these dependencies are noted in the documentation.

Autoconf provides the `AC_BEFORE` macro to warn users when macros with this kind of dependency appear out of order in a 'configure.ac' file. The warning occurs when creating `configure` from 'configure.ac', not when running `configure`.

For example, `AC_PROG_CPP` checks whether the C compiler can run the C preprocessor when given the '-E' option. It should therefore be called after any macros that change which C compiler is being used, such as `AC_PROG_CC`. So `AC_PROG_CC` contains:

        AC_BEFORE([$0], [AC_PROG_CPP])dnl

This warns the user if a call to `AC_PROG_CPP` has already occurred when `AC_PROG_CC` is called.

`AC_BEFORE` (*this-macro-name*, *called-macro-name*)   [Macro]
> Make M4 print a warning message to the standard error output if *called-macro-name* has already been called. *this-macro-name* should be the name of the macro that is calling `AC_BEFORE`. The macro *called-macro-name* must have been defined using `AC_DEFUN` or else contain a call to `AC_PROVIDE` to indicate that it has been called.

10.4.3 One-Shot Macros

Some macros should be called only once, either because calling them multiple time is unsafe, or because it is bad style. For instance Autoconf ensures that `AC_CANONICAL_BUILD` and cousins (see Section 14.2 [Canonicalizing], page 282) are evaluated only once, because it makes no sense to run these expensive checks more than once. Such one-shot macros can be defined using `AC_DEFUN_ONCE`.

`AC_DEFUN_ONCE` (*macro-name*, *macro-body*)   [Macro]
> Declare macro *macro-name* like `AC_DEFUN` would (see Section 10.1 [Macro Definitions], page 177), but add additional logic that guarantees that only the first use of the macro (whether by direct expansion or `AC_REQUIRE`) causes an expansion of *macro-body*; the expansion will occur before the start of any enclosing macro defined by `AC_DEFUN`. Subsequent expansions are silently ignored. Generally, it does not make sense for *macro-body* to use parameters such as $1.

Prior to Autoconf 2.64, a macro defined by `AC_DEFUN_ONCE` would emit a warning if it was directly expanded a second time, so for portability, it is better to use `AC_REQUIRE` than direct invocation of *macro-name* inside a macro defined by `AC_DEFUN` (see Section 10.4.1 [Prerequisite Macros], page 180).

10.5 Obsoleting Macros

Configuration and portability technology has evolved over the years. Often better ways of solving a particular problem are developed, or ad-hoc approaches are systematized. This process has occurred in many parts of Autoconf. One result is that some of the macros are now considered *obsolete*; they still work, but are no longer considered the best thing to do, hence they should be replaced with more modern macros. Ideally, `autoupdate` should replace the old macro calls with their modern implementation.

Autoconf provides a simple means to obsolete a macro.

AU_DEFUN (*old-macro*, *implementation*, [*message*])   [Macro]
> Define *old-macro* as *implementation*. The only difference with `AC_DEFUN` is that the user is warned that *old-macro* is now obsolete.
>
> If she then uses `autoupdate`, the call to *old-macro* is replaced by the modern *implementation*. *message* should include information on what to do after running `autoupdate`; `autoupdate` prints it as a warning, and includes it in the updated 'configure.ac' file.
>
> The details of this macro are hairy: if `autoconf` encounters an `AU_DEFUN`ed macro, all macros inside its second argument are expanded as usual. However, when `autoupdate` is run, only M4 and M4sugar macros are expanded here, while all other macros are disabled and appear literally in the updated 'configure.ac'.

AU_ALIAS (*old-name*, *new-name*)   [Macro]
> Used if the *old-name* is to be replaced by a call to *new-macro* with the same parameters. This happens for example if the macro was renamed.

10.6 Coding Style

The Autoconf macros follow a strict coding style. You are encouraged to follow this style, especially if you intend to distribute your macro, either by contributing it to Autoconf itself or the Autoconf Macro Archive, or by other means.

The first requirement is to pay great attention to the quotation. For more details, see Section 3.1.2 [Autoconf Language], page 7, and Section 8.1 [M4 Quotation], page 123.

Do not try to invent new interfaces. It is likely that there is a macro in Autoconf that resembles the macro you are defining: try to stick to this existing interface (order of arguments, default values, etc.). We *are* conscious that some of these interfaces are not perfect; nevertheless, when harmless, homogeneity should be preferred over creativity.

Be careful about clashes both between M4 symbols and between shell variables.

If you stick to the suggested M4 naming scheme (see Section 10.2 [Macro Names], page 178), you are unlikely to generate conflicts. Nevertheless, when you need to set a special value, *avoid using a regular macro name*; rather, use an "impossible" name. For instance, up to version 2.13, the macro `AC_SUBST` used to remember what *symbol* macros were already defined by setting `AC_SUBST_symbol`, which is a regular macro name. But since there is a macro named `AC_SUBST_FILE`, it was just impossible to 'AC_SUBST(FILE)'! In this case, `AC_SUBST(symbol)` or `_AC_SUBST(symbol)` should have been used (yes, with the parentheses).

No Autoconf macro should ever enter the user-variable name space; i.e., except for the variables that are the actual result of running the macro, all shell variables should start with `ac_`. In addition, small macros or any macro that is likely to be embedded in other macros should be careful not to use obvious names.

Do not use `dnl` to introduce comments: most of the comments you are likely to write are either header comments which are not output anyway, or comments that should make their way into 'configure'. There are exceptional cases where you do want to comment special M4 constructs, in which case `dnl` is right, but keep in mind that it is unlikely.

M4 ignores the leading blanks and newlines before each argument. Use this feature to indent in such a way that arguments are (more or less) aligned with the opening parenthesis of the macro being called. For instance, instead of

```
AC_CACHE_CHECK(for EMX OS/2 environment,
ac_cv_emxos2,
[AC_COMPILE_IFELSE([AC_LANG_PROGRAM(, [return __EMX__;])],
[ac_cv_emxos2=yes], [ac_cv_emxos2=no])])
```

write

```
AC_CACHE_CHECK([for EMX OS/2 environment], [ac_cv_emxos2],
[AC_COMPILE_IFELSE([AC_LANG_PROGRAM([], [return __EMX__;])],
                   [ac_cv_emxos2=yes],
                   [ac_cv_emxos2=no])])
```

or even

```
AC_CACHE_CHECK([for EMX OS/2 environment],
               [ac_cv_emxos2],
               [AC_COMPILE_IFELSE([AC_LANG_PROGRAM([],
                                                   [return __EMX__;])],
                  [ac_cv_emxos2=yes],
                  [ac_cv_emxos2=no])])
```

When using `AC_RUN_IFELSE` or any macro that cannot work when cross-compiling, provide a pessimistic value (typically 'no').

Feel free to use various tricks to prevent auxiliary tools, such as syntax-highlighting editors, from behaving improperly. For instance, instead of:

```
m4_bpatsubst([$1], [$"])
```

use

```
m4_bpatsubst([$1], [$""])
```

so that Emacsen do not open an endless "string" at the first quote. For the same reasons, avoid:

```
test $[#] != 0
```

and use:

```
test $[@%:@] != 0
```

Otherwise, the closing bracket would be hidden inside a '#'-comment, breaking the bracket-matching highlighting from Emacsen. Note the preferred style to escape from M4: '`$[1]`', '`$[@]`', etc. Do not escape when it is unnecessary. Common examples of useless quotation are '`[$]$1`' (write '`$$1`'), '`[$]var`' (use '`$var`'), etc. If you add portability issues to the picture, you'll prefer '${1+"$[@]"}' to '"[$]@"', and you'll prefer do something better than hacking Autoconf :-).

When using sed, don't use '-e' except for indenting purposes. With the s and y commands, the preferred separator is '/' unless '/' itself might appear in the pattern or replacement, in which case you should use '|', or optionally ',' if you know the pattern and replacement cannot contain a file name. If none of these characters will do, choose a printable character that cannot appear in the pattern or replacement. Characters from the set '"#$&'()*;<=>¿|~' are good choices if the pattern or replacement might contain a file name, since they have special meaning to the shell and are less likely to occur in file names.

See Section 10.1 [Macro Definitions], page 177, for details on how to define a macro. If a macro doesn't use AC_REQUIRE, is expected to never be the object of an AC_REQUIRE directive, and macros required by other macros inside arguments do not need to be expanded before this macro, then use m4_define. In case of doubt, use AC_DEFUN. Also take into account that public third-party macros need to use AC_DEFUN in order to be found by aclocal (see Section "Extending aclocal" in *GNU Automake*). All the AC_REQUIRE statements should be at the beginning of the macro, and each statement should be followed by dnl.

You should not rely on the number of arguments: instead of checking whether an argument is missing, test that it is not empty. It provides both a simpler and a more predictable interface to the user, and saves room for further arguments.

Unless the macro is short, try to leave the closing '])' at the beginning of a line, followed by a comment that repeats the name of the macro being defined. This introduces an additional newline in configure; normally, that is not a problem, but if you want to remove it you can use '[]dnl' on the last line. You can similarly use '[]dnl' after a macro call to remove its newline. '[]dnl' is recommended instead of 'dnl' to ensure that M4 does not interpret the 'dnl' as being attached to the preceding text or macro output. For example, instead of:

```
AC_DEFUN([AC_PATH_X],
[AC_MSG_CHECKING([for X])
AC_REQUIRE_CPP()
# ...omitted...
  AC_MSG_RESULT([libraries $x_libraries, headers $x_includes])
fi])
```

you would write:

```
AC_DEFUN([AC_PATH_X],
[AC_REQUIRE_CPP()[]dnl
AC_MSG_CHECKING([for X])
# ...omitted...
  AC_MSG_RESULT([libraries $x_libraries, headers $x_includes])
fi[]dnl
])# AC_PATH_X
```

If the macro is long, try to split it into logical chunks. Typically, macros that check for a bug in a function and prepare its AC_LIBOBJ replacement should have an auxiliary macro to perform this setup. Do not hesitate to introduce auxiliary macros to factor your code.

In order to highlight the recommended coding style, here is a macro written the old way:

```
dnl Check for EMX on OS/2.
dnl _AC_EMXOS2
AC_DEFUN(_AC_EMXOS2,
[AC_CACHE_CHECK(for EMX OS/2 environment, ac_cv_emxos2,
[AC_COMPILE_IFELSE([AC_LANG_PROGRAM(, return __EMX__;)],
ac_cv_emxos2=yes, ac_cv_emxos2=no)])
test "x$ac_cv_emxos2" = xyes && EMXOS2=yes])
```

and the new way:

```
# _AC_EMXOS2
# ----------
# Check for EMX on OS/2.
m4_define([_AC_EMXOS2],
[AC_CACHE_CHECK([for EMX OS/2 environment], [ac_cv_emxos2],
[AC_COMPILE_IFELSE([AC_LANG_PROGRAM([], [return __EMX__;])],
                   [ac_cv_emxos2=yes],
                   [ac_cv_emxos2=no])])
test "x$ac_cv_emxos2" = xyes && EMXOS2=yes[]dnl
])# _AC_EMXOS2
```

11 Portable Shell Programming

When writing your own checks, there are some shell-script programming techniques you should avoid in order to make your code portable. The Bourne shell and upward-compatible shells like the Korn shell and Bash have evolved over the years, and many features added to the original System7 shell are now supported on all interesting porting targets. However, the following discussion between Russ Allbery and Robert Lipe is worth reading:

Russ Allbery:

> The GNU assumption that `/bin/sh` is the one and only shell leads to a permanent deadlock. Vendors don't want to break users' existing shell scripts, and there are some corner cases in the Bourne shell that are not completely compatible with a Posix shell. Thus, vendors who have taken this route will *never* (OK... "never say never") replace the Bourne shell (as `/bin/sh`) with a Posix shell.

Robert Lipe:

> This is exactly the problem. While most (at least most System V's) do have a Bourne shell that accepts shell functions most vendor `/bin/sh` programs are not the Posix shell.
>
> So while most modern systems do have a shell *somewhere* that meets the Posix standard, the challenge is to find it.

For this reason, part of the job of M4sh (see Chapter 9 [Programming in M4sh], page 167) is to find such a shell. But to prevent trouble, if you're not using M4sh you should not take advantage of features that were added after Unix version 7, circa 1977 (see Section 6.7 [Systemology], page 111); you should not use aliases, negated character classes, or even `unset`. `#` comments, while not in Unix version 7, were retrofitted in the original Bourne shell and can be assumed to be part of the least common denominator.

On the other hand, if you're using M4sh you can assume that the shell has the features that were added in SVR2 (circa 1984), including shell functions, `return`, `unset`, and I/O redirection for builtins. For more information, refer to `http://www.in-ulm.de/~mascheck/bourne/`. However, some pitfalls have to be avoided for portable use of these constructs; these will be documented in the rest of this chapter. See in particular Section 11.13 [Shell Functions], page 218 and Section 11.14 [Limitations of Shell Builtins], page 220.

Some ancient systems have quite small limits on the length of the '`#!`' line; for instance, 32 bytes (not including the newline) on SunOS 4. However, these ancient systems are no longer of practical concern.

The set of external programs you should run in a `configure` script is fairly small. See Section "Utilities in Makefiles" in *The GNU Coding Standards*, for the list. This restriction allows users to start out with a fairly small set of programs and build the rest, avoiding too many interdependencies between packages.

Some of these external utilities have a portable subset of features; see Section 11.15 [Limitations of Usual Tools], page 235.

There are other sources of documentation about shells. The specification for the Posix Shell Command Language, though more generous than the restrictive shell subset described above, is fairly portable nowadays. Also please see the Shell FAQs.

11.1 Shellology

There are several families of shells, most prominently the Bourne family and the C shell family which are deeply incompatible. If you want to write portable shell scripts, avoid members of the C shell family. The the Shell difference FAQ includes a small history of Posix shells, and a comparison between several of them.

Below we describe some of the members of the Bourne shell family.

Ash   Ash is often used on GNU/Linux and BSD systems as a light-weight Bourne-compatible shell. Ash 0.2 has some bugs that are fixed in the 0.3.x series, but portable shell scripts should work around them, since version 0.2 is still shipped with many GNU/Linux distributions.

          To be compatible with Ash 0.2:

          − don't use '$?' after expanding empty or unset variables, or at the start of an `eval`:

```
foo=
false
$foo
echo "Do not use it: $?"
false
eval 'echo "Do not use it: $?"'
```

          − don't use command substitution within variable expansion:

```
cat ${FOO='bar'}
```

          − beware that single builtin substitutions are not performed by a subshell, hence their effect applies to the current shell! See Section 11.8 [Shell Substitutions], page 201, item "Command Substitution".

Bash   To detect whether you are running Bash, test whether `BASH_VERSION` is set. To require Posix compatibility, run '`set -o posix`'. See Section "Bash Posix Mode" in *The GNU Bash Reference Manual*, for details.

Bash 2.05 and later

          Versions 2.05 and later of Bash use a different format for the output of the `set` builtin, designed to make evaluating its output easier. However, this output is not compatible with earlier versions of Bash (or with many other shells, probably). So if you use Bash 2.05 or higher to execute `configure`, you'll need to use Bash 2.05 for all other build tasks as well.

Ksh   The Korn shell is compatible with the Bourne family and it mostly conforms to Posix. It has two major variants commonly called 'ksh88' and 'ksh93', named after the years of initial release. It is usually called `ksh`, but is called `sh` on some hosts if you set your path appropriately.

          Solaris systems have three variants: `/usr/bin/ksh` is 'ksh88'; it is standard on Solaris 2.0 and later. `/usr/xpg4/bin/sh` is a Posix-compliant variant of 'ksh88'; it is standard on Solaris 9 and later. `/usr/dt/bin/dtksh` is 'ksh93'. Variants that are not standard may be parts of optional packages. There is no extra charge for these packages, but they are not part of a minimal OS install and therefore some installations may not have it.

Starting with Tru64 Version 4.0, the Korn shell `/usr/bin/ksh` is also available as `/usr/bin/posix/sh`. If the environment variable `BIN_SH` is set to `xpg4`, subsidiary invocations of the standard shell conform to Posix.

Pdksh   A public-domain clone of the Korn shell called `pdksh` is widely available: it has most of the 'ksh88' features along with a few of its own. It usually sets `KSH_VERSION`, except if invoked as `/bin/sh` on OpenBSD, and similarly to Bash you can require Posix compatibility by running 'set -o posix'. Unfortunately, with `pdksh` 5.2.14 (the latest stable version as of January 2007) Posix mode is buggy and causes `pdksh` to depart from Posix in at least one respect, see Section 11.8 [Shell Substitutions], page 201.

Zsh   To detect whether you are running `zsh`, test whether `ZSH_VERSION` is set. By default `zsh` is *not* compatible with the Bourne shell: you must execute 'emulate sh', and for `zsh` versions before 3.1.6-dev-18 you must also set `NULLCMD` to ':'. See Section "Compatibility" in *The Z Shell Manual*, for details.

               The default Mac OS X `sh` was originally Zsh; it was changed to Bash in Mac OS X 10.2.

11.2 Invoking the Shell

The Korn shell (up to at least version M-12/28/93d) has a bug when invoked on a file whose name does not contain a slash. It first searches for the file's name in `PATH`, and if found it executes that rather than the original file. For example, assuming there is a binary executable '/usr/bin/script' in your `PATH`, the last command in the following example fails because the Korn shell finds '/usr/bin/script' and refuses to execute it as a shell script:

```
$ touch xxyzzyz script
$ ksh xxyzzyz
$ ksh ./script
$ ksh script
ksh: script: cannot execute
```

Bash 2.03 has a bug when invoked with the '-c' option: if the option-argument ends in backslash-newline, Bash incorrectly reports a syntax error. The problem does not occur if a character follows the backslash:

```
$ $ bash -c 'echo foo \
> '
bash: -c: line 2: syntax error: unexpected end of file
$ bash -c 'echo foo \
> '
foo
```

See Section 12.4 [Backslash-Newline-Empty], page 254, for how this can cause problems in makefiles.

11.3 Here-Documents

Don't rely on '\' being preserved just because it has no special meaning together with the next symbol. In the native **sh** on OpenBSD 2.7 '\"' expands to '"' in here-documents with unquoted delimiter. As a general rule, if '\\' expands to '\' use '\\' to get '\'.

With OpenBSD 2.7's **sh**

```
$ cat <<EOF
> \" \\
> EOF
" \
```

and with Bash:

```
bash-2.04$ cat <<EOF
> \" \\
> EOF
\" \
```

Using command substitutions in a here-document that is fed to a shell function is not portable. For example, with Solaris 10 **/bin/sh**:

```
$ kitty () { cat; }
$ kitty <<EOF
> `echo ok`
> EOF
/tmp/sh199886: cannot open
$ echo $?
1
```

Some shells mishandle large here-documents: for example, Solaris 10 **dtksh** and the UnixWare 7.1.1 Posix shell, which are derived from Korn shell version M-12/28/93d, mishandle braced variable expansion that crosses a 1024- or 4096-byte buffer boundary within a here-document. Only the part of the variable name after the boundary is used. For example, `${variable}` could be replaced by the expansion of `${ble}`. If the end of the variable name is aligned with the block boundary, the shell reports an error, as if you used `${}`. Instead of `${variable-default}`, the shell may expand `${riable-default}`, or even `${fault}`. This bug can often be worked around by omitting the braces: `$variable`. The bug was fixed in 'ksh93g' (1998-04-30) but as of 2006 many operating systems were still shipping older versions with the bug.

Empty here-documents are not portable either; with the following code, **zsh** up to at least version 4.3.10 creates a file with a single newline, whereas other shells create an empty file:

```
cat >file <<EOF
EOF
```

Many shells (including the Bourne shell) implement here-documents inefficiently. In particular, some shells can be extremely inefficient when a single statement contains many here-documents. For instance if your 'configure.ac' includes something like:

```
if <cross_compiling>; then
  assume this and that
else
  check this
  check that
  check something else
  ...
  on and on forever
  ...
fi
```

A shell parses the whole `if/fi` construct, creating temporary files for each here-document in it. Some shells create links for such here-documents on every `fork`, so that the clean-up code they had installed correctly removes them. It is creating the links that can take the shell forever.

Moving the tests out of the `if/fi`, or creating multiple `if/fi` constructs, would improve the performance significantly. Anyway, this kind of construct is not exactly the typical use of Autoconf. In fact, it's even not recommended, because M4 macros can't look into shell conditionals, so we may fail to expand a macro when it was expanded before in a conditional path, and the condition turned out to be false at runtime, and we end up not executing the macro at all.

Be careful with the use of '<<-' to unindent here-documents. The behavior is only portable for stripping leading TABs, and things can silently break if an overzealous editor converts to using leading spaces (not all shells are nice enough to warn about unterminated here-documents).

```
$ printf 'cat <<-x\n\t1\n\t 2\n\tx\n' | bash && echo done
1
 2
done
$ printf 'cat <<-x\n 1\n  2\n x\n' | bash-3.2 && echo done
 1
  2
 x
done
```

11.4 File Descriptors

Most shells, if not all (including Bash, Zsh, Ash), output traces on stderr, even for subshells. This might result in undesirable content if you meant to capture the standard-error output of the inner command:

```
$ ash -x -c '(eval "echo foo >&2") 2>stderr'
$ cat stderr
+ eval echo foo >&2
+ echo foo
foo
$ bash -x -c '(eval "echo foo >&2") 2>stderr'
$ cat stderr
```

```
+ eval 'echo foo >&2'
++ echo foo
foo
$ zsh -x -c '(eval "echo foo >&2") 2>stderr'
# Traces on startup files deleted here.
$ cat stderr
+zsh:1> eval echo foo >&2
+zsh:1> echo foo
foo
```

One workaround is to grep out uninteresting lines, hoping not to remove good ones.

If you intend to redirect both standard error and standard output, redirect standard output first. This works better with HP-UX, since its shell mishandles tracing if standard error is redirected first:

```
$ sh -x -c ': 2>err >out'
+ :
+ 2> err $ cat err
1> out
```

Don't try to redirect the standard error of a command substitution. It must be done *inside* the command substitution. When running ': `cd /zorglub` 2>/dev/null' expect the error message to escape, while ': `cd /zorglub 2>/dev/null`' works properly.

On the other hand, some shells, such as Solaris or FreeBSD /bin/sh, warn about missing programs before performing redirections. Therefore, to silently check whether a program exists, it is necessary to perform redirections on a subshell or brace group:

```
$ /bin/sh -c 'nosuch 2>/dev/null'
nosuch: not found
$ /bin/sh -c '(nosuch) 2>/dev/null'
$ /bin/sh -c '{ nosuch; } 2>/dev/null'
$ bash -c 'nosuch 2>/dev/null'
```

FreeBSD 6.2 sh may mix the trace output lines from the statements in a shell pipeline.

It is worth noting that Zsh (but not Ash nor Bash) makes it possible in assignments though: 'foo=`cd /zorglub` 2>/dev/null'.

Some shells, like ash, don't recognize bi-directional redirection ('<>'). And even on shells that recognize it, it is not portable to use on fifos: Posix does not require read-write support for named pipes, and Cygwin does not support it:

```
$ mkfifo fifo
$ exec 5<>fifo
$ echo hi >&5
bash: echo: write error: Communication error on send
```

Furthermore, versions of dash before 0.5.6 mistakenly truncate regular files when using '<>':

```
$ echo a > file
$ bash -c ': 1<>file'; cat file
a
$ dash -c ': 1<>file'; cat file
$ rm a
```

When catering to old systems, don't redirect the same file descriptor several times, as you are doomed to failure under Ultrix.

```
ULTRIX V4.4 (Rev. 69) System #31: Thu Aug 10 19:42:23 GMT 1995
UWS V4.4 (Rev. 11)
$ eval 'echo matter >fullness' >void
illegal io
$ eval '(echo matter >fullness)' >void
illegal io
$ (eval '(echo matter >fullness)') >void
Ambiguous output redirect.
```

In each case the expected result is of course 'fullness' containing 'matter' and 'void' being empty. However, this bug is probably not of practical concern to modern platforms.

Solaris 10 sh will try to optimize away a : command (even if it is redirected) in a loop after the first iteration, or in a shell function after the first call:

```
$ for i in 1 2 3 ; do : >x$i; done
$ ls x*
x1
$ f () { : >$1; }; f y1; f y2; f y3;
$ ls y*
y1
```

As a workaround, echo or eval can be used.

Don't rely on file descriptors 0, 1, and 2 remaining closed in a subsidiary program. If any of these descriptors is closed, the operating system may open an unspecified file for the descriptor in the new process image. Posix 2008 says this may be done only if the subsidiary program is set-user-ID or set-group-ID, but HP-UX 11.23 does it even for ordinary programs, and the next version of Posix will allow HP-UX behavior.

If you want a file descriptor above 2 to be inherited into a child process, then you must use redirections specific to that command or a containing subshell or command group, rather than relying on exec in the shell. In ksh as well as HP-UX sh, file descriptors above 2 which are opened using 'exec n>file' are closed by a subsequent 'exec' (such as that involved in the fork-and-exec which runs a program or script):

```
$ echo 'echo hello >&5' >k
$ /bin/sh -c 'exec 5>t; ksh ./k; exec 5>&-; cat t
hello
$ bash -c 'exec 5>t; ksh ./k; exec 5>&-; cat t
hello
$ ksh -c 'exec 5>t; ksh ./k; exec 5>&-; cat t
./k[1]: 5: cannot open [Bad file number]
$ ksh -c '(ksh ./k) 5>t; cat t'
hello
$ ksh -c '{ ksh ./k; } 5>t; cat t'
hello
$ ksh -c '5>t ksh ./k; cat t
hello
```

Don't rely on duplicating a closed file descriptor to cause an error. With Solaris /bin/sh, failed duplication is silently ignored, which can cause unintended leaks to the original file descriptor. In this example, observe the leak to standard output:

```
$ bash -c 'echo hi >&3' 3>&-; echo $?
bash: 3: Bad file descriptor
1
$ /bin/sh -c 'echo hi >&3' 3>&-; echo $?
hi
0
```

Fortunately, an attempt to close an already closed file descriptor will portably succeed. Likewise, it is safe to use either style of 'n<&-' or 'n>&-' for closing a file descriptor, even if it doesn't match the read/write mode that the file descriptor was opened with.

DOS variants cannot rename or remove open files, such as in 'mv foo bar >foo' or 'rm foo >foo', even though this is perfectly portable among Posix hosts.

A few ancient systems reserved some file descriptors. By convention, file descriptor 3 was opened to '/dev/tty' when you logged into Eighth Edition (1985) through Tenth Edition Unix (1989). File descriptor 4 had a special use on the Stardent/Kubota Titan (circa 1990), though we don't now remember what it was. Both these systems are obsolete, so it's now safe to treat file descriptors 3 and 4 like any other file descriptors.

On the other hand, you can't portably use multi-digit file descriptors. Solaris ksh doesn't understand any file descriptor larger than '9':

```
$ bash -c 'exec 10>&-'; echo $?
0
$ ksh -c 'exec 9>&-'; echo $?
0
$ ksh -c 'exec 10>&-'; echo $?
ksh[1]: exec: 10: not found
127
```

11.5 Signal Handling

Portable handling of signals within the shell is another major source of headaches. This is worsened by the fact that various different, mutually incompatible approaches are possible in this area, each with its distinctive merits and demerits. A detailed description of these possible approaches, as well as of their pros and cons, can be found in this article.

Solaris 10 /bin/sh automatically traps most signals by default; the shell still exits with error upon termination by one of those signals, but in such a case the exit status might be somewhat unexpected (even if allowed by POSIX, strictly speaking):

```
$ bash -c 'kill -1 $$'; echo $? # Will exit 128 + (signal number).
Hangup
129
$ /bin/ksh -c 'kill -15 $$'; echo $? # Likewise.
Terminated
143
$ for sig in 1 2 3 15; do
```

```
>    echo $sig:
>    /bin/sh -c "kill -$s \$\$"; echo $?
> done
signal 1:
Hangup
129
signal 2:
208
signal 3:
208
signal 15:
208
```

This gets even worse if one is using the POSIX 'wait' interface to get details about the shell process terminations: it will result in the shell having exited normally, rather than by receiving a signal.

```
$ cat > foo.c <<'END'
#include <stdio.h>    /* for printf */
#include <stdlib.h>   /* for system */
#include <sys/wait.h> /* for WIF* macros */
int main(void)
{
  int status = system ("kill -15 $$");
  printf ("Terminated by signal: %s\n",
          WIFSIGNALED (status) ? "yes" : "no");
  printf ("Exited normally: %s\n",
          WIFEXITED (status) ? "yes" : "no");
  return 0;
}
END
$ cc -o foo foo.c
$ ./a.out # On GNU/Linux
Terminated by signal: no
Exited normally: yes
$ ./a.out # On Solaris 10
Terminated by signal: yes
Exited normally: no
```

Various shells seem to handle SIGQUIT specially: they ignore it even if it is not blocked, and even if the shell is not running interactively (in fact, even if the shell has no attached tty); among these shells are at least Bash (from version 2 onwards), Zsh 4.3.12, Solaris 10 /bin/ksh and /usr/xpg4/bin/sh, and AT&T ksh93 (2011). Still, SIGQUIT seems to be trappable quite portably within all these shells. OTOH, some other shells doesn't special-case the handling of SIGQUIT; among these shells are at least pdksh 5.2.14, Solaris 10 and NetBSD 5.1 /bin/sh, and the Almquist Shell 0.5.5.1.

Some shells (especially Korn shells and derivatives) might try to propagate to themselves a signal that has killed a child process; this is not a bug, but a conscious design choice (although its overall value might be debatable). The exact details of how this is attained vary from shell to shell. For example, upon running `perl -e 'kill 2, $$'`, after the perl process has been interrupted AT&T ksh93 (2011) will proceed to send itself a SIGINT, while Solaris 10 /bin/ksh and /usr/xpg4/bin/sh will proceed to exit with status 130 (i.e., 128 + 2). In any case, if there is an active trap associated with SIGINT, those shells will correctly execute it.

Some Korn shells, when a child process die due receiving a signal with signal number n, can leave in '$?' an exit status of $256+n$ instead of the more common $128+n$. Observe the difference between AT&T ksh93 (2011) and bash 4.1.5 on Debian:

```
$ /bin/ksh -c 'sh -c "kill -1 \$\$"; echo $?'
/bin/ksh: line 1: 7837: Hangup
257
$ /bin/bash -c 'sh -c "kill -1 \$\$"; echo $?'
/bin/bash: line 1:  7861 Hangup        (sh -c "kill -1 \$\$")
129
```

This ksh behavior is allowed by POSIX, if implemented with due care; see this Austin Group discussion for more background. However, if it is not implemented with proper care, such a behavior might cause problems in some corner cases. To see why, assume we have a "wrapper" script like this:

```
#!/bin/sh
# Ignore some signals in the shell only, not in its child processes.
trap : 1 2 13 15
wrapped_command "$@"
ret=$?
other_command
exit $ret
```

If wrapped_command is interrupted by a SIGHUP (which has signal number 1), ret will be set to 257. Unless the exit shell builtin is smart enough to understand that such a value can only have originated from a signal, and adjust the final wait status of the shell appropriately, the value 257 will just get truncated to 1 by the closing exit call, so that a caller of the script will have no way to determine that termination by a signal was involved. Observe the different behavior of AT&T ksh93 (2011) and bash 4.1.5 on Debian:

```
$ cat foo.sh
#!/bin/sh
sh -c 'kill -1 $$'
ret=$?
echo $ret
exit $ret
$ /bin/ksh foo.sh; echo $?
foo.sh: line 2: 12479: Hangup
257
1
$ /bin/bash foo.sh; echo $?
foo.sh: line 2: 12487 Hangup        (sh -c 'kill -1 $$')
129
129
```

11.6 File System Conventions

Autoconf uses shell-script processing extensively, so the file names that it processes should not contain characters that are special to the shell. Special characters include space, tab, newline, NUL, and the following:

```
" # $ & ' ( ) * ; < = > ? [ \ ` |
```

Also, file names should not begin with '~' or '-', and should contain neither '-' immediately after '/' nor '~' immediately after ':'. On Posix-like platforms, directory names should not contain ':', as this runs afoul of ':' used as the path separator.

These restrictions apply not only to the files that you distribute, but also to the absolute file names of your source, build, and destination directories.

On some Posix-like platforms, '!' and '^' are special too, so they should be avoided.

Posix lets implementations treat leading '//' specially, but requires leading '///' and beyond to be equivalent to '/'. Most Unix variants treat '//' like '/'. However, some treat '//' as a "super-root" that can provide access to files that are not otherwise reachable from '/'. The super-root tradition began with Apollo Domain/OS, which died out long ago, but unfortunately Cygwin has revived it.

While `autoconf` and friends are usually run on some Posix variety, they can be used on other systems, most notably DOS variants. This impacts several assumptions regarding file names.

For example, the following code:

```
case $foo_dir in
  /*) # Absolute
     ;;
  *)
     foo_dir=$dots$foo_dir ;;
esac
```

fails to properly detect absolute file names on those systems, because they can use a drivespec, and usually use a backslash as directory separator. If you want to be portable to DOS variants (at the price of rejecting valid but oddball Posix file names like 'a:\b'), you can check for absolute file names like this:

```
case $foo_dir in
  [\\/]* | ?:[\\/]* ) # Absolute
     ;;
  *)
     foo_dir=$dots$foo_dir ;;
esac
```

Make sure you quote the brackets if appropriate and keep the backslash as first character (see [Limitations of Shell Builtins], page 221).

Also, because the colon is used as part of a drivespec, these systems don't use it as path separator. When creating or accessing paths, you can use the `PATH_SEPARATOR` output variable instead. `configure` sets this to the appropriate value for the build system (':' or ';') when it starts up.

File names need extra care as well. While DOS variants that are Posixy enough to run `autoconf` (such as DJGPP) are usually able to handle long file names properly, there are still limitations that can seriously break packages. Several of these issues can be easily detected by the doschk package.

A short overview follows; problems are marked with SFN/LFN to indicate where they apply: SFN means the issues are only relevant to plain DOS, not to DOS under Microsoft Windows variants, while LFN identifies problems that exist even under Microsoft Windows variants.

No multiple dots (SFN)

> DOS cannot handle multiple dots in file names. This is an especially important thing to remember when building a portable configure script, as autoconf uses a .in suffix for template files.
>
> This is perfectly OK on Posix variants:
>
> ```
> AC_CONFIG_HEADERS([config.h])
> AC_CONFIG_FILES([source.c foo.bar])
> AC_OUTPUT
> ```
>
> but it causes problems on DOS, as it requires 'config.h.in', 'source.c.in' and 'foo.bar.in'. To make your package more portable to DOS-based environments, you should use this instead:
>
> ```
> AC_CONFIG_HEADERS([config.h:config.hin])
> AC_CONFIG_FILES([source.c:source.cin foo.bar:foobar.in])
> AC_OUTPUT
> ```

No leading dot (SFN)

> DOS cannot handle file names that start with a dot. This is usually not important for autoconf.

Case insensitivity (LFN)

> DOS is case insensitive, so you cannot, for example, have both a file called 'INSTALL' and a directory called 'install'. This also affects make; if there's a file called 'INSTALL' in the directory, 'make install' does nothing (unless the 'install' target is marked as PHONY).

The 8+3 limit (SFN)

> Because the DOS file system only stores the first 8 characters of the file name and the first 3 of the extension, those must be unique. That means that 'foobar-part1.c', 'foobar-part2.c' and 'foobar-prettybird.c' all resolve to the same file name ('FOOBAR-P.C'). The same goes for 'foo.bar' and 'foo.bartender'.
>
> The 8+3 limit is not usually a problem under Microsoft Windows, as it uses numeric tails in the short version of file names to make them unique. However, a registry setting can turn this behavior off. While this makes it possible to share file trees containing long file names between SFN and LFN environments, it also means the above problem applies there as well.

Invalid characters (LFN)

> Some characters are invalid in DOS file names, and should therefore be avoided. In a LFN environment, these are '/', '\', '?', '*', ':', '<', '>', '|' and '"'. In a SFN environment, other characters are also invalid. These include '+', ',', '[' and ']'.

Invalid names (LFN)

>Some DOS file names are reserved, and cause problems if you try to use files with those names. These names include 'CON', 'AUX', 'COM1', 'COM2', 'COM3', 'COM4', 'LPT1', 'LPT2', 'LPT3', 'NUL', and 'PRN'. File names are case insensitive, so even names like 'aux/config.guess' are disallowed.

11.7 Shell Pattern Matching

Nowadays portable patterns can use negated character classes like '[!-aeiou]'. The older syntax '[^-aeiou]' is supported by some shells but not others; hence portable scripts should never use '^' as the first character of a bracket pattern.

Outside the C locale, patterns like '[a-z]' are problematic since they may match characters that are not lower-case letters.

11.8 Shell Substitutions

Contrary to a persistent urban legend, the Bourne shell does not systematically split variables and back-quoted expressions, in particular on the right-hand side of assignments and in the argument of case. For instance, the following code:

```
case "$given_srcdir" in
.)  top_srcdir="`echo "$dots" | sed 's|/$||'`"  ;;
*)  top_srcdir="$dots$given_srcdir"  ;;
esac
```

is more readable when written as:

```
case $given_srcdir in
.)  top_srcdir=`echo "$dots" | sed 's|/$||'`  ;;
*)  top_srcdir=$dots$given_srcdir  ;;
esac
```

and in fact it is even *more* portable: in the first case of the first attempt, the computation of top_srcdir is not portable, since not all shells properly understand "`..."..."...`", for example Solaris 10 ksh:

```
$ foo="`echo " bar" | sed 's, ,,'`"
ksh:  : cannot execute
ksh: bar | sed 's, ,,': cannot execute
```

Posix does not specify behavior for this sequence. On the other hand, behavior for "`...\"...\"...`" is specified by Posix, but in practice, not all shells understand it the same way: pdksh 5.2.14 prints spurious quotes when in Posix mode:

```
$ echo "`echo \"hello\"`"
hello
$ set -o posix
$ echo "`echo \"hello\"`"
"hello"
```

There is just no portable way to use double-quoted strings inside double-quoted back-quoted expressions (pfew!).

Bash 4.1 has a bug where quoted empty strings adjacent to unquoted parameter expansions are elided during word splitting. Meanwhile, zsh does not perform word splitting except when in Bourne compatibility mode. In the example below, the correct behavior is to have five arguments to the function, and exactly two spaces on either side of the middle '-', since word splitting collapses multiple spaces in '$f' but leaves empty arguments intact.

```
$ bash -c 'n() { echo "$#$@"; }; f="  -  "; n - ""$f"" -'
3- - -
$ ksh -c 'n() { echo "$#$@"; }; f="  -  "; n - ""$f"" -'
5-  -  -
$ zsh -c 'n() { echo "$#$@"; }; f="  -  "; n - ""$f"" -'
3-  -  -
$ zsh -c 'emulate sh;
> n() { echo "$#$@"; }; f="  -  "; n - ""$f"" -'
5-  -  -
```

You can work around this by doing manual word splitting, such as using '"$str" $list' rather than '"$str"$list'.

There are also portability pitfalls with particular expansions:

$@   One of the most famous shell-portability issues is related to '"$@"'. When there are no positional arguments, Posix says that '"$@"' is supposed to be equivalent to nothing, but the original Unix version 7 Bourne shell treated it as equivalent to '""' instead, and this behavior survives in later implementations like Digital Unix 5.0.

The traditional way to work around this portability problem is to use '${1+"$@"}'. Unfortunately this method does not work with Zsh (3.x and 4.x), which is used on Mac OS X. When emulating the Bourne shell, Zsh performs word splitting on '${1+"$@"}':

```
zsh $ emulate sh
zsh $ for i in "$@"; do echo $i; done
Hello World
!
zsh $ for i in ${1+"$@"}; do echo $i; done
Hello
World
!
```

Zsh handles plain '"$@"' properly, but we can't use plain '"$@"' because of the portability problems mentioned above. One workaround relies on Zsh's "global aliases" to convert '${1+"$@"}' into '"$@"' by itself:

```
test "${ZSH_VERSION+set}" = set && alias -g '${1+"$@"}'='"$@"'
```

Zsh only recognizes this alias when a shell word matches it exactly; '"foo"${1+"$@"}' remains subject to word splitting. Since this case always yields at least one shell word, use plain '"$@"'.

A more conservative workaround is to avoid '"$@"' if it is possible that there may be no positional arguments. For example, instead of:

```
cat conftest.c "$@"
```

you can use this instead:

```
case $# in
```

```
0) cat conftest.c;;
*) cat conftest.c "$@";;
esac
```

Autoconf macros often use the **set** command to update '**$@**', so if you are writing shell code intended for **configure** you should not assume that the value of '**$@**' persists for any length of time.

${10}   The 10th, 11th, ... positional parameters can be accessed only after a **shift**. The 7th Edition shell reported an error if given ${10}, and Solaris 10 /bin/sh still acts that way:

```
$ set 1 2 3 4 5 6 7 8 9 10
$ echo ${10}
bad substitution
```

Conversely, not all shells obey the Posix rule that when braces are omitted, multiple digits beyond a '**$**' imply the single-digit positional parameter expansion concatenated with the remaining literal digits. To work around the issue, you must use braces.

```
$ bash -c 'set a b c d e f g h i j; echo $10 ${1}0'
a0 a0
$ dash -c 'set a b c d e f g h i j; echo $10 ${1}0'
j a0
```

${var:-value}
Old BSD shells, including the Ultrix **sh**, don't accept the colon for any shell substitution, and complain and die. Similarly for ${var:=value}, ${var:?value}, etc. However, all shells that support functions allow the use of colon in shell substitution, and since m4sh requires functions, you can portably use null variable substitution patterns in configure scripts.

${var+value}
When using '**${var-value}**' or '**${var-value}**' for providing alternate substitutions, *value* must either be a single shell word, quoted, or in the context of an unquoted here-document. Solaris /bin/sh complains otherwise.

```
$ /bin/sh -c 'echo ${a-b c}'
/bin/sh: bad substitution
$ /bin/sh -c 'echo ${a-'\''b c'\''}'
b c
$ /bin/sh -c 'echo "${a-b c}"'
b c
$ /bin/sh -c 'cat <<EOF
${a-b c}
EOF
b c
```

According to Posix, if an expansion occurs inside double quotes, then the use of unquoted double quotes within *value* is unspecified, and any single quotes become literal characters; in that case, escaping must be done with backslash. Likewise, the use of unquoted here-documents is a case where double quotes have unspecified results:

```
$ /bin/sh -c 'echo "${a-"b   c"}"'
/bin/sh: bad substitution
$ ksh -c 'echo "${a-"b   c"}"'
b c
$ bash -c 'echo "${a-"b   c"}"'
b   c
$ /bin/sh -c 'a=; echo ${a+'\''b   c'\''}'
b c
$ /bin/sh -c 'a=; echo "${a+'\''b   c'\''}"'
'b   c'
$ /bin/sh -c 'a=; echo "${a+\"b   c\"}"'
"b   c"
$ /bin/sh -c 'a=; echo "${a+b   c}"'
b c
$ /bin/sh -c 'cat <<EOF
${a-"b   c"}
EOF'
"b   c"
$ /bin/sh -c 'cat <<EOF
${a-'b   c'}
EOF'
'b   c'
$ bash -c 'cat <<EOF
${a-"b   c"}
EOF'
b   c
$ bash -c 'cat <<EOF
${a-'b   c'}
EOF'
'b   c'
```

Perhaps the easiest way to work around quoting issues in a manner portable
to all shells is to place the results in a temporary variable, then use '$t' as the
value, rather than trying to inline the expression needing quoting.

```
$ /bin/sh -c 't="b   c\"'\''\'\''}\\"; echo "${a-$t}"'
b   c"'\''}\
$ ksh -c 't="b   c\"'\''\'\''}\\"; echo "${a-$t}"'
b   c"'\''}\
$ bash -c 't="b   c\"'\''\'\''}\\"; echo "${a-$t}"'
b   c"'\''}\
```

${var=value}

When using '${var=value}' to assign a default value to *var*, remember that
even though the assignment to *var* does not undergo file name expansion, the
result of the variable expansion does unless the expansion occurred within double quotes. In particular, when using : followed by unquoted variable expansion
for the side effect of setting a default value, if the final value of '$var' contains
any globbing characters (either from *value* or from prior contents), the shell has

to spend time performing file name expansion and field splitting even though those results will not be used. Therefore, it is a good idea to consider double quotes when performing default initialization; while remembering how this impacts any quoting characters appearing in *value*.

```
$ time bash -c ': "${a=/usr/bin/*}"; echo "$a"'
/usr/bin/*

real 0m0.005s
user 0m0.002s
sys 0m0.003s
$ time bash -c ': ${a=/usr/bin/*}; echo "$a"'
/usr/bin/*

real 0m0.039s
user 0m0.026s
sys 0m0.009s
$ time bash -c 'a=/usr/bin/*; : ${a=noglob}; echo "$a"'
/usr/bin/*

real 0m0.031s
user 0m0.020s
sys 0m0.010s

$ time bash -c 'a=/usr/bin/*; : "${a=noglob}"; echo "$a"'
/usr/bin/*

real 0m0.006s
user 0m0.002s
sys 0m0.003s
```

As with '+' and '−', you must use quotes when using '=' if the *value* contains more than one shell word; either single quotes for just the *value*, or double quotes around the entire expansion:

```
$ : ${var1='Some words'}
$ : "${var2=like this}"
$ echo $var1 $var2
Some words like this
```

otherwise some shells, such as Solaris /bin/sh or on Digital Unix V 5.0, die because of a "bad substitution". Meanwhile, Posix requires that with '=', quote removal happens prior to the assignment, and the expansion be the final contents of *var* without quoting (and thus subject to field splitting), in contrast to the behavior with '−' passing the quoting through to the final expansion. However, bash 4.1 does not obey this rule.

```
$ ksh -c 'echo ${var-a\ \ b}'
a  b
$ ksh -c 'echo ${var=a\ \ b}'
a b
```

```
$ bash -c 'echo ${var=a\ \ b}'
a  b
```

Finally, Posix states that when mixing '${a=b}' with regular commands, it is unspecified whether the assignments affect the parent shell environment. It is best to perform assignments independently from commands, to avoid the problems demonstrated in this example:

```
$ bash -c 'x= y=${x:=b} sh -c "echo +\$x+\$y+";echo -$x-'
+b+b+
-b-
$ /bin/sh -c 'x= y=${x:=b} sh -c "echo +\$x+\$y+";echo -$x-'
++b+
--
$ ksh -c 'x= y=${x:=b} sh -c "echo +\$x+\$y+";echo -$x-'
+b+b+
--
```

${var=value}

> Solaris /bin/sh has a frightening bug in its handling of literal assignments. Imagine you need set a variable to a string containing '}'. This '}' character confuses Solaris /bin/sh when the affected variable was already set. This bug can be exercised by running:

```
$ unset foo
$ foo=${foo='}'}
$ echo $foo
}
$ foo=${foo='}'     # no error; this hints to what the bug is
$ echo $foo
}
$ foo=${foo='}'}
$ echo $foo
}}
  ^ ugh!
```

> It seems that '}' is interpreted as matching '${', even though it is enclosed in single quotes. The problem doesn't happen using double quotes, or when using a temporary variable holding the problematic string.

${var=expanded-value}

> On Ultrix, running

```
default="yu,yaa"
: ${var="$default"}
```

> sets var to 'M-yM-uM-,M-yM-aM-a', i.e., the 8th bit of each char is set. You don't observe the phenomenon using a simple 'echo $var' since apparently the shell resets the 8th bit when it expands $var. Here are two means to make this shell confess its sins:

```
$ cat -v <<EOF
$var
EOF
```

and

```
$ set | grep '^var=' | cat -v
```

One classic incarnation of this bug is:

```
default="a b c"
: ${list="$default"}
for c in $list; do
  echo $c
done
```

You'll get 'a b c' on a single line. Why? Because there are no spaces in '$list': there are 'M- ', i.e., spaces with the 8th bit set, hence no IFS splitting is performed!!!

One piece of good news is that Ultrix works fine with ': ${list=$default}'; i.e., if you *don't* quote. The bad news is then that QNX 4.25 then sets *list* to the *last* item of *default*!

The portable way out consists in using a double assignment, to switch the 8th bit twice on Ultrix:

```
list=${list="$default"}
```

. . . but beware of the '}' bug from Solaris (see above). For safety, use:

```
test "${var+set}" = set || var={value}
```

${#var}
${var%word}
${var%%word}
${var#word}
${var##word}

Posix requires support for these usages, but they do not work with many traditional shells, e.g., Solaris 10 /bin/sh.

Also, pdksh 5.2.14 mishandles some *word* forms. For example if '$1' is 'a/b' and '$2' is 'a', then '${1#$2}' should yield '/b', but with pdksh it yields the empty string.

`commands`

Posix requires shells to trim all trailing newlines from command output before substituting it, so assignments like 'dir=`echo "$file" | tr a A`' do not work as expected if '$file' ends in a newline.

While in general it makes no sense, do not substitute a single builtin with side effects, because Ash 0.2, trying to optimize, does not fork a subshell to perform the command.

For instance, if you wanted to check that **cd** is silent, do not use 'test -z "`cd /`"' because the following can happen:

```
$ pwd
/tmp
$ test -z "`cd /`" && pwd
/
```

The result of 'foo=`exit 1`' is left as an exercise to the reader.

The MSYS shell leaves a stray byte in the expansion of a double-quoted command substitution of a native program, if the end of the substitution is not aligned with the end of the double quote. This may be worked around by inserting another pair of quotes:

```
$ echo "`printf 'foo\r\n'` bar" > broken
$ echo "`printf 'foo\r\n'`"" bar" | cmp - broken
- broken differ: char 4, line 1
```

Upon interrupt or SIGTERM, some shells may abort a command substitution, replace it with a null string, and wrongly evaluate the enclosing command before entering the trap or ending the script. This can lead to spurious errors:

```
$ sh -c 'if test `sleep 5; echo hi` = hi; then echo yes; fi'
$ ^C
sh: test: hi: unexpected operator/operand
```

You can avoid this by assigning the command substitution to a temporary variable:

```
$ sh -c 'res=`sleep 5; echo hi`
         if test "x$res" = xhi; then echo yes; fi'
$ ^C
```

$(commands)

This construct is meant to replace '`commands`', and it has most of the problems listed under '`commands`'.

This construct can be nested while this is impossible to do portably with back quotes. Unfortunately it is not yet universally supported. Most notably, even recent releases of Solaris don't support it:

```
$ showrev -c /bin/sh | grep version
Command version: SunOS 5.10 Generic 121005-03 Oct 2006
$ echo $(echo blah)
syntax error: '(' unexpected
```

nor does IRIX 6.5's Bourne shell:

```
$ uname -a
IRIX firebird-image 6.5 07151432 IP22
$ echo $(echo blah)
$(echo blah)
```

If you do use '$(commands)', make sure that the commands do not start with a parenthesis, as that would cause confusion with a different notation '$((expression))' that in modern shells is an arithmetic expression not a command. To avoid the confusion, insert a space between the two opening parentheses.

Avoid *commands* that contain unbalanced parentheses in here-documents, comments, or case statement patterns, as many shells mishandle them. For example, Bash 3.1, 'ksh88', pdksh 5.2.14, and Zsh 4.2.6 all mishandle the following valid command:

```
echo $(case x in x) echo hello;; esac)
```

`$((`*expression*`))`

Arithmetic expansion is not portable as some shells (most notably Solaris 10 /bin/sh) don't support it.

Among shells that do support '`$(( ))`', not all of them obey the Posix rule that octal and hexadecimal constants must be recognized:

```
$ bash -c 'echo $(( 010 + 0x10 ))'
24
$ zsh -c 'echo $(( 010 + 0x10 ))'
26
$ zsh -c 'emulate sh; echo $(( 010 + 0x10 ))'
24
$ pdksh -c 'echo $(( 010 + 0x10 ))'
pdksh:  010 + 0x10 : bad number '0x10'
$ pdksh -c 'echo $(( 010 ))'
10
```

When it is available, using arithmetic expansion provides a noticeable speedup in script execution; but testing for support requires `eval` to avoid syntax errors. The following construct is used by `AS_VAR_ARITH` to provide arithmetic computation when all arguments are provided in decimal and without a leading zero, and all operators are properly quoted and appear as distinct arguments:

```
if ( eval 'test $(( 1 + 1 )) = 2' ) 2>/dev/null; then
  eval 'func_arith ()
  {
    func_arith_result=$(( $* ))
  }'
else
  func_arith ()
  {
    func_arith_result=`expr "$@"`
  }
fi
func_arith 1 + 1
foo=$func_arith_result
```

^   Always quote '`^`', otherwise traditional shells such as /bin/sh on Solaris 10 treat this like '`|`'.

11.9 Assignments

When setting several variables in a row, be aware that the order of the evaluation is undefined. For instance '`foo=1 foo=2; echo $foo`' gives '1' with Solaris /bin/sh, but '2' with Bash. You must use ';' to enforce the order: '`foo=1; foo=2; echo $foo`'.

Don't rely on the following to find '`subdir/program`':

```
PATH=subdir$PATH_SEPARATOR$PATH program
```

as this does not work with Zsh 3.0.6. Use something like this instead:

```
(PATH=subdir$PATH_SEPARATOR$PATH; export PATH; exec program)
```

Don't rely on the exit status of an assignment: Ash 0.2 does not change the status and propagates that of the last statement:

```
$ false || foo=bar; echo $?
1
$ false || foo=':'; echo $?
0
```

and to make things even worse, QNX 4.25 just sets the exit status to 0 in any case:

```
$ foo='exit 1'; echo $?
0
```

To assign default values, follow this algorithm:

1. If the default value is a literal and does not contain any closing brace, use:

   ```
   : "${var='my literal'}"
   ```

2. If the default value contains no closing brace, has to be expanded, and the variable being initialized is not intended to be IFS-split (i.e., it's not a list), then use:

   ```
   : ${var="$default"}
   ```

3. If the default value contains no closing brace, has to be expanded, and the variable being initialized is intended to be IFS-split (i.e., it's a list), then use:

   ```
   var=${var="$default"}
   ```

4. If the default value contains a closing brace, then use:

   ```
   test "${var+set}" = set || var="has a '}'"
   ```

In most cases 'var=${var="$default"}' is fine, but in case of doubt, just use the last form. See Section 11.8 [Shell Substitutions], page 201, items '${var:-value}' and '${var=value}' for the rationale.

11.10 Parentheses in Shell Scripts

Beware of two opening parentheses in a row, as many shell implementations treat them specially, and Posix says that a portable script cannot use '((' outside the '$((' form used for shell arithmetic. In traditional shells, '((cat))' behaves like '(cat)'; but many shells, including Bash and the Korn shell, treat '((cat))' as an arithmetic expression equivalent to 'let "cat"', and may or may not report an error when they detect that 'cat' is not a number. As another example, 'pdksh' 5.2.14 does not treat the following code as a traditional shell would:

```
if ((true) || false); then
   echo ok
fi
```

To work around this problem, insert a space between the two opening parentheses. There is a similar problem and workaround with '$(('; see Section 11.8 [Shell Substitutions], page 201.

11.11 Slashes in Shell Scripts

Unpatched Tru64 5.1 sh omits the last slash of command-line arguments that contain two trailing slashes:

```
$ echo / // /// //// .// //.
/ / // /// ./ //.
$ x=//
$ eval "echo \$x"
/
$ set -x
$ echo abc | tr -t ab //
+ echo abc
+ tr -t ab /
/bc
```

Unpatched Tru64 4.0 **sh** adds a slash after '"**$var**"' if the variable is empty and the second double-quote is followed by a word that begins and ends with slash:

```
$ sh -xc 'p=; echo "$p"/ouch/'
p=
+ echo //ouch/
//ouch/
```

However, our understanding is that patches are available, so perhaps it's not worth worrying about working around these horrendous bugs.

11.12 Special Shell Variables

Some shell variables should not be used, since they can have a deep influence on the behavior of the shell. In order to recover a sane behavior from the shell, some variables should be unset; M4sh takes care of this and provides fallback values, whenever needed, to cater for a very old '/bin/sh' that does not support **unset**. (see Chapter 11 [Portable Shell Programming], page 189).

As a general rule, shell variable names containing a lower-case letter are safe; you can define and use these variables without worrying about their effect on the underlying system, and without worrying about whether the shell changes them unexpectedly. (The exception is the shell variable **status**, as described below.)

Here is a list of names that are known to cause trouble. This list is not exhaustive, but you should be safe if you avoid the name **status** and names containing only upper-case letters and underscores.

?   Not all shells correctly reset '**$?**' after conditionals (see [Limitations of Shell Builtins], page 227). Not all shells manage '**$?**' correctly in shell functions (see Section 11.13 [Shell Functions], page 218) or in traps (see [Limitations of Shell Builtins], page 233). Not all shells reset '**$?**' to zero after an empty command.

```
$ bash -c 'false; $empty; echo $?'
0
$ zsh -c 'false; $empty; echo $?'
1
```

_   Many shells reserve '**$_**' for various purposes, e.g., the name of the last command executed.

BIN_SH   In Tru64, if BIN_SH is set to **xpg4**, subsidiary invocations of the standard shell conform to Posix.

CDPATH   When this variable is set it specifies a list of directories to search when invoking
            `cd` with a relative file name that did not start with '`./`' or '`../`'. Posix 1003.1-
            2001 says that if a nonempty directory name from `CDPATH` is used successfully,
            `cd` prints the resulting absolute file name. Unfortunately this output can break
            idioms like '`abs=`cd src && pwd``' because `abs` receives the name twice. Also,
            many shells do not conform to this part of Posix; for example, `zsh` prints the
            result only if a directory name other than '`.`' was chosen from `CDPATH`.

            In practice the shells that have this problem also support `unset`, so you can
            work around the problem as follows:

            > (unset CDPATH) >/dev/null 2>&1 && unset CDPATH

            You can also avoid output by ensuring that your directory name is absolute or
            anchored at '`./`', as in '`abs=`cd ./src && pwd``'.

            Configure scripts use M4sh, which automatically unsets `CDPATH` if possible, so
            you need not worry about this problem in those scripts.

CLICOLOR_FORCE
            When this variable is set, some implementations of tools like `ls` attempt to
            add color to their output via terminal escape sequences, even when the output
            is not directed to a terminal, and can thus cause spurious failures in scripts.
            Configure scripts use M4sh, which automatically unsets this variable.

DUALCASE   In the MKS shell, case statements and file name generation are case-insensitive
            unless `DUALCASE` is nonzero. Autoconf-generated scripts export this variable
            when they start up.

ENV
MAIL
MAILPATH
PS1
PS2
PS4   These variables should not matter for shell scripts, since they are supposed to
            affect only interactive shells. However, at least one shell (the pre-3.0 UWIN
            Korn shell) gets confused about whether it is interactive, which means that
            (for example) a `PS1` with a side effect can unexpectedly modify '`$?`'. To work
            around this bug, M4sh scripts (including '`configure`' scripts) do something like
            this:

            > (unset ENV) >/dev/null 2>&1 && unset ENV MAIL MAILPATH
            > PS1='$ '
            > PS2='> '
            > PS4='+ '

            (actually, there is some complication due to bugs in `unset`; see [Limitations of
            Shell Builtins], page 234).

FPATH   The Korn shell uses `FPATH` to find shell functions, so avoid `FPATH` in portable
            scripts. `FPATH` is consulted after `PATH`, but you still need to be wary of tests
            that use `PATH` to find whether a command exists, since they might report the
            wrong result if `FPATH` is also set.

GREP_OPTIONS
> When this variable is set, some implementations of **grep** honor these options, even if the options include direction to enable colored output via terminal escape sequences, and the result can cause spurious failures when the output is not directed to a terminal. Configure scripts use M4sh, which automatically unsets this variable.

IFS
> Long ago, shell scripts inherited **IFS** from the environment, but this caused many problems so modern shells ignore any environment settings for **IFS**.
>
> Don't set the first character of **IFS** to backslash. Indeed, Bourne shells use the first character (backslash) when joining the components in '"$@"' and some shells then reinterpret (!) the backslash escapes, so you can end up with backspace and other strange characters.
>
> The proper value for **IFS** (in regular code, not when performing splits) is 'SPCTABRET'. The first character is especially important, as it is used to join the arguments in '$*'; however, note that traditional shells, but also bash-2.04, fail to adhere to this and join with a space anyway.
>
> M4sh guarantees that **IFS** will have the default value at the beginning of a script, and many macros within autoconf rely on this setting. It is okay to use blocks of shell code that temporarily change the value of **IFS** in order to split on another character, but remember to restore it before expanding further macros.
>
> Unsetting **IFS** instead of resetting it to the default sequence is not suggested, since code that tries to save and restore the variable's value will incorrectly reset it to an empty value, thus disabling field splitting:
>
> ```
> unset IFS
> # default separators used for field splitting
>
> save_IFS=$IFS
> IFS=:
> # ...
> IFS=$save_IFS
> # no field splitting performed
> ```

LANG
LC_ALL
LC_COLLATE
LC_CTYPE
LC_MESSAGES
LC_MONETARY
LC_NUMERIC
LC_TIME
> You should set all these variables to 'C' because so much configuration code assumes the C locale and Posix requires that locale environment variables be set to 'C' if the C locale is desired; '**configure**' scripts and M4sh do that for you. Export these variables after setting them.

LANGUAGE

LANGUAGE is not specified by Posix, but it is a GNU extension that overrides LC_ALL in some cases, so you (or M4sh) should set it too.

LC_ADDRESS
LC_IDENTIFICATION
LC_MEASUREMENT
LC_NAME
LC_PAPER
LC_TELEPHONE

These locale environment variables are GNU extensions. They are treated like their Posix brethren (LC_COLLATE, etc.) as described above.

LINENO   Most modern shells provide the current line number in LINENO. Its value is the line number of the beginning of the current command. M4sh, and hence Autoconf, attempts to execute configure with a shell that supports LINENO. If no such shell is available, it attempts to implement LINENO with a Sed prepass that replaces each instance of the string $LINENO (not followed by an alphanumeric character) with the line's number. In M4sh scripts you should execute AS_LINENO_PREPARE so that these workarounds are included in your script; configure scripts do this automatically in AC_INIT.

You should not rely on LINENO within eval or shell functions, as the behavior differs in practice. The presence of a quoted newline within simple commands can alter which line number is used as the starting point for $LINENO substitutions within that command. Also, the possibility of the Sed prepass means that you should not rely on $LINENO when quoted, when in here-documents, or when line continuations are used. Subshells should be OK, though. In the following example, lines 1, 9, and 14 are portable, but the other instances of $LINENO do not have deterministic values:

```
$ cat lineno
echo 1. $LINENO
echo "2. $LINENO
3. $LINENO"
cat <<EOF
5. $LINENO
6. $LINENO
7. \$LINENO
EOF
( echo 9. $LINENO )
eval 'echo 10. $LINENO'
eval 'echo 11. $LINENO
echo 12. $LINENO'
echo 13. '$LINENO'
echo 14. $LINENO '
15.' $LINENO
f () { echo $1 $LINENO;
echo $1 $LINENO }
f 18.
echo 19. \
$LINENO
$ bash-3.2 ./lineno
1. 1
2. 3
3. 3
5. 4
6. 4
7. $LINENO
9. 9
10. 10
11. 12
12. 13
13. $LINENO
14. 14
15. 14
18. 16
18. 17
19. 19
```

```
$ zsh-4.3.4 ./lineno
1.  1
2.  2
3.  2
5.  4
6.  4
7.  $LINENO
9.  9
10. 1
11. 1
12. 2
13. $LINENO
14. 14
15. 14
18. 0
18. 1
19. 19
$ pdksh-5.2.14 ./lineno
1.  1
2.  2
3.  2
5.  4
6.  4
7.  $LINENO
9.  9
10. 0
11. 0
12. 0
13. $LINENO
14. 14
15. 14
18. 16
18. 17
19. 19
```

```
$ sed '=' <lineno |
>   sed '
>     N
>     s,$,-,
>     t loop
>     :loop
>     s,^\([0-9]*\)\(.*\)[$]LINENO\([^a-zA-Z0-9_]\),\1\2\1\3,
>     t loop
>     s,-$,,
>     s,^[0-9]*\n,,
>   ' |
>   sh
1.  1
2.  2
3.  3
5.  5
6.  6
7.  \7
9.  9
10. 10
11. 11
12. 12
13. 13
14. 14
15. 15
18. 16
18. 17
19. 20
```

In particular, note that 'config.status' (and any other subsidiary script created by AS_INIT_GENERATED) might report line numbers relative to the parent script as a result of the potential Sed pass.

NULLCMD   When executing the command '>foo', zsh executes '$NULLCMD >foo' unless it is operating in Bourne shell compatibility mode and the zsh version is newer than 3.1.6-dev-18. If you are using an older zsh and forget to set NULLCMD, your script might be suspended waiting for data on its standard input.

options   For zsh 4.3.10, options is treated as an associative array even after emulate sh, so it should not be used.

PATH_SEPARATOR
           On DJGPP systems, the PATH_SEPARATOR environment variable can be set to either ':' or ';' to control the path separator Bash uses to set up certain environment variables (such as PATH). You can set this variable to ';' if you want configure to use ';' as a separator; this might be useful if you plan to use non-Posix shells to execute files. See Section 11.6 [File System Conventions], page 199, for more information about PATH_SEPARATOR.

POSIXLY_CORRECT

In the GNU environment, exporting `POSIXLY_CORRECT` with any value (even empty) causes programs to try harder to conform to Posix. Autoconf does not directly manipulate this variable, but `bash` ties the shell variable `POSIXLY_CORRECT` to whether the script is running in Posix mode. Therefore, take care when exporting or unsetting this variable, so as not to change whether `bash` is in Posix mode.

```
$ bash --posix -c 'set -o | grep posix
> unset POSIXLY_CORRECT
> set -o | grep posix'
posix           on
posix           off
```

PWD

Posix 1003.1-2001 requires that `cd` and `pwd` must update the `PWD` environment variable to point to the logical name of the current directory, but traditional shells do not support this. This can cause confusion if one shell instance maintains `PWD` but a subsidiary and different shell does not know about `PWD` and executes `cd`; in this case `PWD` points to the wrong directory. Use ``pwd`` rather than '$PWD'.

RANDOM

Many shells provide `RANDOM`, a variable that returns a different integer each time it is used. Most of the time, its value does not change when it is not used, but on IRIX 6.5 the value changes all the time. This can be observed by using `set`. It is common practice to use $RANDOM as part of a file name, but code shouldn't rely on $RANDOM expanding to a nonempty string.

status

This variable is an alias to '$?' for `zsh` (at least 3.1.6), hence read-only. Do not use it.

11.13 Shell Functions

Nowadays, it is difficult to find a shell that does not support shell functions at all. However, some differences should be expected.

When declaring a shell function, you must include whitespace between the ')' after the function name and the start of the compound expression, to avoid upsetting `ksh`. While it is possible to use any compound command, most scripts use '{...}'.

```
$ /bin/sh -c 'a(){ echo hi;}; a'
hi
$ ksh -c 'a(){ echo hi;}; a'
ksh: syntax error at line 1: '}' unexpected
$ ksh -c 'a() { echo hi;}; a'
hi
```

Inside a shell function, you should not rely on the error status of a subshell if the last command of that subshell was `exit` or `trap`, as this triggers bugs in zsh 4.x; while Autoconf tries to find a shell that does not exhibit the bug, zsh might be the only shell present on the user's machine.

Likewise, the state of '$?' is not reliable when entering a shell function. This has the effect that using a function as the first command in a `trap` handler can cause problems.

```
$ bash -c 'foo() { echo $?; }; trap foo 0; (exit 2); exit 2'; echo $?
2
2
$ ash -c 'foo() { echo $?; }; trap foo 0; (exit 2); exit 2'; echo $?
0
2
```

DJGPP bash 2.04 has a bug in that **return** from a shell function which also used a command substitution causes a segmentation fault. To work around the issue, you can use **return** from a subshell, or 'AS_SET_STATUS' as last command in the execution flow of the function (see Section 9.1 [Common Shell Constructs], page 167).

Not all shells treat shell functions as simple commands impacted by 'set -e', for example with Solaris 10 /bin/sh:

```
$ bash -c 'f() { return 1; }; set -e; f; echo oops'
$ /bin/sh -c 'f() { return 1; }; set -e; f; echo oops'
oops
```

Shell variables and functions may share the same namespace, for example with Solaris 10 /bin/sh:

```
$ f () { :; }; f=; f
f: not found
```

For this reason, Autoconf (actually M4sh, see Chapter 9 [Programming in M4sh], page 167) uses the prefix 'as_fn_' for its functions.

Handling of positional parameters and shell options varies among shells. For example, Korn shells reset and restore trace output ('set -x') and other options upon function entry and exit. Inside a function, IRIX sh sets '$0' to the function name.

It is not portable to pass temporary environment variables to shell functions. Solaris /bin/sh does not see the variable. Meanwhile, not all shells follow the Posix rule that the assignment must affect the current environment in the same manner as special built-ins.

```
$ /bin/sh -c 'func() { echo $a;}; a=1 func; echo $a'
⇒
⇒
$ ash -c 'func() { echo $a;}; a=1 func; echo $a'
⇒1
⇒
$ bash -c 'set -o posix; func() { echo $a;}; a=1 func; echo $a'
⇒1
⇒1
```

Some ancient Bourne shell variants with function support did not reset '$i, i >= 0', upon function exit, so effectively the arguments of the script were lost after the first function invocation. It is probably not worth worrying about these shells any more.

With AIX sh, a **trap** on 0 installed in a shell function triggers at function exit rather than at script exit. See [Limitations of Shell Builtins], page 233.

11.14 Limitations of Shell Builtins

No, no, we are serious: some shells do have limitations! :)

You should always keep in mind that any builtin or command may support options, and therefore differ in behavior with arguments starting with a dash. For instance, even the innocent 'echo "$word"' can give unexpected results when `word` starts with a dash. It is often possible to avoid this problem using 'echo "x$word"', taking the 'x' into account later in the pipe. Many of these limitations can be worked around using M4sh (see Chapter 9 [Programming in M4sh], page 167).

.   Use . only with regular files (use 'test -f'). Bash 2.03, for instance, chokes on '. /dev/null'. Remember that . uses PATH if its argument contains no slashes. Also, some shells, including bash 3.2, implicitly append the current directory to this PATH search, even though Posix forbids it. So if you want to use . on a file 'foo' in the current directory, you must use '. ./foo'.

Not all shells gracefully handle syntax errors within a sourced file. On one extreme, some non-interactive shells abort the entire script. On the other, `zsh` 4.3.10 has a bug where it fails to react to the syntax error.

```
$ echo 'fi' > syntax
$ bash -c '. ./syntax; echo $?'
./syntax: line 1: syntax error near unexpected token 'fi'
./syntax: line 1: 'fi'
1
$ ash -c '. ./syntax; echo $?'
./syntax: 1: Syntax error: "fi" unexpected
$ zsh -c '. ./syntax; echo $?'
./syntax:1: parse error near 'fi'
0
```

!   The Unix version 7 shell did not support negating the exit status of commands with !, and this feature is still absent from some shells (e.g., Solaris /bin/sh). Other shells, such as FreeBSD /bin/sh or `ash`, have bugs when using !:

```
$ sh -c '! : | :'; echo $?
1
$ ash -c '! : | :'; echo $?
0
$ sh -c '! { :; }'; echo $?
1
$ ash -c '! { :; }'; echo $?
{: not found
Syntax error: "}" unexpected
2
```

Shell code like this:

```
if ! cmp file1 file2 >/dev/null 2>&1; then
  echo files differ or trouble
fi
```

is therefore not portable in practice. Typically it is easy to rewrite such code, e.g.:

```
cmp file1 file2 >/dev/null 2>&1 ||
  echo files differ or trouble
```

More generally, one can always rewrite '! *command*' as:

```
if command; then (exit 1); else :; fi
```

{...}   Bash 3.2 (and earlier versions) sometimes does not properly set '$?' when failing to write redirected output of a compound command. This problem is most commonly observed with '{...}'; it does not occur with '(...)'. For example:

```
$ bash -c '{ echo foo; } >/bad; echo $?'
bash: line 1: /bad: Permission denied
0
$ bash -c 'while :; do echo; done >/bad; echo $?'
bash: line 1: /bad: Permission denied
0
```

To work around the bug, prepend ':;':

```
$ bash -c ':;{ echo foo; } >/bad; echo $?'
bash: line 1: /bad: Permission denied
1
```

Posix requires a syntax error if a brace list has no contents. However, not all shells obey this rule; and on shells where empty lists are permitted, the effect on '$?' is inconsistent. To avoid problems, ensure that a brace list is never empty.

```
$ bash -c 'false; { }; echo $?' || echo $?
bash: line 1: syntax error near unexpected token '}'
bash: line 1: 'false; { }; echo $?'
2
$ zsh -c 'false; { }; echo $?' || echo $?
1
$ pdksh -c 'false; { }; echo $?' || echo $?
0
```

break   The use of 'break 2' etc. is safe.

case   You don't need to quote the argument; no splitting is performed.

You don't need the final ';;', but you should use it.

Posix requires support for case patterns with opening parentheses like this:

```
case $file_name in
  (*.c) echo "C source code";;
esac
```

but the (in this example is not portable to many Bourne shell implementations, which is a pity for those of us using tools that rely on balanced parentheses. For instance, with Solaris /bin/sh:

```
$ case foo in (foo) echo foo;; esac
error syntax error: '(' unexpected
```

The leading '(' can be omitted safely. Unfortunately, there are contexts where unbalanced parentheses cause other problems, such as when using a syntax-highlighting editor that searches for the balancing counterpart, or more importantly, when using a case statement as an underquoted argument to an Autoconf macro. See Section 8.1.7 [Balancing Parentheses], page 129, for tradeoffs involved in various styles of dealing with unbalanced ')'.

Zsh handles pattern fragments derived from parameter expansions or command substitutions as though quoted:

```
$ pat=\?; case aa in ?$pat) echo match;; esac
$ pat=\?; case a? in ?$pat) echo match;; esac
match
```

Because of a bug in its fnmatch, Bash fails to properly handle backslashes in character classes:

```
bash-2.02$ case /tmp in [/\\]*) echo OK;; esac
bash-2.02$
```

This is extremely unfortunate, since you are likely to use this code to handle Posix or MS-DOS absolute file names. To work around this bug, always put the backslash first:

```
bash-2.02$ case '\TMP' in [\\/]*) echo OK;; esac
OK
bash-2.02$ case /tmp in [\\/]*) echo OK;; esac
OK
```

Many Bourne shells cannot handle closing brackets in character classes correctly.

Some shells also have problems with backslash escaping in case you do not want to match the backslash: both a backslash and the escaped character match this pattern. To work around this, specify the character class in a variable, so that quote removal does not apply afterwards, and the special characters don't have to be backslash-escaped:

```
$ case '\' in [\<]) echo OK;; esac
OK
$ scanset='[<]'; case '\' in $scanset) echo OK;; esac
$
```

Even with this, Solaris ksh matches a backslash if the set contains any of the characters '|', '&', '(', or ')'.

Conversely, Tru64 ksh (circa 2003) erroneously always matches a closing parenthesis if not specified in a character class:

```
$ case foo in *\)*) echo fail ;; esac
fail
$ case foo in *')'*) echo fail ;; esac
fail
```

Some shells, such as Ash 0.3.8, are confused by an empty case/esac:

```
ash-0.3.8 $ case foo in esac;
error Syntax error: ";" unexpected (expecting ")")
```

Posix requires `case` to give an exit status of 0 if no cases match. However, `/bin/sh` in Solaris 10 does not obey this rule. Meanwhile, it is unclear whether a case that matches, but contains no statements, must also change the exit status to 0. The M4sh macro `AS_CASE` works around these inconsistencies.

```
$ bash -c 'case 'false' in ?) ;; esac; echo $?'
0
$ /bin/sh -c 'case 'false' in ?) ;; esac; echo $?'
255
```

cd Posix 1003.1-2001 requires that `cd` must support the '-L' ("logical") and '-P' ("physical") options, with '-L' being the default. However, traditional shells do not support these options, and their `cd` command has the '-P' behavior.

Portable scripts should assume neither option is supported, and should assume neither behavior is the default. This can be a bit tricky, since the Posix default behavior means that, for example, 'ls ..' and 'cd ..' may refer to different directories if the current logical directory is a symbolic link. It is safe to use `cd` *dir* if *dir* contains no '..' components. Also, Autoconf-generated scripts check for this problem when computing variables like `ac_top_srcdir` (see Section 4.6 [Configuration Actions], page 21), so it is safe to `cd` to these variables.

Posix states that behavior is undefined if `cd` is given an explicit empty argument. Some shells do nothing, some change to the first entry in `CDPATH`, some change to `HOME`, and some exit the shell rather than returning an error. Unfortunately, this means that if '$var' is empty, then 'cd "$var"' is less predictable than 'cd $var' (at least the latter is well-behaved in all shells at changing to `HOME`, although this is probably not what you wanted in a script). You should check that a directory name was supplied before trying to change locations.

See Section 11.12 [Special Shell Variables], page 211, for portability problems involving `cd` and the `CDPATH` environment variable. Also please see the discussion of the `pwd` command.

echo The simple `echo` is probably the most surprising source of portability troubles. It is not possible to use 'echo' portably unless both options and escape sequences are omitted. Don't expect any option.

Do not use backslashes in the arguments, as there is no consensus on their handling. For 'echo '\n' | wc -l', the `sh` of Solaris outputs 2, but Bash and Zsh (in `sh` emulation mode) output 1. The problem is truly `echo`: all the shells understand ''\n'' as the string composed of a backslash and an 'n'. Within a command substitution, 'echo 'string\c'' will mess up the internal state of ksh88 on AIX 6.1 so that it will print the first character 's' only, followed by a newline, and then entirely drop the output of the next echo in a command substitution.

Because of these problems, do not pass a string containing arbitrary characters to `echo`. For example, 'echo "$foo"' is safe only if you know that *foo*'s value cannot contain backslashes and cannot start with '-'.

If this may not be true, `printf` is in general safer and easier to use than `echo` and `echo -n`. Thus, scripts where portability is not a major concern should use `printf '%s\n'` whenever echo could fail, and similarly use `printf %s` instead of `echo -n`. For portable shell scripts, instead, it is suggested to use a here-document like this:

```
cat <<EOF
$foo
EOF
```

Alternatively, M4sh provides `AS_ECHO` and `AS_ECHO_N` macros which choose between various portable implementations: 'echo' or 'print' where they work, `printf` if it is available, or else other creative tricks in order to work around the above problems.

eval   The `eval` command is useful in limited circumstances, e.g., using commands like 'eval table_$key=\$value' and 'eval value=table_$key' to simulate a hash table when the key is known to be alphanumeric.

You should also be wary of common bugs in `eval` implementations. In some shell implementations (e.g., older `ash`, OpenBSD 3.8 `sh`, `pdksh` v5.2.14 99/07/13.2, and `zsh` 4.2.5), the arguments of 'eval' are evaluated in a context where '$?' is 0, so they exhibit behavior like this:

```
$ false; eval 'echo $?'
0
```

The correct behavior here is to output a nonzero value, but portable scripts should not rely on this.

You should not rely on `LINENO` within `eval`. See Section 11.12 [Special Shell Variables], page 211.

Note that, even though these bugs are easily avoided, `eval` is tricky to use on arbitrary arguments. It is obviously unwise to use 'eval $cmd' if the string value of 'cmd' was derived from an untrustworthy source. But even if the string value is valid, 'eval $cmd' might not work as intended, since it causes field splitting and file name expansion to occur twice, once for the `eval` and once for the command itself. It is therefore safer to use 'eval "$cmd"'. For example, if *cmd* has the value 'cat test?.c', 'eval $cmd' might expand to the equivalent of 'cat test;.c' if there happens to be a file named 'test;.c' in the current directory; and this in turn mistakenly attempts to invoke `cat` on the file 'test' and then execute the command .c. To avoid this problem, use 'eval "$cmd"' rather than 'eval $cmd'.

However, suppose that you want to output the text of the evaluated command just before executing it. Assuming the previous example, 'echo "Executing: $cmd"' outputs 'Executing: cat test?.c', but this output doesn't show the user that 'test;.c' is the actual name of the copied file. Conversely, 'eval "echo Executing: $cmd"' works on this example, but it fails with 'cmd='cat foo >bar'', since it mistakenly replaces the contents of 'bar' by the string 'cat foo'. No simple, general, and portable solution to this problem is known.

exec   Posix describes several categories of shell built-ins. Special built-ins (such as `exit`) must impact the environment of the current shell, and need not be available through `exec`. All other built-ins are regular, and must not propagate variable assignments to the environment of the current shell. However, the group of regular built-ins is further distinguished by commands that do not require a `PATH` search (such as `cd`), in contrast to built-ins that are offered as a more efficient version of something that must still be found in a `PATH` search (such as `echo`). Posix is not clear on whether `exec` must work with the list of 17 utilities that are invoked without a `PATH` search, and many platforms lack an executable for some of those built-ins:

```
$ sh -c 'exec cd /tmp'
sh: line 0: exec: cd: not found
```

All other built-ins that provide utilities specified by Posix must have a counterpart executable that exists on `PATH`, although Posix allows `exec` to use the built-in instead of the executable. For example, contrast `bash` 3.2 and `pdksh` 5.2.14:

```
$ bash -c 'pwd --version' | head -n1
bash: line 0: pwd: --: invalid option
pwd: usage: pwd [-LP]
$ bash -c 'exec pwd --version' | head -n1
pwd (GNU coreutils) 6.10
$ pdksh -c 'exec pwd --version' | head -n1
pdksh: pwd: --: unknown option
```

When it is desired to avoid a regular shell built-in, the workaround is to use some other forwarding command, such as `env` or `nice`, that will ensure a path search:

```
$ pdksh -c 'exec true --version' | head -n1
$ pdksh -c 'nice true --version' | head -n1
true (GNU coreutils) 6.10
$ pdksh -c 'env true --version' | head -n1
true (GNU coreutils) 6.10
```

`exit`   The default value of `exit` is supposed to be $?; unfortunately, some shells, such as the DJGPP port of Bash 2.04, just perform 'exit 0'.

```
bash-2.04$ foo=`exit 1` || echo fail
fail
bash-2.04$ foo=`(exit 1)` || echo fail
fail
bash-2.04$ foo=`(exit 1); exit` || echo fail
bash-2.04$
```

Using 'exit $?' restores the expected behavior.

Some shell scripts, such as those generated by `autoconf`, use a trap to clean up before exiting. If the last shell command exited with nonzero status, the trap also exits with nonzero status so that the invoker can tell that an error occurred.

Unfortunately, in some shells, such as Solaris `/bin/sh`, an exit trap ignores the `exit` command's argument. In these shells, a trap cannot determine whether it was invoked by plain `exit` or by `exit 1`. Instead of calling `exit` directly, use the `AC_MSG_ERROR` macro that has a workaround for this problem.

export   The builtin `export` dubs a shell variable *environment variable*. Each update of exported variables corresponds to an update of the environment variables. Conversely, each environment variable received by the shell when it is launched should be imported as a shell variable marked as exported.

Alas, many shells, such as Solaris `/bin/sh`, IRIX 6.3, IRIX 5.2, AIX 4.1.5, and Digital Unix 4.0, forget to `export` the environment variables they receive. As a result, two variables coexist: the environment variable and the shell variable. The following code demonstrates this failure:

```
#!/bin/sh
echo $FOO
FOO=bar
echo $FOO
exec /bin/sh $0
```

when run with 'FOO=foo' in the environment, these shells print alternately 'foo' and 'bar', although they should print only 'foo' and then a sequence of 'bar's.

Therefore you should `export` again each environment variable that you update; the export can occur before or after the assignment.

Posix is not clear on whether the **export** of an undefined variable causes the variable to be defined with the value of an empty string, or merely marks any future definition of a variable by that name for export. Various shells behave differently in this regard:

```
$ sh -c 'export foo; env | grep foo'
$ ash -c 'export foo; env | grep foo'
foo=
```

Posix requires `export` to honor assignments made as arguments, but older shells do not support this, including `/bin/sh` in Solaris 10. Portable scripts should separate assignments and exports into different statements.

```
$ bash -c 'export foo=bar; echo $foo'
bar
$ /bin/sh -c 'export foo=bar; echo $foo'
/bin/sh: foo=bar: is not an identifier
$ /bin/sh -c 'export foo; foo=bar; echo $foo'
bar
```

false   Don't expect `false` to exit with status 1: in native Solaris '`/bin/false`' exits with status 255.

for   To loop over positional arguments, use:

```
for arg
do
  echo "$arg"
done
```

You may *not* leave the `do` on the same line as `for`, since some shells improperly grok:

```
for arg; do
  echo "$arg"
```

```
done
```

If you want to explicitly refer to the positional arguments, given the '$@' bug (see Section 11.8 [Shell Substitutions], page 201), use:

```
for arg in ${1+"$@"}; do
  echo "$arg"
done
```

But keep in mind that Zsh, even in Bourne shell emulation mode, performs word splitting on '${1+"$@"}'; see Section 11.8 [Shell Substitutions], page 201, item '$@', for more.

In Solaris /bin/sh, when the list of arguments of a for loop starts with *unquoted* tokens looking like variable assignments, the loop is not executed on those tokens:

```
$ /bin/sh -c 'for v in a=b c=d x e=f; do echo $v; done'
x
e=f
```

Thankfully, quoting the assignment-like tokens, or starting the list with other tokens (including unquoted variable expansion that results in an assignment-like result), avoids the problem, so it is easy to work around:

```
$ /bin/sh -c 'for v in "a=b"; do echo $v; done'
a=b
$ /bin/sh -c 'x=a=b; for v in $x c=d; do echo $v; done'
a=b
c=d
```

if   Using '!' is not portable. Instead of:

```
if ! cmp -s file file.new; then
  mv file.new file
fi
```

use:

```
if cmp -s file file.new; then :; else
  mv file.new file
fi
```

Or, especially if the *else* branch is short, you can use ||. In M4sh, the AS_IF macro provides an easy way to write these kinds of conditionals:

```
AS_IF([cmp -s file file.new], [], [mv file.new file])
```

This is especially useful in other M4 macros, where the *then* and *else* branches might be macro arguments.

Some very old shells did not reset the exit status from an if with no else:

```
$ if (exit 42); then true; fi; echo $?
42
```

whereas a proper shell should have printed '0'. But this is no longer a portability problem; any shell that supports functions gets it correct. However, it explains why some makefiles have lengthy constructs:

```
        if test -f "$file"; then
          install "$file" "$dest"
        else
          :
        fi
```

printf A format string starting with a '-' can cause problems. Bash interprets it as an option and gives an error. And '--' to mark the end of options is not good in the NetBSD Almquist shell (e.g., 0.4.6) which takes that literally as the format string. Putting the '-' in a '%c' or '%s' is probably easiest:

```
        printf %s -foo
```

Bash 2.03 mishandles an escape sequence that happens to evaluate to '%':

```
        $ printf '\045'
        bash: printf: '%': missing format character
```

Large outputs may cause trouble. On Solaris 2.5.1 through 10, for example, '/usr/bin/printf' is buggy, so when using /bin/sh the command 'printf %010000x 123' normally dumps core.

Since printf is not always a shell builtin, there is a potential speed penalty for using printf '%s\n' as a replacement for an echo that does not interpret '\' or leading '-'. With Solaris ksh, it is possible to use print -r -- for this role instead.

See [Limitations of Shell Builtins], page 223, for a discussion of portable alternatives to both printf and echo.

pwd With modern shells, plain pwd outputs a "logical" directory name, some of whose components may be symbolic links. These directory names are in contrast to "physical" directory names, whose components are all directories.

Posix 1003.1-2001 requires that pwd must support the '-L' ("logical") and '-P' ("physical") options, with '-L' being the default. However, traditional shells do not support these options, and their pwd command has the '-P' behavior.

Portable scripts should assume neither option is supported, and should assume neither behavior is the default. Also, on many hosts '/bin/pwd' is equivalent to 'pwd -P', but Posix does not require this behavior and portable scripts should not rely on it.

Typically it's best to use plain pwd. On modern hosts this outputs logical directory names, which have the following advantages:

- Logical names are what the user specified.
- Physical names may not be portable from one installation host to another due to network file system gymnastics.
- On modern hosts 'pwd -P' may fail due to lack of permissions to some parent directory, but plain pwd cannot fail for this reason.

Also please see the discussion of the cd command.

read No options are portable, not even support '-r' (Solaris /bin/sh for example). Tru64/OSF 5.1 sh treats read as a special built-in, so it may exit if input is redirected from a non-existent or unreadable file.

`set`   With the FreeBSD 6.0 shell, the `set` command (without any options) does not
sort its output.

The `set` builtin faces the usual problem with arguments starting with a dash.
Modern shells such as Bash or Zsh understand '--' to specify the end of the
options (any argument after '--' is a parameter, even '-x' for instance), but
many traditional shells (e.g., Solaris 10 `/bin/sh`) simply stop option processing
as soon as a non-option argument is found. Therefore, use '`dummy`' or simply
'`x`' to end the option processing, and use `shift` to pop it out:

```
set x $my_list; shift
```

Avoid '`set -`', e.g., '`set - $my_list`'. Posix no longer requires support for this
command, and in traditional shells '`set - $my_list`' resets the '-v' and '-x'
options, which makes scripts harder to debug.

Some nonstandard shells do not recognize more than one option (e.g., '`set -e`
`-x`' assigns '-x' to the command line). It is better to combine them:

```
set -ex
```

The option '-e' has historically been underspecified, with enough ambiguities
to cause numerous differences across various shell implementations; see for example this overview, or this link, documenting a change to Posix 2008 to match
`ksh88` behavior. Note that mixing `set -e` and shell functions is asking for
surprises:

```
set -e
doit()
{
  rm file
  echo one
}
doit || echo two
```

According to the recommendation, '`one`' should always be output regardless of
whether the `rm` failed, because it occurs within the body of the shell function
'`doit`' invoked on the left side of '||', where the effects of '`set -e`' are not
enforced. Likewise, '`two`' should never be printed, since the failure of `rm` does
not abort the function, such that the status of '`doit`' is 0.

The BSD shell has had several problems with the '-e' option. Older versions of
the BSD shell (circa 1990) mishandled '&&', '||', '`if`', and '`case`' when '-e' was
in effect, causing the shell to exit unexpectedly in some cases. This was particularly a problem with makefiles, and led to circumlocutions like '`sh -c 'test -f`
`file || touch file'`', where the seemingly-unnecessary '`sh -c '...'`' wrapper works around the bug (see Section 12.2 [Failure in Make Rules], page 253).

Even relatively-recent versions of the BSD shell (e.g., OpenBSD 3.4) wrongly
exit with '-e' if the last command within a compound statement fails and is
guarded by an '&&' only. For example:

```
#! /bin/sh
set -e
foo=''
test -n "$foo" && exit 1
```

```
echo one
if :; then
  test -n "$foo" && exit 1
  echo two
  test -n "$foo" && exit 1
fi
echo three
```

does not print 'three'. One workaround is to change the last instance of 'test -n "$foo" && exit 1' to be 'if test -n "$foo"; then exit 1; fi' instead. Another possibility is to warn BSD users not to use 'sh -e'.

When 'set -e' is in effect, a failed command substitution in Solaris /bin/sh cannot be ignored, even with '||'.

```
$ /bin/sh -c 'set -e; foo=`false` || echo foo; echo bar'
$ bash -c 'set -e; foo=`false` || echo foo; echo bar'
foo
bar
```

Moreover, a command substitution, successful or not, causes this shell to exit from a failing outer command even in presence of an '&&' list:

```
$ bash -c 'set -e; false `true` && echo notreached; echo ok'
ok
$ sh -c 'set -e; false `true` && echo notreached; echo ok'
$
```

Portable scripts should not use 'set -e' if trap is used to install an exit handler. This is because Tru64/OSF 5.1 sh sometimes enters the trap handler with the exit status of the command prior to the one that triggered the errexit handler:

```
$ sh -ec 'trap '\''echo $?'\'' 0; false'
0
$ sh -c 'set -e; trap '\''echo $?'\'' 0; false'
1
```

Thus, when writing a script in M4sh, rather than trying to rely on 'set -e', it is better to append '|| AS_EXIT' to any statement where it is desirable to abort on failure.

Job control is not provided by all shells, so the use of 'set -m' or 'set -b' must be done with care. When using zsh in native mode, asynchronous notification ('set -b') is enabled by default, and using 'emulate sh' to switch to Posix mode does not clear this setting (although asynchronous notification has no impact unless job monitoring is also enabled). Also, zsh 4.3.10 and earlier have a bug where job control can be manipulated in interactive shells, but not in subshells or scripts. Furthermore, some shells, like pdksh, fail to treat subshells as interactive, even though the parent shell was.

```
$ echo $ZSH_VERSION
4.3.10
$ set -m; echo $?
0
$ zsh -c 'set -m; echo $?'
```

```
set: can't change option: -m
$ (set -m); echo $?
set: can't change option: -m
1
$ pdksh -ci 'echo $-; (echo $-)'
cim
c
```

Use of `set -n` (typically via `sh -n script`) to validate a script is not foolproof. Modern `ksh93` tries to be helpful by informing you about better syntax, but switching the script to use the suggested syntax in order to silence the warnings would render the script no longer portable to older shells:

```
$ ksh -nc '``'
ksh: warning: line 1: '...' obsolete, use $(...)
0
```

Furthermore, on ancient hosts, such as SunOS 4, `sh -n` could go into an infinite loop; even with that bug fixed, Solaris 8 `/bin/sh` takes extremely long to parse large scripts. Autoconf itself uses `sh -n` within its testsuite to check that correct scripts were generated, but only after first probing for other shell features (such as `test -n "${BASH_VERSION+set}"`) that indicate a reasonably fast and working implementation.

`shift`
Not only is `shift`ing a bad idea when there is nothing left to shift, but in addition it is not portable: the shell of MIPS RISC/OS 4.52 refuses to do it.

Don't use '`shift 2`' etc.; while it in the SVR1 shell (1983), it is also absent in many pre-Posix shells.

`source`
This command is not portable, as Posix does not require it; use . instead.

`test`
The `test` program is the way to perform many file and string tests. It is often invoked by the alternate name '`[`', but using that name in Autoconf code is asking for trouble since it is an M4 quote character.

The '`-a`', '`-o`', '`(`', and '`)`' operands are not present in all implementations, and have been marked obsolete by Posix 2008. This is because there are inherent ambiguities in using them. For example, '`test "$1" -a "$2"`' looks like a binary operator to check whether two strings are both non-empty, but if '`$1`' is the literal '`!`', then some implementations of `test` treat it as a negation of the unary operator '`-a`'.

Thus, portable uses of `test` should never have more than four arguments, and scripts should use shell constructs like '`&&`' and '`||`' instead. If you combine '`&&`' and '`||`' in the same statement, keep in mind that they have equal precedence, so it is often better to parenthesize even when this is redundant. For example:

```
# Not portable:
test "X$a" = "X$b" -a \
  '(' "X$c" != "X$d" -o "X$e" = "X$f" ')'

# Portable:
test "X$a" = "X$b" &&
  { test "X$c" != "X$d" || test "X$e" = "X$f"; }
```

`test` does not process options like most other commands do; for example, it does not recognize the '`--`' argument as marking the end of options.

It is safe to use '`!`' as a `test` operator. For example, '`if test ! -d foo; ...`' is portable even though '`if ! test -d foo; ...`' is not.

test (files)

To enable `configure` scripts to support cross-compilation, they shouldn't do anything that tests features of the build system instead of the host system. But occasionally you may find it necessary to check whether some arbitrary file exists. To do so, use '`test -f`', '`test -r`', or '`test -x`'. Do not use '`test -e`', because Solaris 10 `/bin/sh` lacks it. To test for symbolic links on systems that have them, use '`test -h`' rather than '`test -L`'; either form conforms to Posix 1003.1-2001, but older shells like Solaris 8 `/bin/sh` support only '`-h`'.

For historical reasons, Posix reluctantly allows implementations of '`test -x`' that will succeed for the root user, even if no execute permissions are present. Furthermore, shells do not all agree on whether Access Control Lists should affect '`test -r`', '`test -w`', and '`test -x`'; some shells base test results strictly on the current user id compared to file owner and mode, as if by `stat(2)`; while other shells base test results on whether the current user has the given right, even if that right is only granted by an ACL, as if by `faccessat(2)`. Furthermore, there is a classic time of check to time of use race between any use of `test` followed by operating on the just-checked file. Therefore, it is a good idea to write scripts that actually attempt an operation, and are prepared for the resulting failure if permission is denied, rather than trying to avoid an operation based solely on whether `test` guessed that it might not be permitted.

test (strings)

Posix says that '`test "string"`' succeeds if *string* is not null, but this usage is not portable to traditional platforms like Solaris 10 `/bin/sh`, which mishandle strings like '`!`' and '`-n`'.

Posix also says that '`test ! "string"`', '`test -n "string"`' and '`test -z "string"`' work with any string, but many shells (such as Solaris, AIX 3.2, UNICOS 10.0.0.6, Digital Unix 4, etc.) get confused if *string* looks like an operator:

```
$ test -n =
test: argument expected
$ test ! -n
test: argument expected
$ test -z ")"; echo $?
0
```

Similarly, Posix says that both '`test "string1" = "string2"`' and '`test "string1" != "string2"`' work for any pairs of strings, but in practice this is not true for troublesome strings that look like operators or parentheses, or that begin with '`-`'.

It is best to protect such strings with a leading '`X`', e.g., '`test "Xstring" != X`' rather than '`test -n "string"`' or '`test ! "string"`'.

It is common to find variations of the following idiom:

```
test -n "`echo $ac_feature | sed 's/[-a-zA-Z0-9_]//g'`" &&
  action
```

to take an action when a token matches a given pattern. Such constructs should be avoided by using:

```
case $ac_feature in
  *[!-a-zA-Z0-9_]*) action;;
esac
```

If the pattern is a complicated regular expression that cannot be expressed as a shell pattern, use something like this instead:

```
expr "X$ac_feature" : 'X.*[^-a-zA-Z0-9_]' >/dev/null &&
  action
```

'expr "X*foo*" : "X*bar*"' is more robust than 'echo "X*foo*" | grep "^X*bar*"', because it avoids problems when '*foo*' contains backslashes.

trap   It is safe to trap at least the signals 1, 2, 13, and 15. You can also trap 0, i.e., have the **trap** run when the script ends (either via an explicit **exit**, or the end of the script). The trap for 0 should be installed outside of a shell function, or AIX 5.3 **/bin/sh** will invoke the trap at the end of this function.

Posix says that 'trap − 1 2 13 15' resets the traps for the specified signals to their default values, but many common shells (e.g., Solaris **/bin/sh**) misinterpret this and attempt to execute a "command" named − when the specified conditions arise. Posix 2008 also added a requirement to support 'trap 1 2 13 15' to reset traps, as this is supported by a larger set of shells, but there are still shells like **dash** that mistakenly try to execute 1 instead of resetting the traps. Therefore, there is no portable workaround, except for 'trap − 0', for which 'trap '' 0' is a portable substitute.

Although Posix is not absolutely clear on this point, it is widely admitted that when entering the trap '$?' should be set to the exit status of the last command run before the trap. The ambiguity can be summarized as: "when the trap is launched by an **exit**, what is the *last* command run: that before **exit**, or **exit** itself?"

Bash considers **exit** to be the last command, while Zsh and Solaris **/bin/sh** consider that when the trap is run it is *still* in the **exit**, hence it is the previous exit status that the trap receives:

```
$ cat trap.sh
trap 'echo $?' 0
(exit 42); exit 0
$ zsh trap.sh
42
$ bash trap.sh
0
```

The portable solution is then simple: when you want to 'exit 42', run '(exit 42); exit 42', the first **exit** being used to set the exit status to 42 for Zsh, and the second to trigger the trap and pass 42 as exit status for Bash. In M4sh, this is covered by using **AS_EXIT**.

The shell in FreeBSD 4.0 has the following bug: '$?' is reset to 0 by empty lines if the code is inside trap.

```
$ trap 'false

echo $?' 0
$ exit
0
```

Fortunately, this bug only affects trap.

Several shells fail to execute an exit trap that is defined inside a subshell, when the last command of that subshell is not a builtin. A workaround is to use 'exit $?' as the shell builtin.

```
$ bash -c '(trap "echo hi" 0; /bin/true)'
hi
$ /bin/sh -c '(trap "echo hi" 0; /bin/true)'
$ /bin/sh -c '(trap "echo hi" 0; /bin/true; exit $?)'
hi
```

Likewise, older implementations of bash failed to preserve '$?' across an exit trap consisting of a single cleanup command.

```
$ bash -c 'trap "/bin/true" 0; exit 2'; echo $?
2
$ bash-2.05b -c 'trap "/bin/true" 0; exit 2'; echo $?
0
$ bash-2.05b -c 'trap ":; /bin/true" 0; exit 2'; echo $?
2
```

true   Don't worry: as far as we know true is portable. Nevertheless, it's not always a builtin (e.g., Bash 1.x), and the portable shell community tends to prefer using :. This has a funny side effect: when asked whether false is more portable than true Alexandre Oliva answered:

> In a sense, yes, because if it doesn't exist, the shell will produce an exit status of failure, which is correct for false, but not for true.

Remember that even though ':' ignores its arguments, it still takes time to compute those arguments. It is a good idea to use double quotes around any arguments to ':' to avoid time spent in field splitting and file name expansion.

unset   In some nonconforming shells (e.g., Solaris 10 /bin/ksh and /usr/xpg4/bin/sh, NetBSD 5.99.43 sh, or Bash 2.05a), unset FOO fails when FOO is not set. This can interfere with set -e operation. You can use

```
FOO=; unset FOO
```

if you are not sure that FOO is set.

A few ancient shells lack unset entirely. For some variables such as PS1, you can use a neutralizing value instead:

```
PS1='$ '
```

Usually, shells that do not support unset need less effort to make the environment sane, so for example is not a problem if you cannot unset CDPATH on

those shells. However, Bash 2.01 mishandles unset MAIL and unset MAILPATH
in some cases and dumps core. So, you should do something like

```
( (unset MAIL) || exit 1) >/dev/null 2>&1 && unset MAIL || :
```

See Section 11.12 [Special Shell Variables], page 211, for some neutralizing
values. Also, see [Limitations of Builtins], page 225, for the case of environment
variables.

wait   The exit status of wait is not always reliable.

11.15 Limitations of Usual Tools

The small set of tools you can expect to find on any machine can still include some limitations you should be aware of.

awk   Don't leave white space before the opening parenthesis in a user function call.
Posix does not allow this and GNU Awk rejects it:

```
$ gawk 'function die () { print "Aaaaarg!"  }
        BEGIN { die () }'
gawk: cmd. line:2:         BEGIN { die () }
gawk: cmd. line:2:                         ^ parse error
$ gawk 'function die () { print "Aaaaarg!"  }
        BEGIN { die() }'
Aaaaarg!
```

Posix says that if a program contains only 'BEGIN' actions, and contains no
instances of getline, then the program merely executes the actions without
reading input. However, traditional Awk implementations (such as Solaris 10
awk) read and discard input in this case. Portable scripts can redirect input
from '/dev/null' to work around the problem. For example:

```
awk 'BEGIN {print "hello world"}' </dev/null
```

Posix says that in an 'END' action, '$NF' (and presumably, '$1') retain their
value from the last record read, if no intervening 'getline' occurred. However,
some implementations (such as Solaris 10 '/usr/bin/awk', 'nawk', or Darwin
'awk') reset these variables. A workaround is to use an intermediate variable
prior to the 'END' block. For example:

```
$ cat end.awk
{ tmp = $1 }
END { print "a", $1, $NF, "b", tmp }
$ echo 1 | awk -f end.awk
a    b 1
$ echo 1 | gawk -f end.awk
a 1 1 b 1
```

If you want your program to be deterministic, don't depend on for on arrays:

```
$ cat for.awk
END {
  arr["foo"] = 1
  arr["bar"] = 1
  for (i in arr)
```

```
        print i
    }
$ gawk -f for.awk </dev/null
foo
bar
$ nawk -f for.awk </dev/null
bar
foo
```

Some Awk implementations, such as HP-UX 11.0's native one, mishandle anchors:

```
$ echo xfoo | $AWK '/foo|^bar/ { print }'
$ echo bar | $AWK '/foo|^bar/ { print }'
bar
$ echo xfoo | $AWK '/^bar|foo/ { print }'
xfoo
$ echo bar | $AWK '/^bar|foo/ { print }'
bar
```

Either do not depend on such patterns (i.e., use '/^(.*foo|bar)/', or use a simple test to reject such implementations.

On 'ia64-hp-hpux11.23', Awk mishandles printf conversions after %u:

```
$ awk 'BEGIN { printf "%u %d\n", 0, -1 }'
0 0
```

AIX version 5.2 has an arbitrary limit of 399 on the length of regular expressions and literal strings in an Awk program.

Traditional Awk implementations derived from Unix version 7, such as Solaris /bin/awk, have many limitations and do not conform to Posix. Nowadays AC_PROG_AWK (see Section 5.2.1 [Particular Programs], page 43) finds you an Awk that doesn't have these problems, but if for some reason you prefer not to use AC_PROG_AWK you may need to address them. For more detailed descriptions, see Section "awk language history" in *GNU Awk User's Guide*.

Traditional Awk does not support multidimensional arrays or user-defined functions.

Traditional Awk does not support the '-v' option. You can use assignments after the program instead, e.g., $AWK '{print v $1}' v=x; however, don't forget that such assignments are not evaluated until they are encountered (e.g., after any BEGIN action).

Traditional Awk does not support the keywords delete or do.

Traditional Awk does not support the expressions a?b:c, !a, a^b, or a^=b.

Traditional Awk does not support the predefined CONVFMT or ENVIRON variables.

Traditional Awk supports only the predefined functions exp, index, int, length, log, split, sprintf, sqrt, and substr.

Traditional Awk getline is not at all compatible with Posix; avoid it.

Traditional Awk has for (i in a) ... but no other uses of the in keyword. For example, it lacks if (i in a) ....

In code portable to both traditional and modern Awk, FS must be a string containing just one ordinary character, and similarly for the field-separator argument to split.

Traditional Awk has a limit of 99 fields in a record. Since some Awk implementations, like Tru64's, split the input even if you don't refer to any field in the script, to circumvent this problem, set 'FS' to an unusual character and use split.

Traditional Awk has a limit of at most 99 bytes in a number formatted by OFMT; for example, OFMT="%.300e"; print 0.1; typically dumps core.

The original version of Awk had a limit of at most 99 bytes per split field, 99 bytes per substr substring, and 99 bytes per run of non-special characters in a printf format, but these bugs have been fixed on all practical hosts that we know of.

HP-UX 11.00 and IRIX 6.5 Awk require that input files have a line length of at most 3070 bytes.

basename   Not all hosts have a working basename. You can use expr instead.

cat   Don't rely on any option.

cc   The command 'cc -c foo.c' traditionally produces an object file named 'foo.o'. Most compilers allow '-c' to be combined with '-o' to specify a different object file name, but Posix does not require this combination and a few compilers lack support for it. See Section 5.10.3 [C Compiler], page 80, for how GNU Make tests for this feature with AC_PROG_CC_C_O.

When a compilation such as 'cc -o foo foo.c' fails, some compilers (such as CDS on Reliant Unix) leave a 'foo.o'.

HP-UX cc doesn't accept '.S' files to preprocess and assemble. 'cc -c foo.S' appears to succeed, but in fact does nothing.

The default executable, produced by 'cc foo.c', can be

- 'a.out' — usual Posix convention.
- 'b.out' — i960 compilers (including gcc).
- 'a.exe' — DJGPP port of gcc.
- 'a_out.exe' — GNV cc wrapper for DEC C on OpenVMS.
- 'foo.exe' — various MS-DOS compilers.

The C compiler's traditional name is cc, but other names like gcc are common. Posix 1003.1-2001 specifies the name c99, but older Posix editions specified c89 and anyway these standard names are rarely used in practice. Typically the C compiler is invoked from makefiles that use '$(CC)', so the value of the 'CC' make variable selects the compiler name.

chgrp
chown   It is not portable to change a file's group to a group that the owner does not belong to.

chmod   Avoid usages like 'chmod -w file'; use 'chmod a-w file' instead, for two reasons. First, plain '-w' does not necessarily make the file unwritable, since it does not affect mode bits that correspond to bits in the file mode creation mask. Second, Posix says that the '-w' might be interpreted as an implementation-specific option, not as a mode; Posix suggests using 'chmod -- -w file' to avoid this confusion, but unfortunately '--' does not work on some older hosts.

cmp
    cmp performs a raw data comparison of two files, while diff compares two text files. Therefore, if you might compare DOS files, even if only checking whether two files are different, use diff to avoid spurious differences due to differences of newline encoding.

cp
    Avoid the '-r' option, since Posix 1003.1-2004 marks it as obsolescent and its behavior on special files is implementation-defined. Use '-R' instead. On GNU hosts the two options are equivalent, but on Solaris hosts (for example) cp -r reads from pipes instead of replicating them. AIX 5.3 cp -R may corrupt its own memory with some directory hierarchies and error out or dump core:

```
mkdir -p 12345678/12345678/12345678/12345678
touch 12345678/12345678/x
cp -R 12345678 t
cp: 0653-440 12345678/12345678/: name too long.
```

Some cp implementations (e.g., BSD/OS 4.2) do not allow trailing slashes at the end of nonexistent destination directories. To avoid this problem, omit the trailing slashes. For example, use 'cp -R source /tmp/newdir' rather than 'cp -R source /tmp/newdir/' if '/tmp/newdir' does not exist.

The ancient SunOS 4 cp does not support '-f', although its mv does.

Traditionally, file timestamps had 1-second resolution, and 'cp -p' copied the timestamps exactly. However, many modern file systems have timestamps with 1-nanosecond resolution. Unfortunately, some older 'cp -p' implementations truncate timestamps when copying files, which can cause the destination file to appear to be older than the source. The exact amount of truncation depends on the resolution of the system calls that cp uses. Traditionally this was utime, which has 1-second resolution. Less-ancient cp implementations such as GNU Core Utilities 5.0.91 (2003) use utimes, which has 1-microsecond resolution. Modern implementations such as GNU Core Utilities 6.12 (2008) can set timestamps to the full nanosecond resolution, using the modern system calls futimens and utimensat when they are available. As of 2011, though, many platforms do not yet fully support these new system calls.

Bob Proulx notes that 'cp -p' always *tries* to copy ownerships. But whether it actually does copy ownerships or not is a system dependent policy decision implemented by the kernel. If the kernel allows it then it happens. If the kernel does not allow it then it does not happen. It is not something cp itself has control over.

In Unix System V any user can chown files to any other user, and System V also has a non-sticky '/tmp'. That probably derives from the heritage of System V in a business environment without hostile users. BSD changed this to be a more secure model where only root can chown files and a sticky '/tmp' is used. That undoubtedly derives from the heritage of BSD in a campus environment.

GNU/Linux and Solaris by default follow BSD, but can be configured to allow a System V style **chown**. On the other hand, HP-UX follows System V, but can be configured to use the modern security model and disallow **chown**. Since it is an administrator-configurable parameter you can't use the name of the kernel as an indicator of the behavior.

date   Some versions of **date** do not recognize special '%' directives, and unfortunately, instead of complaining, they just pass them through, and exit with success:

```
$ uname -a
OSF1 medusa.sis.pasteur.fr V5.1 732 alpha
$ date "+%s"
%s
```

diff   Option '-u' is nonportable.

Some implementations, such as Tru64's, fail when comparing to '/dev/null'. Use an empty file instead.

dirname   Not all hosts have a working **dirname**, and you should instead use **AS_DIRNAME** (see Chapter 9 [Programming in M4sh], page 167). For example:

```
dir=`dirname "$file"`        # This is not portable.
dir=`AS_DIRNAME(["$file"])`  # This is more portable.
```

egrep   Posix 1003.1-2001 no longer requires **egrep**, but many hosts do not yet support the Posix replacement **grep -E**. Also, some traditional implementations do not work on long input lines. To work around these problems, invoke **AC_PROG_EGREP** and then use **$EGREP**.

Portable extended regular expressions should use '\' only to escape characters in the string '$()*+.?[\^{|'. For example, '\}' is not portable, even though it typically matches '}'.

The empty alternative is not portable. Use '?' instead. For instance with Digital Unix v5.0:

```
> printf "foo\n|foo\n" | $EGREP '^(|foo|bar)$'
|foo
> printf "bar\nbar|\n" | $EGREP '^(foo|bar|)$'
bar|
> printf "foo\nfoo|\n|bar\nbar\n" | $EGREP '^(foo||bar)$'
foo
|bar
```

$EGREP also suffers the limitations of **grep** (see [Limitations of Usual Tools], page 242).

expr   Not all implementations obey the Posix rule that '--' separates options from arguments; likewise, not all implementations provide the extension to Posix that the first argument can be treated as part of a valid expression rather than an invalid option if it begins with '-'. When performing arithmetic, use 'expr 0 + $var' if '$var' might be a negative number, to keep **expr** from interpreting it as an option.

No **expr** keyword starts with 'X', so use 'expr X"*word*" : 'X*regex*'' to keep **expr** from misinterpreting *word*.

Don't use `length`, `substr`, `match` and `index`.

expr ('|')   You can use '|'. Although Posix does require that 'expr ''' return the empty string, it does not specify the result when you '|' together the empty string (or zero) with the empty string. For example:

```
expr '' \| ''
```

Posix 1003.2-1992 returns the empty string for this case, but traditional Unix returns '0' (Solaris is one such example). In Posix 1003.1-2001, the specification was changed to match traditional Unix's behavior (which is bizarre, but it's too late to fix this). Please note that the same problem does arise when the empty string results from a computation, as in:

```
expr bar : foo \| foo : bar
```

Avoid this portability problem by avoiding the empty string.

expr (':')   Portable `expr` regular expressions should use '\' to escape only characters in the string '$()*.0123456789[\^n{}'. For example, alternation, '\|', is common but Posix does not require its support, so it should be avoided in portable scripts. Similarly, '\+' and '\?' should be avoided.

Portable `expr` regular expressions should not begin with '^'. Patterns are automatically anchored so leading '^' is not needed anyway.

On the other hand, the behavior of the '$' anchor is not portable on multi-line strings. Posix is ambiguous whether the anchor applies to each line, as was done in older versions of the GNU Core Utilities, or whether it applies only to the end of the overall string, as in Coreutils 6.0 and most other implementations.

```
$ baz='foo
> bar'
$ expr "X$baz" : 'X\(foo\)$'

$ expr-5.97 "X$baz" : 'X\(foo\)$'
foo
```

The Posix standard is ambiguous as to whether 'expr 'a' : '\(b\)'' outputs '0' or the empty string. In practice, it outputs the empty string on most platforms, but portable scripts should not assume this. For instance, the QNX 4.25 native `expr` returns '0'.

One might think that a way to get a uniform behavior would be to use the empty string as a default value:

```
expr a : '\(b\)' \| ''
```

Unfortunately this behaves exactly as the original expression; see the expr ('|') entry for more information.

Some ancient `expr` implementations (e.g., SunOS 4 `expr` and Solaris 8 `/usr/ucb/expr`) have a silly length limit that causes `expr` to fail if the matched substring is longer than 120 bytes. In this case, you might want to fall back on 'echo|sed' if expr fails. Nowadays this is of practical importance only for the rare installer who mistakenly puts '/usr/ucb' before '/usr/bin' in PATH.

On Mac OS X 10.4, `expr` mishandles the pattern '[^-]' in some cases. For example, the command

```
expr Xpowerpc-apple-darwin8.1.0 : 'X[^-]*-[^-]*-\(.*\)'
```

outputs 'apple-darwin8.1.0' rather than the correct 'darwin8.1.0'. This particular case can be worked around by substituting '[^--]' for '[^-]'.

Don't leave, there is some more!

The QNX 4.25 `expr`, in addition of preferring '0' to the empty string, has a funny behavior in its exit status: it's always 1 when parentheses are used!

```
$ val=`expr 'a' : 'a'`; echo "$?: $val"
0: 1
$ val=`expr 'a' : 'b'`; echo "$?: $val"
1: 0

$ val=`expr 'a' : '\(a\)'`; echo "?: $val"
1: a
$ val=`expr 'a' : '\(b\)'`; echo "?: $val"
1: 0
```

In practice this can be a big problem if you are ready to catch failures of `expr` programs with some other method (such as using `sed`), since you may get twice the result. For instance

```
$ expr 'a' : '\(a\)' || echo 'a' | sed 's/^\(a\)$/\1/'
```

outputs 'a' on most hosts, but 'aa' on QNX 4.25. A simple workaround consists of testing `expr` and using a variable set to `expr` or to `false` according to the result.

Tru64 `expr` incorrectly treats the result as a number, if it can be interpreted that way:

```
$ expr 00001 : '.*\(...\)'
1
```

On HP-UX 11, `expr` only supports a single sub-expression.

```
$ expr 'Xfoo' : 'X\(f\(oo\)*\)$'
expr: More than one '\(' was used.
```

`fgrep`   Posix 1003.1-2001 no longer requires `fgrep`, but many hosts do not yet support the Posix replacement `grep -F`. Also, some traditional implementations do not work on long input lines. To work around these problems, invoke `AC_PROG_FGREP` and then use `$FGREP`.

Tru64/OSF 5.1 `fgrep` does not match an empty pattern.

`find`   The option '-maxdepth' seems to be GNU specific. Tru64 v5.1, NetBSD 1.5 and Solaris `find` commands do not understand it.

The replacement of '{}' is guaranteed only if the argument is exactly {}, not if it's only a part of an argument. For instance on DU, and HP-UX 10.20 and HP-UX 11:

```
$ touch foo
$ find . -name foo -exec echo "{}-{}" \;
```

```
{}-{}
```
while GNU `find` reports '`./foo-./foo`'.

grep   Portable scripts can rely on the `grep` options '`-c`', '`-l`', '`-n`', and '`-v`', but should avoid other options. For example, don't use '`-w`', as Posix does not require it and Irix 6.5.16m's `grep` does not support it. Also, portable scripts should not combine '`-c`' with '`-l`', as Posix does not allow this.

Some of the options required by Posix are not portable in practice. Don't use '`grep -q`' to suppress output, because many `grep` implementations (e.g., Solaris) do not support '`-q`'. Don't use '`grep -s`' to suppress output either, because Posix says '`-s`' does not suppress output, only some error messages; also, the '`-s`' option of traditional `grep` behaved like '`-q`' does in most modern implementations. Instead, redirect the standard output and standard error (in case the file doesn't exist) of `grep` to '`/dev/null`'. Check the exit status of `grep` to determine whether it found a match.

The QNX4 implementation fails to count lines with `grep -c '$'`, but works with `grep -c '^'`. Other alternatives for counting lines are to use `sed -n '$='` or `wc -l`.

Some traditional `grep` implementations do not work on long input lines. On AIX the default `grep` silently truncates long lines on the input before matching.

Also, many implementations do not support multiple regexps with '`-e`': they either reject '`-e`' entirely (e.g., Solaris) or honor only the last pattern (e.g., IRIX 6.5 and NeXT). To work around these problems, invoke `AC_PROG_GREP` and then use `$GREP`.

Another possible workaround for the multiple '`-e`' problem is to separate the patterns by newlines, for example:

```
grep 'foo
bar' in.txt
```

except that this fails with traditional `grep` implementations and with OpenBSD 3.8 `grep`.

Traditional `grep` implementations (e.g., Solaris) do not support the '`-E`' or '`-F`' options. To work around these problems, invoke `AC_PROG_EGREP` and then use `$EGREP`, and similarly for `AC_PROG_FGREP` and `$FGREP`. Even if you are willing to require support for Posix `grep`, your script should not use both '`-E`' and '`-F`', since Posix does not allow this combination.

Portable `grep` regular expressions should use '`\`' only to escape characters in the string '`$()*.0123456789[\^{}`'. For example, alternation, '`\|`', is common but Posix does not require its support in basic regular expressions, so it should be avoided in portable scripts. Solaris and HP-UX `grep` do not support it. Similarly, the following escape sequences should also be avoided: '`\<`', '`\>`', '`\+`', '`\?`', '`` \` ``', '`\'`', '`\B`', '`\b`', '`\S`', '`\s`', '`\W`', and '`\w`'.

Posix does not specify the behavior of `grep` on binary files. An example where this matters is using BSD `grep` to search text that includes embedded ANSI escape sequences for colored output to terminals ('`\033[m`' is the sequence to restore normal output); the behavior depends on whether input is seekable:

```
$ printf 'esc\033[mape\n' > sample
$ grep . sample
Binary file sample matches
$ cat sample | grep .
escape
```

join   Solaris 8 `join` has bugs when the second operand is standard input, and when standard input is a pipe. For example, the following shell script causes Solaris 8 `join` to loop forever:

```
cat >file <<'EOF'
1 x
2 y
EOF
cat file | join file -
```

Use 'join - file' instead.

On NetBSD, `join -a 1 file1 file2` mistakenly behaves like `join -a 1 -a 2 1 file1 file2`, resulting in a usage warning; the workaround is to use `join -a1 file1 file2` instead.

ln   Don't rely on `ln` having a '-f' option. Symbolic links are not available on old systems; use '$(LN_S)' as a portable substitute.

For versions of the DJGPP before 2.04, `ln` emulates symbolic links to executables by generating a stub that in turn calls the real program. This feature also works with nonexistent files like in the Posix spec. So 'ln -s file link' generates 'link.exe', which attempts to call 'file.exe' if run. But this feature only works for executables, so 'cp -p' is used instead for these systems. DJGPP versions 2.04 and later have full support for symbolic links.

ls   The portable options are '-acdilrtu'. Current practice is for '-l' to output both owner and group, even though ancient versions of `ls` omitted the group.

On ancient hosts, 'ls foo' sent the diagnostic 'foo not found' to standard output if 'foo' did not exist. Hence a shell command like 'sources=`ls *.c 2>/dev/null`' did not always work, since it was equivalent to 'sources='*.c not found'' in the absence of '.c' files. This is no longer a practical problem, since current `ls` implementations send diagnostics to standard error.

The behavior of `ls` on a directory that is being concurrently modified is not always predictable, because of a data race where cached information returned by `readdir` does not match the current directory state. In fact, MacOS 10.5 has an intermittent bug where `readdir`, and thus `ls`, sometimes lists a file more than once if other files were added or removed from the directory immediately prior to the `ls` call. Since `ls` already sorts its output, the duplicate entries can be avoided by piping the results through `uniq`.

mkdir   No `mkdir` option is portable to older systems. Instead of 'mkdir -p file-name', you should use `AS_MKDIR_P(file-name)` (see Chapter 9 [Programming in M4sh], page 167) or `AC_PROG_MKDIR_P` (see Section 5.2.1 [Particular Programs], page 43).

Combining the '-m' and '-p' options, as in 'mkdir -m go-w -p *dir*', often leads to trouble. FreeBSD mkdir incorrectly attempts to change the permissions of *dir* even if it already exists. HP-UX 11.23 and IRIX 6.5 mkdir often assign the wrong permissions to any newly-created parents of *dir*.

Posix does not clearly specify whether 'mkdir -p foo' should succeed when 'foo' is a symbolic link to an already-existing directory. The GNU Core Utilities 5.1.0 mkdir succeeds, but Solaris mkdir fails.

Traditional mkdir -p implementations suffer from race conditions. For example, if you invoke mkdir -p a/b and mkdir -p a/c at the same time, both processes might detect that 'a' is missing, one might create 'a', then the other might try to create 'a' and fail with a File exists diagnostic. The GNU Core Utilities ('fileutils' version 4.1), FreeBSD 5.0, NetBSD 2.0.2, and OpenBSD 2.4 are known to be race-free when two processes invoke mkdir -p simultaneously, but earlier versions are vulnerable. Solaris mkdir is still vulnerable as of Solaris 10, and other traditional Unix systems are probably vulnerable too. This possible race is harmful in parallel builds when several Make rules call mkdir -p to construct directories. You may use install-sh -d as a safe replacement, provided this script is recent enough; the copy shipped with Autoconf 2.60 and Automake 1.10 is OK, but copies from older versions are vulnerable.

mkfifo
mknod

The GNU Coding Standards state that mknod is safe to use on platforms where it has been tested to exist; but it is generally portable only for creating named FIFOs, since device numbers are platform-specific. Autotest uses mkfifo to implement parallel testsuites. Posix states that behavior is unspecified when opening a named FIFO for both reading and writing; on at least Cygwin, this results in failure on any attempt to read or write to that file descriptor.

mktemp

Shell scripts can use temporary files safely with mktemp, but it does not exist on all systems. A portable way to create a safe temporary file name is to create a temporary directory with mode 700 and use a file inside this directory. Both methods prevent attackers from gaining control, though mktemp is far less likely to fail gratuitously under attack.

Here is sample code to create a new temporary directory '$dir' safely:

```
# Create a temporary directory $dir in $TMPDIR (default /tmp).
# Use mktemp if possible; otherwise fall back on mkdir,
# with $RANDOM to make collisions less likely.
: "${TMPDIR:=/tmp}"
{
  dir=`
    (umask 077 && mktemp -d "$TMPDIR/fooXXXXXX") 2>/dev/null
  ` &&
  test -d "$dir"
} || {
  dir=$TMPDIR/foo$$-$RANDOM
  (umask 077 && mkdir "$dir")
} || exit $?
```

mv   The only portable options are '-f' and '-i'.

Moving individual files between file systems is portable (it was in Unix version 6), but it is not always atomic: when doing 'mv new existing', there's a critical section where neither the old nor the new version of 'existing' actually exists.

On some systems moving files from '/tmp' can sometimes cause undesirable (but perfectly valid) warnings, even if you created these files. This is because '/tmp' belongs to a group that ordinary users are not members of, and files created in '/tmp' inherit the group of '/tmp'. When the file is copied, mv issues a diagnostic without failing:

```
$ touch /tmp/foo
$ mv /tmp/foo .
error  mv: ./foo: set owner/group (was: 100/0): Operation not permitted
$ echo $?
0
$ ls foo
foo
```

This annoying behavior conforms to Posix, unfortunately.

Moving directories across mount points is not portable, use cp and rm.

DOS variants cannot rename or remove open files, and do not support commands like 'mv foo bar >foo', even though this is perfectly portable among Posix hosts.

od

In Mac OS X 10.3, od does not support the standard Posix options '-A', '-j', '-N', or '-t', or the XSI option '-s'. The only supported Posix option is '-v', and the only supported XSI options are those in '-bcdox'. The BSD hexdump program can be used instead.

This problem no longer exists in Mac OS X 10.4.3.

rm   The '-f' and '-r' options are portable.

It is not portable to invoke rm without options or operands. On the other hand, Posix now requires rm -f to silently succeed when there are no operands (useful for constructs like rm -rf $filelist without first checking if '$filelist' was empty). But this was not always portable; at least NetBSD rm built before 2008 would fail with a diagnostic.

A file might not be removed even if its parent directory is writable and searchable. Many Posix hosts cannot remove a mount point, a named stream, a working directory, or a last link to a file that is being executed.

DOS variants cannot rename or remove open files, and do not support commands like 'rm foo >foo', even though this is perfectly portable among Posix hosts.

rmdir   Just as with rm, some platforms refuse to remove a working directory.

sed   Patterns should not include the separator (unless escaped), even as part of a character class. In conformance with Posix, the Cray sed rejects 's/[^/]*$//': use 's%[^/]*$%%'. Even when escaped, patterns should not include separators that are also used as sed metacharacters. For example, GNU sed 4.0.9 rejects 's,x\{1\,\},,', while sed 4.1 strips the backslash before the comma before evaluating the basic regular expression.

Avoid empty patterns within parentheses (i.e., '\(\)'). Posix does not require support for empty patterns, and Unicos 9 sed rejects them.

Unicos 9 sed loops endlessly on patterns like '.*\n.*'.

Sed scripts should not use branch labels longer than 7 characters and should not contain comments; AIX 5.3 sed rejects indented comments. HP-UX sed has a limit of 99 commands (not counting ':' commands) and 48 labels, which cannot be circumvented by using more than one script file. It can execute up to 19 reads with the 'r' command per cycle. Solaris /usr/ucb/sed rejects usages that exceed a limit of about 6000 bytes for the internal representation of commands.

Avoid redundant ';', as some sed implementations, such as NetBSD 1.4.2's, incorrectly try to interpret the second ';' as a command:

```
$ echo a | sed 's/x/x/;;s/x/x/'
sed: 1: "s/x/x/;;s/x/x/": invalid command code ;
```

Some sed implementations have a buffer limited to 4000 bytes, and this limits the size of input lines, output lines, and internal buffers that can be processed portably. Likewise, not all sed implementations can handle embedded NUL or a missing trailing newline.

Remember that ranges within a bracket expression of a regular expression are only well-defined in the 'C' (or 'POSIX') locale. Meanwhile, support for character classes like '[[:upper:]]' is not yet universal, so if you cannot guarantee the setting of LC_ALL, it is better to spell out a range '[ABCDEFGHIJKLMNOPQRSTUVWXYZ]' than to rely on '[A-Z]'.

Additionally, Posix states that regular expressions are only well-defined on characters. Unfortunately, there exist platforms such as MacOS X 10.5 where not all 8-bit byte values are valid characters, even though that platform has a single-byte 'C' locale. And Posix allows the existence of a multi-byte 'C' locale, although that does not yet appear to be a common implementation. At any rate, it means that not all bytes will be matched by the regular expression '.':

```
$ printf '\200\n' | LC_ALL=C sed -n /./p | wc -l
0
$ printf '\200\n' | LC_ALL=en_US.ISO8859-1 sed -n /./p | wc -l
1
```

Portable sed regular expressions should use '\' only to escape characters in the string '$()*.0123456789[\^n{}'. For example, alternation, '\|', is common but Posix does not require its support, so it should be avoided in portable scripts. Solaris sed does not support alternation; e.g., 'sed '/a\|b/d'' deletes only lines that contain the literal string 'a|b'. Similarly, '\+' and '\?' should be avoided.

Anchors ('^' and '$') inside groups are not portable.

Nested parentheses in patterns (e.g., '\(\(a*\)b*\)\)') are quite portable to current hosts, but was not supported by some ancient **sed** implementations like SVR3.

Some **sed** implementations, e.g., Solaris, restrict the special role of the asterisk '*' to one-character regular expressions and back-references, and the special role of interval expressions '\{m\}', '\{m,\}', or '\{m,n\}' to one-character regular expressions. This may lead to unexpected behavior:

```
$ echo '1*23*4' | /usr/bin/sed 's/\(.\)*/x/g'
x2x4
$ echo '1*23*4' | /usr/xpg4/bin/sed 's/\(.\)*/x/g'
x
```

The '-e' option is mostly portable. However, its argument cannot start with 'a', 'c', or 'i', as this runs afoul of a Tru64 5.1 bug. Also, its argument cannot be empty, as this fails on AIX 5.3. Some people prefer to use '-e':

```
sed -e 'command-1' \
    -e 'command-2'
```

as opposed to the equivalent:

```
sed '
  command-1
  command-2
'
```

The following usage is sometimes equivalent:

```
sed 'command-1;command-2'
```

but Posix says that this use of a semicolon has undefined effect if *command-1*'s verb is '{', 'a', 'b', 'c', 'i', 'r', 't', 'w', ':', or '#', so you should use semicolon only with simple scripts that do not use these verbs.

Posix up to the 2008 revision requires the argument of the '-e' option to be a syntactically complete script. GNU **sed** allows to pass multiple script fragments, each as argument of a separate '-e' option, that are then combined, with newlines between the fragments, and a future Posix revision may allow this as well. This approach is not portable with script fragments ending in backslash; for example, the **sed** programs on Solaris 10, HP-UX 11, and AIX don't allow splitting in this case:

```
$ echo a | sed -n -e 'i\
0'
0
$ echo a | sed -n -e 'i\' -e 0
Unrecognized command: 0
```

In practice, however, this technique of joining fragments through '-e' works for multiple **sed** functions within '{' and '}', even if that is not specified by Posix:

```
$ echo a | sed -n -e '/a/{' -e s/a/b/ -e p -e '}'
b
```

Commands inside { } brackets are further restricted. Posix 2008 says that they cannot be preceded by addresses, '!', or ';', and that each command must be followed immediately by a newline, without any intervening blanks or semicolons. The closing bracket must be alone on a line, other than white space preceding or following it. However, a future version of Posix may standardize the use of addresses within brackets.

Contrary to yet another urban legend, you may portably use '&' in the replacement part of the s command to mean "what was matched". All descendants of Unix version 7 sed (at least; we don't have first hand experience with older sed implementations) have supported it.

Posix requires that you must not have any white space between '!' and the following command. It is OK to have blanks between the address and the '!'. For instance, on Solaris:

```
$ echo "foo" | sed -n '/bar/ ! p'
error Unrecognized command: /bar/ ! p
$ echo "foo" | sed -n '/bar/! p'
error Unrecognized command: /bar/! p
$ echo "foo" | sed -n '/bar/ !p'
foo
```

Posix also says that you should not combine '!' and ';'. If you use '!', it is best to put it on a command that is delimited by newlines rather than ';'.

Also note that Posix requires that the 'b', 't', 'r', and 'w' commands be followed by exactly one space before their argument. On the other hand, no white space is allowed between ':' and the subsequent label name.

If a sed script is specified on the command line and ends in an 'a', 'c', or 'i' command, the last line of inserted text should be followed by a newline. Otherwise some sed implementations (e.g., OpenBSD 3.9) do not append a newline to the inserted text.

Many sed implementations (e.g., MacOS X 10.4, OpenBSD 3.9, Solaris 10 /usr/ucb/sed) strip leading white space from the text of 'a', 'c', and 'i' commands. Prepend a backslash to work around this incompatibility with Posix:

```
$ echo flushleft | sed 'a\
>    indented
> '
flushleft
indented
$ echo foo | sed 'a\
> \    indented
> '
flushleft
    indented
```

Posix requires that with an empty regular expression, the last non-empty regular expression from either an address specification or substitution command is applied. However, busybox 1.6.1 complains when using a substitution command with a replacement containing a back-reference to an empty regular expression; the workaround is repeating the regular expression.

```
$ echo abc | busybox sed '/a\(b\)c/ s//\1/'
```

```
                     sed: No previous regexp.
                     $ echo abc | busybox sed '/a\(b\)c/ s/a\(b\)c/\1/'
                     b
```

sed ('t')   Some old systems have **sed** that "forget" to reset their 't' flag when starting a
new cycle. For instance on MIPS RISC/OS, and on IRIX 5.3, if you run the
following **sed** script (the line numbers are not actual part of the texts):

```
            s/keep me/kept/g    # a
            t end               # b
            s/.*/deleted/g      # c
            :end                # d
```

on

```
            delete me           # 1
            delete me           # 2
            keep me             # 3
            delete me           # 4
```

you get

```
            deleted
            delete me
            kept
            deleted
```

instead of

```
            deleted
            deleted
            kept
            deleted
```

Why? When processing line 1, (c) matches, therefore sets the 't' flag, and the
output is produced. When processing line 2, the 't' flag is still set (this is the
bug). Command (a) fails to match, but **sed** is not supposed to clear the 't'
flag when a substitution fails. Command (b) sees that the flag is set, therefore
it clears it, and jumps to (d), hence you get 'delete me' instead of 'deleted'.
When processing line (3), 't' is clear, (a) matches, so the flag is set, hence (b)
clears the flags and jumps. Finally, since the flag is clear, line 4 is processed
properly.

There are two things one should remember about 't' in **sed**. Firstly, always
remember that 't' jumps if *some* substitution succeeded, not only the immediately preceding substitution. Therefore, always use a fake 't clear' followed
by a ':clear' on the next line, to reset the 't' flag where needed.

Secondly, you cannot rely on **sed** to clear the flag at each new cycle.

One portable implementation of the script above is:

```
             t clear
             :clear
             s/keep me/kept/g
             t end
             s/.*/deleted/g
```

```
      :end
```

sleep   Using `sleep` is generally portable. However, remember that adding a `sleep` to work around timestamp issues, with a minimum granularity of one second, doesn't scale well for parallel builds on modern machines with sub-second process completion.

sort   Remember that sort order is influenced by the current locale. Inside 'configure', the C locale is in effect, but in Makefile snippets, you may need to specify `LC_ALL=C sort`.

tar   There are multiple file formats for `tar`; if you use Automake, the macro `AM_INIT_AUTOMAKE` has some options controlling which level of portability to use.

touch   If you specify the desired timestamp (e.g., with the '-r' option), older `touch` implementations use the `utime` or `utimes` system call, which can result in the same kind of timestamp truncation problems that 'cp -p' has.

         On ancient BSD systems, `touch` or any command that results in an empty file does not update the timestamps, so use a command like `echo` as a workaround. Also, GNU `touch` 3.16r (and presumably all before that) fails to work on SunOS 4.1.3 when the empty file is on an NFS-mounted 4.2 volume. However, these problems are no longer of practical concern.

tr   Not all versions of `tr` handle all backslash character escapes. For example, Solaris 10 `/usr/ucb/tr` falls over, even though Solaris contains more modern `tr` in other locations. Using octal escapes is more portable for carriage returns, since '\015' is the same for both ASCII and EBCDIC, and since use of literal carriage returns in scripts causes a number of other problems. But for other characters, like newline, using octal escapes ties the operation to ASCII, so it is better to use literal characters.

```
$ { echo moon; echo light; } | /usr/ucb/tr -d '\n' ; echo
moo
light
$ { echo moon; echo light; } | /usr/bin/tr -d '\n' ; echo
moonlight
$ { echo moon; echo light; } | /usr/ucb/tr -d '\012' ; echo
moonlight
$ nl='
'; { echo moon; echo light; } | /usr/ucb/tr -d "$nl" ; echo
moonlight
```

Not all versions of `tr` recognize direct ranges of characters: at least Solaris `/usr/bin/tr` still fails to do so. But you can use `/usr/xpg4/bin/tr` instead, or add brackets (which in Posix transliterate to themselves).

```
$ echo "Hazy Fantazy" | LC_ALL=C /usr/bin/tr a-z A-Z
HAZy FAntAZy
$ echo "Hazy Fantazy" | LC_ALL=C /usr/bin/tr '[a-z]' '[A-Z]'
HAZY FANTAZY
$ echo "Hazy Fantazy" | LC_ALL=C /usr/xpg4/bin/tr a-z A-Z
HAZY FANTAZY
```

When providing two arguments, be sure the second string is at least as long as the first.

```
$ echo abc | /usr/xpg4/bin/tr bc d
adc
$ echo abc | coreutils/tr bc d
add
```

Posix requires `tr` to operate on binary files. But at least Solaris `/usr/ucb/tr` and `/usr/bin/tr` silently discard NUL in the input prior to doing any translation. When using `tr` to process a binary file that may contain NUL bytes, it is necessary to use `/usr/xpg4/bin/tr` instead, or `/usr/xpg6/bin/tr` if that is available.

```
$ printf 'a\0b' | /usr/ucb/tr x x | od -An -tx1
 61 62
$ printf 'a\0b' | /usr/bin/tr x x | od -An -tx1
 61 62
$ printf 'a\0b' | /usr/xpg4/bin/tr x x | od -An -tx1
 61 00 62
```

Solaris `/usr/ucb/tr` additionally fails to handle '\0' as the octal escape for NUL.

```
$ printf 'abc' | /usr/ucb/tr 'bc' '\0d' | od -An -tx1
 61 62 63
$ printf 'abc' | /usr/bin/tr 'bc' '\0d' | od -An -tx1
 61 00 64
$ printf 'abc' | /usr/xpg4/bin/tr 'bc' '\0d' | od -An -tx1
 61 00 64
```

12 Portable Make Programming

Writing portable makefiles is an art. Since a makefile's commands are executed by the shell, you must consider the shell portability issues already mentioned. However, other issues are specific to make itself.

12.1 $< in Ordinary Make Rules

Posix says that the '$<' construct in makefiles can be used only in inference rules and in the '.DEFAULT' rule; its meaning in ordinary rules is unspecified. Solaris make for instance replaces it with the empty string. OpenBSD (3.0 and later) make diagnoses these uses and errors out.

12.2 Failure in Make Rules

Posix 2008 requires that make must invoke each command with the equivalent of a 'sh -e -c' subshell, which causes the subshell to exit immediately if a subsidiary simple-command fails, although not all make implementations have historically followed this rule. For example, the command 'touch T; rm -f U' may attempt to remove 'U' even if the touch fails, although this is not permitted with Posix make. One way to work around failures in simple commands is to reword them so that they always succeed, e.g., 'touch T || :; rm -f U'. However, even this approach can run into common bugs in BSD implementations of the '-e' option of sh and set (see [Limitations of Shell Builtins], page 228), so if you are worried about porting to buggy BSD shells it may be simpler to migrate complicated make actions into separate scripts.

12.3 Special Characters in Make Macro Names

Posix limits macro names to nonempty strings containing only ASCII letters and digits, '.', and '_'. Many make implementations allow a wider variety of characters, but portable makefiles should avoid them. It is portable to start a name with a special character, e.g., '$(.FOO)'.

Some ancient make implementations don't support leading underscores in macro names. An example is NEWS-OS 4.2R.

```
$ cat Makefile
_am_include = #
_am_quote =
all:; @echo this is test
$ make
Make: Must be a separator on rules line 2.  Stop.
$ cat Makefile2
am_include = #
am_quote =
all:; @echo this is test
$ make -f Makefile2
this is test
```

However, this problem is no longer of practical concern.

12.4 Backslash-Newline Before Empty Lines

A bug in Bash 2.03 can cause problems if a Make rule contains a backslash-newline followed by line that expands to nothing. For example, on Solaris 8:

```
SHELL = /bin/bash
EMPTY =
foo:
touch foo \
$(EMPTY)
```

executes

```
/bin/bash -c 'touch foo \
'
```

which fails with a syntax error, due to the Bash bug. To avoid this problem, avoid nullable macros in the last line of a multiline command.

On some versions of HP-UX, make reads multiple newlines following a backslash, continuing to the next non-empty line. For example,

```
FOO = one \

BAR = two


test:
        : FOO is "$(FOO)"
        : BAR is "$(BAR)"
```

shows FOO equal to one BAR = two. Other implementations sensibly let a backslash continue only to the immediately following line.

12.5 Backslash-Newline in Make Comments

According to Posix, Make comments start with # and continue until an unescaped newline is reached.

```
$ cat Makefile
# A = foo \
        bar \
        baz

all:
        @echo ok
$ make    # GNU make
ok
```

However this is not always the case. Some implementations discard everything from # through the end of the line, ignoring any trailing backslash.

```
$ pmake  # BSD make
"Makefile", line 3: Need an operator
Fatal errors encountered -- cannot continue
```

Therefore, if you want to comment out a multi-line definition, prefix each line with #, not only the first.

```
# A = foo \
#     bar \
#     baz
```

12.6 Long Lines in Makefiles

Tru64 5.1's **make** has been reported to crash when given a makefile with lines longer than around 20 kB. Earlier versions are reported to exit with `Line too long` diagnostics.

12.7 `make macro=value` and Submakes

A command-line variable definition such as **foo=bar** overrides any definition of **foo** in a makefile. Some **make** implementations (such as GNU **make**) propagate this override to subsidiary invocations of **make**. Some other implementations do not pass the substitution along to submakes.

```
$ cat Makefile
foo = foo
one:
        @echo $(foo)
        $(MAKE) two
two:
        @echo $(foo)
$ make foo=bar           # GNU make 3.79.1
bar
make two
make[1]: Entering directory '/home/adl'
bar
make[1]: Leaving directory '/home/adl'
$ pmake foo=bar          # BSD make
bar
pmake two
foo
```

You have a few possibilities if you do want the **foo=bar** override to propagate to submakes. One is to use the '-e' option, which causes all environment variables to have precedence over the makefile macro definitions, and declare foo as an environment variable:

```
$ env foo=bar make -e
```

The '-e' option is propagated to submakes automatically, and since the environment is inherited between **make** invocations, the **foo** macro is overridden in submakes as expected.

This syntax (**foo=bar make -e**) is portable only when used outside of a makefile, for instance from a script or from the command line. When run inside a **make** rule, GNU **make** 3.80 and prior versions forget to propagate the '-e' option to submakes.

Moreover, using '-e' could have unexpected side effects if your environment contains some other macros usually defined by the makefile. (See also the note about **make -e** and **SHELL** below.)

If you can foresee all macros that a user might want to override, then you can propagate them to submakes manually, from your makefile:

```
foo = foo
one:
        @echo $(foo)
        $(MAKE) foo=$(foo) two
two:
        @echo $(foo)
```

Another way to propagate a variable to submakes in a portable way is to expand an extra variable in every invocation of '$(MAKE)' within your makefile:

```
foo = foo
one:
        @echo $(foo)
        $(MAKE) $(SUBMAKEFLAGS) two
two:
        @echo $(foo)
```

Users must be aware that this technique is in use to take advantage of it, e.g. with `make foo=bar SUBMAKEFLAGS='foo=bar'`, but it allows any macro to be overridden. Makefiles generated by `automake` use this technique, expanding `$(AM_MAKEFLAGS)` on the command lines of submakes (see Section "Automake" in *GNU Automake*).

12.8 The Make Macro MAKEFLAGS

Posix requires `make` to use `MAKEFLAGS` to affect the current and recursive invocations of make, but allows implementations several formats for the variable. It is tricky to parse `$MAKEFLAGS` to determine whether '-s' for silent execution or '-k' for continued execution are in effect. For example, you cannot assume that the first space-separated word in `$MAKEFLAGS` contains single-letter options, since in the Cygwin version of GNU `make` it is either '--unix' or '--win32' with the second word containing single-letter options.

```
$ cat Makefile
all:
        @echo MAKEFLAGS = $(MAKEFLAGS)
$ make
MAKEFLAGS = --unix
$ make -k
MAKEFLAGS = --unix -k
```

12.9 The Make Macro SHELL

Posix-compliant `make` internally uses the `$(SHELL)` macro to spawn shell processes and execute Make rules. This is a builtin macro supplied by `make`, but it can be modified by a makefile or by a command-line argument.

Not all `make` implementations define this `SHELL` macro. Tru64 `make` is an example; this implementation always uses `/bin/sh`. So it's a good idea to always define `SHELL` in your makefiles. If you use Autoconf, do

```
SHELL = @SHELL@
```

If you use Automake, this is done for you.

Do not force `SHELL = /bin/sh` because that is not correct everywhere. Remember, '/bin/sh' is not Posix compliant on many systems, such as FreeBSD 4, NetBSD 3, AIX 3, Solaris 10, or Tru64. Additionally, DJGPP lacks `/bin/sh`, and when its GNU `make` port sees such a setting it enters a special emulation mode where features like pipes and redirections are emulated on top of DOS's `command.com`. Unfortunately this emulation is incomplete; for instance it does not handle command substitutions. Using `@SHELL@` means that your makefile will benefit from the same improved shell, such as `bash` or `ksh`, that was discovered during `configure`, so that you aren't fighting two different sets of shell bugs between the two contexts.

Posix-compliant `make` should never acquire the value of $(SHELL) from the environment, even when `make -e` is used (otherwise, think about what would happen to your rules if `SHELL=/bin/tcsh`).

However not all `make` implementations have this exception. For instance it's not surprising that Tru64 `make` doesn't protect SHELL, since it doesn't use it.

```
$ cat Makefile
SHELL = /bin/sh
FOO = foo
all:
        @echo $(SHELL)
        @echo $(FOO)
$ env SHELL=/bin/tcsh FOO=bar make -e    # Tru64 Make
/bin/tcsh
bar
$ env SHELL=/bin/tcsh FOO=bar gmake -e   # GNU make
/bin/sh
bar
```

Conversely, `make` is not supposed to export any changes to the macro SHELL to child processes. Again, many implementations break this rule:

```
$ cat Makefile
all:
        @echo $(SHELL)
        @printenv SHELL
$ env SHELL=sh make -e SHELL=/bin/ksh    # BSD Make, GNU make 3.80
/bin/ksh
/bin/ksh
$ env SHELL=sh gmake -e SHELL=/bin/ksh   # GNU make 3.81
/bin/ksh
sh
```

12.10 Parallel Make

Support for parallel execution in `make` implementation varies. Generally, using GNU make is your best bet.

When NetBSD or FreeBSD `make` are run in parallel mode, they will reuse the same shell for multiple commands within one recipe. This can have various unexpected consequences. For example, changes of directories or variables persist between recipes, so that:

```
all:
        @var=value; cd /; pwd; echo $$var; echo $$$$
        @pwd; echo $$var; echo $$$$
```

may output the following with `make -j1`, at least on NetBSD up to 5.1 and FreeBSD up to 8.2:

```
/
value
32235
/
value
32235
```

while without '`-j1`', or with '`-B`', the output looks less surprising:

```
/
value
32238
/tmp

32239
```

Another consequence is that, if one command in a recipe uses `exit 0` to indicate a successful exit, the shell will be gone and the remaining commands of this recipe will not be executed.

The BSD `make` implementations, when run in parallel mode, will also pass the `Makefile` recipes to the shell through its standard input, thus making it unusable from the recipes:

```
$ cat Makefile
read:
        @read line; echo LINE: $$line
$ echo foo | make read
LINE: foo
$ echo foo | make -j1 read # NetBSD 5.1 and FreeBSD 8.2
LINE:
```

Moreover, when FreeBSD `make` (up at least to 8.2) is run in parallel mode, it implements the `@` and `-` "recipe modifiers" by dynamically modifying the active shell flags. This behavior has the effects of potentially clobbering the exit status of recipes silenced with the `@` modifier if they also unset the '`errexit`' shell flag, and of mangling the output in unexpected ways:

```
$ cat Makefile
a:
        @echo $$-; set +e; false
b:
        -echo $$-; false; echo set -
$ make a; echo status: $?
ehBc
*** Error code 1
status: 1
$ make -j1 a; echo status: $?
ehB
status: 0
```

```
$ make b
echo $-; echo set -
hBc
set -
$ make -j1 b
echo $-; echo hvB
```

You can avoid all these issues by using the '-B' option to enable compatibility semantics. However, that will effectively also disable all parallelism as that will cause prerequisites to be updated in the order they are listed in a rule.

Some make implementations (among them, FreeBSD **make**, NetBSD **make**, and Solaris **dmake**), when invoked with a '-j*N*' option, connect the standard output and standard error of all their child processes to pipes or temporary regular files. This can lead to subtly different semantics in the behavior of the spawned processes. For example, even if the **make** standard output is connected to a tty, the recipe command will not be:

```
$ cat Makefile
all:
        @test -t 1 && echo "Is a tty" || echo "Is not a tty"
$ make -j 2 # FreeBSD 8.2 make
Is not a tty
$ make -j 2 # NetBSD 5.1 make
--- all ---
Is not a tty
$ dmake -j 2 # Solaris 10 dmake
hostname --> 1 job
hostname --> Job output
Is not a tty
```

On the other hand:

```
$ make -j 2 # GNU make, Heirloom make
Is a tty
```

The above examples also show additional status output produced in parallel mode for targets being updated by Solaris **dmake** and NetBSD **make** (but *not* by FreeBSD **make**).

Furthermore, parallel runs of those **make** implementations will route standard error from commands that they spawn into their own standard output, and may remove leading whitespace from output lines.

12.11 Comments in Make Rules

Never put comments in a rule.

Some **make** treat anything starting with a tab as a command for the current rule, even if the tab is immediately followed by a **#**. The **make** from Tru64 Unix V5.1 is one of them. The following makefile runs **# foo** through the shell.

```
all:
        # foo
```

As a workaround, you can use the : no-op command with a string argument that gets ignored:

```
all:
        : "foo"
```

Conversely, if you want to use the '#' character in some command, you can only do so by expanding it inside a rule (see Section 12.13 [Comments in Make Macros], page 260). So for example, if 'COMMENT_CHAR' is substituted by `config.status` as '#', then the following substitutes '@COMMENT_CHAR@' in a generated header:

```
foo.h: foo.h.in
        sed -e 's|@''COMMENT_CHAR''@|@COMMENT_CHAR@|g' \
            $(srcdir)/foo.h.in > $@
```

The funny shell quoting avoids a substitution at `config.status` run time of the left-hand side of the `sed` 's' command.

12.12 Newlines in Make Rules

In shell scripts, newlines can be used inside string literals. But in the shell statements of 'Makefile' rules, this is not possible: A newline not preceded by a backslash is a separator between shell statements. Whereas a newline that is preceded by a backslash becomes part of the shell statement according to POSIX, but gets replaced, together with the backslash that precedes it, by a space in GNU `make` 3.80 and older. So, how can a newline be used in a string literal?

The trick is to set up a shell variable that contains a newline:

```
nlinit=`echo 'nl="'; echo '"'`; eval "$$nlinit"
```

For example, in order to create a multiline 'sed' expression that inserts a blank line after every line of a file, this code can be used:

```
nlinit=`echo 'nl="'; echo '"'`; eval "$$nlinit"; \
sed -e "s/\$$/\\$${nl}/" < input > output
```

12.13 Comments in Make Macros

Avoid putting comments in macro values as far as possible. Posix specifies that the text starting from the '#' sign until the end of the line is to be ignored, which has the unfortunate effect of disallowing them even within quotes. Thus, the following might lead to a syntax error at compile time:

```
CPPFLAGS = "-DCOMMENT_CHAR='#'"
```

as 'CPPFLAGS' may be expanded to '"-DCOMMENT_CHAR='.

Most `make` implementations disregard this and treat single and double quotes specially here. Also, GNU `make` lets you put '#' into a macro value by escaping it with a backslash, i.e., '\#'. However, neither of these usages are portable. See Section 12.11 [Comments in Make Rules], page 259, for a portable alternative.

Even without quoting involved, comments can have surprising effects, because the white-space before them is part of the variable value:

```
foo = bar # trailing comment
print: ; @echo "$(foo)."
```

prints 'bar .', which is usually not intended, and can expose `make` bugs as described below.

12.14 Trailing whitespace in Make Macros

GNU make 3.80 mistreats trailing whitespace in macro substitutions and appends another spurious suffix:

```
empty =
foo = bar $(empty)
print: ; @echo $(foo:=.test)
```

prints 'bar.test .test'.

BSD and Solaris make implementations do not honor trailing whitespace in macro definitions as Posix requires:

```
foo = bar # Note the space after "bar".
print: ; @echo $(foo)t
```

prints 'bart' instead of 'bar t'. To work around this, you can use a helper macro as in the previous example.

12.15 Command-line Macros and whitespace

Some make implementations may strip trailing whitespace off of macros set on the command line in addition to leading whitespace. Further, some may strip leading whitespace off of macros set from environment variables:

```
$ echo 'print: ; @echo "x$(foo)x$(bar)x"' |
  foo=' f f ' make -f - bar=' b b '
x f f xb b x  # AIX, BSD, GNU make
xf f xb b x   # HP-UX, IRIX, Tru64/OSF make
x f f xb bx   # Solaris make
```

12.16 The 'obj/' Subdirectory and Make

Never name one of your subdirectories 'obj/' if you don't like surprises.

If an 'obj/' directory exists, BSD make enters it before reading the makefile. Hence the makefile in the current directory is not read.

```
$ cat Makefile
all:
        echo Hello
$ cat obj/Makefile
all:
        echo World
$ make       # GNU make
echo Hello
Hello
$ pmake      # BSD make
echo World
World
```

12.17 Exit Status of `make -k`

Do not rely on the exit status of `make -k`. Some implementations reflect whether they encountered an error in their exit status; other implementations always succeed.

```
$ cat Makefile
all:
        false
$ make -k; echo exit status: $?    # GNU make
false
make: *** [all] Error 1
exit status: 2
$ pmake -k; echo exit status: $?    # BSD make
false
*** Error code 1 (continuing)
exit status: 0
```

12.18 `VPATH` and Make

Posix does not specify the semantics of `VPATH`. Typically, `make` supports `VPATH`, but its implementation is not consistent.

Autoconf and Automake support makefiles whose usages of `VPATH` are portable to recent-enough popular implementations of `make`, but to keep the resulting makefiles portable, a package's makefile prototypes must take the following issues into account. These issues are complicated and are often poorly understood, and installers who use `VPATH` should expect to find many bugs in this area. If you use `VPATH`, the simplest way to avoid these portability bugs is to stick with GNU `make`, since it is the most commonly-used `make` among Autoconf users.

Here are some known issues with some `VPATH` implementations.

12.18.1 Variables listed in `VPATH`

Do not set `VPATH` to the value of another variable, for example 'VPATH = $(srcdir)', because some ancient versions of `make` do not do variable substitutions on the value of `VPATH`. For example, use this

```
srcdir = @srcdir@
VPATH = @srcdir@
```

rather than 'VPATH = $(srcdir)'. Note that with GNU Automake, there is no need to set this yourself.

12.18.2 `VPATH` and Double-colon Rules

With ancient versions of Sun `make`, any assignment to `VPATH` causes `make` to execute only the first set of double-colon rules. However, this problem is no longer of practical concern.

12.18.3 `$<` Not Supported in Explicit Rules

Using `$<` in explicit rules is not portable. The prerequisite file must be named explicitly in the rule. If you want to find the prerequisite via a `VPATH` search, you have to code the whole thing manually. See Section 4.8.4 [Build Directories], page 31.

12.18.4 Automatic Rule Rewriting

Some make implementations, such as Solaris and Tru64, search for prerequisites in VPATH and then rewrite each occurrence as a plain word in the rule. For instance:

```
# This isn't portable to GNU make.
VPATH = ../pkg/src
f.c: if.c
        cp if.c f.c
```

executes `cp ../pkg/src/if.c f.c` if 'if.c' is found in '../pkg/src'.

However, this rule leads to real problems in practice. For example, if the source directory contains an ordinary file named 'test' that is used in a dependency, Solaris make rewrites commands like 'if test -r foo; ...' to 'if ../pkg/src/test -r foo; ...', which is typically undesirable. In fact, make is completely unaware of shell syntax used in the rules, so the VPATH rewrite can potentially apply to *any* whitespace-separated word in a rule, including shell variables, functions, and keywords.

```
$ mkdir build
$ cd build
$ cat > Makefile <<'END'
VPATH = ..
all: arg func for echo
        func () { for arg in "$$@"; do echo $$arg; done; }; \
        func "hello world"
END
$ touch ../arg ../func ../for ../echo
$ make
../func () { ../for ../arg in "$@"; do ../echo $arg; done; }; \
../func "hello world"
sh: syntax error at line 1: 'do' unexpected
*** Error code 2
```

To avoid this problem, portable makefiles should never mention a source file or dependency whose name is that of a shell keyword like 'for' or 'until', a shell command like cat or gcc or test, or a shell function or variable used in the corresponding Makefile recipe.

Because of these problems GNU make and many other make implementations do not rewrite commands, so portable makefiles should search VPATH manually. It is tempting to write this:

```
# This isn't portable to Solaris make.
VPATH = ../pkg/src
f.c: if.c
        cp `test -f if.c || echo $(VPATH)/`if.c f.c
```

However, the "prerequisite rewriting" still applies here. So if 'if.c' is in '../pkg/src', Solaris and Tru64 make execute

```
cp `test -f ../pkg/src/if.c || echo ../pkg/src/`if.c f.c
```

which reduces to

```
cp if.c f.c
```

and thus fails. Oops.

A simple workaround, and good practice anyway, is to use '$?' and '$@' when possible:

```
VPATH = ../pkg/src
f.c: if.c
        cp $? $@
```

but this does not generalize well to commands with multiple prerequisites. A more general workaround is to rewrite the rule so that the prerequisite 'if.c' never appears as a plain word. For example, these three rules would be safe, assuming 'if.c' is in '../pkg/src' and the other files are in the working directory:

```
VPATH = ../pkg/src
f.c: if.c f1.c
        cat `test -f ./if.c || echo $(VPATH)/`if.c f1.c >$@
g.c: if.c g1.c
        cat `test -f 'if.c' || echo $(VPATH)/`if.c g1.c >$@
h.c: if.c h1.c
        cat `test -f "if.c" || echo $(VPATH)/`if.c h1.c >$@
```

Things get worse when your prerequisites are in a macro.

```
VPATH = ../pkg/src
HEADERS = f.h g.h h.h
install-HEADERS: $(HEADERS)
        for i in $(HEADERS); do \
          $(INSTALL) -m 644 \
            `test -f $$i || echo $(VPATH)/`$$i \
            $(DESTDIR)$(includedir)/$$i; \
        done
```

The above `install-HEADERS` rule is not Solaris-proof because `for i in $(HEADERS);` is expanded to `for i in f.h g.h h.h;` where `f.h` and `g.h` are plain words and are hence subject to `VPATH` adjustments.

If the three files are in '../pkg/src', the rule is run as:

```
for i in ../pkg/src/f.h ../pkg/src/g.h h.h; do \
  install -m 644 \
      `test -f $i || echo ../pkg/src/`$i \
      /usr/local/include/$i; \
done
```

where the two first `install` calls fail. For instance, consider the `f.h` installation:

```
install -m 644 \
  `test -f ../pkg/src/f.h || \
    echo ../pkg/src/ \
  `../pkg/src/f.h \
  /usr/local/include/../pkg/src/f.h;
```

It reduces to:

```
install -m 644 \
  ../pkg/src/f.h \
  /usr/local/include/../pkg/src/f.h;
```

Note that the manual `VPATH` search did not cause any problems here; however this command installs 'f.h' in an incorrect directory.

Trying to quote `$(HEADERS)` in some way, as we did for `foo.c` a few makefiles ago, does not help:

```
install-HEADERS: $(HEADERS)
        headers='$(HEADERS)'; \
        for i in $$headers; do \
          $(INSTALL) -m 644 \
            `test -f $$i || echo $(VPATH)/`$$i \
            $(DESTDIR)$(includedir)/$$i; \
        done
```

Now, `headers='$(HEADERS)'` macro-expands to:

```
headers='f.h g.h h.h'
```

but `g.h` is still a plain word. (As an aside, the idiom `headers='$(HEADERS)'; for i in $$headers;` is a good idea if `$(HEADERS)` can be empty, because some shells diagnose a syntax error on `for i in;`.)

One workaround is to strip this unwanted '`../pkg/src/`' prefix manually:

```
VPATH = ../pkg/src
HEADERS = f.h g.h h.h
install-HEADERS: $(HEADERS)
        headers='$(HEADERS)'; \
        for i in $$headers; do \
          i=`expr "$$i" : '$(VPATH)/\(.*\)'`; \
          $(INSTALL) -m 644 \
            `test -f $$i || echo $(VPATH)/`$$i \
            $(DESTDIR)$(includedir)/$$i; \
        done
```

Automake does something similar. However the above hack works only if the files listed in HEADERS are in the current directory or a subdirectory; they should not be in an enclosing directory. If we had `HEADERS = ../f.h`, the above fragment would fail in a VPATH build with Tru64 make. The reason is that not only does Tru64 make rewrite dependencies, but it also simplifies them. Hence `../f.h` becomes `../pkg/f.h` instead of `../pkg/src/../f.h`. This obviously defeats any attempt to strip a leading '`../pkg/src/`' component.

The following example makes the behavior of Tru64 make more apparent.

```
$ cat Makefile
VPATH = sub
all: ../foo
        echo ../foo
$ ls
Makefile foo
$ make
echo foo
foo
```

Dependency '`../foo`' was found in '`sub/../foo`', but Tru64 make simplified it as '`foo`'. (Note that the '`sub/`' directory does not even exist, this just means that the simplification occurred before the file was checked for.)

For the record here is how SunOS 4 make behaves on this example.

```
$ make
make: Fatal error: Don't know how to make target `../foo'
```

```
$ mkdir sub
$ make
echo sub/../foo
sub/../foo
```

12.18.5 Tru64 make Creates Prerequisite Directories Magically

When a prerequisite is a subdirectory of VPATH, Tru64 make creates it in the current directory.

```
$ mkdir -p foo/bar build
$ cd build
$ cat >Makefile <<END
VPATH = ..
all: foo/bar
END
$ make
mkdir foo
mkdir foo/bar
```

This can yield unexpected results if a rule uses a manual VPATH search as presented before.

```
VPATH = ..
all : foo/bar
            command `test -d foo/bar || echo ../`foo/bar
```

The above command is run on the empty 'foo/bar' directory that was created in the current directory.

12.18.6 Make Target Lookup

GNU make uses a complex algorithm to decide when it should use files found via a VPATH search. See Section "How Directory Searches are Performed" in *The GNU Make Manual*.

If a target needs to be rebuilt, GNU make discards the file name found during the VPATH search for this target, and builds the file locally using the file name given in the makefile. If a target does not need to be rebuilt, GNU make uses the file name found during the VPATH search.

Other make implementations, like NetBSD make, are easier to describe: the file name found during the VPATH search is used whether the target needs to be rebuilt or not. Therefore new files are created locally, but existing files are updated at their VPATH location.

OpenBSD and FreeBSD make, however, never perform a VPATH search for a dependency that has an explicit rule. This is extremely annoying.

When attempting a VPATH build for an autoconfiscated package (e.g., mkdir build && cd build && ../configure), this means GNU make builds everything locally in the 'build' directory, while BSD make builds new files locally and updates existing files in the source directory.

```
$ cat Makefile
VPATH = ..
all: foo.x bar.x
foo.x bar.x: newer.x
```

```
            @echo Building $@
$ touch ../bar.x
$ touch ../newer.x
$ make          # GNU make
Building foo.x
Building bar.x
$ pmake         # NetBSD make
Building foo.x
Building ../bar.x
$ fmake         # FreeBSD make, OpenBSD make
Building foo.x
Building bar.x
$ tmake         # Tru64 make
Building foo.x
Building bar.x
$ touch ../bar.x
$ make          # GNU make
Building foo.x
$ pmake         # NetBSD make
Building foo.x
$ fmake         # FreeBSD make, OpenBSD make
Building foo.x
Building bar.x
$ tmake         # Tru64 make
Building foo.x
Building bar.x
```

Note how NetBSD make updates '../bar.x' in its VPATH location, and how FreeBSD, OpenBSD, and Tru64 make always update 'bar.x', even when '../bar.x' is up to date.

Another point worth mentioning is that once GNU make has decided to ignore a VPATH file name (e.g., it ignored '../bar.x' in the above example) it continues to ignore it when the target occurs as a prerequisite of another rule.

The following example shows that GNU make does not look up 'bar.x' in VPATH before performing the .x.y rule, because it ignored the VPATH result of 'bar.x' while running the bar.x: newer.x rule.

```
$ cat Makefile
VPATH = ..
all: bar.y
bar.x: newer.x
        @echo Building $@
.SUFFIXES: .x .y
.x.y:
        cp $< $@
$ touch ../bar.x
$ touch ../newer.x
$ make          # GNU make
Building bar.x
```

```
cp bar.x bar.y
cp: cannot stat 'bar.x': No such file or directory
make: *** [bar.y] Error 1
$ pmake          # NetBSD make
Building ../bar.x
cp ../bar.x bar.y
$ rm bar.y
$ fmake          # FreeBSD make, OpenBSD make
echo Building bar.x
cp bar.x bar.y
cp: cannot stat 'bar.x': No such file or directory
*** Error code 1
$ tmake          # Tru64 make
Building bar.x
cp: bar.x: No such file or directory
*** Exit 1
```

Note that if you drop away the command from the bar.x: newer.x rule, GNU make
magically starts to work: it knows that bar.x hasn't been updated, therefore it doesn't
discard the result from VPATH ('../bar.x') in succeeding uses. Tru64 also works, but
FreeBSD and OpenBSD still don't.

```
$ cat Makefile
VPATH = ..
all: bar.y
bar.x: newer.x
.SUFFIXES: .x .y
.x.y:
        cp $< $@
$ touch ../bar.x
$ touch ../newer.x
$ make           # GNU make
cp ../bar.x bar.y
$ rm bar.y
$ pmake          # NetBSD make
cp ../bar.x bar.y
$ rm bar.y
$ fmake          # FreeBSD make, OpenBSD make
cp bar.x bar.y
cp: cannot stat 'bar.x': No such file or directory
*** Error code 1
$ tmake          # Tru64 make
cp ../bar.x bar.y
```

It seems the sole solution that would please every make implementation is to never rely
on VPATH searches for targets. In other words, VPATH should be reserved to unbuilt sources.

12.19 Single Suffix Rules and Separated Dependencies

A *Single Suffix Rule* is basically a usual suffix (inference) rule ('.from.to:'), but which *destination* suffix is empty ('.from:').

Separated dependencies simply refers to listing the prerequisite of a target, without defining a rule. Usually one can list on the one hand side, the rules, and on the other hand side, the dependencies.

Solaris `make` does not support separated dependencies for targets defined by single suffix rules:

```
$ cat Makefile
.SUFFIXES: .in
foo: foo.in
.in:
        cp $< $@
$ touch foo.in
$ make
$ ls
Makefile  foo.in
```

while GNU Make does:

```
$ gmake
cp foo.in foo
$ ls
Makefile  foo         foo.in
```

Note it works without the 'foo: foo.in' dependency.

```
$ cat Makefile
.SUFFIXES: .in
.in:
        cp $< $@
$ make foo
cp foo.in foo
```

and it works with double suffix inference rules:

```
$ cat Makefile
foo.out: foo.in
.SUFFIXES: .in .out
.in.out:
        cp $< $@
$ make
cp foo.in foo.out
```

As a result, in such a case, you have to write target rules.

12.20 Timestamp Resolution and Make

Traditionally, file timestamps had 1-second resolution, and `make` used those timestamps to determine whether one file was newer than the other. However, many modern file systems have timestamps with 1-nanosecond resolution. Some `make` implementations look at the entire timestamp; others ignore the fractional part, which can lead to incorrect results.

Normally this is not a problem, but in some extreme cases you may need to use tricks like 'sleep 1' to work around timestamp truncation bugs.

Commands like 'cp -p' and 'touch -r' typically do not copy file timestamps to their full resolutions (see [Limitations of Usual Tools], page 250). Hence you should be wary of rules like this:

```
dest: src
        cp -p src dest
```

as 'dest' often appears to be older than 'src' after the timestamp is truncated, and this can cause make to do needless rework the next time it is invoked. To work around this problem, you can use a timestamp file, e.g.:

```
dest-stamp: src
        cp -p src dest
        date >dest-stamp
```

Apart from timestamp resolution, there are also differences in handling equal time-stamps. HP-UX make updates targets if it has the same time stamp as one of its prerequisites, in violation of Posix rules.

This can cause spurious rebuilds for repeated runs of make. This in turn can cause make to fail if it tries to rebuild generated files in a possibly read-only source tree with tools not present on the end-user machine. Use GNU make instead.

13 Portable C and C++ Programming

C and C++ programs often use low-level features of the underlying system, and therefore are often more difficult to make portable to other platforms.

Several standards have been developed to help make your programs more portable. If you write programs with these standards in mind, you can have greater confidence that your programs work on a wide variety of systems. See Section "Language Standards Supported by GCC" in *Using the GNU Compiler Collection (GCC)*, for a list of C-related standards. Many programs also assume the Posix standard.

Some old code is written to be portable to K&R C, which predates any C standard. K&R C compilers are no longer of practical interest, though, and the rest of section assumes at least C89, the first C standard.

Program portability is a huge topic, and this section can only briefly introduce common pitfalls. See Section "Portability between System Types" in *The GNU Coding Standards*, for more information.

13.1 Varieties of Unportability

Autoconf tests and ordinary programs often need to test what is allowed on a system, and therefore they may need to deliberately exceed the boundaries of what the standards allow, if only to see whether an optional feature is present. When you write such a program, you should keep in mind the difference between constraints, unspecified behavior, and undefined behavior.

In C, a *constraint* is a rule that the compiler must enforce. An example constraint is that C programs must not declare a bit-field with negative width. Tests can therefore reliably assume that programs with negative-width bit-fields are rejected by a compiler that conforms to the standard.

Unspecified behavior is valid behavior, where the standard allows multiple possibilities. For example, the order of evaluation of function arguments is unspecified. Some unspecified behavior is *implementation-defined*, i.e., documented by the implementation, but since Autoconf tests cannot read the documentation they cannot distinguish between implementation-defined and other unspecified behavior. It is common for Autoconf tests to probe implementations to determine otherwise-unspecified behavior.

Undefined behavior is invalid behavior, where the standard allows the implementation to do anything it pleases. For example, dereferencing a null pointer leads to undefined behavior. If possible, test programs should avoid undefined behavior, since a program with undefined behavior might succeed on a test that should fail.

The above rules apply to programs that are intended to conform to the standard. However, strictly-conforming programs are quite rare, since the standards are so limiting. A major goal of Autoconf is to support programs that use implementation features not described by the standard, and it is fairly common for test programs to violate the above rules, if the programs work well enough in practice.

13.2 Integer Overflow

In practice many portable C programs assume that signed integer overflow wraps around reliably using two's complement arithmetic. Yet the C standard says that program behavior is undefined on overflow, and in a few cases C programs do not work on some modern implementations because their overflows do not wrap around as their authors expected. Conversely, in signed integer remainder, the C standard requires overflow behavior that is commonly not implemented.

13.2.1 Basics of Integer Overflow

In languages like C, unsigned integer overflow reliably wraps around; e.g., `UINT_MAX + 1` yields zero. This is guaranteed by the C standard and is portable in practice, unless you specify aggressive, nonstandard optimization options suitable only for special applications.

In contrast, the C standard says that signed integer overflow leads to undefined behavior where a program can do anything, including dumping core or overrunning a buffer. The misbehavior can even precede the overflow. Such an overflow can occur during addition, subtraction, multiplication, division, and left shift.

Despite this requirement of the standard, many C programs and Autoconf tests assume that signed integer overflow silently wraps around modulo a power of two, using two's complement arithmetic, so long as you cast the resulting value to a signed integer type or store it into a signed integer variable. If you use conservative optimization flags, such programs are generally portable to the vast majority of modern platforms, with a few exceptions discussed later.

For historical reasons the C standard also allows implementations with ones' complement or signed magnitude arithmetic, but it is safe to assume two's complement nowadays.

Also, overflow can occur when converting an out-of-range value to a signed integer type. Here a standard implementation must define what happens, but this might include raising an exception. In practice all known implementations support silent wraparound in this case, so you need not worry about other possibilities.

13.2.2 Examples of Code Assuming Wraparound Overflow

There has long been a tension between what the C standard requires for signed integer overflow, and what C programs commonly assume. The standard allows aggressive optimizations based on assumptions that overflow never occurs, but many practical C programs rely on overflow wrapping around. These programs do not conform to the standard, but they commonly work in practice because compiler writers are understandably reluctant to implement optimizations that would break many programs, unless perhaps a user specifies aggressive optimization.

The C Standard says that if a program has signed integer overflow its behavior is undefined, and the undefined behavior can even precede the overflow. To take an extreme example:

```
if (password == expected_password)
  allow_superuser_privileges ();
else if (counter++ == INT_MAX)
  abort ();
else
```

```
printf ("%d password mismatches\n", counter);
```

If the `int` variable `counter` equals `INT_MAX`, `counter++` must overflow and the behavior is undefined, so the C standard allows the compiler to optimize away the test against `INT_MAX` and the `abort` call. Worse, if an earlier bug in the program lets the compiler deduce that `counter == INT_MAX` or that `counter` previously overflowed, the C standard allows the compiler to optimize away the password test and generate code that allows superuser privileges unconditionally.

Despite this requirement by the standard, it has long been common for C code to assume wraparound arithmetic after signed overflow, and all known practical C implementations support some C idioms that assume wraparound signed arithmetic, even if the idioms do not conform strictly to the standard. If your code looks like the following examples it will almost surely work with real-world compilers.

Here is an example derived from the 7th Edition Unix implementation of `atoi` (1979-01-10):

```
char *p;
int f, n;
...
while (*p >= '0' && *p <= '9')
  n = n * 10 + *p++ - '0';
return (f ? -n : n);
```

Even if the input string is in range, on most modern machines this has signed overflow when computing the most negative integer (the `-n` overflows) or a value near an extreme integer (the first `+` overflows).

Here is another example, derived from the 7th Edition implementation of `rand` (1979-01-10). Here the programmer expects both multiplication and addition to wrap on overflow:

```
static long int randx = 1;
...
randx = randx * 1103515245 + 12345;
return (randx >> 16) & 077777;
```

In the following example, derived from the GNU C Library 2.5 implementation of `mktime` (2006-09-09), the code assumes wraparound arithmetic in `+` to detect signed overflow:

```
time_t t, t1, t2;
int sec_requested, sec_adjustment;
...
t1 = t + sec_requested;
t2 = t1 + sec_adjustment;
if (((t1 < t) != (sec_requested < 0))
    | ((t2 < t1) != (sec_adjustment < 0)))
  return -1;
```

If your code looks like these examples, it is probably safe even though it does not strictly conform to the C standard. This might lead one to believe that one can generally assume wraparound on overflow, but that is not always true, as can be seen in the next section.

13.2.3 Optimizations That Break Wraparound Arithmetic

Compilers sometimes generate code that is incompatible with wraparound integer arithmetic. A simple example is an algebraic simplification: a compiler might translate (i * 2000) / 1000 to i * 2 because it assumes that i * 2000 does not overflow. The translation is not equivalent to the original when overflow occurs: e.g., in the typical case of 32-bit signed two's complement wraparound int, if i has type int and value 1073742, the original expression returns −2147483 but the optimized version returns the mathematically correct value 2147484.

More subtly, loop induction optimizations often exploit the undefined behavior of signed overflow. Consider the following contrived function sumc:

```
int
sumc (int lo, int hi)
{
  int sum = 0;
  int i;
  for (i = lo; i <= hi; i++)
    sum ^= i * 53;
  return sum;
}
```

To avoid multiplying by 53 each time through the loop, an optimizing compiler might internally transform sumc to the equivalent of the following:

```
int
transformed_sumc (int lo, int hi)
{
  int sum = 0;
  int hic = hi * 53;
  int ic;
  for (ic = lo * 53; ic <= hic; ic += 53)
    sum ^= ic;
  return sum;
}
```

This transformation is allowed by the C standard, but it is invalid for wraparound arithmetic when INT_MAX / 53 < hi, because then the overflow in computing expressions like hi * 53 can cause the expression i <= hi to yield a different value from the transformed expression ic <= hic.

For this reason, compilers that use loop induction and similar techniques often do not support reliable wraparound arithmetic when a loop induction variable like ic is involved. Since loop induction variables are generated by the compiler, and are not visible in the source code, it is not always trivial to say whether the problem affects your code.

Hardly any code actually depends on wraparound arithmetic in cases like these, so in practice these loop induction optimizations are almost always useful. However, edge cases in this area can cause problems. For example:

```
int j;
for (j = 1; 0 < j; j *= 2)
  test (j);
```

Here, the loop attempts to iterate through all powers of 2 that int can represent, but the C standard allows a compiler to optimize away the comparison and generate an infinite loop, under the argument that behavior is undefined on overflow. As of this writing this optimization is not done by any production version of GCC with '-O2', but it might be performed by other compilers, or by more aggressive GCC optimization options, and the GCC developers have not decided whether it will continue to work with GCC and '-O2'.

13.2.4 Practical Advice for Signed Overflow Issues

Ideally the safest approach is to avoid signed integer overflow entirely. For example, instead of multiplying two signed integers, you can convert them to unsigned integers, multiply the unsigned values, then test whether the result is in signed range.

Rewriting code in this way will be inconvenient, though, particularly if the signed values might be negative. Also, it may hurt performance. Using unsigned arithmetic to check for overflow is particularly painful to do portably and efficiently when dealing with an integer type like uid_t whose width and signedness vary from platform to platform.

Furthermore, many C applications pervasively assume wraparound behavior and typically it is not easy to find and remove all these assumptions. Hence it is often useful to maintain nonstandard code that assumes wraparound on overflow, instead of rewriting the code. The rest of this section attempts to give practical advice for this situation.

If your code wants to detect signed integer overflow in sum = a + b, it is generally safe to use an expression like (sum < a) != (b < 0).

If your code uses a signed loop index, make sure that the index cannot overflow, along with all signed expressions derived from the index. Here is a contrived example of problematic code with two instances of overflow.

```
for (i = INT_MAX - 10; i <= INT_MAX; i++)
  if (i + 1 < 0)
    {
      report_overflow ();
      break;
    }
```

Because of the two overflows, a compiler might optimize away or transform the two comparisons in a way that is incompatible with the wraparound assumption.

If your code uses an expression like (i * 2000) / 1000 and you actually want the multiplication to wrap around on overflow, use unsigned arithmetic to do it, e.g., ((int) (i * 2000u)) / 1000.

If your code assumes wraparound behavior and you want to insulate it against any GCC optimizations that would fail to support that behavior, you should use GCC's '-fwrapv' option, which causes signed overflow to wrap around reliably (except for division and remainder, as discussed in the next section).

If you need to port to platforms where signed integer overflow does not reliably wrap around (e.g., due to hardware overflow checking, or to highly aggressive optimizations), you should consider debugging with GCC's '-ftrapv' option, which causes signed overflow to raise an exception.

13.2.5 Signed Integer Division and Integer Overflow

Overflow in signed integer division is not always harmless: for example, on CPUs of the i386 family, dividing `INT_MIN` by `-1` yields a SIGFPE signal which by default terminates the program. Worse, taking the remainder of these two values typically yields the same signal on these CPUs, even though the C standard requires `INT_MIN % -1` to yield zero because the expression does not overflow.

13.3 Preprocessor Arithmetic

In C99, preprocessor arithmetic, used for `#if` expressions, must be evaluated as if all signed values are of type `intmax_t` and all unsigned values of type `uintmax_t`. Many compilers are buggy in this area, though. For example, as of 2007, Sun C mishandles `#if LLONG_MIN < 0` on a platform with 32-bit `long int` and 64-bit `long long int`. Also, some older preprocessors mishandle constants ending in `LL`. To work around these problems, you can compute the value of expressions like `LONG_MAX < LLONG_MAX` at `configure`-time rather than at `#if`-time.

13.4 Properties of Null Pointers

Most modern hosts reliably fail when you attempt to dereference a null pointer.

On almost all modern hosts, null pointers use an all-bits-zero internal representation, so you can reliably use `memset` with 0 to set all the pointers in an array to null values.

If `p` is a null pointer to an object type, the C expression `p + 0` always evaluates to `p` on modern hosts, even though the standard says that it has undefined behavior.

13.5 Buffer Overruns and Subscript Errors

Buffer overruns and subscript errors are the most common dangerous errors in C programs. They result in undefined behavior because storing outside an array typically modifies storage that is used by some other object, and most modern systems lack runtime checks to catch these errors. Programs should not rely on buffer overruns being caught.

There is one exception to the usual rule that a portable program cannot address outside an array. In C, it is valid to compute the address just past an object, e.g., `&a[N]` where `a` has N elements, so long as you do not dereference the resulting pointer. But it is not valid to compute the address just before an object, e.g., `&a[-1]`; nor is it valid to compute two past the end, e.g., `&a[N+1]`. On most platforms `&a[-1] < &a[0] && &a[N] < &a[N+1]`, but this is not reliable in general, and it is usually easy enough to avoid the potential portability problem, e.g., by allocating an extra unused array element at the start or end.

Valgrind can catch many overruns. GCC users might also consider using the '`-fmudflap`' option to catch overruns.

Buffer overruns are usually caused by off-by-one errors, but there are more subtle ways to get them.

Using `int` values to index into an array or compute array sizes causes problems on typical 64-bit hosts where an array index might be 2^{31} or larger. Index values of type `size_t` avoid this problem, but cannot be negative. Index values of type `ptrdiff_t` are signed, and are wide enough in practice.

If you add or multiply two numbers to calculate an array size, e.g., `malloc (x * sizeof y + z)`, havoc ensues if the addition or multiplication overflows.

Many implementations of the `alloca` function silently misbehave and can generate buffer overflows if given sizes that are too large. The size limits are implementation dependent, but are at least 4000 bytes on all platforms that we know about.

The standard functions `asctime`, `asctime_r`, `ctime`, `ctime_r`, and `gets` are prone to buffer overflows, and portable code should not use them unless the inputs are known to be within certain limits. The time-related functions can overflow their buffers if given timestamps out of range (e.g., a year less than -999 or greater than 9999). Time-related buffer overflows cannot happen with recent-enough versions of the GNU C library, but are possible with other implementations. The `gets` function is the worst, since it almost invariably overflows its buffer when presented with an input line larger than the buffer.

13.6 Volatile Objects

The keyword `volatile` is often misunderstood in portable code. Its use inhibits some memory-access optimizations, but programmers often wish that it had a different meaning than it actually does.

`volatile` was designed for code that accesses special objects like memory-mapped device registers whose contents spontaneously change. Such code is inherently low-level, and it is difficult to specify portably what `volatile` means in these cases. The C standard says, "What constitutes an access to an object that has volatile-qualified type is implementation-defined," so in theory each implementation is supposed to fill in the gap by documenting what `volatile` means for that implementation. In practice, though, this documentation is usually absent or incomplete.

One area of confusion is the distinction between objects defined with volatile types, and volatile lvalues. From the C standard's point of view, an object defined with a volatile type has externally visible behavior. You can think of such objects as having little oscilloscope probes attached to them, so that the user can observe some properties of accesses to them, just as the user can observe data written to output files. However, the standard does not make it clear whether users can observe accesses by volatile lvalues to ordinary objects. For example:

```
/* Declare and access a volatile object.
   Accesses to X are "visible" to users.  */
static int volatile x;
x = 1;

/* Access two ordinary objects via a volatile lvalue.
   It's not clear whether accesses to *P are "visible".  */
int y;
int *z = malloc (sizeof (int));
int volatile *p;
p = &y;
*p = 1;
p = z;
*p = 1;
```

Programmers often wish that `volatile` meant "Perform the memory access here and now, without merging several memory accesses, without changing the memory word size, and without reordering." But the C standard does not require this. For objects defined with a volatile type, accesses must be done before the next sequence point; but otherwise merging, reordering, and word-size change is allowed. Worse, it is not clear from the standard whether volatile lvalues provide more guarantees in general than nonvolatile lvalues, if the underlying objects are ordinary.

Even when accessing objects defined with a volatile type, the C standard allows only extremely limited signal handlers: the behavior is undefined if a signal handler reads any nonlocal object, or writes to any nonlocal object whose type is not `sig_atomic_t volatile`, or calls any standard library function other than **abort**, **signal**, and (if C99) **_Exit**. Hence C compilers need not worry about a signal handler disturbing ordinary computation, unless the computation accesses a `sig_atomic_t volatile` lvalue that is not a local variable. (There is an obscure exception for accesses via a pointer to a volatile character, since it may point into part of a `sig_atomic_t volatile` object.) Posix adds to the list of library functions callable from a portable signal handler, but otherwise is like the C standard in this area.

Some C implementations allow memory-access optimizations within each translation unit, such that actual behavior agrees with the behavior required by the standard only when calling a function in some other translation unit, and a signal handler acts like it was called from a different translation unit. The C standard hints that in these implementations, objects referred to by signal handlers "would require explicit specification of **volatile** storage, as well as other implementation-defined restrictions." But unfortunately even for this special case these other restrictions are often not documented well. See Section "When is a Volatile Object Accessed?" in *Using the GNU Compiler Collection (GCC)*, for some restrictions imposed by GCC. See Section "Defining Signal Handlers" in *The GNU C Library*, for some restrictions imposed by the GNU C library. Restrictions differ on other platforms.

If possible, it is best to use a signal handler that fits within the limits imposed by the C and Posix standards.

If this is not practical, you can try the following rules of thumb. A signal handler should access only volatile lvalues, preferably lvalues that refer to objects defined with a volatile type, and should not assume that the accessed objects have an internally consistent state if they are larger than a machine word. Furthermore, installers should employ compilers and compiler options that are commonly used for building operating system kernels, because kernels often need more from **volatile** than the C Standard requires, and installers who compile an application in a similar environment can sometimes benefit from the extra constraints imposed by kernels on compilers. Admittedly we are handwaving somewhat here, as there are few guarantees in this area; the rules of thumb may help to fix some bugs but there is a good chance that they will not fix them all.

For `volatile`, C++ has the same problems that C does. Multithreaded applications have even more problems with `volatile`, but they are beyond the scope of this section.

The bottom line is that using `volatile` typically hurts performance but should not hurt correctness. In some cases its use does help correctness, but these cases are often so poorly understood that all too often adding `volatile` to a data structure merely alleviates some symptoms of a bug while not fixing the bug in general.

13.7 Floating Point Portability

Almost all modern systems use IEEE-754 floating point, and it is safe to assume IEEE-754 in most portable code these days. For more information, please see David Goldberg's classic paper *What Every Computer Scientist Should Know About Floating-Point Arithmetic*.

13.8 Exiting Portably

A C or C++ program can exit with status N by returning N from the `main` function. Portable programs are supposed to exit either with status 0 or `EXIT_SUCCESS` to succeed, or with status `EXIT_FAILURE` to fail, but in practice it is portable to fail by exiting with status 1, and test programs that assume Posix can fail by exiting with status values from 1 through 255. Programs on SunOS 2.0 (1985) through 3.5.2 (1988) incorrectly exited with zero status when `main` returned nonzero, but ancient systems like these are no longer of practical concern.

A program can also exit with status N by passing N to the `exit` function, and a program can fail by calling the `abort` function. If a program is specialized to just some platforms, it can fail by calling functions specific to those platforms, e.g., `_exit` (Posix) and `_Exit` (C99). However, like other functions, an exit function should be declared, typically by including a header. For example, if a C program calls `exit`, it should include 'stdlib.h' either directly or via the default includes (see Section 5.1.2 [Default Includes], page 41).

A program can fail due to undefined behavior such as dereferencing a null pointer, but this is not recommended as undefined behavior allows an implementation to do whatever it pleases and this includes exiting successfully.

14 Manual Configuration

A few kinds of features can't be guessed automatically by running test programs. For example, the details of the object-file format, or special options that need to be passed to the compiler or linker. You can check for such features using ad-hoc means, such as having `configure` check the output of the `uname` program, or looking for libraries that are unique to particular systems. However, Autoconf provides a uniform method for handling unguessable features.

14.1 Specifying target triplets

Autoconf-generated `configure` scripts can make decisions based on a canonical name for the system type, or *target triplet*, which has the form: '*cpu-vendor-os*', where *os* can be '*system*' or '*kernel-system*'

`configure` can usually guess the canonical name for the type of system it's running on. To do so it runs a script called `config.guess`, which infers the name using the `uname` command or symbols predefined by the C preprocessor.

Alternately, the user can specify the system type with command line arguments to `configure` (see Section 16.7 [System Type], page 298. Doing so is necessary when cross-compiling. In the most complex case of cross-compiling, three system types are involved. The options to specify them are:

'`--build=build-type`'

> the type of system on which the package is being configured and compiled. It defaults to the result of running `config.guess`. Specifying a *build-type* that differs from *host-type* enables cross-compilation mode.

'`--host=host-type`'

> the type of system on which the package runs. By default it is the same as the build machine. Specifying a *host-type* that differs from *build-type*, when *build-type* was also explicitly specified, enables cross-compilation mode.

'`--target=target-type`'

> the type of system for which any compiler tools in the package produce code (rarely needed). By default, it is the same as host.

If you mean to override the result of `config.guess`, use '`--build`', not '`--host`', since the latter enables cross-compilation. For historical reasons, whenever you specify '`--host`', be sure to specify '`--build`' too; this will be fixed in the future. So, to enter cross-compilation mode, use a command like this

```
./configure --build=i686-pc-linux-gnu --host=m68k-coff
```

Note that if you do not specify '`--host`', `configure` fails if it can't run the code generated by the specified compiler. For example, configuring as follows fails:

```
./configure CC=m68k-coff-gcc
```

When cross-compiling, `configure` will warn about any tools (compilers, linkers, assemblers) whose name is not prefixed with the host type. This is an aid to users performing cross-compilation. Continuing the example above, if a cross-compiler named `cc` is used with a native `pkg-config`, then libraries found by `pkg-config` will likely cause subtle build failures; but using the names `m68k-coff-cc` and `m68k-coff-pkg-config` avoids any confusion. Avoiding the warning is as simple as creating the correct symlinks naming the cross tools.

`configure` recognizes short aliases for many system types; for example, 'decstation' can be used instead of 'mips-dec-ultrix4.2'. `configure` runs a script called `config.sub` to canonicalize system type aliases.

This section deliberately omits the description of the obsolete interface; see Section 18.6.3 [Hosts and Cross-Compilation], page 322.

14.2 Getting the Canonical System Type

The following macros make the system type available to `configure` scripts.

The variables 'build_alias', 'host_alias', and 'target_alias' are always exactly the arguments of '--build', '--host', and '--target'; in particular, they are left empty if the user did not use them, even if the corresponding AC_CANONICAL macro was run. Any configure script may use these variables anywhere. These are the variables that should be used when in interaction with the user.

If you need to recognize some special environments based on their system type, run the following macros to get canonical system names. These variables are not set before the macro call.

If you use these macros, you must distribute `config.guess` and `config.sub` along with your source code. See Section 4.5 [Output], page 20, for information about the AC_CONFIG_AUX_DIR macro which you can use to control in which directory `configure` looks for those scripts.

AC_CANONICAL_BUILD   [Macro]
> Compute the canonical build-system type variable, `build`, and its three individual parts `build_cpu`, `build_vendor`, and `build_os`.
>
> If '--build' was specified, then `build` is the canonicalization of `build_alias` by `config.sub`, otherwise it is determined by the shell script `config.guess`.

AC_CANONICAL_HOST   [Macro]
> Compute the canonical host-system type variable, `host`, and its three individual parts `host_cpu`, `host_vendor`, and `host_os`.
>
> If '--host' was specified, then `host` is the canonicalization of `host_alias` by `config.sub`, otherwise it defaults to `build`.

AC_CANONICAL_TARGET   [Macro]
> Compute the canonical target-system type variable, `target`, and its three individual parts `target_cpu`, `target_vendor`, and `target_os`.
>
> If '--target' was specified, then `target` is the canonicalization of `target_alias` by `config.sub`, otherwise it defaults to `host`.

Note that there can be artifacts due to the backward compatibility code. See Section 18.6.3 [Hosts and Cross-Compilation], page 322, for more.

14.3 Using the System Type

In 'configure.ac' the system type is generally used by one or more **case** statements to select system-specifics. Shell wildcards can be used to match a group of system types.

For example, an extra assembler code object file could be chosen, giving access to a CPU cycle counter register. **$(CYCLE_OBJ)** in the following would be used in a makefile to add the object to a program or library.

```
AS_CASE([$host],
    [alpha*-*-*], [CYCLE_OBJ=rpcc.o],
    [i?86-*-*],   [CYCLE_OBJ=rdtsc.o],
    [CYCLE_OBJ=""]
)
AC_SUBST([CYCLE_OBJ])
```

AC_CONFIG_LINKS (see Section 4.11 [Configuration Links], page 38) is another good way to select variant source files, for example optimized code for some CPUs. The configured CPU type doesn't always indicate exact CPU types, so some runtime capability checks may be necessary too.

```
case $host in
    alpha*-*-*)   AC_CONFIG_LINKS([dither.c:alpha/dither.c]) ;;
    powerpc*-*-*) AC_CONFIG_LINKS([dither.c:powerpc/dither.c]) ;;
    *-*-*)        AC_CONFIG_LINKS([dither.c:generic/dither.c]) ;;
esac
```

The host system type can also be used to find cross-compilation tools with **AC_CHECK_TOOL** (see Section 5.2.2 [Generic Programs], page 46).

The above examples all show '**$host**', since this is where the code is going to run. Only rarely is it necessary to test '**$build**' (which is where the build is being done).

Whenever you're tempted to use '**$host**' it's worth considering whether some sort of probe would be better. New system types come along periodically or previously missing features are added. Well-written probes can adapt themselves to such things, but hard-coded lists of names can't. Here are some guidelines,

- Availability of libraries and library functions should always be checked by probing.

- Variant behavior of system calls is best identified with runtime tests if possible, but bug workarounds or obscure difficulties might have to be driven from '**$host**'.

- Assembler code is inevitably highly CPU-specific and is best selected according to '**$host_cpu**'.

- Assembler variations like underscore prefix on globals or ELF versus COFF type directives are however best determined by probing, perhaps even examining the compiler output.

'**$target**' is for use by a package creating a compiler or similar. For ordinary packages it's meaningless and should not be used. It indicates what the created compiler should generate code for, if it can cross-compile. '**$target**' generally selects various hard-coded CPU and system conventions, since usually the compiler or tools under construction themselves determine how the target works.

15 Site Configuration

`configure` scripts support several kinds of local configuration decisions. There are ways for users to specify where external software packages are, include or exclude optional features, install programs under modified names, and set default values for `configure` options.

15.1 Controlling Help Output

Users consult '`configure --help`' to learn of configuration decisions specific to your package. By default, `configure` breaks this output into sections for each type of option; within each section, help strings appear in the order '`configure.ac`' defines them:

```
Optional Features:
  ...
  --enable-bar            include bar

Optional Packages:
  ...
  --with-foo              use foo
```

`AC_PRESERVE_HELP_ORDER`   [Macro]
> Request an alternate '`--help`' format, in which options of all types appear together, in the order defined. Call this macro before any `AC_ARG_ENABLE` or `AC_ARG_WITH`.
>
> ```
> Optional Features and Packages:
>   ...
>   --enable-bar            include bar
>   --with-foo              use foo
> ```

15.2 Working With External Software

Some packages require, or can optionally use, other software packages that are already installed. The user can give `configure` command line options to specify which such external software to use. The options have one of these forms:

```
--with-package[=arg]
--without-package
```

For example, '`--with-gnu-ld`' means work with the GNU linker instead of some other linker. '`--with-x`' means work with The X Window System.

The user can give an argument by following the package name with '=' and the argument. Giving an argument of '`no`' is for packages that are used by default; it says to *not* use the package. An argument that is neither '`yes`' nor '`no`' could include a name or number of a version of the other package, to specify more precisely which other package this program is supposed to work with. If no argument is given, it defaults to '`yes`'. '`--without-package`' is equivalent to '`--with-package=no`'.

Normally `configure` scripts complain about '`--with-package`' options that they do not support. See Section 15.5 [Option Checking], page 289, for details, and for how to override the defaults.

For each external software package that may be used, 'configure.ac' should call AC_ARG_WITH to detect whether the configure user asked to use it. Whether each package is used or not by default, and which arguments are valid, is up to you.

AC_ARG_WITH (*package*, *help-string*, [*action-if-given*],   [Macro]
        [*action-if-not-given*])

> If the user gave configure the option '--with-*package*' or '--without-*package*', run shell commands *action-if-given*. If neither option was given, run shell commands *action-if-not-given*. The name *package* indicates another software package that this program should work with. It should consist only of alphanumeric characters, dashes, plus signs, and dots.
>
> The option's argument is available to the shell commands *action-if-given* in the shell variable withval, which is actually just the value of the shell variable named with_*package*, with any non-alphanumeric characters in *package* changed into '_'. You may use that variable instead, if you wish.
>
> The argument *help-string* is a description of the option that looks like this:
>
> > --with-readline   support fancy command line editing
>
> *help-string* may be more than one line long, if more detail is needed. Just make sure the columns line up in 'configure --help'. Avoid tabs in the help string. The easiest way to provide the proper leading whitespace is to format your *help-string* with the macro AS_HELP_STRING (see Section 15.4 [Pretty Help Strings], page 288).
>
> The following example shows how to use the AC_ARG_WITH macro in a common situation. You want to let the user decide whether to enable support for an external library (e.g., the readline library); if the user specified neither '--with-readline' nor '--without-readline', you want to enable support for readline only if the library is available on the system.
>
> ```
> AC_ARG_WITH([readline],
>   [AS_HELP_STRING([--with-readline],
>     [support fancy command line editing @<:@default=check@:>@])],
>   [],
>   [with_readline=check])
>
> LIBREADLINE=
> AS_IF([test "x$with_readline" != xno],
>   [AC_CHECK_LIB([readline], [main],
>     [AC_SUBST([LIBREADLINE], ["-lreadline -lncurses"])
>     AC_DEFINE([HAVE_LIBREADLINE], [1],
>               [Define if you have libreadline])
>     ],
>     [if test "x$with_readline" != xcheck; then
>        AC_MSG_FAILURE(
>          [--with-readline was given, but test for readline failed])
>      fi
>     ], -lncurses)])
> ```

The next example shows how to use `AC_ARG_WITH` to give the user the possibility to enable support for the readline library, in case it is still experimental and not well tested, and is therefore disabled by default.

```
AC_ARG_WITH([readline],
  [AS_HELP_STRING([--with-readline],
    [enable experimental support for readline])],
  [],
  [with_readline=no])

LIBREADLINE=
AS_IF([test "x$with_readline" != xno],
  [AC_CHECK_LIB([readline], [main],
    [AC_SUBST([LIBREADLINE], ["-lreadline -lncurses"])
    AC_DEFINE([HAVE_LIBREADLINE], [1],
               [Define if you have libreadline])
    ],
    [AC_MSG_FAILURE(
       [--with-readline was given, but test for readline failed])],
    [-lncurses])])
```

The last example shows how to use `AC_ARG_WITH` to give the user the possibility to disable support for the readline library, given that it is an important feature and that it should be enabled by default.

```
AC_ARG_WITH([readline],
  [AS_HELP_STRING([--without-readline],
    [disable support for readline])],
  [],
  [with_readline=yes])

LIBREADLINE=
AS_IF([test "x$with_readline" != xno],
  [AC_CHECK_LIB([readline], [main],
    [AC_SUBST([LIBREADLINE], ["-lreadline -lncurses"])
    AC_DEFINE([HAVE_LIBREADLINE], [1],
               [Define if you have libreadline])
    ],
    [AC_MSG_FAILURE(
       [readline test failed (--without-readline to disable)])],
    [-lncurses])])
```

These three examples can be easily adapted to the case where `AC_ARG_ENABLE` should be preferred to `AC_ARG_WITH` (see Section 15.3 [Package Options], page 287).

15.3 Choosing Package Options

If a software package has optional compile-time features, the user can give `configure` command line options to specify whether to compile them. The options have one of these forms:

```
--enable-feature[=arg]
--disable-feature
```

These options allow users to choose which optional features to build and install. '--enable-*feature*' options should never make a feature behave differently or cause one feature to replace another. They should only cause parts of the program to be built rather than left out.

The user can give an argument by following the feature name with '=' and the argument. Giving an argument of 'no' requests that the feature *not* be made available. A feature with an argument looks like '--enable-debug=stabs'. If no argument is given, it defaults to 'yes'. '--disable-*feature*' is equivalent to '--enable-*feature*=no'.

Normally **configure** scripts complain about '--enable-*package*' options that they do not support. See Section 15.5 [Option Checking], page 289, for details, and for how to override the defaults.

For each optional feature, 'configure.ac' should call AC_ARG_ENABLE to detect whether the **configure** user asked to include it. Whether each feature is included or not by default, and which arguments are valid, is up to you.

AC_ARG_ENABLE (*feature*, *help-string*, [*action-if-given*],   [Macro]
      [*action-if-not-given*])

> If the user gave **configure** the option '--enable-*feature*' or '--disable-*feature*', run shell commands *action-if-given*. If neither option was given, run shell commands *action-if-not-given*. The name *feature* indicates an optional user-level facility. It should consist only of alphanumeric characters, dashes, plus signs, and dots.
>
> The option's argument is available to the shell commands *action-if-given* in the shell variable **enableval**, which is actually just the value of the shell variable named **enable_*feature***, with any non-alphanumeric characters in *feature* changed into '_'. You may use that variable instead, if you wish. The *help-string* argument is like that of **AC_ARG_WITH** (see Section 15.2 [External Software], page 285).
>
> You should format your *help-string* with the macro **AS_HELP_STRING** (see Section 15.4 [Pretty Help Strings], page 288).
>
> See the examples suggested with the definition of **AC_ARG_WITH** (see Section 15.2 [External Software], page 285) to get an idea of possible applications of **AC_ARG_ENABLE**.

15.4 Making Your Help Strings Look Pretty

Properly formatting the '**help strings**' which are used in **AC_ARG_WITH** (see Section 15.2 [External Software], page 285) and **AC_ARG_ENABLE** (see Section 15.3 [Package Options], page 287) can be challenging. Specifically, you want your own '**help strings**' to line up in the appropriate columns of '**configure --help**' just like the standard Autoconf '**help strings**' do. This is the purpose of the **AS_HELP_STRING** macro.

AS_HELP_STRING (*left-hand-side*, *right-hand-side* [*indent-column*   [Macro]
    = '26'], [*wrap-column* = '79'])

> Expands into a help string that looks pretty when the user executes '**configure --help**'. It is typically used in **AC_ARG_WITH** (see Section 15.2 [External Software],

page 285) or `AC_ARG_ENABLE` (see Section 15.3 [Package Options], page 287). The following example makes this clearer.

```
AC_ARG_WITH([foo],
  [AS_HELP_STRING([--with-foo],
    [use foo (default is no)]))],
  [use_foo=$withval],
  [use_foo=no])
```

Then the last few lines of 'configure --help' appear like this:

```
--enable and --with options recognized:
  --with-foo              use foo (default is no)
```

Macro expansion is performed on the first argument. However, the second argument of `AS_HELP_STRING` is treated as a whitespace separated list of text to be reformatted, and is not subject to macro expansion. Since it is not expanded, it should not be double quoted. See Section 3.1.2 [Autoconf Language], page 7, for a more detailed explanation.

The `AS_HELP_STRING` macro is particularly helpful when the *left-hand-side* and/or *right-hand-side* are composed of macro arguments, as shown in the following example. Be aware that *left-hand-side* may not expand to unbalanced quotes, although quadrigraphs can be used.

```
AC_DEFUN([MY_ARG_WITH],
  [AC_ARG_WITH(m4_translit([[$1]], [_], [-]),
    [AS_HELP_STRING([--with-m4_translit([$1], [_], [-])],
                    [use $1 (default is $2)])],
    [use_[]$1=$withval],
    [use_[]$1=$2])])
MY_ARG_WITH([a_b], [no])
```

Here, the last few lines of 'configure --help' will include:

```
--enable and --with options recognized:
  --with-a-b              use a_b (default is no)
```

The parameters *indent-column* and *wrap-column* were introduced in Autoconf 2.62. Generally, they should not be specified; they exist for fine-tuning of the wrapping.

```
AS_HELP_STRING([--option], [description of option])
⇒  --option                description of option
AS_HELP_STRING([--option], [description of option], [15], [30])
⇒  --option     description of
⇒               option
```

15.5 Controlling Checking of `configure` Options

The `configure` script checks its command-line options against a list of known options, like '--help' or '--config-cache'. An unknown option ordinarily indicates a mistake by the user and `configure` halts with an error. However, by default unknown '--with-*package*' and '--enable-*feature*' options elicit only a warning, to support configuring entire source trees.

Source trees often contain multiple packages with a top-level `configure` script that uses the `AC_CONFIG_SUBDIRS` macro (see Section 4.12 [Subdirectories], page 38). Because the packages generally support different '`--with-`*package*' and '`--enable-`*feature*' options, the GNU Coding Standards say they must accept unrecognized options without halting. Even a warning message is undesirable here, so `AC_CONFIG_SUBDIRS` automatically disables the warnings.

This default behavior may be modified in two ways. First, the installer can invoke `configure --disable-option-checking` to disable these warnings, or invoke `configure --enable-option-checking=fatal` options to turn them into fatal errors, respectively. Second, the maintainer can use `AC_DISABLE_OPTION_CHECKING`.

`AC_DISABLE_OPTION_CHECKING`   [Macro]

> By default, disable warnings related to any unrecognized '`--with-`*package*' or '`--enable-`*feature*' options. This is implied by `AC_CONFIG_SUBDIRS`.
>
> The installer can override this behavior by passing '`--enable-option-checking`' (enable warnings) or '`--enable-option-checking=fatal`' (enable errors) to `configure`.

15.6 Configuring Site Details

Some software packages require complex site-specific information. Some examples are host names to use for certain services, company names, and email addresses to contact. Since some configuration scripts generated by Metaconfig ask for such information interactively, people sometimes wonder how to get that information in Autoconf-generated configuration scripts, which aren't interactive.

Such site configuration information should be put in a file that is edited *only by users*, not by programs. The location of the file can either be based on the `prefix` variable, or be a standard location such as the user's home directory. It could even be specified by an environment variable. The programs should examine that file at runtime, rather than at compile time. Runtime configuration is more convenient for users and makes the configuration process simpler than getting the information while configuring. See Section "Variables for Installation Directories" in *The GNU Coding Standards*, for more information on where to put data files.

15.7 Transforming Program Names When Installing

Autoconf supports changing the names of programs when installing them. In order to use these transformations, '`configure.ac`' must call the macro `AC_ARG_PROGRAM`.

`AC_ARG_PROGRAM`   [Macro]

> Place in output variable `program_transform_name` a sequence of `sed` commands for changing the names of installed programs.
>
> If any of the options described below are given to `configure`, program names are transformed accordingly. Otherwise, if `AC_CANONICAL_TARGET` has been called and a '`--target`' value is given, the target type followed by a dash is used as a prefix. Otherwise, no program name transformation is done.

15.7.1 Transformation Options

You can specify name transformations by giving `configure` these command line options:

'`--program-prefix=`*`prefix`*'
> prepend *prefix* to the names;

'`--program-suffix=`*`suffix`*'
> append *suffix* to the names;

'`--program-transform-name=`*`expression`*'
> perform `sed` substitution *expression* on the names.

15.7.2 Transformation Examples

These transformations are useful with programs that can be part of a cross-compilation development environment. For example, a cross-assembler running on a Sun 4 configured with '`--target=i960-vxworks`' is normally installed as '`i960-vxworks-as`', rather than '`as`', which could be confused with a native Sun 4 assembler.

You can force a program name to begin with '`g`', if you don't want GNU programs installed on your system to shadow other programs with the same name. For example, if you configure GNU `diff` with '`--program-prefix=g`', then when you run '`make install`' it is installed as '`/usr/local/bin/gdiff`'.

As a more sophisticated example, you could use

```
--program-transform-name='s/^/g/; s/^gg/g/; s/^gless/less/'
```

to prepend '`g`' to most of the program names in a source tree, excepting those like `gdb` that already have one and those like `less` and `lesskey` that aren't GNU programs. (That is assuming that you have a source tree containing those programs that is set up to use this feature.)

One way to install multiple versions of some programs simultaneously is to append a version number to the name of one or both. For example, if you want to keep Autoconf version 1 around for awhile, you can configure Autoconf version 2 using '`--program-suffix=2`' to install the programs as '`/usr/local/bin/autoconf2`', '`/usr/local/bin/autoheader2`', etc. Nevertheless, pay attention that only the binaries are renamed, therefore you'd have problems with the library files which might overlap.

15.7.3 Transformation Rules

Here is how to use the variable `program_transform_name` in a '`Makefile.in`':

```
PROGRAMS = cp ls rm
transform = @program_transform_name@
install:
        for p in $(PROGRAMS); do \
          $(INSTALL_PROGRAM) $$p $(DESTDIR)$(bindir)/`echo $$p | \
                                          sed '$(transform)'`; \
        done

uninstall:
        for p in $(PROGRAMS); do \
```

```
        rm -f $(DESTDIR)$(bindir)/`echo $$p | sed '$(transform)'`; \
    done
```

It is guaranteed that `program_transform_name` is never empty, and that there are no useless separators. Therefore you may safely embed `program_transform_name` within a sed program using ';':

```
transform = @program_transform_name@
transform_exe = s/$(EXEEXT)$$//;$(transform);s/$$/$(EXEEXT)/
```

Whether to do the transformations on documentation files (Texinfo or `man`) is a tricky question; there seems to be no perfect answer, due to the several reasons for name transforming. Documentation is not usually particular to a specific architecture, and Texinfo files do not conflict with system documentation. But they might conflict with earlier versions of the same files, and `man` pages sometimes do conflict with system documentation. As a compromise, it is probably best to do name transformations on `man` pages but not on Texinfo manuals.

15.8 Setting Site Defaults

Autoconf-generated `configure` scripts allow your site to provide default values for some configuration values. You do this by creating site- and system-wide initialization files.

If the environment variable `CONFIG_SITE` is set, `configure` uses its value as the name of a shell script to read; it is recommended that this be an absolute file name. Otherwise, it reads the shell script '*prefix*/`share/config.site`' if it exists, then '*prefix*/`etc/config.site`' if it exists. Thus, settings in machine-specific files override those in machine-independent ones in case of conflict.

Site files can be arbitrary shell scripts, but only certain kinds of code are really appropriate to be in them. Because `configure` reads any cache file after it has read any site files, a site file can define a default cache file to be shared between all Autoconf-generated `configure` scripts run on that system (see Section 7.4.2 [Cache Files], page 119). If you set a default cache file in a site file, it is a good idea to also set the output variable `CC` in that site file, because the cache file is only valid for a particular compiler, but many systems have several available.

You can examine or override the value set by a command line option to `configure` in a site file; options set shell variables that have the same names as the options, with any dashes turned into underscores. The exceptions are that '`--without-`' and '`--disable-`' options are like giving the corresponding '`--with-`' or '`--enable-`' option and the value 'no'. Thus, '`--cache-file=localcache`' sets the variable `cache_file` to the value '`localcache`'; '`--enable-warnings=no`' or '`--disable-warnings`' sets the variable `enable_warnings` to the value 'no'; '`--prefix=/usr`' sets the variable `prefix` to the value '`/usr`'; etc.

Site files are also good places to set default values for other output variables, such as `CFLAGS`, if you need to give them non-default values: anything you would normally do, repetitively, on the command line. If you use non-default values for *prefix* or *exec_prefix* (wherever you locate the site file), you can set them in the site file if you specify it with the `CONFIG_SITE` environment variable.

You can set some cache values in the site file itself. Doing this is useful if you are cross-compiling, where it is impossible to check features that require running a test program. You could "prime the cache" by setting those values correctly for that system in '*prefix*/etc/config.site'. To find out the names of the cache variables you need to set, see the documentation of the respective Autoconf macro. If the variables or their semantics are undocumented, you may need to look for shell variables with '_cv_' in their names in the affected `configure` scripts, or in the Autoconf M4 source code for those macros; but in that case, their name or semantics may change in a future Autoconf version.

The cache file is careful to not override any variables set in the site files. Similarly, you should not override command-line options in the site files. Your code should check that variables such as `prefix` and `cache_file` have their default values (as set near the top of `configure`) before changing them.

Here is a sample file '/usr/share/local/gnu/share/config.site'. The command 'configure --prefix=/usr/share/local/gnu' would read this file (if CONFIG_SITE is not set to a different file).

```
# /usr/share/local/gnu/share/config.site for configure
#
# Change some defaults.
test "$prefix" = NONE && prefix=/usr/share/local/gnu
test "$exec_prefix" = NONE && exec_prefix=/usr/local/gnu
test "$sharedstatedir" = '${prefix}/com' && sharedstatedir=/var
test "$localstatedir" = '${prefix}/var' && localstatedir=/var

# Give Autoconf 2.x generated configure scripts a shared default
# cache file for feature test results, architecture-specific.
if test "$cache_file" = /dev/null; then
  cache_file="$prefix/var/config.cache"
  # A cache file is only valid for one C compiler.
  CC=gcc
fi
```

Another use of 'config.site' is for priming the directory variables in a manner consistent with the Filesystem Hierarchy Standard (FHS). Once the following file is installed at '/usr/share/config.site', a user can execute simply ./configure --prefix=/usr to get all the directories chosen in the locations recommended by FHS.

```
# /usr/share/config.site for FHS defaults when installing below /usr,
# and the respective settings were not changed on the command line.
if test "$prefix" = /usr; then
  test "$sysconfdir" = '${prefix}/etc' && sysconfdir=/etc
  test "$sharedstatedir" = '${prefix}/com' && sharedstatedir=/var
  test "$localstatedir" = '${prefix}/var' && localstatedir=/var
fi
```

Likewise, on platforms where 64-bit libraries are built by default, then installed in '/usr/local/lib64' instead of '/usr/local/lib', it is appropriate to install '/usr/local/share/config.site':

```
# /usr/local/share/config.site for platforms that prefer
# the directory /usr/local/lib64 over /usr/local/lib.
test "$libdir" = '${exec_prefix}/lib' && libdir='${exec_prefix}/lib64'
```

16 Running `configure` Scripts

Below are instructions on how to configure a package that uses a `configure` script, suitable for inclusion as an 'INSTALL' file in the package. A plain-text version of 'INSTALL' which you may use comes with Autoconf.

16.1 Basic Installation

Briefly, the shell commands './configure; make; make install' should configure, build, and install this package. The following more-detailed instructions are generic; see the 'README' file for instructions specific to this package. More recommendations for GNU packages can be found in Section "Makefile Conventions" in *GNU Coding Standards*.

The `configure` shell script attempts to guess correct values for various system-dependent variables used during compilation. It uses those values to create a 'Makefile' in each directory of the package. It may also create one or more '.h' files containing system-dependent definitions. Finally, it creates a shell script 'config.status' that you can run in the future to recreate the current configuration, and a file 'config.log' containing compiler output (useful mainly for debugging `configure`).

It can also use an optional file (typically called 'config.cache' and enabled with '--cache-file=config.cache' or simply '-C') that saves the results of its tests to speed up reconfiguring. Caching is disabled by default to prevent problems with accidental use of stale cache files.

If you need to do unusual things to compile the package, please try to figure out how `configure` could check whether to do them, and mail diffs or instructions to the address given in the 'README' so they can be considered for the next release. If you are using the cache, and at some point 'config.cache' contains results you don't want to keep, you may remove or edit it.

The file 'configure.ac' (or 'configure.in') is used to create 'configure' by a program called `autoconf`. You need 'configure.ac' if you want to change it or regenerate 'configure' using a newer version of `autoconf`.

The simplest way to compile this package is:

1. `cd` to the directory containing the package's source code and type './configure' to configure the package for your system.

   Running `configure` might take a while. While running, it prints some messages telling which features it is checking for.

2. Type 'make' to compile the package.

3. Optionally, type 'make check' to run any self-tests that come with the package, generally using the just-built uninstalled binaries.

4. Type 'make install' to install the programs and any data files and documentation. When installing into a prefix owned by root, it is recommended that the package be configured and built as a regular user, and only the 'make install' phase executed with root privileges.

5. Optionally, type 'make installcheck' to repeat any self-tests, but this time using the binaries in their final installed location. This target does not install anything.

Running this target as a regular user, particularly if the prior 'make install' required root privileges, verifies that the installation completed correctly.

6. You can remove the program binaries and object files from the source code directory by typing 'make clean'. To also remove the files that configure created (so you can compile the package for a different kind of computer), type 'make distclean'. There is also a 'make maintainer-clean' target, but that is intended mainly for the package's developers. If you use it, you may have to get all sorts of other programs in order to regenerate files that came with the distribution.

7. Often, you can also type 'make uninstall' to remove the installed files again. In practice, not all packages have tested that uninstallation works correctly, even though it is required by the GNU Coding Standards.

8. Some packages, particularly those that use Automake, provide 'make distcheck', which can by used by developers to test that all other targets like 'make install' and 'make uninstall' work correctly. This target is generally not run by end users.

16.2 Compilers and Options

Some systems require unusual options for compilation or linking that the configure script does not know about. Run './configure --help' for details on some of the pertinent environment variables.

You can give configure initial values for configuration parameters by setting variables in the command line or in the environment. Here is an example:

```
./configure CC=c99 CFLAGS=-g LIBS=-lposix
```

See Section 16.9 [Defining Variables], page 299, for more details.

16.3 Compiling For Multiple Architectures

You can compile the package for more than one kind of computer at the same time, by placing the object files for each architecture in their own directory. To do this, you can use GNU make. cd to the directory where you want the object files and executables to go and run the configure script. configure automatically checks for the source code in the directory that configure is in and in '..'. This is known as a *VPATH* build.

With a non-GNU make, it is safer to compile the package for one architecture at a time in the source code directory. After you have installed the package for one architecture, use 'make distclean' before reconfiguring for another architecture.

On MacOS X 10.5 and later systems, you can create libraries and executables that work on multiple system types—known as *fat* or *universal* binaries—by specifying multiple '-arch' options to the compiler but only a single '-arch' option to the preprocessor. Like this:

```
./configure CC="gcc -arch i386 -arch x86_64 -arch ppc -arch ppc64" \
            CXX="g++ -arch i386 -arch x86_64 -arch ppc -arch ppc64" \
            CPP="gcc -E" CXXCPP="g++ -E"
```

This is not guaranteed to produce working output in all cases, you may have to build one architecture at a time and combine the results using the lipo tool if you have problems.

16.4 Installation Names

By default, '`make install`' installs the package's commands under '`/usr/local/bin`', include files under '`/usr/local/include`', etc. You can specify an installation prefix other than '`/usr/local`' by giving `configure` the option '`--prefix=prefix`', where *prefix* must be an absolute file name.

You can specify separate installation prefixes for architecture-specific files and architecture-independent files. If you pass the option '`--exec-prefix=prefix`' to `configure`, the package uses *prefix* as the prefix for installing programs and libraries. Documentation and other data files still use the regular prefix.

In addition, if you use an unusual directory layout you can give options like '`--bindir=dir`' to specify different values for particular kinds of files. Run '`configure --help`' for a list of the directories you can set and what kinds of files go in them. In general, the default for these options is expressed in terms of '`${prefix}`', so that specifying just '`--prefix`' will affect all of the other directory specifications that were not explicitly provided.

The most portable way to affect installation locations is to pass the correct locations to `configure`; however, many packages provide one or both of the following shortcuts of passing variable assignments to the '`make install`' command line to change installation locations without having to reconfigure or recompile.

The first method involves providing an override variable for each affected directory. For example, '`make install prefix=/alternate/directory`' will choose an alternate location for all directory configuration variables that were expressed in terms of '`${prefix}`'. Any directories that were specified during `configure`, but not in terms of '`${prefix}`', must each be overridden at install time for the entire installation to be relocated. The approach of makefile variable overrides for each directory variable is required by the GNU Coding Standards, and ideally causes no recompilation. However, some platforms have known limitations with the semantics of shared libraries that end up requiring recompilation when using this method, particularly noticeable in packages that use GNU Libtool.

The second method involves providing the '`DESTDIR`' variable. For example, '`make install DESTDIR=/alternate/directory`' will prepend '`/alternate/directory`' before all installation names. The approach of '`DESTDIR`' overrides is not required by the GNU Coding Standards, and does not work on platforms that have drive letters. On the other hand, it does better at avoiding recompilation issues, and works well even when some directory options were not specified in terms of '`${prefix}`' at `configure` time.

16.5 Optional Features

If the package supports it, you can cause programs to be installed with an extra prefix or suffix on their names by giving `configure` the option '`--program-prefix=PREFIX`' or '`--program-suffix=SUFFIX`'.

Some packages pay attention to '`--enable-feature`' options to `configure`, where *feature* indicates an optional part of the package. They may also pay attention to '`--with-package`' options, where *package* is something like '`gnu-as`' or '`x`' (for the X Window System). The '`README`' should mention any '`--enable-`' and '`--with-`' options that the package recognizes.

For packages that use the X Window System, `configure` can usually find the X include and library files automatically, but if it doesn't, you can use the `configure` options '`--x-includes=dir`' and '`--x-libraries=dir`' to specify their locations.

Some packages offer the ability to configure how verbose the execution of `make` will be. For these packages, running '`./configure --enable-silent-rules`' sets the default to minimal output, which can be overridden with `make V=1`; while running '`./configure --disable-silent-rules`' sets the default to verbose, which can be overridden with `make V=0`.

16.6 Particular systems

On HP-UX, the default C compiler is not ANSI C compatible. If GNU CC is not installed, it is recommended to use the following options in order to use an ANSI C compiler:

```
./configure CC="cc -Ae -D_XOPEN_SOURCE=500"
```

and if that doesn't work, install pre-built binaries of GCC for HP-UX.

HP-UX `make` updates targets which have the same time stamps as their prerequisites, which makes it generally unusable when shipped generated files such as `configure` are involved. Use GNU `make` instead.

On OSF/1 a.k.a. Tru64, some versions of the default C compiler cannot parse its `<wchar.h>` header file. The option '`-nodtk`' can be used as a workaround. If GNU CC is not installed, it is therefore recommended to try

```
./configure CC="cc"
```

and if that doesn't work, try

```
./configure CC="cc -nodtk"
```

On Solaris, don't put `/usr/ucb` early in your `PATH`. This directory contains several dysfunctional programs; working variants of these programs are available in `/usr/bin`. So, if you need `/usr/ucb` in your `PATH`, put it *after* `/usr/bin`.

On Haiku, software installed for all users goes in '`/boot/common`', not '`/usr/local`'. It is recommended to use the following options:

```
./configure --prefix=/boot/common
```

16.7 Specifying the System Type

There may be some features `configure` cannot figure out automatically, but needs to determine by the type of machine the package will run on. Usually, assuming the package is built to be run on the *same* architectures, `configure` can figure that out, but if it prints a message saying it cannot guess the machine type, give it the '`--build=type`' option. *type* can either be a short name for the system type, such as '`sun4`', or a canonical name which has the form:

```
cpu-company-system
```

where *system* can have one of these forms:

```
os
kernel-os
```

See the file '`config.sub`' for the possible values of each field. If '`config.sub`' isn't included in this package, then this package doesn't need to know the machine type.

If you are *building* compiler tools for cross-compiling, you should use the option '`--target=type`' to select the type of system they will produce code for.

If you want to *use* a cross compiler, that generates code for a platform different from the build platform, you should specify the *host* platform (i.e., that on which the generated programs will eventually be run) with '`--host=type`'.

16.8 Sharing Defaults

If you want to set default values for `configure` scripts to share, you can create a site shell script called '`config.site`' that gives default values for variables like `CC`, `cache_file`, and `prefix`. `configure` looks for '*prefix*`/share/config.site`' if it exists, then '*prefix*`/etc/config.site`' if it exists. Or, you can set the `CONFIG_SITE` environment variable to the location of the site script. A warning: not all `configure` scripts look for a site script.

16.9 Defining Variables

Variables not defined in a site shell script can be set in the environment passed to `configure`. However, some packages may run configure again during the build, and the customized values of these variables may be lost. In order to avoid this problem, you should set them in the `configure` command line, using '`VAR=value`'. For example:

    ./configure CC=/usr/local2/bin/gcc

causes the specified `gcc` to be used as the C compiler (unless it is overridden in the site shell script).

Unfortunately, this technique does not work for `CONFIG_SHELL` due to an Autoconf limitation. Until the limitation is lifted, you can use this workaround:

    CONFIG_SHELL=/bin/bash ./configure CONFIG_SHELL=/bin/bash

16.10 `configure` Invocation

`configure` recognizes the following options to control how it operates.

'`--help`'
'`-h`'   Print a summary of all of the options to `configure`, and exit.

'`--help=short`'
'`--help=recursive`'
                   Print a summary of the options unique to this package's `configure`, and exit. The `short` variant lists options used only in the top level, while the `recursive` variant lists options also present in any nested packages.

'`--version`'
'`-V`'   Print the version of Autoconf used to generate the `configure` script, and exit.

'`--cache-file=file`'
                   Enable the cache: use and save the results of the tests in *file*, traditionally '`config.cache`'. *file* defaults to '`/dev/null`' to disable caching.

'`--config-cache`'
'`-C`'   Alias for '`--cache-file=config.cache`'.

'`--quiet`'
'`--silent`'
'`-q`'   Do not print messages saying which checks are being made. To suppress all nor-
                 mal output, redirect it to '`/dev/null`' (any error messages will still be shown).

'`--srcdir=dir`'
                 Look for the package's source code in directory *dir*. Usually `configure` can
                 determine that directory automatically.

'`--prefix=dir`'
                 Use *dir* as the installation prefix. Section 16.4 [Installation Names], page 297 for
                 more details, including other options available for fine-tuning the installation
                 locations.

'`--no-create`'
'`-n`'   Run the configure checks, but stop before creating any output files.

`configure` also accepts some other, not widely useful, options. Run '`configure --help`'
for more details.

17 config.status Invocation

The `configure` script creates a file named 'config.status', which actually configures, *instantiates*, the template files. It also records the configuration options that were specified when the package was last configured in case reconfiguring is needed.

Synopsis:

    ./config.status [*option*]... [*tag*]...

It configures each *tag*; if none are specified, all the templates are instantiated. A *tag* refers to a file or other tag associated with a configuration action, as specified by an `AC_CONFIG_ITEMS` macro (see Section 4.6 [Configuration Actions], page 21). The files must be specified without their dependencies, as in

    ./config.status foobar

not

    ./config.status foobar:foo.in:bar.in

The supported options are:

'--help'
'-h'   Print a summary of the command line options, the list of the template files, and exit.

'--version'
'-V'   Print the version number of Autoconf and the configuration settings, and exit.

'--config'
            Print the configuration settings in reusable way, quoted for the shell, and exit. For example, for a debugging build that otherwise reuses the configuration from a different build directory *build-dir* of a package in *src-dir*, you could use the following:

                args='*build-dir*/config.status --config'
                eval *src-dir*/configure "$args" CFLAGS=-g --srcdir=*src-dir*

            Note that it may be necessary to override a '--srcdir' setting that was saved in the configuration, if the arguments are used in a different build directory.

'--silent'
'--quiet'
'-q'   Do not print progress messages.

'--debug'
'-d'   Don't remove the temporary files.

'--file=*file*[:*template*]'
            Require that *file* be instantiated as if 'AC_CONFIG_FILES(*file*:*template*)' was used. Both *file* and *template* may be '-' in which case the standard output and/or standard input, respectively, is used. If a *template* file name is relative, it is first looked for in the build tree, and then in the source tree. See Section 4.6 [Configuration Actions], page 21, for more details.

            This option and the following ones provide one way for separately distributed packages to share the values computed by `configure`. Doing so can be useful if some of the packages need a superset of the features that one of them, perhaps a common library, does. These options allow a 'config.status' file to create files other than the ones that its 'configure.ac' specifies, so it can be used for a different package, or for extracting a subset of values. For example,

```
echo '@CC@' | ./config.status --file=-
```

provides the value of @CC@ on standard output.

'--header=*file*[:*template*]'
    Same as '--file' above, but with 'AC_CONFIG_HEADERS'.

'--recheck'
    Ask 'config.status' to update itself and exit (no instantiation). This option is useful if you change configure, so that the results of some tests might be different from the previous run. The '--recheck' option reruns configure with the same arguments you used before, plus the '--no-create' option, which prevents configure from running 'config.status' and creating 'Makefile' and other files, and the '--no-recursion' option, which prevents configure from running other configure scripts in subdirectories. (This is so other Make rules can run 'config.status' when it changes; see Section 4.8.5 [Automatic Remaking], page 32, for an example).

'config.status' checks several optional environment variables that can alter its behavior:

CONFIG_SHELL   [Variable]
    The shell with which to run configure. It must be Bourne-compatible, and the absolute name of the shell should be passed. The default is a shell that supports LINENO if available, and '/bin/sh' otherwise.

CONFIG_STATUS   [Variable]
    The file name to use for the shell script that records the configuration. The default is './config.status'. This variable is useful when one package uses parts of another and the configure scripts shouldn't be merged because they are maintained separately.

You can use './config.status' in your makefiles. For example, in the dependencies given above (see Section 4.8.5 [Automatic Remaking], page 32), 'config.status' is run twice when 'configure.ac' has changed. If that bothers you, you can make each run only regenerate the files for that rule:

```
config.h: stamp-h
stamp-h: config.h.in config.status
        ./config.status config.h
        echo > stamp-h

Makefile: Makefile.in config.status
        ./config.status Makefile
```

The calling convention of 'config.status' has changed; see Section 18.1 [Obsolete config.status Use], page 303, for details.

18 Obsolete Constructs

Autoconf changes, and throughout the years some constructs have been obsoleted. Most of the changes involve the macros, but in some cases the tools themselves, or even some concepts, are now considered obsolete.

You may completely skip this chapter if you are new to Autoconf. Its intention is mainly to help maintainers updating their packages by understanding how to move to more modern constructs.

18.1 Obsolete 'config.status' Invocation

'config.status' now supports arguments to specify the files to instantiate; see Chapter 17 [config.status Invocation], page 301, for more details. Before, environment variables had to be used.

CONFIG_COMMANDS   [Variable]
> The tags of the commands to execute. The default is the arguments given to AC_OUTPUT and AC_CONFIG_COMMANDS in 'configure.ac'.

CONFIG_FILES   [Variable]
> The files in which to perform '@variable@' substitutions. The default is the arguments given to AC_OUTPUT and AC_CONFIG_FILES in 'configure.ac'.

CONFIG_HEADERS   [Variable]
> The files in which to substitute C #define statements. The default is the arguments given to AC_CONFIG_HEADERS; if that macro was not called, 'config.status' ignores this variable.

CONFIG_LINKS   [Variable]
> The symbolic links to establish. The default is the arguments given to AC_CONFIG_LINKS; if that macro was not called, 'config.status' ignores this variable.

In Chapter 17 [config.status Invocation], page 301, using this old interface, the example would be:

```
config.h: stamp-h
stamp-h: config.h.in config.status
        CONFIG_COMMANDS= CONFIG_LINKS= CONFIG_FILES= \
          CONFIG_HEADERS=config.h ./config.status
        echo > stamp-h

Makefile: Makefile.in config.status
        CONFIG_COMMANDS= CONFIG_LINKS= CONFIG_HEADERS= \
          CONFIG_FILES=Makefile ./config.status
```

(If 'configure.ac' does not call AC_CONFIG_HEADERS, there is no need to set CONFIG_HEADERS in the make rules. Equally for CONFIG_COMMANDS, etc.)

18.2 'acconfig.h'

In order to produce 'config.h.in', autoheader needs to build or to find templates for each symbol. Modern releases of Autoconf use AH_VERBATIM and AH_TEMPLATE (see Section 4.9.3 [Autoheader Macros], page 36), but in older releases a file, 'acconfig.h', contained the list of needed templates. autoheader copied comments and #define and #undef statements from 'acconfig.h' in the current directory, if present. This file used to be mandatory if you AC_DEFINE any additional symbols.

Modern releases of Autoconf also provide AH_TOP and AH_BOTTOM if you need to prepend/append some information to 'config.h.in'. Ancient versions of Autoconf had a similar feature: if './acconfig.h' contains the string '@TOP@', autoheader copies the lines before the line containing '@TOP@' into the top of the file that it generates. Similarly, if './acconfig.h' contains the string '@BOTTOM@', autoheader copies the lines after that line to the end of the file it generates. Either or both of those strings may be omitted. An even older alternate way to produce the same effect in ancient versions of Autoconf is to create the files 'file.top' (typically 'config.h.top') and/or 'file.bot' in the current directory. If they exist, autoheader copies them to the beginning and end, respectively, of its output.

In former versions of Autoconf, the files used in preparing a software package for distribution were:

```
configure.ac --.    .------> autoconf* -----> configure
               +---+
[aclocal.m4] --+   '---.
[acsite.m4] ---'       |
                       +--> [autoheader*] -> [config.h.in]
[acconfig.h] ----.     |
              +-----'
[config.h.top] --+
[config.h.bot] --'
```

Using only the AH_ macros, 'configure.ac' should be self-contained, and should not depend upon 'acconfig.h' etc.

18.3 Using autoupdate to Modernize 'configure.ac'

The autoupdate program updates a 'configure.ac' file that calls Autoconf macros by their old names to use the current macro names. In version 2 of Autoconf, most of the macros were renamed to use a more uniform and descriptive naming scheme. See Section 10.2 [Macro Names], page 178, for a description of the new scheme. Although the old names still work (see Section 18.4 [Obsolete Macros], page 305, for a list of the old macros and the corresponding new names), you can make your 'configure.ac' files more readable and make it easier to use the current Autoconf documentation if you update them to use the new macro names.

If given no arguments, autoupdate updates 'configure.ac', backing up the original version with the suffix '~' (or the value of the environment variable SIMPLE_BACKUP_SUFFIX, if that is set). If you give autoupdate an argument, it reads that file instead of 'configure.ac' and writes the updated file to the standard output.

autoupdate accepts the following options:

'`--help`'
'`-h`'   Print a summary of the command line options and exit.

'`--version`'
'`-V`'   Print the version number of Autoconf and exit.

'`--verbose`'
'`-v`'   Report processing steps.

'`--debug`'
'`-d`'   Don't remove the temporary files.

'`--force`'
'`-f`'   Force the update even if the file has not changed. Disregard the cache.

'`--include=`*dir*'
'`-I `*dir*'   Also look for input files in *dir*. Multiple invocations accumulate. Directories are browsed from last to first.

'`--prepend-include=`*dir*'
'`-B `*dir*'   Prepend directory *dir* to the search path. This is used to include the language-specific files before any third-party macros.

18.4 Obsolete Macros

Several macros are obsoleted in Autoconf, for various reasons (typically they failed to quote properly, couldn't be extended for more recent issues, etc.). They are still supported, but deprecated: their use should be avoided.

During the jump from Autoconf version 1 to version 2, most of the macros were renamed to use a more uniform and descriptive naming scheme, but their signature did not change. See Section 10.2 [Macro Names], page 178, for a description of the new naming scheme. Below, if there is just the mapping from old names to new names for these macros, the reader is invited to refer to the definition of the new macro for the signature and the description.

AC_AIX   [Macro]
    This macro is a platform-specific subset of `AC_USE_SYSTEM_EXTENSIONS` (see [AC_USE_SYSTEM_EXTENSIONS], page 98).

AC_ALLOCA   [Macro]
    Replaced by `AC_FUNC_ALLOCA` (see [AC_FUNC_ALLOCA], page 53).

AC_ARG_ARRAY   [Macro]
    Removed because of limited usefulness.

AC_C_CROSS   [Macro]
    This macro is obsolete; it does nothing.

AC_C_LONG_DOUBLE   [Macro]
    If the C compiler supports a working `long double` type with more range or precision than the `double` type, define `HAVE_LONG_DOUBLE`.

    You should use `AC_TYPE_LONG_DOUBLE` or `AC_TYPE_LONG_DOUBLE_WIDER` instead. See Section 5.9.1 [Particular Types], page 74.

AC_CANONICAL_SYSTEM   [Macro]

Determine the system type and set output variables to the names of the canonical system types. See Section 14.2 [Canonicalizing], page 282, for details about the variables this macro sets.

The user is encouraged to use either **AC_CANONICAL_BUILD**, or **AC_CANONICAL_HOST**, or **AC_CANONICAL_TARGET**, depending on the needs. Using **AC_CANONICAL_TARGET** is enough to run the two other macros (see Section 14.2 [Canonicalizing], page 282).

AC_CHAR_UNSIGNED   [Macro]

Replaced by **AC_C_CHAR_UNSIGNED** (see [AC_C_CHAR_UNSIGNED], page 84).

AC_CHECK_TYPE (*type*, *default*)   [Macro]

Autoconf, up to 2.13, used to provide this version of **AC_CHECK_TYPE**, deprecated because of its flaws. First, although it is a member of the **CHECK** clan, it does more than just checking. Secondly, missing types are defined using **#define**, not **typedef**, and this can lead to problems in the case of pointer types.

This use of **AC_CHECK_TYPE** is obsolete and discouraged; see Section 5.9.2 [Generic Types], page 77, for the description of the current macro.

If the type *type* is not defined, define it to be the C (or C++) builtin type *default*, e.g., 'short int' or 'unsigned int'.

This macro is equivalent to:

```
AC_CHECK_TYPE([type], [],
  [AC_DEFINE_UNQUOTED([type], [default],
    [Define to 'default'
     if <sys/types.h> does not define.])])
```

In order to keep backward compatibility, the two versions of **AC_CHECK_TYPE** are implemented, selected using these heuristics:

1. If there are three or four arguments, the modern version is used.

2. If the second argument appears to be a C or C++ type, then the obsolete version is used. This happens if the argument is a C or C++ *builtin* type or a C identifier ending in '_t', optionally followed by one of '[(* ' and then by a string of zero or more characters taken from the set '[]()* _a-zA-Z0-9'.

3. If the second argument is spelled with the alphabet of valid C and C++ types, the user is warned and the modern version is used.

4. Otherwise, the modern version is used.

You are encouraged either to use a valid builtin type, or to use the equivalent modern code (see above), or better yet, to use **AC_CHECK_TYPES** together with

```
#ifndef HAVE_LOFF_T
typedef loff_t off_t;
#endif
```

AC_CHECKING (*feature-description*)   [Macro]

Same as

```
AC_MSG_NOTICE([checking feature-description...]
```

See [AC_MSG_NOTICE], page 121.

AC_COMPILE_CHECK (*echo-text, includes, function-body,*   [Macro]
    action-if-true, [*action-if-false*])

This is an obsolete version of `AC_TRY_COMPILE` itself replaced by `AC_COMPILE_IFELSE`
(see Section 6.4 [Running the Compiler], page 108), with the addition that it prints
'`checking for` *echo-text*' to the standard output first, if *echo-text* is non-empty.
Use `AC_MSG_CHECKING` and `AC_MSG_RESULT` instead to print messages (see Section 7.5
[Printing Messages], page 120).

AC_CONST   [Macro]

Replaced by `AC_C_CONST` (see [AC_C_CONST], page 83).

AC_CROSS_CHECK   [Macro]

Same as `AC_C_CROSS`, which is obsolete too, and does nothing :-).

AC_CYGWIN   [Macro]

Check for the Cygwin environment in which case the shell variable `CYGWIN` is set to
'`yes`'. Don't use this macro, the dignified means to check the nature of the host is
using `AC_CANONICAL_HOST` (see Section 14.2 [Canonicalizing], page 282). As a matter
of fact this macro is defined as:

```
AC_REQUIRE([AC_CANONICAL_HOST])[]dnl
case $host_os in
  *cygwin* ) CYGWIN=yes;;
         * ) CYGWIN=no;;
esac
```

Beware that the variable `CYGWIN` has a special meaning when running Cygwin, and
should not be changed. That's yet another reason not to use this macro.

AC_DECL_SYS_SIGLIST   [Macro]

Same as:

```
AC_CHECK_DECLS([sys_siglist], [], [],
[#include <signal.h>
/* NetBSD declares sys_siglist in unistd.h.  */
#ifdef HAVE_UNISTD_H
# include <unistd.h>
#endif
])
```

See [AC_CHECK_DECLS], page 72.

AC_DECL_YYTEXT   [Macro]

Does nothing, now integrated in `AC_PROG_LEX` (see [AC_PROG_LEX], page 44).

AC_DIR_HEADER   [Macro]

Like calling `AC_FUNC_CLOSEDIR_VOID` (see [AC_FUNC_CLOSEDIR_VOID], page 55)
and `AC_HEADER_DIRENT` (see [AC_HEADER_DIRENT], page 65), but defines a different set of C preprocessor macros to indicate which header file is found:

Header	Old Symbol	New Symbol
'dirent.h'	DIRENT	HAVE_DIRENT_H
'sys/ndir.h'	SYSNDIR	HAVE_SYS_NDIR_H

| `'sys/dir.h'` | `SYSDIR` | `HAVE_SYS_DIR_H` |
| `'ndir.h'` | `NDIR` | `HAVE_NDIR_H` |

`AC_DYNIX_SEQ`   [Macro]

If on DYNIX/ptx, add '`-lseq`' to output variable `LIBS`. This macro used to be defined as

```
AC_CHECK_LIB([seq], [getmntent], [LIBS="-lseq $LIBS"])
```

now it is just `AC_FUNC_GETMNTENT` (see [AC_FUNC_GETMNTENT], page 57).

`AC_EXEEXT`   [Macro]

Defined the output variable `EXEEXT` based on the output of the compiler, which is now done automatically. Typically set to empty string if Posix and '`.exe`' if a DOS variant.

`AC_EMXOS2`   [Macro]

Similar to `AC_CYGWIN` but checks for the EMX environment on OS/2 and sets `EMXOS2`. Don't use this macro, the dignified means to check the nature of the host is using `AC_CANONICAL_HOST` (see Section 14.2 [Canonicalizing], page 282).

`AC_ENABLE (feature, action-if-given, [action-if-not-given])`   [Macro]

This is an obsolete version of `AC_ARG_ENABLE` that does not support providing a help string (see [AC_ARG_ENABLE], page 288).

`AC_ERROR`   [Macro]

Replaced by `AC_MSG_ERROR` (see [AC_MSG_ERROR], page 121).

`AC_FIND_X`   [Macro]

Replaced by `AC_PATH_X` (see [AC_PATH_X], page 96).

`AC_FIND_XTRA`   [Macro]

Replaced by `AC_PATH_XTRA` (see [AC_PATH_XTRA], page 97).

`AC_FOREACH`   [Macro]

Replaced by `m4_foreach_w` (see [m4_foreach_w], page 148).

`AC_FUNC_CHECK`   [Macro]

Replaced by `AC_CHECK_FUNC` (see [AC_CHECK_FUNC], page 61).

`AC_FUNC_SETVBUF_REVERSED`   [Macro]

Do nothing. Formerly, this macro checked whether `setvbuf` takes the buffering type as its second argument and the buffer pointer as the third, instead of the other way around, and defined `SETVBUF_REVERSED`. However, the last systems to have the problem were those based on SVR2, which became obsolete in 1987, and the macro is no longer needed.

`AC_FUNC_WAIT3`   [Macro]

If `wait3` is found and fills in the contents of its third argument (a '`struct rusage *`'), which HP-UX does not do, define `HAVE_WAIT3`.

These days portable programs should use `waitpid`, not `wait3`, as `wait3` has been removed from Posix.

AC_GCC_TRADITIONAL   [Macro]
    Replaced by AC_PROG_GCC_TRADITIONAL (see [AC_PROG_GCC_TRADITIONAL], page 85).

AC_GETGROUPS_T   [Macro]
    Replaced by AC_TYPE_GETGROUPS (see [AC_TYPE_GETGROUPS], page 74).

AC_GETLOADAVG   [Macro]
    Replaced by AC_FUNC_GETLOADAVG (see [AC_FUNC_GETLOADAVG], page 56).

AC_GNU_SOURCE   [Macro]
    This macro is a platform-specific subset of AC_USE_SYSTEM_EXTENSIONS (see [AC_USE_SYSTEM_EXTENSIONS], page 98).

AC_HAVE_FUNCS   [Macro]
    Replaced by AC_CHECK_FUNCS (see [AC_CHECK_FUNCS], page 61).

AC_HAVE_HEADERS   [Macro]
    Replaced by AC_CHECK_HEADERS (see [AC_CHECK_HEADERS], page 70).

AC_HAVE_LIBRARY (*library*, [*action-if-found*],   [Macro]
    [*action-if-not-found*], [*other-libraries*])
    This macro is equivalent to calling AC_CHECK_LIB with a *function* argument of main. In addition, *library* can be written as any of 'foo', '-lfoo', or 'libfoo.a'. In all of those cases, the compiler is passed '-lfoo'. However, *library* cannot be a shell variable; it must be a literal name. See [AC_CHECK_LIB], page 49.

AC_HAVE_POUNDBANG   [Macro]
    Replaced by AC_SYS_INTERPRETER (see [AC_SYS_INTERPRETER], page 97).

AC_HEADER_CHECK   [Macro]
    Replaced by AC_CHECK_HEADER (see [AC_CHECK_HEADER], page 70).

AC_HEADER_EGREP   [Macro]
    Replaced by AC_EGREP_HEADER (see [AC_EGREP_HEADER], page 107).

AC_HELP_STRING   [Macro]
    Replaced by AS_HELP_STRING (see [AS_HELP_STRING], page 288).

AC_INIT (*unique-file-in-source-dir*)   [Macro]
    Formerly AC_INIT used to have a single argument, and was equivalent to:

```
AC_INIT
AC_CONFIG_SRCDIR(unique-file-in-source-dir)
```

    See [AC_INIT], page 17 and [AC_CONFIG_SRCDIR], page 19.

AC_INLINE   [Macro]
    Replaced by AC_C_INLINE (see [AC_C_INLINE], page 84).

AC_INT_16_BITS   [Macro]
    If the C type int is 16 bits wide, define INT_16_BITS. Use 'AC_CHECK_SIZEOF(int)' instead (see [AC_CHECK_SIZEOF], page 78).

AC_IRIX_SUN   [Macro]

If on IRIX (Silicon Graphics Unix), add '-lsun' to output LIBS. If you were using it to get `getmntent`, use `AC_FUNC_GETMNTENT` instead. If you used it for the NIS versions of the password and group functions, use 'AC_CHECK_LIB(sun, getpwnam)'. Up to Autoconf 2.13, it used to be

```
AC_CHECK_LIB([sun], [getmntent], [LIBS="-lsun $LIBS"])
```

now it is defined as

```
AC_FUNC_GETMNTENT
AC_CHECK_LIB([sun], [getpwnam])
```

See [AC_FUNC_GETMNTENT], page 57 and [AC_CHECK_LIB], page 49.

AC_ISC_POSIX   [Macro]

This macro adds '-lcposix' to output variable LIBS if necessary for Posix facilities. Sun dropped support for the obsolete INTERACTIVE Systems Corporation Unix on 2006-07-23. New programs need not use this macro. It is implemented as `AC_SEARCH_LIBS([strerror], [cposix])` (see [AC_SEARCH_LIBS], page 50).

AC_LANG_C   [Macro]

Same as 'AC_LANG([C])' (see [AC_LANG], page 101).

AC_LANG_CPLUSPLUS   [Macro]

Same as 'AC_LANG([C++])' (see [AC_LANG], page 101).

AC_LANG_FORTRAN77   [Macro]

Same as 'AC_LANG([Fortran 77])' (see [AC_LANG], page 101).

AC_LANG_RESTORE   [Macro]

Select the *language* that is saved on the top of the stack, as set by `AC_LANG_SAVE`, remove it from the stack, and call `AC_LANG(language)`. See Section 6.1 [Language Choice], page 101, for the preferred way to change languages.

AC_LANG_SAVE   [Macro]

Remember the current language (as set by `AC_LANG`) on a stack. The current language does not change. `AC_LANG_PUSH` is preferred (see [AC_LANG_PUSH], page 102).

AC_LINK_FILES (*source...***, ***dest...***)**   [Macro]

This is an obsolete version of `AC_CONFIG_LINKS` (see [AC_CONFIG_LINKS], page 38. An updated version of:

```
AC_LINK_FILES(config/$machine.h config/$obj_format.h,
              host.h          object.h)
```

is:

```
AC_CONFIG_LINKS([host.h:config/$machine.h
                object.h:config/$obj_format.h])
```

AC_LN_S   [Macro]

Replaced by `AC_PROG_LN_S` (see [AC_PROG_LN_S], page 45).

AC_LONG_64_BITS   [Macro]

> Define `LONG_64_BITS` if the C type `long int` is 64 bits wide. Use the generic macro '`AC_CHECK_SIZEOF([long int])`' instead (see [AC_CHECK_SIZEOF], page 78).

AC_LONG_DOUBLE   [Macro]

> If the C compiler supports a working `long double` type with more range or precision than the `double` type, define `HAVE_LONG_DOUBLE`.
>
> You should use `AC_TYPE_LONG_DOUBLE` or `AC_TYPE_LONG_DOUBLE_WIDER` instead. See Section 5.9.1 [Particular Types], page 74.

AC_LONG_FILE_NAMES   [Macro]

> Replaced by
>
>   `AC_SYS_LONG_FILE_NAMES`
>
> See [AC_SYS_LONG_FILE_NAMES], page 97.

AC_MAJOR_HEADER   [Macro]

> Replaced by `AC_HEADER_MAJOR` (see [AC_HEADER_MAJOR], page 66).

AC_MEMORY_H   [Macro]

> Used to define `NEED_MEMORY_H` if the `mem` functions were defined in '`memory.h`'. Today it is equivalent to '`AC_CHECK_HEADERS([memory.h])`' (see [AC_CHECK_HEADERS], page 70). Adjust your code to depend upon `HAVE_MEMORY_H`, not `NEED_MEMORY_H`; see Section 5.1.1 [Standard Symbols], page 41.

AC_MINGW32   [Macro]

> Similar to `AC_CYGWIN` but checks for the MinGW compiler environment and sets `MINGW32`. Don't use this macro, the dignified means to check the nature of the host is using `AC_CANONICAL_HOST` (see Section 14.2 [Canonicalizing], page 282).

AC_MINIX   [Macro]

> This macro is a platform-specific subset of `AC_USE_SYSTEM_EXTENSIONS` (see [AC_USE_SYSTEM_EXTENSIONS], page 98).

AC_MINUS_C_MINUS_O   [Macro]

> Replaced by `AC_PROG_CC_C_O` (see [AC_PROG_CC_C_O], page 81).

AC_MMAP   [Macro]

> Replaced by `AC_FUNC_MMAP` (see [AC_FUNC_MMAP], page 58).

AC_MODE_T   [Macro]

> Replaced by `AC_TYPE_MODE_T` (see [AC_TYPE_MODE_T], page 76).

AC_OBJEXT   [Macro]

> Defined the output variable `OBJEXT` based on the output of the compiler, after .c files have been excluded. Typically set to 'o' if Posix, 'obj' if a DOS variant. Now the compiler checking macros handle this automatically.

AC_OBSOLETE (*this-macro-name*, [*suggestion*])   [Macro]

> Make M4 print a message to the standard error output warning that *this-macro-name* is obsolete, and giving the file and line number where it was called. *this-macro-name*

should be the name of the macro that is calling `AC_OBSOLETE`. If *suggestion* is given, it is printed at the end of the warning message; for example, it can be a suggestion for what to use instead of *this-macro-name*.

For instance

```
AC_OBSOLETE([$0], [; use AC_CHECK_HEADERS(unistd.h) instead])dnl
```

You are encouraged to use `AU_DEFUN` instead, since it gives better services to the user (see [AU_DEFUN], page 184).

`AC_OFF_T`   [Macro]

    Replaced by `AC_TYPE_OFF_T` (see [AC_TYPE_OFF_T], page 76).

`AC_OUTPUT ([file]..., [extra-cmds], [init-cmds])`   [Macro]

    The use of `AC_OUTPUT` with arguments is deprecated. This obsoleted interface is equivalent to:

```
AC_CONFIG_FILES(file...)
AC_CONFIG_COMMANDS([default],
                   extra-cmds, init-cmds)
AC_OUTPUT
```

See [AC_CONFIG_FILES], page 23, [AC_CONFIG_COMMANDS], page 37, and [AC_OUTPUT], page 20.

`AC_OUTPUT_COMMANDS (extra-cmds, [init-cmds])`   [Macro]

    Specify additional shell commands to run at the end of 'config.status', and shell commands to initialize any variables from `configure`. This macro may be called multiple times. It is obsolete, replaced by `AC_CONFIG_COMMANDS` (see [AC_CONFIG_COMMANDS], page 37).

Here is an unrealistic example:

```
fubar=27
AC_OUTPUT_COMMANDS([echo this is extra $fubar, and so on.],
                   [fubar=$fubar])
AC_OUTPUT_COMMANDS([echo this is another, extra, bit],
                   [echo init bit])
```

Aside from the fact that `AC_CONFIG_COMMANDS` requires an additional key, an important difference is that `AC_OUTPUT_COMMANDS` is quoting its arguments twice, unlike `AC_CONFIG_COMMANDS`. This means that `AC_CONFIG_COMMANDS` can safely be given macro calls as arguments:

```
AC_CONFIG_COMMANDS(foo, [my_FOO()])
```

Conversely, where one level of quoting was enough for literal strings with `AC_OUTPUT_COMMANDS`, you need two with `AC_CONFIG_COMMANDS`. The following lines are equivalent:

```
AC_OUTPUT_COMMANDS([echo "Square brackets: []"])
AC_CONFIG_COMMANDS([default], [[echo "Square brackets: []"]])
```

`AC_PID_T`   [Macro]

    Replaced by `AC_TYPE_PID_T` (see [AC_TYPE_PID_T], page 76).

AC_PREFIX [Macro]

    Replaced by `AC_PREFIX_PROGRAM` (see [AC_PREFIX_PROGRAM], page 39).

AC_PROGRAMS_CHECK [Macro]

    Replaced by `AC_CHECK_PROGS` (see [AC_CHECK_PROGS], page 46).

AC_PROGRAMS_PATH [Macro]

    Replaced by `AC_PATH_PROGS` (see [AC_PATH_PROGS], page 48).

AC_PROGRAM_CHECK [Macro]

    Replaced by `AC_CHECK_PROG` (see [AC_CHECK_PROG], page 46).

AC_PROGRAM_EGREP [Macro]

    Replaced by `AC_EGREP_CPP` (see [AC_EGREP_CPP], page 108).

AC_PROGRAM_PATH [Macro]

    Replaced by `AC_PATH_PROG` (see [AC_PATH_PROG], page 48).

AC_REMOTE_TAPE [Macro]

    Removed because of limited usefulness.

AC_RESTARTABLE_SYSCALLS [Macro]

    This macro was renamed `AC_SYS_RESTARTABLE_SYSCALLS`. However, these days portable programs should use `sigaction` with `SA_RESTART` if they want restartable system calls. They should not rely on `HAVE_RESTARTABLE_SYSCALLS`, since nowadays whether a system call is restartable is a dynamic issue, not a configuration-time issue.

AC_RETSIGTYPE [Macro]

    Replaced by `AC_TYPE_SIGNAL` (see [AC_TYPE_SIGNAL], page 316), which itself is obsolete when assuming C89 or better.

AC_RSH [Macro]

    Removed because of limited usefulness.

AC_SCO_INTL [Macro]

    If on SCO Unix, add '-lintl' to output variable `LIBS`. This macro used to do this:

        `AC_CHECK_LIB([intl], [strftime], [LIBS="-lintl $LIBS"])`

    Now it just calls `AC_FUNC_STRFTIME` instead (see [AC_FUNC_STRFTIME], page 60).

AC_SETVBUF_REVERSED [Macro]

    Replaced by

        `AC_FUNC_SETVBUF_REVERSED`

    See [AC_FUNC_SETVBUF_REVERSED], page 308.

AC_SET_MAKE [Macro]

    Replaced by `AC_PROG_MAKE_SET` (see [AC_PROG_MAKE_SET], page 20).

AC_SIZEOF_TYPE [Macro]

    Replaced by `AC_CHECK_SIZEOF` (see [AC_CHECK_SIZEOF], page 78).

AC_SIZE_T   [Macro]

> Replaced by `AC_TYPE_SIZE_T` (see [AC_TYPE_SIZE_T], page 76).

AC_STAT_MACROS_BROKEN   [Macro]

> Replaced by `AC_HEADER_STAT` (see [AC_HEADER_STAT], page 66).

AC_STDC_HEADERS   [Macro]

> Replaced by `AC_HEADER_STDC` (see [AC_HEADER_STDC], page 67).

AC_STRCOLL   [Macro]

> Replaced by `AC_FUNC_STRCOLL` (see [AC_FUNC_STRCOLL], page 59).

AC_STRUCT_ST_BLKSIZE   [Macro]

> If `struct stat` contains an `st_blksize` member, define `HAVE_STRUCT_STAT_ST_BLKSIZE`. The former name, `HAVE_ST_BLKSIZE` is to be avoided, as its support will cease in the future. This macro is obsoleted, and should be replaced by
>
>   AC_CHECK_MEMBERS([struct stat.st_blksize])
>
> See [AC_CHECK_MEMBERS], page 74.

AC_STRUCT_ST_RDEV   [Macro]

> If `struct stat` contains an `st_rdev` member, define `HAVE_STRUCT_STAT_ST_RDEV`. The former name for this macro, `HAVE_ST_RDEV`, is to be avoided as it will cease to be supported in the future. Actually, even the new macro is obsolete and should be replaced by:
>
>   AC_CHECK_MEMBERS([struct stat.st_rdev])
>
> See [AC_CHECK_MEMBERS], page 74.

AC_ST_BLKSIZE   [Macro]

> Replaced by `AC_CHECK_MEMBERS` (see [AC_CHECK_MEMBERS], page 74).

AC_ST_BLOCKS   [Macro]

> Replaced by `AC_STRUCT_ST_BLOCKS` (see [AC_STRUCT_ST_BLOCKS], page 73).

AC_ST_RDEV   [Macro]

> Replaced by `AC_CHECK_MEMBERS` (see [AC_CHECK_MEMBERS], page 74).

AC_SYS_RESTARTABLE_SYSCALLS   [Macro]

> If the system automatically restarts a system call that is interrupted by a signal, define `HAVE_RESTARTABLE_SYSCALLS`. This macro does not check whether system calls are restarted in general—it checks whether a signal handler installed with `signal` (but not `sigaction`) causes system calls to be restarted. It does not check whether system calls can be restarted when interrupted by signals that have no handler.
>
> These days portable programs should use `sigaction` with `SA_RESTART` if they want restartable system calls. They should not rely on `HAVE_RESTARTABLE_SYSCALLS`, since nowadays whether a system call is restartable is a dynamic issue, not a configuration-time issue.

AC_SYS_SIGLIST_DECLARED   [Macro]

> This macro was renamed `AC_DECL_SYS_SIGLIST`. However, even that name is obsolete, as the same functionality is now achieved via `AC_CHECK_DECLS` (see [AC_CHECK_DECLS], page 72).

AC_TEST_CPP   [Macro]

    This macro was renamed **AC_TRY_CPP**, which in turn was replaced by **AC_PREPROC_IFELSE** (see [AC_PREPROC_IFELSE], page 107).

AC_TEST_PROGRAM   [Macro]

    This macro was renamed **AC_TRY_RUN**, which in turn was replaced by **AC_RUN_IFELSE** (see [AC_RUN_IFELSE], page 109).

AC_TIMEZONE   [Macro]

    Replaced by **AC_STRUCT_TIMEZONE** (see [AC_STRUCT_TIMEZONE], page 73).

AC_TIME_WITH_SYS_TIME   [Macro]

    Replaced by **AC_HEADER_TIME** (see [AC_HEADER_TIME], page 69).

AC_TRY_COMPILE (*includes*, *function-body*, [*action-if-true*],   [Macro]
    [*action-if-false*])

    Same as:

```
AC_COMPILE_IFELSE(
  [AC_LANG_PROGRAM([[includes]],
    [[function-body]])],
  [action-if-true],
  [action-if-false])
```

    See Section 6.4 [Running the Compiler], page 108.

    This macro double quotes both *includes* and *function-body*.

    For C and C++, *includes* is any #include statements needed by the code in *function-body* (*includes* is ignored if the currently selected language is Fortran or Fortran 77). The compiler and compilation flags are determined by the current language (see Section 6.1 [Language Choice], page 101).

AC_TRY_CPP (*input*, [*action-if-true*], [*action-if-false*])   [Macro]
    Same as:

```
AC_PREPROC_IFELSE(
  [AC_LANG_SOURCE([[input]])],
  [action-if-true],
  [action-if-false])
```

    See Section 6.3 [Running the Preprocessor], page 107.

    This macro double quotes the *input*.

AC_TRY_LINK (*includes*, *function-body*, [*action-if-true*],   [Macro]
    [*action-if-false*])

    Same as:

```
AC_LINK_IFELSE(
  [AC_LANG_PROGRAM([[includes]],
    [[function-body]])],
  [action-if-true],
  [action-if-false])
```

    See Section 6.4 [Running the Compiler], page 108.

This macro double quotes both *includes* and *function-body*.

Depending on the current language (see Section 6.1 [Language Choice], page 101), create a test program to see whether a function whose body consists of *function-body* can be compiled and linked. If the file compiles and links successfully, run shell commands *action-if-found*, otherwise run *action-if-not-found*.

This macro double quotes both *includes* and *function-body*.

For C and C++, *includes* is any `#include` statements needed by the code in *function-body* (*includes* is ignored if the currently selected language is Fortran or Fortran 77). The compiler and compilation flags are determined by the current language (see Section 6.1 [Language Choice], page 101), and in addition `LDFLAGS` and `LIBS` are used for linking.

AC_TRY_LINK_FUNC (*function*, [*action-if-found*],   [Macro]
    [*action-if-not-found*])
    This macro is equivalent to

        `AC_LINK_IFELSE([AC_LANG_CALL([], [`*function*`])],`
          `[`*action-if-found*`], [`*action-if-not-found*`])`

    See [AC_LINK_IFELSE], page 109.

AC_TRY_RUN (*program*, [*action-if-true*], [*action-if-false*],   [Macro]
    [*action-if-cross-compiling* = 'AC_MSG_FAILURE'])
    Same as:

        `AC_RUN_IFELSE(`
        `[AC_LANG_SOURCE([[`*program*`]])],`
        `[`*action-if-true*`],`
        `[`*action-if-false*`],`
        `[`*action-if-cross-compiling*`])`

    See Section 6.6 [Runtime], page 109.

AC_TYPE_SIGNAL   [Macro]
    If 'signal.h' declares `signal` as returning a pointer to a function returning `void`, define `RETSIGTYPE` to be `void`; otherwise, define it to be `int`. These days, it is portable to assume C89, and that signal handlers return `void`, without needing to use this macro or `RETSIGTYPE`.

    When targeting older K&R C, it is possible to define signal handlers as returning type `RETSIGTYPE`, and omit a return statement:

        `RETSIGTYPE`
        `hup_handler ()`
        `{`
        `...`
        `}`

AC_UID_T   [Macro]
    Replaced by `AC_TYPE_UID_T` (see [AC_TYPE_UID_T], page 76).

AC_UNISTD_H   [Macro]
    Same as 'AC_CHECK_HEADERS([unistd.h])' (see [AC_CHECK_HEADERS], page 70).

AC_USG   [Macro]

Define USG if the BSD string functions are defined in 'strings.h'. You should no longer depend upon USG, but on HAVE_STRING_H; see Section 5.1.1 [Standard Symbols], page 41.

AC_UTIME_NULL   [Macro]

Replaced by AC_FUNC_UTIME_NULL (see [AC_FUNC_UTIME_NULL], page 60).

AC_VALIDATE_CACHED_SYSTEM_TUPLE ([cmd])   [Macro]

If the cache file is inconsistent with the current host, target and build system types, it used to execute *cmd* or print a default error message. This is now handled by default.

AC_VERBOSE (result-description)   [Macro]

Replaced by AC_MSG_RESULT (see [AC_MSG_RESULT], page 121).

AC_VFORK   [Macro]

Replaced by AC_FUNC_FORK (see [AC_FUNC_FORK], page 55).

AC_VPRINTF   [Macro]

Replaced by AC_FUNC_VPRINTF (see [AC_FUNC_VPRINTF], page 60).

AC_WAIT3   [Macro]

This macro was renamed AC_FUNC_WAIT3. However, these days portable programs should use waitpid, not wait3, as wait3 has been removed from Posix.

AC_WARN   [Macro]

Replaced by AC_MSG_WARN (see [AC_MSG_WARN], page 121).

AC_WITH (package, action-if-given, [action-if-not-given])   [Macro]

This is an obsolete version of AC_ARG_WITH that does not support providing a help string (see [AC_ARG_WITH], page 286).

AC_WORDS_BIGENDIAN   [Macro]

Replaced by AC_C_BIGENDIAN (see [AC_C_BIGENDIAN], page 83).

AC_XENIX_DIR   [Macro]

This macro used to add '-lx' to output variable LIBS if on Xenix. Also, if 'dirent.h' is being checked for, added '-ldir' to LIBS. Now it is merely an alias of AC_HEADER_DIRENT instead, plus some code to detect whether running XENIX on which you should not depend:

```
AC_MSG_CHECKING([for Xenix])
AC_EGREP_CPP([yes],
[#if defined M_XENIX && !defined M_UNIX
  yes
#endif],
                [AC_MSG_RESULT([yes]); XENIX=yes],
                [AC_MSG_RESULT([no]); XENIX=])
```

Don't use this macro, the dignified means to check the nature of the host is using AC_CANONICAL_HOST (see Section 14.2 [Canonicalizing], page 282).

`AC_YYTEXT_POINTER`   [Macro]

This macro was renamed `AC_DECL_YYTEXT`, which in turn was integrated into `AC_PROG_LEX` (see [AC_PROG_LEX], page 44).

18.5 Upgrading From Version 1

Autoconf version 2 is mostly backward compatible with version 1. However, it introduces better ways to do some things, and doesn't support some of the ugly things in version 1. So, depending on how sophisticated your 'configure.ac' files are, you might have to do some manual work in order to upgrade to version 2. This chapter points out some problems to watch for when upgrading. Also, perhaps your configure scripts could benefit from some of the new features in version 2; the changes are summarized in the file 'NEWS' in the Autoconf distribution.

18.5.1 Changed File Names

If you have an 'aclocal.m4' installed with Autoconf (as opposed to in a particular package's source directory), you must rename it to 'acsite.m4'. See Section 3.4 [autoconf Invocation], page 11.

If you distribute 'install.sh' with your package, rename it to 'install-sh' so make builtin rules don't inadvertently create a file called 'install' from it. AC_PROG_INSTALL looks for the script under both names, but it is best to use the new name.

If you were using 'config.h.top', 'config.h.bot', or 'acconfig.h', you still can, but you have less clutter if you use the AH_ macros. See Section 4.9.3 [Autoheader Macros], page 36.

18.5.2 Changed Makefiles

Add '@CFLAGS@', '@CPPFLAGS@', and '@LDFLAGS@' in your 'Makefile.in' files, so they can take advantage of the values of those variables in the environment when configure is run. Doing this isn't necessary, but it's a convenience for users.

Also add '@configure_input@' in a comment to each input file for AC_OUTPUT, so that the output files contain a comment saying they were produced by configure. Automatically selecting the right comment syntax for all the kinds of files that people call AC_OUTPUT on became too much work.

Add 'config.log' and 'config.cache' to the list of files you remove in distclean targets.

If you have the following in 'Makefile.in':

```
prefix = /usr/local
exec_prefix = $(prefix)
```

you must change it to:

```
prefix = @prefix@
exec_prefix = @exec_prefix@
```

The old behavior of replacing those variables without '@' characters around them has been removed.

18.5.3 Changed Macros

Many of the macros were renamed in Autoconf version 2. You can still use the old names, but the new ones are clearer, and it's easier to find the documentation for them. See Section 18.4 [Obsolete Macros], page 305, for a table showing the new names for the old macros. Use the `autoupdate` program to convert your 'configure.ac' to using the new macro names. See Section 18.3 [autoupdate Invocation], page 304.

Some macros have been superseded by similar ones that do the job better, but are not call-compatible. If you get warnings about calling obsolete macros while running `autoconf`, you may safely ignore them, but your `configure` script generally works better if you follow the advice that is printed about what to replace the obsolete macros with. In particular, the mechanism for reporting the results of tests has changed. If you were using `echo` or `AC_VERBOSE` (perhaps via `AC_COMPILE_CHECK`), your `configure` script's output looks better if you switch to `AC_MSG_CHECKING` and `AC_MSG_RESULT`. See Section 7.5 [Printing Messages], page 120. Those macros work best in conjunction with cache variables. See Section 7.4 [Caching Results], page 117.

18.5.4 Changed Results

If you were checking the results of previous tests by examining the shell variable `DEFS`, you need to switch to checking the values of the cache variables for those tests. `DEFS` no longer exists while `configure` is running; it is only created when generating output files. This difference from version 1 is because properly quoting the contents of that variable turned out to be too cumbersome and inefficient to do every time `AC_DEFINE` is called. See Section 7.4.1 [Cache Variable Names], page 118.

For example, here is a 'configure.ac' fragment written for Autoconf version 1:

```
AC_HAVE_FUNCS(syslog)
case "$DEFS" in
*-DHAVE_SYSLOG*) ;;
*) # syslog is not in the default libraries.  See if it's in some other.
  saved_LIBS="$LIBS"
  for lib in bsd socket inet; do
    AC_CHECKING(for syslog in -l$lib)
    LIBS="-l$lib $saved_LIBS"
    AC_HAVE_FUNCS(syslog)
    case "$DEFS" in
    *-DHAVE_SYSLOG*) break ;;
    *) ;;
    esac
    LIBS="$saved_LIBS"
  done ;;
esac
```

Here is a way to write it for version 2:

```
AC_CHECK_FUNCS([syslog])
if test "x$ac_cv_func_syslog" = xno; then
  # syslog is not in the default libraries.  See if it's in some other.
  for lib in bsd socket inet; do
```

```
            AC_CHECK_LIB([$lib], [syslog], [AC_DEFINE([HAVE_SYSLOG])
              LIBS="-l$lib $LIBS"; break])
         done
      fi
```

If you were working around bugs in `AC_DEFINE_UNQUOTED` by adding backslashes before quotes, you need to remove them. It now works predictably, and does not treat quotes (except back quotes) specially. See Section 7.2 [Setting Output Variables], page 114.

All of the Boolean shell variables set by Autoconf macros now use 'yes' for the true value. Most of them use 'no' for false, though for backward compatibility some use the empty string instead. If you were relying on a shell variable being set to something like 1 or 't' for true, you need to change your tests.

18.5.5 Changed Macro Writing

When defining your own macros, you should now use `AC_DEFUN` instead of `define`. `AC_DEFUN` automatically calls `AC_PROVIDE` and ensures that macros called via `AC_REQUIRE` do not interrupt other macros, to prevent nested 'checking...' messages on the screen. There's no actual harm in continuing to use the older way, but it's less convenient and attractive. See Section 10.1 [Macro Definitions], page 177.

You probably looked at the macros that came with Autoconf as a guide for how to do things. It would be a good idea to take a look at the new versions of them, as the style is somewhat improved and they take advantage of some new features.

If you were doing tricky things with undocumented Autoconf internals (macros, variables, diversions), check whether you need to change anything to account for changes that have been made. Perhaps you can even use an officially supported technique in version 2 instead of kludging. Or perhaps not.

To speed up your locally written feature tests, add caching to them. See whether any of your tests are of general enough usefulness to encapsulate them into macros that you can share.

18.6 Upgrading From Version 2.13

The introduction of the previous section (see Section 18.5 [Autoconf 1], page 318) perfectly suits this section...

> Autoconf version 2.50 is mostly backward compatible with version 2.13. However, it introduces better ways to do some things, and doesn't support some of the ugly things in version 2.13. So, depending on how sophisticated your 'configure.ac' files are, you might have to do some manual work in order to upgrade to version 2.50. This chapter points out some problems to watch for when upgrading. Also, perhaps your `configure` scripts could benefit from some of the new features in version 2.50; the changes are summarized in the file 'NEWS' in the Autoconf distribution.

18.6.1 Changed Quotation

The most important changes are invisible to you: the implementation of most macros have completely changed. This allowed more factorization of the code, better error messages, a higher uniformity of the user's interface etc. Unfortunately, as a side effect, some construct which used to (miraculously) work might break starting with Autoconf 2.50. The most common culprit is bad quotation.

For instance, in the following example, the message is not properly quoted:

```
AC_INIT
AC_CHECK_HEADERS(foo.h, ,
  AC_MSG_ERROR(cannot find foo.h, bailing out))
AC_OUTPUT
```

Autoconf 2.13 simply ignores it:

```
$ autoconf-2.13; ./configure --silent
creating cache ./config.cache
configure: error: cannot find foo.h
$
```

while Autoconf 2.50 produces a broken 'configure':

```
$ autoconf-2.50; ./configure --silent
configure: error: cannot find foo.h
./configure: exit: bad non-numeric arg 'bailing'
./configure: exit: bad non-numeric arg 'bailing'
$
```

The message needs to be quoted, and the AC_MSG_ERROR invocation too!

```
AC_INIT([Example], [1.0], [bug-example@example.org])
AC_CHECK_HEADERS([foo.h], [],
  [AC_MSG_ERROR([cannot find foo.h, bailing out])])
AC_OUTPUT
```

Many many (and many more) Autoconf macros were lacking proper quotation, including no less than... AC_DEFUN itself!

```
$ cat configure.in
AC_DEFUN([AC_PROG_INSTALL],
[# My own much better version
])
AC_INIT
AC_PROG_INSTALL
AC_OUTPUT
$ autoconf-2.13
autoconf: Undefined macros:
***BUG in Autoconf--please report*** AC_FD_MSG
***BUG in Autoconf--please report*** AC_EPI
configure.in:1:AC_DEFUN([AC_PROG_INSTALL],
configure.in:5:AC_PROG_INSTALL
$ autoconf-2.50
$
```

18.6.2 New Macros

While Autoconf was relatively dormant in the late 1990s, Automake provided Autoconf-like macros for a while. Starting with Autoconf 2.50 in 2001, Autoconf provided versions of these macros, integrated in the `AC_` namespace, instead of `AM_`. But in order to ease the upgrading via `autoupdate`, bindings to such `AM_` macros are provided.

Unfortunately older versions of Automake (e.g., Automake 1.4) did not quote the names of these macros. Therefore, when `m4` finds something like 'AC_DEFUN(AM_TYPE_PTRDIFF_T, ...)' in 'aclocal.m4', AM_TYPE_PTRDIFF_T is expanded, replaced with its Autoconf definition.

Fortunately Autoconf catches pre-`AC_INIT` expansions, and complains, in its own words:

```
$ cat configure.ac
AC_INIT([Example], [1.0], [bug-example@example.org])
AM_TYPE_PTRDIFF_T
$ aclocal-1.4
$ autoconf
aclocal.m4:17: error: m4_defn: undefined macro: _m4_divert_diversion
aclocal.m4:17: the top level
autom4te: m4 failed with exit status: 1
$
```

Modern versions of Automake no longer define most of these macros, and properly quote the names of the remaining macros. If you must use an old Automake, do not depend upon macros from Automake as it is simply not its job to provide macros (but the one it requires itself):

```
$ cat configure.ac
AC_INIT([Example], [1.0], [bug-example@example.org])
AM_TYPE_PTRDIFF_T
$ rm aclocal.m4
$ autoupdate
autoupdate: 'configure.ac' is updated
$ cat configure.ac
AC_INIT([Example], [1.0], [bug-example@example.org])
AC_CHECK_TYPES([ptrdiff_t])
$ aclocal-1.4
$ autoconf
$
```

18.6.3 Hosts and Cross-Compilation

Based on the experience of compiler writers, and after long public debates, many aspects of the cross-compilation chain have changed:

— the relationship between the build, host, and target architecture types,

— the command line interface for specifying them to `configure`,

— the variables defined in `configure`,

— the enabling of cross-compilation mode.

The relationship between build, host, and target have been cleaned up: the chain of default is now simply: target defaults to host, host to build, and build to the result of `config.guess`. Nevertheless, in order to ease the transition from 2.13 to 2.50, the following transition scheme is implemented. *Do not rely on it*, as it will be completely disabled in a couple of releases (we cannot keep it, as it proves to cause more problems than it cures).

They all default to the result of running `config.guess`, unless you specify either '`--build`' or '`--host`'. In this case, the default becomes the system type you specified. If you specify both, and they're different, `configure` enters cross compilation mode, so it doesn't run any tests that require execution.

Hint: if you mean to override the result of `config.guess`, prefer '`--build`' over '`--host`'.

For backward compatibility, `configure` accepts a system type as an option by itself. Such an option overrides the defaults for build, host, and target system types. The following configure statement configures a cross toolchain that runs on NetBSD/alpha but generates code for GNU Hurd/sparc, which is also the build platform.

```
./configure --host=alpha-netbsd sparc-gnu
```

In Autoconf 2.13 and before, the variables `build`, `host`, and `target` had a different semantics before and after the invocation of `AC_CANONICAL_BUILD` etc. Now, the argument of '`--build`' is strictly copied into `build_alias`, and is left empty otherwise. After the `AC_CANONICAL_BUILD`, `build` is set to the canonicalized build type. To ease the transition, before, its contents is the same as that of `build_alias`. Do *not* rely on this broken feature.

For consistency with the backward compatibility scheme exposed above, when '`--host`' is specified but '`--build`' isn't, the build system is assumed to be the same as '`--host`', and '`build_alias`' is set to that value. Eventually, this historically incorrect behavior will go away.

The former scheme to enable cross-compilation proved to cause more harm than good, in particular, it used to be triggered too easily, leaving regular end users puzzled in front of cryptic error messages. `configure` could even enter cross-compilation mode only because the compiler was not functional. This is mainly because `configure` used to try to detect cross-compilation, instead of waiting for an explicit flag from the user.

Now, `configure` enters cross-compilation mode if and only if '`--host`' is passed.

That's the short documentation. To ease the transition between 2.13 and its successors, a more complicated scheme is implemented. *Do not rely on the following*, as it will be removed in the near future.

If you specify '`--host`', but not '`--build`', when `configure` performs the first compiler test it tries to run an executable produced by the compiler. If the execution fails, it enters cross-compilation mode. This is fragile. Moreover, by the time the compiler test is performed, it may be too late to modify the build-system type: other tests may have already been performed. Therefore, whenever you specify '`--host`', be sure to specify '`--build`' too.

```
./configure --build=i686-pc-linux-gnu --host=m68k-coff
```

enters cross-compilation mode. The former interface, which consisted in setting the compiler to a cross-compiler without informing `configure` is obsolete. For instance, `configure` fails if it can't run the code generated by the specified compiler if you configure as follows:

```
./configure CC=m68k-coff-gcc
```

18.6.4 AC_LIBOBJ vs. LIBOBJS

Up to Autoconf 2.13, the replacement of functions was triggered via the variable LIBOBJS. Since Autoconf 2.50, the macro AC_LIBOBJ should be used instead (see Section 5.5.3 [Generic Functions], page 61). Starting at Autoconf 2.53, the use of LIBOBJS is an error.

This change is mandated by the unification of the GNU Build System components. In particular, the various fragile techniques used to parse a 'configure.ac' are all replaced with the use of traces. As a consequence, any action must be traceable, which obsoletes critical variable assignments. Fortunately, LIBOBJS was the only problem, and it can even be handled gracefully (read, "without your having to change something").

There were two typical uses of LIBOBJS: asking for a replacement function, and adjusting LIBOBJS for Automake and/or Libtool.

As for function replacement, the fix is immediate: use AC_LIBOBJ. For instance:

```
LIBOBJS="$LIBOBJS fnmatch.o"
LIBOBJS="$LIBOBJS malloc.$ac_objext"
```

should be replaced with:

```
AC_LIBOBJ([fnmatch])
AC_LIBOBJ([malloc])
```

When used with Automake 1.10 or newer, a suitable value for LIBOBJDIR is set so that the LIBOBJS and LTLIBOBJS can be referenced from any 'Makefile.am'. Even without Automake, arranging for LIBOBJDIR to be set correctly enables referencing LIBOBJS and LTLIBOBJS in another directory. The LIBOBJDIR feature is experimental.

18.6.5 AC_ACT_IFELSE vs. AC_TRY_ACT

Since Autoconf 2.50, internal codes uses AC_PREPROC_IFELSE, AC_COMPILE_IFELSE, AC_LINK_IFELSE, and AC_RUN_IFELSE on one hand and AC_LANG_SOURCE, and AC_LANG_PROGRAM on the other hand instead of the deprecated AC_TRY_CPP, AC_TRY_COMPILE, AC_TRY_LINK, and AC_TRY_RUN. The motivations where:

— a more consistent interface: AC_TRY_COMPILE etc. were double quoting their arguments;

— the combinatoric explosion is solved by decomposing on the one hand the generation of sources, and on the other hand executing the program;

— this scheme helps supporting more languages than plain C and C++.

In addition to the change of syntax, the philosophy has changed too: while emphasis was put on speed at the expense of accuracy, today's Autoconf promotes accuracy of the testing framework at, ahem..., the expense of speed.

As a perfect example of what is *not* to be done, here is how to find out whether a header file contains a particular declaration, such as a typedef, a structure, a structure member, or a function. Use AC_EGREP_HEADER instead of running grep directly on the header file; on some systems the symbol might be defined in another header file that the file you are checking includes.

As a (bad) example, here is how you should not check for C preprocessor symbols, either defined by header files or predefined by the C preprocessor: using AC_EGREP_CPP:

```
AC_EGREP_CPP(yes,
[#ifdef _AIX
  yes
#endif
], is_aix=yes, is_aix=no)
```

The above example, properly written would (i) use `AC_LANG_PROGRAM`, and (ii) run the compiler:

```
AC_COMPILE_IFELSE([AC_LANG_PROGRAM(
[[#ifndef _AIX
 error: This isn't AIX!
#endif
]])],
                    [is_aix=yes],
                    [is_aix=no])
```

19 Generating Test Suites with Autotest

N.B.: This section describes a feature which is still stabilizing. Although we believe that Autotest is useful as-is, this documentation describes an interface which might change in the future: do not depend upon Autotest without subscribing to the Autoconf mailing lists.

It is paradoxical that portable projects depend on nonportable tools to run their test suite. Autoconf by itself is the paragon of this problem: although it aims at perfectly portability, up to 2.13 its test suite was using DejaGNU, a rich and complex testing framework, but which is far from being standard on Posix systems. Worse yet, it was likely to be missing on the most fragile platforms, the very platforms that are most likely to torture Autoconf and exhibit deficiencies.

To circumvent this problem, many package maintainers have developed their own testing framework, based on simple shell scripts whose sole outputs are exit status values describing whether the test succeeded. Most of these tests share common patterns, and this can result in lots of duplicated code and tedious maintenance.

Following exactly the same reasoning that yielded to the inception of Autoconf, Autotest provides a test suite generation framework, based on M4 macros building a portable shell script. The suite itself is equipped with automatic logging and tracing facilities which greatly diminish the interaction with bug reporters, and simple timing reports.

Autoconf itself has been using Autotest for years, and we do attest that it has considerably improved the strength of the test suite and the quality of bug reports. Other projects are known to use some generation of Autotest, such as Bison, Free Recode, Free Wdiff, GNU Tar, each of them with different needs, and this usage has validated Autotest as a general testing framework.

Nonetheless, compared to DejaGNU, Autotest is inadequate for interactive tool testing, which is probably its main limitation.

19.1 Using an Autotest Test Suite

19.1.1 `testsuite` Scripts

Generating testing or validation suites using Autotest is rather easy. The whole validation suite is held in a file to be processed through `autom4te`, itself using GNU M4 under the hood, to produce a stand-alone Bourne shell script which then gets distributed. Neither `autom4te` nor GNU M4 are needed at the installer's end.

Each test of the validation suite should be part of some test group. A *test group* is a sequence of interwoven tests that ought to be executed together, usually because one test in the group creates data files that a later test in the same group needs to read. Complex test groups make later debugging more tedious. It is much better to keep only a few tests per test group. Ideally there is only one test per test group.

For all but the simplest packages, some file such as '`testsuite.at`' does not fully hold all test sources, as these are often easier to maintain in separate files. Each of these separate files holds a single test group, or a sequence of test groups all addressing some common functionality in the package. In such cases, '`testsuite.at`' merely initializes the validation suite, and sometimes does elementary health checking, before listing include statements for all other test files. The special file 'package.m4', containing the identification of the package, is automatically included if found.

A convenient alternative consists in moving all the global issues (local Autotest macros, elementary health checking, and AT_INIT invocation) into the file local.at, and making 'testsuite.at' be a simple list of m4_includes of sub test suites. In such case, generating the whole test suite or pieces of it is only a matter of choosing the autom4te command line arguments.

The validation scripts that Autotest produces are by convention called testsuite. When run, testsuite executes each test group in turn, producing only one summary line per test to say if that particular test succeeded or failed. At end of all tests, summarizing counters get printed. One debugging directory is left for each test group which failed, if any: such directories are named 'testsuite.dir/nn', where nn is the sequence number of the test group, and they include:

- a debugging script named 'run' which reruns the test in *debug mode* (see Section 19.3 [testsuite Invocation], page 335). The automatic generation of debugging scripts has the purpose of easing the chase for bugs.
- all the files created with AT_DATA
- all the Erlang source code files created with AT_CHECK_EUNIT
- a log of the run, named 'testsuite.log'

In the ideal situation, none of the tests fail, and consequently no debugging directory is left behind for validation.

It often happens in practice that individual tests in the validation suite need to get information coming out of the configuration process. Some of this information, common for all validation suites, is provided through the file 'atconfig', automatically created by AC_CONFIG_TESTDIR. For configuration information which your testing environment specifically needs, you might prepare an optional file named 'atlocal.in', instantiated by AC_CONFIG_FILES. The configuration process produces 'atconfig' and 'atlocal' out of these two input files, and these two produced files are automatically read by the 'testsuite' script.

Here is a diagram showing the relationship between files.

Files used in preparing a software package for distribution:

```
                [package.m4] -->.
                                  \
    subfile-1.at ->.  [local.at] ---->+
        ...           \               \
    subfile-i.at ---->-- testsuite.at -->-- autom4te* -->testsuite
        ...           /
    subfile-n.at ->'
```

Files used in configuring a software package:

```
                                   .--> atconfig
                                  /
    [atlocal.in] --> config.status* --<
                                  \
                                   '--> [atlocal]
```

Files created during test suite execution:

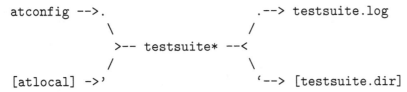

```
atconfig -->.                            .--> testsuite.log
             \                          /
              >-- testsuite* --<
             /                          \
[atlocal] ->'                            '--> [testsuite.dir]
```

19.1.2 Autotest Logs

When run, the test suite creates a log file named after itself, e.g., a test suite named testsuite creates 'testsuite.log'. It contains a lot of information, usually more than maintainers actually need, but therefore most of the time it contains all that is needed:

command line arguments

> A bad but unfortunately widespread habit consists of setting environment variables before the command, such as in 'CC=my-home-grown-cc ./testsuite'. The test suite does not know this change, hence (i) it cannot report it to you, and (ii) it cannot preserve the value of CC for subsequent runs. Autoconf faced exactly the same problem, and solved it by asking users to pass the variable definitions as command line arguments. Autotest requires this rule, too, but has no means to enforce it; the log then contains a trace of the variables that were changed by the user.

'ChangeLog' excerpts

> The topmost lines of all the 'ChangeLog' files found in the source hierarchy. This is especially useful when bugs are reported against development versions of the package, since the version string does not provide sufficient information to know the exact state of the sources the user compiled. Of course, this relies on the use of a 'ChangeLog'.

build machine

> Running a test suite in a cross-compile environment is not an easy task, since it would mean having the test suite run on a machine *build*, while running programs on a machine *host*. It is much simpler to run both the test suite and the programs on *host*, but then, from the point of view of the test suite, there remains a single environment, *host = build*. The log contains relevant information on the state of the *build* machine, including some important environment variables.

tested programs

> The absolute file name and answers to '--version' of the tested programs (see Section 19.2 [Writing Testsuites], page 329, AT_TESTED).

configuration log

> The contents of 'config.log', as created by configure, are appended. It contains the configuration flags and a detailed report on the configuration itself.

19.2 Writing 'testsuite.at'

The 'testsuite.at' is a Bourne shell script making use of special Autotest M4 macros. It often contains a call to AT_INIT near its beginning followed by one call to m4_include per source file for tests. Each such included file, or the remainder of 'testsuite.at' if include files are not used, contain a sequence of test groups. Each test group begins with a call to AT_SETUP, then an arbitrary number of shell commands or calls to AT_CHECK, and then completes with a call to AT_CLEANUP. Multiple test groups can be categorized by a call to AT_BANNER.

All of the public Autotest macros have all-uppercase names in the namespace '^AT_' to prevent them from accidentally conflicting with other text; Autoconf also reserves the namespace '^_AT_' for internal macros. All shell variables used in the testsuite for internal purposes have mostly-lowercase names starting with 'at_'. Autotest also uses here-document delimiters in the namespace '^_AT[A-Z]', and makes use of the file system namespace '^at-'.

Since Autoconf is built on top of M4sugar (see Section 8.3 [Programming in M4sugar], page 137) and M4sh (see Chapter 9 [Programming in M4sh], page 167), you must also be aware of those namespaces ('^_?\(m4\|AS\)_'). In general, you *should not use* the namespace of a package that does not own the macro or shell code you are writing.

AT_INIT ([*name*])   [Macro]

Initialize Autotest. Giving a *name* to the test suite is encouraged if your package includes several test suites. Before this macro is called, AT_PACKAGE_STRING and AT_PACKAGE_BUGREPORT must be defined, which are used to display information about the testsuite to the user. Typically, these macros are provided by a file 'package.m4' built by make (see Section 19.4 [Making testsuite Scripts], page 337), in order to inherit the package name, version, and bug reporting address from 'configure.ac'.

AT_COPYRIGHT (*copyright-notice*)   [Macro]

State that, in addition to the Free Software Foundation's copyright on the Autotest macros, parts of your test suite are covered by *copyright-notice*.

The *copyright-notice* shows up in both the head of testsuite and in 'testsuite --version'.

AT_ARG_OPTION (*options*, *help-text*, [*action-if-given*],   [Macro]
    [*action-if-not-given*])

Accept options from the space-separated list *options*, a list that has leading dashes removed from the options. Long options will be prefixed with '--', single-character options with '-'. The first word in this list is the primary *option*, any others are assumed to be short-hand aliases. The variable associated with it is at_arg_*option*, with any dashes in *option* replaced with underscores.

If the user passes '--*option*' to the testsuite, the variable will be set to ':'. If the user does not pass the option, or passes '--no-*option*', then the variable will be set to 'false'.

action-if-given is run each time the option is encountered; here, the variable at_optarg will be set to ':' or 'false' as appropriate. at_optarg is actually just a copy of at_arg_*option*.

action-if-not-given will be run once after option parsing is complete and if no option from *options* was used.

help-text is added to the end of the list of options shown in testsuite --help (see [AS_HELP_STRING], page 288).

It is recommended that you use a package-specific prefix to *options* names in order to avoid clashes with future Autotest built-in options.

AT_ARG_OPTION_ARG (*options*, *help-text*, [*action-if-given*],   [Macro]
          [*action-if-not-given*])

Accept options with arguments from the space-separated list *options*, a list that has leading dashes removed from the options. Long options will be prefixed with '`--`', single-character options with '`-`'. The first word in this list is the primary *option*, any others are assumed to be short-hand aliases. The variable associated with it is `at_arg_option`, with any dashes in *option* replaced with underscores.

If the user passes '`--option=arg`' or '`--option arg`' to the `testsuite`, the variable will be set to '`arg`'.

action-if-given is run each time the option is encountered; here, the variable `at_optarg` will be set to '`arg`'. `at_optarg` is actually just a copy of `at_arg_option`.

action-if-not-given will be run once after option parsing is complete and if no option from *options* was used.

help-text is added to the end of the list of options shown in `testsuite --help` (see [AS_HELP_STRING], page 288).

It is recommended that you use a package-specific prefix to *options* names in order to avoid clashes with future Autotest built-in options.

AT_COLOR_TESTS   [Macro]

Enable colored test results by default when the output is connected to a terminal.

AT_TESTED (*executables*)   [Macro]

Log the file name and answer to '`--version`' of each program in space-separated list *executables*. Several invocations register new executables, in other words, don't fear registering one program several times.

Autotest test suites rely on `PATH` to find the tested program. This avoids the need to generate absolute names of the various tools, and makes it possible to test installed programs. Therefore, knowing which programs are being exercised is crucial to understanding problems in the test suite itself, or its occasional misuses. It is a good idea to also subscribe foreign programs you depend upon, to avoid incompatible diagnostics.

AT_BANNER (*test-category-name*)   [Macro]

This macro identifies the start of a category of related test groups. When the resulting '`testsuite`' is invoked with more than one test group to run, its output will include a banner containing *test-category-name* prior to any tests run from that category. The banner should be no more than about 40 or 50 characters. A blank banner indicates uncategorized tests; an empty line will be inserted after tests from an earlier category, effectively ending that category.

AT_SETUP (*test-group-name*)   [Macro]

This macro starts a group of related tests, all to be executed in the same subshell. It accepts a single argument, which holds a few words (no more than about 30 or

40 characters) quickly describing the purpose of the test group being started. *test-group-name* must not expand to unbalanced quotes, although quadrigraphs can be used.

AT_KEYWORDS (*keywords*)   [Macro]

Associate the space-separated list of *keywords* to the enclosing test group. This makes it possible to run "slices" of the test suite. For instance, if some of your test groups exercise some 'foo' feature, then using 'AT_KEYWORDS(foo)' lets you run './testsuite -k foo' to run exclusively these test groups. The *test-group-name* of the test group is automatically recorded to AT_KEYWORDS.

Several invocations within a test group accumulate new keywords. In other words, don't fear registering the same keyword several times in a test group.

AT_CAPTURE_FILE (*file*)   [Macro]

If the current test group fails, log the contents of *file*. Several identical calls within one test group have no additional effect.

AT_FAIL_IF (*shell-condition*)   [Macro]

Make the test group fail and skip the rest of its execution, if *shell-condition* is true. *shell-condition* is a shell expression such as a **test** command. Tests before AT_FAIL_IF will be executed and may still cause the test group to be skipped. You can instantiate this macro many times from within the same test group.

You should use this macro only for very simple failure conditions. If the *shell-condition* could emit any kind of output you should instead use AT_CHECK like

        AT_CHECK([if *shell-condition*; then exit 99; fi])

so that such output is properly recorded in the 'testsuite.log' file.

AT_SKIP_IF (*shell-condition*)   [Macro]

Determine whether the test should be skipped because it requires features that are unsupported on the machine under test. *shell-condition* is a shell expression such as a **test** command. Tests before AT_SKIP_IF will be executed and may still cause the test group to fail. You can instantiate this macro many times from within the same test group.

You should use this macro only for very simple skip conditions. If the *shell-condition* could emit any kind of output you should instead use AT_CHECK like

        AT_CHECK([if *shell-condition*; then exit 77; fi])

so that such output is properly recorded in the 'testsuite.log' file.

AT_XFAIL_IF (*shell-condition*)   [Macro]

Determine whether the test is expected to fail because it is a known bug (for unsupported features, you should skip the test). *shell-condition* is a shell expression such as a **test** command; you can instantiate this macro many times from within the same test group, and one of the conditions is enough to turn the test into an expected failure.

AT_CLEANUP   [Macro]

End the current test group.

AT_DATA (*file*, *contents*)   [Macro]

> Initialize an input data *file* with given *contents*. Of course, the *contents* have to be properly quoted between square brackets to protect against included commas or spurious M4 expansion. *contents* must be empty or end with a newline. *file* must be a single shell word that expands into a single file name.

AT_CHECK (*commands*, [*status* = '0'], [*stdout*], [*stderr*],   [Macro]
         [*run-if-fail*], [*run-if-pass*])
AT_CHECK_UNQUOTED (*commands*, [*status* = '0'], [*stdout*], [*stderr*],   [Macro]
         [*run-if-fail*], [*run-if-pass*])

> Execute a test by performing given shell *commands* in a subshell. *commands* is output as-is, so shell expansions are honored. These commands should normally exit with *status*, while producing expected *stdout* and *stderr* contents. If *commands* exit with unexpected status 77, then the rest of the test group is skipped. If *commands* exit with unexpected status 99, then the test group is immediately failed. Otherwise, if this test fails, run shell commands *run-if-fail* or, if this test passes, run shell commands *run-if-pass*, both inside the current shell execution environment. At the beginning of *run-if-fail* and *run-if-pass*, the status of *commands* is available in the **at_status** shell variable.
>
> This macro must be invoked in between **AT_SETUP** and **AT_CLEANUP**.
>
> If *status* is the literal '**ignore**', then the corresponding exit status is not checked, except for the special cases of 77 (skip) and 99 (hard failure). The existence of hard failures allows one to mark a test as an expected failure with **AT_XFAIL_IF** because a feature has not yet been implemented, but to still distinguish between gracefully handling the missing feature and dumping core. A hard failure also inhibits post-test actions in *run-if-fail*.
>
> If the value of the *stdout* or *stderr* parameter is one of the literals in the following table, then the test treats the output according to the rules of that literal. Otherwise, the value of the parameter is treated as text that must exactly match the output given by *commands* on standard output and standard error (including an empty parameter for no output); any differences are captured in the testsuite log and the test is failed (unless an unexpected exit status of 77 skipped the test instead). The difference between **AT_CHECK** and **AT_CHECK_UNQUOTED** is that only the latter performs shell variable expansion ('$'), command substitution ('` `'), and backslash escaping ('\') on comparison text given in the *stdout* and *stderr* arguments; if the text includes a trailing newline, this would be the same as if it were specified via an unquoted here-document. (However, there is no difference in the interpretation of *commands*).
>
> '**ignore**'   The content of the output is ignored, but still captured in the test group log (if the testsuite is run with option '**-v**', the test group log is displayed as the test is run; if the test group later fails, the test group log is also copied into the overall testsuite log). This action is valid for both *stdout* and *stderr*.
>
> '**ignore-nolog**'
>   The content of the output is ignored, and nothing is captured in the log files. If *commands* are likely to produce binary output (including long lines) or large amounts of output, then logging the output can make it

harder to locate details related to subsequent tests within the group, and could potentially corrupt terminal display of a user running `testsuite -v`.

'stdout'   For the *stdout* parameter, capture the content of standard output to both the file 'stdout' and the test group log. Subsequent commands in the test group can then post-process the file. This action is often used when it is desired to use `grep` to look for a substring in the output, or when the output must be post-processed to normalize error messages into a common form.

'stderr'   Like 'stdout', except that it only works for the *stderr* parameter, and the standard error capture file will be named 'stderr'.

'stdout-nolog'
'stderr-nolog'
             Like 'stdout' or 'stderr', except that the captured output is not duplicated into the test group log. This action is particularly useful for an intermediate check that produces large amounts of data, which will be followed by another check that filters down to the relevant data, as it makes it easier to locate details in the log.

'expout'   For the *stdout* parameter, compare standard output contents with the previously created file 'expout', and list any differences in the testsuite log.

'experr'   Like 'expout', except that it only works for the *stderr* parameter, and the standard error contents are compared with 'experr'.

AT_CHECK_EUNIT (*module*, *test-spec*, [*erlflags*], [*run-if-fail*],   [Macro]
    [*run-if-pass*])
Initialize and execute an Erlang module named *module* that performs tests following the *test-spec* EUnit test specification. *test-spec* must be a valid EUnit test specification, as defined in the EUnit Reference Manual. *erlflags* are optional command-line options passed to the Erlang interpreter to execute the test Erlang module. Typically, *erlflags* defines at least the paths to directories containing the compiled Erlang modules under test, as '-pa path1 path2 ...'.

For example, the unit tests associated with Erlang module 'testme', which compiled code is in subdirectory 'src', can be performed with:

```
AT_CHECK_EUNIT([testme_testsuite], [{module, testme}],
               [-pa "${abs_top_builddir}/src"])
```

This macro must be invoked in between **AT_SETUP** and **AT_CLEANUP**.

Variables ERL, ERLC, and (optionally) ERLCFLAGS must be defined as the path of the Erlang interpreter, the path of the Erlang compiler, and the command-line flags to pass to the compiler, respectively. Those variables should be configured in 'configure.ac' using the **AC_ERLANG_PATH_ERL** and **AC_ERLANG_PATH_ERLC** macros, and the configured values of those variables are automatically defined in the testsuite. If ERL or ERLC is not defined, the test group is skipped.

If the EUnit library cannot be found, i.e. if module **eunit** cannot be loaded, the test group is skipped. Otherwise, if *test-spec* is an invalid EUnit test specification, the test group fails. Otherwise, if the EUnit test passes, shell commands *run-if-pass* are executed or, if the EUnit test fails, shell commands *run-if-fail* are executed and the test group fails.

Only the generated test Erlang module is automatically compiled and executed. If *test-spec* involves testing other Erlang modules, e.g. module '**testme**' in the example above, those modules must be already compiled.

If the testsuite is run in verbose mode, with option '**--verbose**', EUnit is also run in verbose mode to output more details about individual unit tests.

19.3 Running `testsuite` Scripts

Autotest test suites support the following options:

'**--help**'
'**-h**'   Display the list of options and exit successfully.

'**--version**'
'**-V**'   Display the version of the test suite and exit successfully.

'**--directory=***dir*'
'**-C** *dir*'   Change the current directory to *dir* before creating any files. Useful for running the testsuite in a subdirectory from a top-level Makefile.

'**--jobs[=***n***]**'
'**-j[***n***]**' Run *n* tests in parallel, if possible. If *n* is not given, run all given tests in parallel. Note that there should be no space before the argument to '**-j**', as '**-j** *number*' denotes the separate arguments '**-j**' and '*number*', see below.

In parallel mode, the standard input device of the testsuite script is not available to commands inside a test group. Furthermore, banner lines are not printed, and the summary line for each test group is output after the test group completes. Summary lines may appear unordered. If verbose and trace output are enabled (see below), they may appear intermixed from concurrently running tests.

Parallel mode requires the **mkfifo** command to work, and will be silently disabled otherwise.

'**--clean**'
'**-c**'   Remove all the files the test suite might have created and exit. Meant for **clean** Make targets.

'**--list**'
'**-l**'   List all the tests (or only the selection), including their possible keywords.

By default all tests are performed (or described with '**--list**') silently in the default environment, but the environment, set of tests, and verbosity level can be tuned:

'*variable=value*'
          Set the environment *variable* to *value*. Use this rather than '**FOO=foo** ./**testsuite**' as debugging scripts would then run in a different environment.

The variable `AUTOTEST_PATH` specifies the testing path to prepend to `PATH`. Relative directory names (not starting with '/') are considered to be relative to the top level of the package being built. All directories are made absolute, first starting from the top level *build* tree, then from the *source* tree. For instance './testsuite AUTOTEST_PATH=tests:bin' for a '/src/foo-1.0' source package built in '/tmp/foo' results in '/tmp/foo/tests:/tmp/foo/bin' and then '/src/foo-1.0/tests:/src/foo-1.0/bin' being prepended to `PATH`.

'*number*'
'*number-number*'
'*number-*'
'*-number*' Add the corresponding test groups, with obvious semantics, to the selection.

'--keywords=*keywords*'
'-k *keywords*'
Add to the selection the test groups with title or keywords (arguments to `AT_SETUP` or `AT_KEYWORDS`) that match *all* keywords of the comma separated list *keywords*, case-insensitively. Use '!' immediately before the keyword to invert the selection for this keyword. By default, the keywords match whole words; enclose them in '.*' to also match parts of words.

For example, running

> ./testsuite -k 'autoupdate,.*FUNC.*'

selects all tests tagged 'autoupdate' *and* with tags containing 'FUNC' (as in 'AC_CHECK_FUNC', 'AC_FUNC_ALLOCA', etc.), while

> ./testsuite -k '!autoupdate' -k '.*FUNC.*'

selects all tests not tagged 'autoupdate' *or* with tags containing 'FUNC'.

'--errexit'
'-e' If any test fails, immediately abort testing. This implies '--debug': post test group clean up, and top-level logging are inhibited. This option is meant for the full test suite, it is not really useful for generated debugging scripts. If the testsuite is run in parallel mode using '--jobs', then concurrently running tests will finish before exiting.

'--verbose'
'-v' Force more verbosity in the detailed output of what is being done. This is the default for debugging scripts.

'--color'
'--color[=never|auto|always]'
Enable colored test results. Without an argument, or with 'always', test results will be colored. With 'never', color mode is turned off. Otherwise, if either the macro `AT_COLOR_TESTS` is used by the testsuite author, or the argument 'auto' is given, then test results are colored if standard output is connected to a terminal.

'--debug'
'-d' Do not remove the files after a test group was performed—but they are still removed *before*, therefore using this option is sane when running several test

groups. Create debugging scripts. Do not overwrite the top-level log (in order to preserve a supposedly existing full log file). This is the default for debugging scripts, but it can also be useful to debug the testsuite itself.

'--recheck'
>Add to the selection all test groups that failed or passed unexpectedly during the last non-debugging test run.

'--trace'
'-x'   Trigger shell tracing of the test groups.

Besides these options accepted by every Autotest testsuite, the testsuite author might have added package-specific options via the `AT_ARG_OPTION` and `AT_ARG_OPTION_ARG` macros (see Section 19.2 [Writing Testsuites], page 329); refer to `testsuite --help` and the package documentation for details.

19.4 Making `testsuite` Scripts

For putting Autotest into movement, you need some configuration and makefile machinery. We recommend, at least if your package uses deep or shallow hierarchies, that you use 'tests/' as the name of the directory holding all your tests and their makefile. Here is a check list of things to do.

— Make sure to create the file 'package.m4', which defines the identity of the package. It must define `AT_PACKAGE_STRING`, the full signature of the package, and `AT_PACKAGE_BUGREPORT`, the address to which bug reports should be sent. For sake of completeness, we suggest that you also define `AT_PACKAGE_NAME`, `AT_PACKAGE_TARNAME`, `AT_PACKAGE_VERSION`, and `AT_PACKAGE_URL`. See Section 4.1 [Initializing configure], page 17, for a description of these variables. Be sure to distribute 'package.m4' and to put it into the source hierarchy: the test suite ought to be shipped! See below for an example 'Makefile' excerpt.

— Invoke `AC_CONFIG_TESTDIR`.

`AC_CONFIG_TESTDIR` (*directory*, [*test-path* = 'directory'])   [Macro]
>An Autotest test suite is to be configured in *directory*. This macro causes '*directory*/atconfig' to be created by `config.status` and sets the default `AUTOTEST_PATH` to *test-path* (see Section 19.3 [testsuite Invocation], page 335).

— Still within 'configure.ac', as appropriate, ensure that some `AC_CONFIG_FILES` command includes substitution for 'tests/atlocal'.

— The appropriate 'Makefile' should be modified so the validation in your package is triggered by 'make check'. An example is provided below.

With Automake, here is a minimal example for inclusion in 'tests/Makefile.am', in order to link 'make check' with a validation suite.

```
# The ':;' works around a Bash 3.2 bug when the output is not writable.
$(srcdir)/package.m4: $(top_srcdir)/configure.ac
        :;{ \
          echo '# Signature of the current package.' && \
          echo 'm4_define([AT_PACKAGE_NAME],' && \
          echo '  [$(PACKAGE_NAME)])' && \
```

```
            echo 'm4_define([AT_PACKAGE_TARNAME],' && \
            echo '  [$(PACKAGE_TARNAME)])' && \
            echo 'm4_define([AT_PACKAGE_VERSION],' && \
            echo '  [$(PACKAGE_VERSION)])' && \
            echo 'm4_define([AT_PACKAGE_STRING],' && \
            echo '  [$(PACKAGE_STRING)])' && \
            echo 'm4_define([AT_PACKAGE_BUGREPORT],' && \
            echo '  [$(PACKAGE_BUGREPORT)])'; \
            echo 'm4_define([AT_PACKAGE_URL],' && \
            echo '  [$(PACKAGE_URL)])'; \
        } >'$(srcdir)/package.m4'

EXTRA_DIST = testsuite.at $(srcdir)/package.m4 $(TESTSUITE) atlocal.in
TESTSUITE = $(srcdir)/testsuite

check-local: atconfig atlocal $(TESTSUITE)
        $(SHELL) '$(TESTSUITE)' $(TESTSUITEFLAGS)

installcheck-local: atconfig atlocal $(TESTSUITE)
        $(SHELL) '$(TESTSUITE)' AUTOTEST_PATH='$(bindir)' \
          $(TESTSUITEFLAGS)

clean-local:
        test ! -f '$(TESTSUITE)' || \
          $(SHELL) '$(TESTSUITE)' --clean

AUTOM4TE = $(SHELL) $(srcdir)/build-aux/missing --run autom4te
AUTOTEST = $(AUTOM4TE) --language=autotest
$(TESTSUITE): $(srcdir)/testsuite.at $(srcdir)/package.m4
        $(AUTOTEST) -I '$(srcdir)' -o $@.tmp $@.at
        mv $@.tmp $@
```

Note that the built testsuite is distributed; this is necessary because users might not have Autoconf installed, and thus would not be able to rebuild it. Likewise, the use of 'missing' provides the user with a nicer error message if they modify a source file to the testsuite, and accidentally trigger the rebuild rules.

You might want to list explicitly the dependencies, i.e., the list of the files 'testsuite.at' includes.

If you don't use Automake, you should include the above example in 'tests/ Makefile.in', along with additional lines inspired from the following:

```
subdir = tests
PACKAGE_NAME = @PACKAGE_NAME@
PACKAGE_TARNAME = @PACKAGE_TARNAME@
PACKAGE_VERSION = @PACKAGE_VERSION@
PACKAGE_STRING = @PACKAGE_STRING@
PACKAGE_BUGREPORT = @PACKAGE_BUGREPORT@
PACKAGE_URL = @PACKAGE_URL@
```

```
atconfig: $(top_builddir)/config.status
        cd $(top_builddir) && \
          $(SHELL) ./config.status $(subdir)/$@

atlocal: $(srcdir)/atlocal.in $(top_builddir)/config.status
        cd $(top_builddir) && \
          $(SHELL) ./config.status $(subdir)/$@
```

and manage to have `$(EXTRA_DIST)` distributed. You will also want to distribute the file
'`build-aux/missing`' from the Automake project; a copy of this file resides in the Autoconf
source tree.

With all this in place, and if you have not initialized 'TESTSUITEFLAGS' within your
makefile, you can fine-tune test suite execution with this variable, for example:

```
make check TESTSUITEFLAGS='-v -d -x 75 -k AC_PROG_CC CFLAGS=-g'
```

20 Frequent Autoconf Questions, with answers

Several questions about Autoconf come up occasionally. Here some of them are addressed.

20.1 Distributing `configure` Scripts

> What are the restrictions on distributing `configure`
> scripts that Autoconf generates? How does that affect my
> programs that use them?

There are no restrictions on how the configuration scripts that Autoconf produces may be distributed or used. In Autoconf version 1, they were covered by the GNU General Public License. We still encourage software authors to distribute their work under terms like those of the GPL, but doing so is not required to use Autoconf.

Of the other files that might be used with `configure`, 'config.h.in' is under whatever copyright you use for your 'configure.ac'. 'config.sub' and 'config.guess' have an exception to the GPL when they are used with an Autoconf-generated `configure` script, which permits you to distribute them under the same terms as the rest of your package. 'install-sh' is from the X Consortium and is not copyrighted.

20.2 Why Require GNU M4?

> Why does Autoconf require GNU M4?

Many M4 implementations have hard-coded limitations on the size and number of macros that Autoconf exceeds. They also lack several builtin macros that it would be difficult to get along without in a sophisticated application like Autoconf, including:

```
m4_builtin
m4_indir
m4_bpatsubst
__file__
__line__
```

Autoconf requires version 1.4.6 or later of GNU M4.

Since only software maintainers need to use Autoconf, and since GNU M4 is simple to configure and install, it seems reasonable to require GNU M4 to be installed also. Many maintainers of GNU and other free software already have most of the GNU utilities installed, since they prefer them.

20.3 How Can I Bootstrap?

> If Autoconf requires GNU M4 and GNU M4 has an Autoconf
> `configure` script, how do I bootstrap? It seems like a chicken
> and egg problem!

This is a misunderstanding. Although GNU M4 does come with a `configure` script produced by Autoconf, Autoconf is not required in order to run the script and install GNU M4. Autoconf is only required if you want to change the M4 `configure` script, which few people have to do (mainly its maintainer).

20.4 Why Not Imake?

Why not use Imake instead of `configure` scripts?

Several people have written addressing this question, so adaptations of their explanations are included here.

The following answer is based on one written by Richard Pixley:

Autoconf generated scripts frequently work on machines that it has never been set up to handle before. That is, it does a good job of inferring a configuration for a new system. Imake cannot do this.

Imake uses a common database of host specific data. For X11, this makes sense because the distribution is made as a collection of tools, by one central authority who has control over the database.

GNU tools are not released this way. Each GNU tool has a maintainer; these maintainers are scattered across the world. Using a common database would be a maintenance nightmare. Autoconf may appear to be this kind of database, but in fact it is not. Instead of listing host dependencies, it lists program requirements.

If you view the GNU suite as a collection of native tools, then the problems are similar. But the GNU development tools can be configured as cross tools in almost any host+target permutation. All of these configurations can be installed concurrently. They can even be configured to share host independent files across hosts. Imake doesn't address these issues.

Imake templates are a form of standardization. The GNU coding standards address the same issues without necessarily imposing the same restrictions.

Here is some further explanation, written by Per Bothner:

One of the advantages of Imake is that it is easy to generate large makefiles using the '`#include`' and macro mechanisms of `cpp`. However, `cpp` is not programmable: it has limited conditional facilities, and no looping. And `cpp` cannot inspect its environment.

All of these problems are solved by using `sh` instead of `cpp`. The shell is fully programmable, has macro substitution, can execute (or source) other shell scripts, and can inspect its environment.

Paul Eggert elaborates more:

With Autoconf, installers need not assume that Imake itself is already installed and working well. This may not seem like much of an advantage to people who are accustomed to Imake. But on many hosts Imake is not installed or the default installation is not working well, and requiring Imake to install a package hinders the acceptance of that package on those hosts. For example, the Imake template and configuration files might not be installed properly on a host, or the Imake build procedure might wrongly assume that all source files are in one big directory tree, or the Imake configuration might assume one compiler whereas the package or the installer needs to use another, or there might be a version mismatch between the Imake expected by the package and the Imake supported by the host. These problems are much rarer with Autoconf, where each package comes with its own independent configuration processor.

Also, Imake often suffers from unexpected interactions between **make** and the installer's C preprocessor. The fundamental problem here is that the C pre-processor was designed to preprocess C programs, not makefiles. This is much less of a problem with Autoconf, which uses the general-purpose preproces-sor M4, and where the package's author (rather than the installer) does the preprocessing in a standard way.

Finally, Mark Eichin notes:

Imake isn't all that extensible, either. In order to add new features to Imake, you need to provide your own project template, and duplicate most of the features of the existing one. This means that for a sophisticated project, using the vendor-provided Imake templates fails to provide any leverage—since they don't cover anything that your own project needs (unless it is an X11 program).

On the other side, though:

The one advantage that Imake has over **configure**: 'Imakefile' files tend to be much shorter (likewise, less redundant) than 'Makefile.in' files. There is a fix to this, however—at least for the Kerberos V5 tree, we've modified things to call in common 'post.in' and 'pre.in' makefile fragments for the entire tree. This means that a lot of common things don't have to be duplicated, even though they normally are in **configure** setups.

20.5 How Do I #define Installation Directories?

My program needs library files, installed in **datadir** and similar. If I use

```
AC_DEFINE_UNQUOTED([DATADIR], [$datadir],
    [Define to the read-only architecture-independent
    data directory.])
```

I get

```
#define DATADIR "${prefix}/share"
```

As already explained, this behavior is on purpose, mandated by the GNU Coding Stan-dards, see Section 4.8.2 [Installation Directory Variables], page 27. There are several means to achieve a similar goal:

— Do not use **AC_DEFINE** but use your makefile to pass the actual value of **datadir** via compilation flags. See Section 4.8.2 [Installation Directory Variables], page 27, for the details.

— This solution can be simplified when compiling a program: you may either extend the CPPFLAGS:

```
CPPFLAGS = -DDATADIR='"$(datadir)"' @CPPFLAGS@
```

If you are using Automake, you should use AM_CPPFLAGS instead:

```
AM_CPPFLAGS = -DDATADIR='"$(datadir)"'
```

Alternatively, create a dedicated header file:

```
DISTCLEANFILES = myprog-paths.h
myprog-paths.h: Makefile
        echo '#define DATADIR "$(datadir)"' >$@
```

The gnulib module 'configmake' provides such a header with all the standard directory variables defined, see Section "configmake" in *GNU Gnulib*.

— Use AC_DEFINE but have configure compute the literal value of datadir and others. Many people have wrapped macros to automate this task; for an example, see the macro AC_DEFINE_DIR from the Autoconf Macro Archive.

This solution does not conform to the GNU Coding Standards.

— Note that all the previous solutions hard wire the absolute name of these directories in the executables, which is not a good property. You may try to compute the names relative to prefix, and try to find prefix at runtime, this way your package is relocatable.

20.6 What is 'autom4te.cache'?

What is this directory 'autom4te.cache'? Can I safely remove it?

In the GNU Build System, 'configure.ac' plays a central role and is read by many tools: autoconf to create 'configure', autoheader to create 'config.h.in', automake to create 'Makefile.in', autoscan to check the completeness of 'configure.ac', autoreconf to check the GNU Build System components that are used. To "read 'configure.ac'" actually means to compile it with M4, which can be a long process for complex 'configure.ac'.

This is why all these tools, instead of running directly M4, invoke autom4te (see Section 8.2.1 [autom4te Invocation], page 132) which, while answering to a specific demand, stores additional information in 'autom4te.cache' for future runs. For instance, if you run autoconf, behind the scenes, autom4te also stores information for the other tools, so that when you invoke autoheader or automake etc., reprocessing 'configure.ac' is not needed. The speed up is frequently 30%, and is increasing with the size of 'configure.ac'.

But it is and remains being simply a cache: you can safely remove it.

Can I permanently get rid of it?

The creation of this cache can be disabled from '~/.autom4te.cfg', see Section 8.2.2 [Customizing autom4te], page 136, for more details. You should be aware that disabling the cache slows down the Autoconf test suite by 40%. The more GNU Build System components are used, the more the cache is useful; for instance running 'autoreconf -f' on the Core Utilities is twice slower without the cache *although '--force' implies that the cache is not fully exploited*, and eight times slower than without '--force'.

20.7 Header Present But Cannot Be Compiled

The most important guideline to bear in mind when checking for features is to mimic as much as possible the intended use. Unfortunately, old versions of AC_CHECK_HEADER and AC_CHECK_HEADERS failed to follow this idea, and called the preprocessor, instead of the compiler, to check for headers. As a result, incompatibilities between headers went unnoticed during configuration, and maintainers finally had to deal with this issue elsewhere.

The transition began with Autoconf 2.56. As of Autoconf 2.64 both checks are performed, and `configure` complains loudly if the compiler and the preprocessor do not agree. However, only the compiler result is considered.

Consider the following example:

```
$ cat number.h
typedef int number;
$ cat pi.h
const number pi = 3;
$ cat configure.ac
AC_INIT([Example], [1.0], [bug-example@example.org])
AC_CHECK_HEADERS([pi.h])
$ autoconf -Wall
$ ./configure
checking for gcc... gcc
checking for C compiler default output file name... a.out
checking whether the C compiler works... yes
checking whether we are cross compiling... no
checking for suffix of executables...
checking for suffix of object files... o
checking whether we are using the GNU C compiler... yes
checking whether gcc accepts -g... yes
checking for gcc option to accept ISO C89... none needed
checking how to run the C preprocessor... gcc -E
checking for grep that handles long lines and -e... grep
checking for egrep... grep -E
checking for ANSI C header files... yes
checking for sys/types.h... yes
checking for sys/stat.h... yes
checking for stdlib.h... yes
checking for string.h... yes
checking for memory.h... yes
checking for strings.h... yes
checking for inttypes.h... yes
checking for stdint.h... yes
checking for unistd.h... yes
checking pi.h usability... no
checking pi.h presence... yes
configure: WARNING: pi.h: present but cannot be compiled
configure: WARNING: pi.h:     check for missing prerequisite headers?
configure: WARNING: pi.h: see the Autoconf documentation
configure: WARNING: pi.h:     section "Present But Cannot Be Compiled"
configure: WARNING: pi.h: proceeding with the compiler's result
configure: WARNING:     ## ------------------------------------- ##
configure: WARNING:     ## Report this to bug-example@example.org ##
configure: WARNING:     ## ------------------------------------- ##
checking for pi.h... yes
```

The proper way the handle this case is using the fourth argument (see Section 5.6.3 [Generic Headers], page 70):

```
$ cat configure.ac
AC_INIT([Example], [1.0], [bug-example@example.org])
AC_CHECK_HEADERS([number.h pi.h], [], [],
[[#ifdef HAVE_NUMBER_H
# include <number.h>
#endif
```

```
]])
$ autoconf -Wall
$ ./configure
checking for gcc... gcc
checking for C compiler default output... a.out
checking whether the C compiler works... yes
checking whether we are cross compiling... no
checking for suffix of executables...
checking for suffix of object files... o
checking whether we are using the GNU C compiler... yes
checking whether gcc accepts -g... yes
checking for gcc option to accept ANSI C... none needed
checking for number.h... yes
checking for pi.h... yes
```

See Section 5.6.2 [Particular Headers], page 65, for a list of headers with their prerequisites.

20.8 Expanded Before Required

Older versions of Autoconf silently built files with incorrect ordering between dependent macros if an outer macro first expanded, then later indirectly required, an inner macro. Starting with Autoconf 2.64, this situation no longer generates out-of-order code, but results in duplicate output and a syntax warning:

```
$ cat configure.ac
⇒AC_DEFUN([TESTA], [[echo in A
⇒if test -n "$SEEN_A" ; then echo duplicate ; fi
⇒SEEN_A=:]])
⇒AC_DEFUN([TESTB], [AC_REQUIRE([TESTA])[echo in B
⇒if test -z "$SEEN_A" ; then echo bug ; fi]])
⇒AC_DEFUN([TESTC], [AC_REQUIRE([TESTB])[echo in C]])
⇒AC_DEFUN([OUTER], [[echo in OUTER]
⇒TESTA
⇒TESTC])
⇒AC_INIT
⇒OUTER
⇒AC_OUTPUT
$ autoconf
⇒configure.ac:11: warning: AC_REQUIRE:
⇒ 'TESTA' was expanded before it was required
⇒configure.ac:4: TESTB is expanded from...
⇒configure.ac:6: TESTC is expanded from...
⇒configure.ac:7: OUTER is expanded from...
⇒configure.ac:11: the top level
```

To avoid this warning, decide what purpose the macro in question serves. If it only needs to be expanded once (for example, if it provides initialization text used by later macros), then the simplest fix is to change the macro to be declared with AC_DEFUN_ONCE (see Section 10.4.3 [One-Shot Macros], page 183), although this only works in Autoconf 2.64

and newer. A more portable fix is to change all instances of direct calls to instead go through `AC_REQUIRE` (see Section 10.4.1 [Prerequisite Macros], page 180). If, instead, the macro is parameterized by arguments or by the current definition of other macros in the m4 environment, then the macro should always be directly expanded instead of required.

For another case study, consider this example trimmed down from an actual package. Originally, the package contained shell code and multiple macro invocations at the top level of 'configure.ac':

```
AC_DEFUN([FOO], [AC_COMPILE_IFELSE([...])])
foobar=
AC_PROG_CC
FOO
```

but that was getting complex, so the author wanted to offload some of the text into a new macro in another file included via 'aclocal.m4'. The naïve approach merely wraps the text in a new macro:

```
AC_DEFUN([FOO], [AC_COMPILE_IFELSE([...])])
AC_DEFUN([BAR], [
foobar=
AC_PROG_CC
FOO
])
BAR
```

With older versions of Autoconf, the setting of 'foobar=' occurs before the single compiler check, as the author intended. But with Autoconf 2.64, this issues the "expanded before it was required" warning for `AC_PROG_CC`, and outputs two copies of the compiler check, one before 'foobar=', and one after. To understand why this is happening, remember that the use of `AC_COMPILE_IFELSE` includes a call to `AC_REQUIRE([AC_PROG_CC])` under the hood. According to the documented semantics of `AC_REQUIRE`, this means that `AC_PROG_CC` *must* occur before the body of the outermost `AC_DEFUN`, which in this case is BAR, thus preceding the use of 'foobar='. The older versions of Autoconf were broken with regards to the rules of `AC_REQUIRE`, which explains why the code changed from one over to two copies of `AC_PROG_CC` when upgrading autoconf. In other words, the author was unknowingly relying on a bug exploit to get the desired results, and that exploit broke once the bug was fixed.

So, what recourse does the author have, to restore their intended semantics of setting 'foobar=' prior to a single compiler check, regardless of whether Autoconf 2.63 or 2.64 is used? One idea is to remember that only `AC_DEFUN` is impacted by `AC_REQUIRE`; there is always the possibility of using the lower-level `m4_define`:

```
AC_DEFUN([FOO], [AC_COMPILE_IFELSE([...])])
m4_define([BAR], [
foobar=
AC_PROG_CC
FOO
])
BAR
```

This works great if everything is in the same file. However, it does not help in the case where the author wants to have `aclocal` find the definition of BAR from its own file, since `aclocal` requires the use of `AC_DEFUN`. In this case, a better fix is to recognize that if `BAR` also uses `AC_REQUIRE`, then there will no longer be direct expansion prior to a subsequent require. Then, by creating yet another helper macro, the author can once again guarantee a single invocation of `AC_PROG_CC`, which will still occur after `foobar=`. The author can also use `AC_BEFORE` to make sure no other macro appearing before `BAR` has triggered an unwanted expansion of `AC_PROG_CC`.

```
AC_DEFUN([FOO], [AC_COMPILE_IFELSE([...])])
AC_DEFUN([BEFORE_CC], [
foobar=
])
AC_DEFUN([BAR], [
AC_BEFORE([$0], [AC_PROG_CC])dnl
AC_REQUIRE([BEFORE_CC])dnl
AC_REQUIRE([AC_PROG_CC])dnl
FOO
])
BAR
```

20.9 Debugging `configure` scripts

While in general, `configure` scripts generated by Autoconf strive to be fairly portable to various systems, compilers, shells, and other tools, it may still be necessary to debug a failing test, broken script or makefile, or fix or override an incomplete, faulty, or erroneous test, especially during macro development. Failures can occur at all levels, in M4 syntax or semantics, shell script issues, or due to bugs in the test or the tools invoked by `configure`. Together with the rather arcane error message that `m4` and `make` may produce when their input contains syntax errors, this can make debugging rather painful.

Nevertheless, here is a list of hints and strategies that may help:

- When `autoconf` fails, common causes for error include:
  - mismatched or unbalanced parentheses or braces (see Section 8.1.7 [Balancing Parentheses], page 129),
  - under- or overquoted macro arguments (see Section 3.1.2 [Autoconf Language], page 7, see Section 8.1.3 [Quoting and Parameters], page 125, see Section 8.1.4 [Quotation and Nested Macros], page 126),
  - spaces between macro name and opening parenthesis (see Section 3.1.2 [Autoconf Language], page 7).

  Typically, it helps to go back to the last working version of the input and compare the differences for each of these errors. Another possibility is to sprinkle pairs of `m4_traceon` and `m4_traceoff` judiciously in the code, either without a parameter or listing some macro names and watch `m4` expand its input verbosely (see Section 8.4 [Debugging via autom4te], page 164).

- Sometimes `autoconf` succeeds but the generated `configure` script has invalid shell syntax. You can detect this case by running 'bash -n configure' or 'sh -n configure'. If this command fails, the same tips apply, as if `autoconf` had failed.

- Debugging `configure` script execution may be done by sprinkling pairs of `set -x` and `set +x` into the shell script before and after the region that contains a bug. Running the whole script with '`shell -vx ./configure 2>&1 | tee log-file`' with a decent *shell* may work, but produces lots of output. Here, it can help to search for markers like '`checking for`' a particular test in the *log-file*.

- Alternatively, you might use a shell with debugging capabilities like bashdb.

- When `configure` tests produce invalid results for your system, it may be necessary to override them:

  - For programs, tools or libraries variables, preprocessor, compiler, or linker flags, it is often sufficient to override them at `make` run time with some care (see Section 12.7 [Macros and Submakes], page 255). Since this normally won't cause `configure` to be run again with these changed settings, it may fail if the changed variable would have caused different test results from `configure`, so this may work only for simple differences.

  - Most tests which produce their result in a substituted variable allow to override the test by setting the variable on the `configure` command line (see Section 16.2 [Compilers and Options], page 296, see Section 16.9 [Defining Variables], page 299, see Section 16.6 [Particular Systems], page 298).

  - Many tests store their result in a cache variable (see Section 7.4 [Caching Results], page 117). This lets you override them either on the `configure` command line as above, or through a primed cache or site file (see Section 7.4.2 [Cache Files], page 119, see Section 15.8 [Site Defaults], page 292). The name of a cache variable is documented with a test macro or may be inferred from Section 7.4.1 [Cache Variable Names], page 118; the precise semantics of undocumented variables are often internal details, subject to change.

- Alternatively, `configure` may produce invalid results because of uncaught programming errors, in your package or in an upstream library package. For example, when `AC_CHECK_LIB` fails to find a library with a specified function, always check '`config.log`'. This will reveal the exact error that produced the failing result: the library linked by `AC_CHECK_LIB` probably has a fatal bug.

Conversely, as macro author, you can make it easier for users of your macro:

- by minimizing dependencies between tests and between test results as far as possible,

- by using `make` variables to factorize and allow override of settings at `make` run time,

- by honoring the GNU Coding Standards and not overriding flags reserved for the user except temporarily during `configure` tests,

- by not requiring users of your macro to use the cache variables. Instead, expose the result of the test via *run-if-true* and *run-if-false* parameters. If the result is not a boolean, then provide it through documented shell variables.

21 History of Autoconf

This chapter was written by the original author, David MacKenzie.

You may be wondering, Why was Autoconf originally written? How did it get into its present form? (Why does it look like gorilla spit?) If you're not wondering, then this chapter contains no information useful to you, and you might as well skip it. If you *are* wondering, then let there be light...

21.1 Genesis

In June 1991 I was maintaining many of the GNU utilities for the Free Software Foundation. As they were ported to more platforms and more programs were added, the number of '-D' options that users had to select in the makefile (around 20) became burdensome. Especially for me—I had to test each new release on a bunch of different systems. So I wrote a little shell script to guess some of the correct settings for the fileutils package, and released it as part of fileutils 2.0. That `configure` script worked well enough that the next month I adapted it (by hand) to create similar `configure` scripts for several other GNU utilities packages. Brian Berliner also adapted one of my scripts for his CVS revision control system.

Later that summer, I learned that Richard Stallman and Richard Pixley were developing similar scripts to use in the GNU compiler tools; so I adapted my `configure` scripts to support their evolving interface: using the file name '`Makefile.in`' as the templates; adding '`+srcdir`', the first option (of many); and creating '`config.status`' files.

21.2 Exodus

As I got feedback from users, I incorporated many improvements, using Emacs to search and replace, cut and paste, similar changes in each of the scripts. As I adapted more GNU utilities packages to use `configure` scripts, updating them all by hand became impractical. Rich Murphey, the maintainer of the GNU graphics utilities, sent me mail saying that the `configure` scripts were great, and asking if I had a tool for generating them that I could send him. No, I thought, but I should! So I started to work out how to generate them. And the journey from the slavery of hand-written `configure` scripts to the abundance and ease of Autoconf began.

Cygnus `configure`, which was being developed at around that time, is table driven; it is meant to deal mainly with a discrete number of system types with a small number of mainly unguessable features (such as details of the object file format). The automatic configuration system that Brian Fox had developed for Bash takes a similar approach. For general use, it seems to me a hopeless cause to try to maintain an up-to-date database of which features each variant of each operating system has. It's easier and more reliable to check for most features on the fly—especially on hybrid systems that people have hacked on locally or that have patches from vendors installed.

I considered using an architecture similar to that of Cygnus `configure`, where there is a single `configure` script that reads pieces of '`configure.in`' when run. But I didn't want to have to distribute all the feature tests with every package, so I settled on having a different `configure` made from each '`configure.in`' by a preprocessor. That approach also offered more control and flexibility.

I looked briefly into using the Metaconfig package, by Larry Wall, Harlan Stenn, and Raphael Manfredi, but I decided not to for several reasons. The `Configure` scripts it produces are interactive, which I find quite inconvenient; I didn't like the ways it checked for some features (such as library functions); I didn't know that it was still being maintained, and the `Configure` scripts I had seen didn't work on many modern systems (such as System V R4 and NeXT); it wasn't flexible in what it could do in response to a feature's presence or absence; I found it confusing to learn; and it was too big and complex for my needs (I didn't realize then how much Autoconf would eventually have to grow).

I considered using Perl to generate my style of `configure` scripts, but decided that M4 was better suited to the job of simple textual substitutions: it gets in the way less, because output is implicit. Plus, everyone already has it. (Initially I didn't rely on the GNU extensions to M4.) Also, some of my friends at the University of Maryland had recently been putting M4 front ends on several programs, including `tvtwm`, and I was interested in trying out a new language.

21.3 Leviticus

Since my `configure` scripts determine the system's capabilities automatically, with no interactive user intervention, I decided to call the program that generates them Autoconfig. But with a version number tacked on, that name would be too long for old Unix file systems, so I shortened it to Autoconf.

In the fall of 1991 I called together a group of fellow questers after the Holy Grail of portability (er, that is, alpha testers) to give me feedback as I encapsulated pieces of my handwritten scripts in M4 macros and continued to add features and improve the techniques used in the checks. Prominent among the testers were François Pinard, who came up with the idea of making an Autoconf shell script to run M4 and check for unresolved macro calls; Richard Pixley, who suggested running the compiler instead of searching the file system to find include files and symbols, for more accurate results; Karl Berry, who got Autoconf to configure TEX and added the macro index to the documentation; and Ian Lance Taylor, who added support for creating a C header file as an alternative to putting '-D' options in a makefile, so he could use Autoconf for his UUCP package. The alpha testers cheerfully adjusted their files again and again as the names and calling conventions of the Autoconf macros changed from release to release. They all contributed many specific checks, great ideas, and bug fixes.

21.4 Numbers

In July 1992, after months of alpha testing, I released Autoconf 1.0, and converted many GNU packages to use it. I was surprised by how positive the reaction to it was. More people started using it than I could keep track of, including people working on software that wasn't part of the GNU Project (such as TCL, FSP, and Kerberos V5). Autoconf continued to improve rapidly, as many people using the `configure` scripts reported problems they encountered.

Autoconf turned out to be a good torture test for M4 implementations. Unix M4 started to dump core because of the length of the macros that Autoconf defined, and several bugs showed up in GNU M4 as well. Eventually, we realized that we needed to use some features that only GNU M4 has. 4.3BSD M4, in particular, has an impoverished set of builtin macros; the System V version is better, but still doesn't provide everything we need.

More development occurred as people put Autoconf under more stresses (and to uses I hadn't anticipated). Karl Berry added checks for X11. david zuhn contributed C++ support. François Pinard made it diagnose invalid arguments. Jim Blandy bravely coerced it into configuring GNU Emacs, laying the groundwork for several later improvements. Roland McGrath got it to configure the GNU C Library, wrote the `autoheader` script to automate the creation of C header file templates, and added a '`--verbose`' option to `configure`. Noah Friedman added the '`--autoconf-dir`' option and `AC_MACRODIR` environment variable. (He also coined the term *autoconfiscate* to mean "adapt a software package to use Autoconf".) Roland and Noah improved the quoting protection in `AC_DEFINE` and fixed many bugs, especially when I got sick of dealing with portability problems from February through June, 1993.

21.5 Deuteronomy

A long wish list for major features had accumulated, and the effect of several years of patching by various people had left some residual cruft. In April 1994, while working for Cygnus Support, I began a major revision of Autoconf. I added most of the features of the Cygnus `configure` that Autoconf had lacked, largely by adapting the relevant parts of Cygnus `configure` with the help of david zuhn and Ken Raeburn. These features include support for using '`config.sub`', '`config.guess`', '`--host`', and '`--target`'; making links to files; and running `configure` scripts in subdirectories. Adding these features enabled Ken to convert GNU `as`, and Rob Savoye to convert DejaGNU, to using Autoconf.

I added more features in response to other peoples' requests. Many people had asked for `configure` scripts to share the results of the checks between runs, because (particularly when configuring a large source tree, like Cygnus does) they were frustratingly slow. Mike Haertel suggested adding site-specific initialization scripts. People distributing software that had to unpack on MS-DOS asked for a way to override the '`.in`' extension on the file names, which produced file names like '`config.h.in`' containing two dots. Jim Avera did an extensive examination of the problems with quoting in `AC_DEFINE` and `AC_SUBST`; his insights led to significant improvements. Richard Stallman asked that compiler output be sent to '`config.log`' instead of '`/dev/null`', to help people debug the Emacs `configure` script.

I made some other changes because of my dissatisfaction with the quality of the program. I made the messages showing results of the checks less ambiguous, always printing a result. I regularized the names of the macros and cleaned up coding style inconsistencies. I added some auxiliary utilities that I had developed to help convert source code packages to use Autoconf. With the help of François Pinard, I made the macros not interrupt each others' messages. (That feature revealed some performance bottlenecks in GNU M4, which he hastily corrected!) I reorganized the documentation around problems people want to solve. And I began a test suite, because experience had shown that Autoconf has a pronounced tendency to regress when we change it.

Again, several alpha testers gave invaluable feedback, especially François Pinard, Jim Meyering, Karl Berry, Rob Savoye, Ken Raeburn, and Mark Eichin.

Finally, version 2.0 was ready. And there was much rejoicing. (And I have free time again. I think. Yeah, right.)

Appendix A GNU Free Documentation License

Version 1.3, 3 November 2008

Copyright © 2000, 2001, 2002, 2007, 2008 Free Software Foundation, Inc.
http://fsf.org/

0. PREAMBLE

The purpose of this License is to make a manual, textbook, or other functional and useful document *free* in the sense of freedom: to assure everyone the effective freedom to copy and redistribute it, with or without modifying it, either commercially or non-commercially. Secondarily, this License preserves for the author and publisher a way to get credit for their work, while not being considered responsible for modifications made by others.

This License is a kind of "copyleft", which means that derivative works of the document must themselves be free in the same sense. It complements the GNU General Public License, which is a copyleft license designed for free software.

We have designed this License in order to use it for manuals for free software, because free software needs free documentation: a free program should come with manuals providing the same freedoms that the software does. But this License is not limited to software manuals; it can be used for any textual work, regardless of subject matter or whether it is published as a printed book. We recommend this License principally for works whose purpose is instruction or reference.

1. APPLICABILITY AND DEFINITIONS

This License applies to any manual or other work, in any medium, that contains a notice placed by the copyright holder saying it can be distributed under the terms of this License. Such a notice grants a world-wide, royalty-free license, unlimited in duration, to use that work under the conditions stated herein. The "Document", below, refers to any such manual or work. Any member of the public is a licensee, and is addressed as "you". You accept the license if you copy, modify or distribute the work in a way requiring permission under copyright law.

A "Modified Version" of the Document means any work containing the Document or a portion of it, either copied verbatim, or with modifications and/or translated into another language.

A "Secondary Section" is a named appendix or a front-matter section of the Document that deals exclusively with the relationship of the publishers or authors of the Document to the Document's overall subject (or to related matters) and contains nothing that could fall directly within that overall subject. (Thus, if the Document is in part a textbook of mathematics, a Secondary Section may not explain any mathematics.) The relationship could be a matter of historical connection with the subject or with related matters, or of legal, commercial, philosophical, ethical or political position regarding them.

The "Invariant Sections" are certain Secondary Sections whose titles are designated, as being those of Invariant Sections, in the notice that says that the Document is released under this License. If a section does not fit the above definition of Secondary then it is not allowed to be designated as Invariant. The Document may contain zero Invariant Sections. If the Document does not identify any Invariant Sections then there are none.

The "Cover Texts" are certain short passages of text that are listed, as Front-Cover Texts or Back-Cover Texts, in the notice that says that the Document is released under this License. A Front-Cover Text may be at most 5 words, and a Back-Cover Text may be at most 25 words.

A "Transparent" copy of the Document means a machine-readable copy, represented in a format whose specification is available to the general public, that is suitable for revising the document straightforwardly with generic text editors or (for images composed of pixels) generic paint programs or (for drawings) some widely available drawing editor, and that is suitable for input to text formatters or for automatic translation to a variety of formats suitable for input to text formatters. A copy made in an otherwise Transparent file format whose markup, or absence of markup, has been arranged to thwart or discourage subsequent modification by readers is not Transparent. An image format is not Transparent if used for any substantial amount of text. A copy that is not "Transparent" is called "Opaque".

Examples of suitable formats for Transparent copies include plain ASCII without markup, Texinfo input format, LaTeX input format, SGML or XML using a publicly available DTD, and standard-conforming simple HTML, PostScript or PDF designed for human modification. Examples of transparent image formats include PNG, XCF and JPG. Opaque formats include proprietary formats that can be read and edited only by proprietary word processors, SGML or XML for which the DTD and/or processing tools are not generally available, and the machine-generated HTML, PostScript or PDF produced by some word processors for output purposes only.

The "Title Page" means, for a printed book, the title page itself, plus such following pages as are needed to hold, legibly, the material this License requires to appear in the title page. For works in formats which do not have any title page as such, "Title Page" means the text near the most prominent appearance of the work's title, preceding the beginning of the body of the text.

The "publisher" means any person or entity that distributes copies of the Document to the public.

A section "Entitled XYZ" means a named subunit of the Document whose title either is precisely XYZ or contains XYZ in parentheses following text that translates XYZ in another language. (Here XYZ stands for a specific section name mentioned below, such as "Acknowledgements", "Dedications", "Endorsements", or "History".) To "Preserve the Title" of such a section when you modify the Document means that it remains a section "Entitled XYZ" according to this definition.

The Document may include Warranty Disclaimers next to the notice which states that this License applies to the Document. These Warranty Disclaimers are considered to be included by reference in this License, but only as regards disclaiming warranties: any other implication that these Warranty Disclaimers may have is void and has no effect on the meaning of this License.

2. VERBATIM COPYING

You may copy and distribute the Document in any medium, either commercially or noncommercially, provided that this License, the copyright notices, and the license notice saying this License applies to the Document are reproduced in all copies, and that you add no other conditions whatsoever to those of this License. You may not use technical measures to obstruct or control the reading or further copying of the copies you make or distribute. However, you may accept compensation in exchange for copies. If you distribute a large enough number of copies you must also follow the conditions in section 3.

You may also lend copies, under the same conditions stated above, and you may publicly display copies.

3. COPYING IN QUANTITY

If you publish printed copies (or copies in media that commonly have printed covers) of the Document, numbering more than 100, and the Document's license notice requires Cover Texts, you must enclose the copies in covers that carry, clearly and legibly, all these Cover Texts: Front-Cover Texts on the front cover, and Back-Cover Texts on the back cover. Both covers must also clearly and legibly identify you as the publisher of these copies. The front cover must present the full title with all words of the title equally prominent and visible. You may add other material on the covers in addition. Copying with changes limited to the covers, as long as they preserve the title of the Document and satisfy these conditions, can be treated as verbatim copying in other respects.

If the required texts for either cover are too voluminous to fit legibly, you should put the first ones listed (as many as fit reasonably) on the actual cover, and continue the rest onto adjacent pages.

If you publish or distribute Opaque copies of the Document numbering more than 100, you must either include a machine-readable Transparent copy along with each Opaque copy, or state in or with each Opaque copy a computer-network location from which the general network-using public has access to download using public-standard network protocols a complete Transparent copy of the Document, free of added material. If you use the latter option, you must take reasonably prudent steps, when you begin distribution of Opaque copies in quantity, to ensure that this Transparent copy will remain thus accessible at the stated location until at least one year after the last time you distribute an Opaque copy (directly or through your agents or retailers) of that edition to the public.

It is requested, but not required, that you contact the authors of the Document well before redistributing any large number of copies, to give them a chance to provide you with an updated version of the Document.

4. MODIFICATIONS

You may copy and distribute a Modified Version of the Document under the conditions of sections 2 and 3 above, provided that you release the Modified Version under precisely this License, with the Modified Version filling the role of the Document, thus licensing distribution and modification of the Modified Version to whoever possesses a copy of it. In addition, you must do these things in the Modified Version:

A. Use in the Title Page (and on the covers, if any) a title distinct from that of the Document, and from those of previous versions (which should, if there were any, be listed in the History section of the Document). You may use the same title as a previous version if the original publisher of that version gives permission.

B. List on the Title Page, as authors, one or more persons or entities responsible for authorship of the modifications in the Modified Version, together with at least five of the principal authors of the Document (all of its principal authors, if it has fewer than five), unless they release you from this requirement.

C. State on the Title page the name of the publisher of the Modified Version, as the publisher.

D. Preserve all the copyright notices of the Document.

E. Add an appropriate copyright notice for your modifications adjacent to the other copyright notices.

F. Include, immediately after the copyright notices, a license notice giving the public permission to use the Modified Version under the terms of this License, in the form shown in the Addendum below.

G. Preserve in that license notice the full lists of Invariant Sections and required Cover Texts given in the Document's license notice.

H. Include an unaltered copy of this License.

I. Preserve the section Entitled "History", Preserve its Title, and add to it an item stating at least the title, year, new authors, and publisher of the Modified Version as given on the Title Page. If there is no section Entitled "History" in the Document, create one stating the title, year, authors, and publisher of the Document as given on its Title Page, then add an item describing the Modified Version as stated in the previous sentence.

J. Preserve the network location, if any, given in the Document for public access to a Transparent copy of the Document, and likewise the network locations given in the Document for previous versions it was based on. These may be placed in the "History" section. You may omit a network location for a work that was published at least four years before the Document itself, or if the original publisher of the version it refers to gives permission.

K. For any section Entitled "Acknowledgements" or "Dedications", Preserve the Title of the section, and preserve in the section all the substance and tone of each of the contributor acknowledgements and/or dedications given therein.

L. Preserve all the Invariant Sections of the Document, unaltered in their text and in their titles. Section numbers or the equivalent are not considered part of the section titles.

M. Delete any section Entitled "Endorsements". Such a section may not be included in the Modified Version.

N. Do not retitle any existing section to be Entitled "Endorsements" or to conflict in title with any Invariant Section.

O. Preserve any Warranty Disclaimers.

If the Modified Version includes new front-matter sections or appendices that qualify as Secondary Sections and contain no material copied from the Document, you may at your option designate some or all of these sections as invariant. To do this, add their titles to the list of Invariant Sections in the Modified Version's license notice. These titles must be distinct from any other section titles.

You may add a section Entitled "Endorsements", provided it contains nothing but endorsements of your Modified Version by various parties—for example, statements of peer review or that the text has been approved by an organization as the authoritative definition of a standard.

You may add a passage of up to five words as a Front-Cover Text, and a passage of up to 25 words as a Back-Cover Text, to the end of the list of Cover Texts in the Modified Version. Only one passage of Front-Cover Text and one of Back-Cover Text may be added by (or through arrangements made by) any one entity. If the Document already includes a cover text for the same cover, previously added by you or by arrangement made by the same entity you are acting on behalf of, you may not add another; but you may replace the old one, on explicit permission from the previous publisher that added the old one.

The author(s) and publisher(s) of the Document do not by this License give permission to use their names for publicity for or to assert or imply endorsement of any Modified Version.

5. COMBINING DOCUMENTS

You may combine the Document with other documents released under this License, under the terms defined in section 4 above for modified versions, provided that you include in the combination all of the Invariant Sections of all of the original documents, unmodified, and list them all as Invariant Sections of your combined work in its license notice, and that you preserve all their Warranty Disclaimers.

The combined work need only contain one copy of this License, and multiple identical Invariant Sections may be replaced with a single copy. If there are multiple Invariant Sections with the same name but different contents, make the title of each such section unique by adding at the end of it, in parentheses, the name of the original author or publisher of that section if known, or else a unique number. Make the same adjustment to the section titles in the list of Invariant Sections in the license notice of the combined work.

In the combination, you must combine any sections Entitled "History" in the various original documents, forming one section Entitled "History"; likewise combine any sections Entitled "Acknowledgements", and any sections Entitled "Dedications". You must delete all sections Entitled "Endorsements."

6. COLLECTIONS OF DOCUMENTS

You may make a collection consisting of the Document and other documents released under this License, and replace the individual copies of this License in the various documents with a single copy that is included in the collection, provided that you follow the rules of this License for verbatim copying of each of the documents in all other respects.

You may extract a single document from such a collection, and distribute it individually under this License, provided you insert a copy of this License into the extracted document, and follow this License in all other respects regarding verbatim copying of that document.

7. AGGREGATION WITH INDEPENDENT WORKS

A compilation of the Document or its derivatives with other separate and independent documents or works, in or on a volume of a storage or distribution medium, is called an "aggregate" if the copyright resulting from the compilation is not used to limit the legal rights of the compilation's users beyond what the individual works permit. When the Document is included in an aggregate, this License does not apply to the other works in the aggregate which are not themselves derivative works of the Document.

If the Cover Text requirement of section 3 is applicable to these copies of the Document, then if the Document is less than one half of the entire aggregate, the Document's Cover Texts may be placed on covers that bracket the Document within the aggregate, or the electronic equivalent of covers if the Document is in electronic form. Otherwise they must appear on printed covers that bracket the whole aggregate.

8. TRANSLATION

Translation is considered a kind of modification, so you may distribute translations of the Document under the terms of section 4. Replacing Invariant Sections with translations requires special permission from their copyright holders, but you may include translations of some or all Invariant Sections in addition to the original versions of these Invariant Sections. You may include a translation of this License, and all the license notices in the Document, and any Warranty Disclaimers, provided that you also include the original English version of this License and the original versions of those notices and disclaimers. In case of a disagreement between the translation and the original version of this License or a notice or disclaimer, the original version will prevail.

If a section in the Document is Entitled "Acknowledgements", "Dedications", or "History", the requirement (section 4) to Preserve its Title (section 1) will typically require changing the actual title.

9. TERMINATION

You may not copy, modify, sublicense, or distribute the Document except as expressly provided under this License. Any attempt otherwise to copy, modify, sublicense, or distribute it is void, and will automatically terminate your rights under this License.

However, if you cease all violation of this License, then your license from a particular copyright holder is reinstated (a) provisionally, unless and until the copyright holder explicitly and finally terminates your license, and (b) permanently, if the copyright holder fails to notify you of the violation by some reasonable means prior to 60 days after the cessation.

Moreover, your license from a particular copyright holder is reinstated permanently if the copyright holder notifies you of the violation by some reasonable means, this is the first time you have received notice of violation of this License (for any work) from that copyright holder, and you cure the violation prior to 30 days after your receipt of the notice.

Termination of your rights under this section does not terminate the licenses of parties who have received copies or rights from you under this License. If your rights have been terminated and not permanently reinstated, receipt of a copy of some or all of the same material does not give you any rights to use it.

10. FUTURE REVISIONS OF THIS LICENSE

The Free Software Foundation may publish new, revised versions of the GNU Free Documentation License from time to time. Such new versions will be similar in spirit to the present version, but may differ in detail to address new problems or concerns. See `http://www.gnu.org/copyleft/`.

Each version of the License is given a distinguishing version number. If the Document specifies that a particular numbered version of this License "or any later version" applies to it, you have the option of following the terms and conditions either of that specified version or of any later version that has been published (not as a draft) by the Free Software Foundation. If the Document does not specify a version number of this License, you may choose any version ever published (not as a draft) by the Free Software Foundation. If the Document specifies that a proxy can decide which future versions of this License can be used, that proxy's public statement of acceptance of a version permanently authorizes you to choose that version for the Document.

11. RELICENSING

"Massive Multiauthor Collaboration Site" (or "MMC Site") means any World Wide Web server that publishes copyrightable works and also provides prominent facilities for anybody to edit those works. A public wiki that anybody can edit is an example of such a server. A "Massive Multiauthor Collaboration" (or "MMC") contained in the site means any set of copyrightable works thus published on the MMC site.

"CC-BY-SA" means the Creative Commons Attribution-Share Alike 3.0 license published by Creative Commons Corporation, a not-for-profit corporation with a principal place of business in San Francisco, California, as well as future copyleft versions of that license published by that same organization.

"Incorporate" means to publish or republish a Document, in whole or in part, as part of another Document.

An MMC is "eligible for relicensing" if it is licensed under this License, and if all works that were first published under this License somewhere other than this MMC, and subsequently incorporated in whole or in part into the MMC, (1) had no cover texts or invariant sections, and (2) were thus incorporated prior to November 1, 2008.

The operator of an MMC Site may republish an MMC contained in the site under CC-BY-SA on the same site at any time before August 1, 2009, provided the MMC is eligible for relicensing.

ADDENDUM: How to use this License for your documents

To use this License in a document you have written, include a copy of the License in the document and put the following copyright and license notices just after the title page:

```
Copyright (C)  year  your name.
Permission is granted to copy, distribute and/or modify this document
under the terms of the GNU Free Documentation License, Version 1.3
or any later version published by the Free Software Foundation;
with no Invariant Sections, no Front-Cover Texts, and no Back-Cover
Texts.  A copy of the license is included in the section entitled ''GNU
Free Documentation License''.
```

If you have Invariant Sections, Front-Cover Texts and Back-Cover Texts, replace the "with...Texts." line with this:

```
with the Invariant Sections being list their titles, with
the Front-Cover Texts being list, and with the Back-Cover Texts
being list.
```

If you have Invariant Sections without Cover Texts, or some other combination of the three, merge those two alternatives to suit the situation.

If your document contains nontrivial examples of program code, we recommend releasing these examples in parallel under your choice of free software license, such as the GNU General Public License, to permit their use in free software.

Appendix B Indices

B.1 Environment Variable Index

This is an alphabetical list of the environment variables that might influence Autoconf checks.

_

_ 211

B

BIN_SH 211

C

CC 81
CDPATH 212
CFLAGS 24, 81
CLICOLOR_FORCE 212
CONFIG_COMMANDS 303
CONFIG_FILES 303
CONFIG_HEADERS 303
CONFIG_LINKS 303
CONFIG_SHELL 302
CONFIG_SITE 292
CONFIG_STATUS 302
CPP 82
CPPFLAGS 24
CXX 86
CXXCPP 86
CXXFLAGS 25, 86
CYGWIN 307

D

DUALCASE 212

E

ENV 212
ERL 88
ERLC 87
ERLCFLAGS 25, 87

F

F77 88
FC 88
FCFLAGS 25, 88
FFLAGS 25, 88
FPATH 212

G

GOFLAGS 26
GREP_OPTIONS 213

I

IFS 213

L

LANG 213
LANGUAGE 213
LC_ADDRESS 214
LC_ALL 173, 213
LC_COLLATE 213
LC_CTYPE 213
LC_IDENTIFICATION 214
LC_MEASUREMENT 214
LC_MESSAGES 213
LC_MONETARY 213
LC_NAME 214
LC_NUMERIC 213
LC_PAPER 214
LC_TELEPHONE 214
LC_TIME 213
LDFLAGS 26
LIBS 26
LINENO 174, 214

M

M4 132
MAIL 212
MAILPATH 212

N

NULLCMD 217

O

OBJC 86
OBJCFLAGS 26, 86
OBJCPP 87
OBJCXX 87
OBJCXXCPP 87
OBJCXXFLAGS 26, 87
options 217

P

PATH_SEPARATOR 217
POSIXLY_CORRECT 218
PS1 212
PS2 212
PS4 212
PWD 218

R

RANDOM 218

S

SHELL 173
SIMPLE_BACKUP_SUFFIX 304
status 218

T

TMPDIR 174

W

WARNINGS 12, 15, 36, 133

X

XMKMF 96

Y

YACC 46
YFLAGS 46

B.2 Output Variable Index

This is an alphabetical list of the variables that Autoconf can substitute into files that it creates, typically one or more makefiles. See Section 7.2 [Setting Output Variables], page 114, for more information on how this is done.

A

abs_builddir 26
abs_srcdir 27
abs_top_builddir 26
abs_top_srcdir 27
ac_empty 95
ALLOCA 54
AWK 43

B

bindir 27
build 282
build_alias 282
build_cpu 282
build_os 282
build_vendor 282
builddir 26

C

CC 81, 85, 97
CFLAGS 24, 81
configure_input 24
CPP 82
CPPFLAGS 24
cross_compiling 110
CXX 86
CXXCPP 86
CXXFLAGS 25, 86

D

datadir 27
datarootdir 27
DEFS 25
docdir 27
dvidir 27

E

ECHO_C 25
ECHO_N 25
ECHO_T 25
EGREP 43
ERL 88, 102, 108
ERLANG_ERTS_VER 98
ERLANG_INSTALL_LIB_DIR 30, 100
ERLANG_INSTALL_LIB_DIR_library 30, 100
ERLANG_LIB_DIR 99
ERLANG_LIB_DIR_library 99
ERLANG_LIB_VER_library 99
ERLANG_ROOT_DIR 98
ERLC 87, 102
ERLCFLAGS 25, 87, 102
exec_prefix 27
EXEEXT 78, 308

F

F77 88
FC 88
FC_MODEXT 95
FC_MODINC 95

FC_MODOUT 96
FCFLAGS 25, 88
FCLIBS 89
FFLAGS 25, 88
FGREP 43
FLIBS 89

G

GETGROUPS_LIBS 56
GETLOADAVG_LIBS 56
GOFLAGS 26
GREP 43

H

host 282
host_alias 282
host_cpu 282
host_os 282
host_vendor 282
htmldir 27

I

includedir 27
infodir 27
INSTALL 43
INSTALL_DATA 43
INSTALL_PROGRAM 43
INSTALL_SCRIPT 43

K

KMEM_GROUP 56

L

LDFLAGS 26
LEX 44
LEX_OUTPUT_ROOT 44
LEXLIB 44
libdir 27
libexecdir 27
LIBOBJDIR 324
LIBOBJS 56, 58, 62, 63, 73
LIBS 26, 310, 313, 317
LN_S 45
localedir 28
localstatedir 28

M

mandir 28
MKDIR_P 44

N

NEED_SETGID 56

O

OBJC 86
OBJCFLAGS 26, 86
OBJCPP 87
OBJCXX 87
OBJCXXCPP 87
OBJCXXFLAGS 26, 87
OBJEXT 78, 311
oldincludedir 28
OPENMP_CFLAGS 79
OPENMP_CXXFLAGS 79
OPENMP_FCFLAGS 79
OPENMP_FFLAGS 79

P

PACKAGE_BUGREPORT 17
PACKAGE_NAME 17
PACKAGE_STRING 17
PACKAGE_TARNAME 17
PACKAGE_URL 18
PACKAGE_VERSION 17
pdfdir 28
POW_LIB 60
prefix 28
program_transform_name 290
psdir 28

R

RANLIB 46

S

sbindir 28
SED 46
SET_MAKE 20
sharedstatedir 28
srcdir 26
subdirs 39
sysconfdir 28

T

target 282
target_alias 282
target_cpu 282
target_os 282
target_vendor 282
tmp 174
top_build_prefix 26
top_builddir 26
top_srcdir 27

X

X_CFLAGS 97
X_EXTRA_LIBS 97
X_LIBS 97

X_PRE_LIBS 97

Y

YACC 46

B.3 Preprocessor Symbol Index

This is an alphabetical list of the C preprocessor symbols that the Autoconf macros define. To work with Autoconf, C source code needs to use these names in `#if` or `#ifdef` directives.

–

__CHAR_UNSIGNED__ 84
__EXTENSIONS__ 98
__PROTOTYPES 85
_ALL_SOURCE 98, 305
_FILE_OFFSET_BITS 97
_GNU_SOURCE 98, 309
_LARGE_FILES 97
_LARGEFILE_SOURCE 56
_MINIX 98, 311
_OPENMP 79
_POSIX_1_SOURCE 98, 311
_POSIX_PTHREAD_SEMANTICS 98
_POSIX_SOURCE 98, 311
_POSIX_VERSION 69
_TANDEM_SOURCE 98

A

ALIGNOF_*type* 79

C

C_ALLOCA 54
C_GETLOADAVG 56
CLOSEDIR_VOID 55
const 83
CXX_NO_MINUS_C_MINUS_O 86

D

DGUX 56
DIRENT 307

F

F77_DUMMY_MAIN 90
F77_FUNC 91
F77_FUNC_ 91
F77_MAIN 91
F77_NO_MINUS_C_MINUS_O 89
FC_DUMMY_MAIN 90
FC_FUNC 91
FC_FUNC_ 91
FC_MAIN 91

FC_NO_MINUS_C_MINUS_O 89
FLEXIBLE_ARRAY_MEMBER 85

G

GETGROUPS_T 75
GETLOADAVG_PRIVILEGED 56
GETPGRP_VOID 57
gid_t 76
GWINSZ_IN_SYS_IOCTL 69

H

HAVE__BOOL 65, 66
HAVE_*aggregate_member* 74
HAVE_ALLOCA_H 54
HAVE_C_BACKSLASH_A 83
HAVE_C_VARARRAYS 85
HAVE_CHOWN 55
HAVE_CONFIG_H 34
HAVE_DECL_STRERROR_R 59
HAVE_DECL_*symbol* 72, 73
HAVE_DECL_TZNAME 73
HAVE_DIRENT_H 65
HAVE_DOPRNT 60
HAVE_FSEEKO 56
HAVE_*function* 61, 63
HAVE_GETGROUPS 56
HAVE_GETMNTENT 57
HAVE_*header* 70, 71
HAVE_INT16_T 75
HAVE_INT32_T 75
HAVE_INT64_T 75
HAVE_INT8_T 75
HAVE_INTMAX_T 75
HAVE_INTPTR_T 75
HAVE_LONG_DOUBLE 75, 305
HAVE_LONG_DOUBLE_WIDER 75
HAVE_LONG_FILE_NAMES 97
HAVE_LONG_LONG_INT 76
HAVE_LSTAT_EMPTY_STRING_BUG 59
HAVE_MALLOC 57
HAVE_MBRTOWC 58
HAVE_MMAP 58
HAVE_NDIR_H 65

HAVE_NLIST_H 56
HAVE_OBSTACK 58
HAVE_REALLOC 59
HAVE_RESOLV_H 66
HAVE_RESTARTABLE_SYSCALLS 314
HAVE_ST_BLKSIZE 314
HAVE_ST_BLOCKS 73
HAVE_ST_RDEV 314
HAVE_STAT_EMPTY_STRING_BUG 59
HAVE_STDBOOL_H 66
HAVE_STRCOLL 59
HAVE_STRERROR_R 59
HAVE_STRFTIME 60
HAVE_STRINGIZE 85
HAVE_STRNLEN 60
HAVE_STRTOLD 60
HAVE_STRUCT_DIRENT_D_INO 73
HAVE_STRUCT_DIRENT_D_TYPE 73
HAVE_STRUCT_STAT_ST_BLKSIZE 314
HAVE_STRUCT_STAT_ST_BLOCKS 73
HAVE_STRUCT_STAT_ST_RDEV 314
HAVE_STRUCT_TM_TM_ZONE 73
HAVE_SYS_DIR_H 65
HAVE_SYS_NDIR_H 65
HAVE_SYS_WAIT_H 68
HAVE_TM_ZONE 73
HAVE_type 77
HAVE_TYPEOF 85
HAVE_TZNAME 73
HAVE_UINT16_T 76
HAVE_UINT32_T 76
HAVE_UINT64_T 76
HAVE_UINT8_T 76
HAVE_UINTMAX_T 77
HAVE_UINTPTR_T 77
HAVE_UNSIGNED_LONG_LONG_INT 77
HAVE_UTIME_NULL 60
HAVE_VFORK_H 55
HAVE_VPRINTF 60
HAVE_WAIT3 308
HAVE_WORKING_FORK 55
HAVE_WORKING_VFORK 55

I

inline 84
INT_16_BITS 309
int16_t 75
int32_t 75
int64_t 75
int8_t 75
intmax_t 75
intptr_t 75

L

LONG_64_BITS 311
LSTAT_FOLLOWS_SLASHED_SYMLINK 57

M

MAJOR_IN_MKDEV 66
MAJOR_IN_SYSMACROS 66
malloc 57
mbstate_t 76
mode_t 76

N

NDEBUG 65
NDIR 307
NEED_MEMORY_H 311
NEED_SETGID 56
NLIST_NAME_UNION 56
NO_MINUS_C_MINUS_O 81

O

off_t 76

P

PACKAGE_BUGREPORT 17
PACKAGE_NAME 17
PACKAGE_STRING 17
PACKAGE_TARNAME 17
PACKAGE_URL 18
PACKAGE_VERSION 17
PARAMS 85
pid_t 76
PROTOTYPES 85

R

realloc 59
restrict 84
RETSIGTYPE 316

S

SELECT_TYPE_ARG1 59
SELECT_TYPE_ARG234 59
SELECT_TYPE_ARG5 59
SETPGRP_VOID 59
SETVBUF_REVERSED 308
size_t 76
SIZEOF_type-or-expr 78
ssize_t 76
STAT_MACROS_BROKEN 66
STDC_HEADERS 67
STRERROR_R_CHAR_P 59
SVR4 56
SYS_SIGLIST_DECLARED 307
SYSDIR 307
SYSNDIR 307

T

TIME_WITH_SYS_TIME 69
TM_IN_SYS_TIME 73
typeof 85

U

uid_t 76
uint16_t 76
uint32_t 76
uint64_t 76
uint8_t 76
uintmax_t 77
uintptr_t 77
UMAX 56
UMAX4_3 56
USG 317

V

variable 113, 114
vfork 55
volatile 84

W

WORDS_BIGENDIAN 83

X

X_DISPLAY_MISSING 97

Y

YYTEXT_POINTER 44

B.4 Cache Variable Index

This is an alphabetical list of documented cache variables used by macros defined in Autoconf. Autoconf macros may use additional cache variables internally. To make the list easier to use, the variables are listed without their preceding 'ac_cv_'.

A

alignof_*type-or-expr* 79

C

c_const 83
c_int16_t 75
c_int32_t 75
c_int64_t 75
c_int8_t 75
c_restrict 84
c_uint16_t 76
c_uint32_t 76
c_uint64_t 76
c_uint8_t 76

F

f77_compiler_gnu 88
f77_dummy_main 90
f77_implicit_none 95
f77_libs 89
f77_main 91
f77_mangling 91
fc_check_bounds 94
fc_compiler_gnu 88
fc_dummy_main 90
fc_fixedform 94
fc_freeform 93
fc_implicit_none 95
fc_libs 89

fc_line_length 94
fc_main 91
fc_mangling 91
fc_module_ext 95
fc_module_flag 95
fc_module_output_flag 96
fc_pp_define 93
fc_pp_srcext_*ext* 92
fc_srcext_*ext* 92
file_*file* 49
func_chown_works 55
func_closedir_void 55
func_fnmatch_gnu 55
func_fnmatch_works 55, 60
func_*function* 61
func_getgroups_works 56
func_getpgrp_void 57
func_lstat_dereferences_slashed_symlink .. 57
func_lstat_empty_string_bug 59
func_malloc_0_nonnull 57
func_mbrtowc 58
func_memcmp_working 58
func_mmap_fixed_mapped 58
func_obstack 58
func_pow 60
func_realloc_0_nonnull 59
func_setpgrp_void 59
func_stat_empty_string_bug 59
func_strcoll_works 59
func_strerror_r_char_p 59
func_strnlen_working 60
func_strtod 60

func_strtold 60
func_utime_null 60
func_working_mktime 58

H

have_decl_*symbol* 71, 72
header_*header-file* 70
header_stdbool_h 65, 66
header_stdc 67
header_sys_wait_h 68
header_time 69

L

lib_error_at_line 55
lib_*library_function* 49

M

member_*aggregate_member* 74
member_struct_stat_st_blocks 73

P

path_install 43
path_mkdir 44
path_SED 46
path_*variable* 48
prog_AWK 43
prog_c_openmp 79
prog_cc_c89 .... 81, 82
prog_cc_c99 82
prog_cc_*compiler_c_o* 81
prog_cc_stdc 82
prog_cxx_openmp 79

prog_EGREP 43
prog_f77_c_o 89
prog_f77_g 88
prog_f77_openmp 79
prog_f77_v 89
prog_fc_c_o 89
prog_fc_g 88
prog_fc_openmp 79
prog_fc_v 89
prog_FGREP 43
prog_GREP 43
prog_LEX 44
prog_*variable* 46
prog_YACC 46

S

search_*function* 50
search_getmntent 57
sizeof_*type-or-expr* 78
sys_posix_termios 97

T

type_getgroups 75
type_long_double 75
type_long_double_wider 75
type_long_long_int 76
type_mbstate_t 76
type_mode_t 76
type_off_t 76
type_pid_t 76
type_size_t 76
type_ssize_t 76
type_*type* 77
type_uid_t 76
type_unsigned_long_long_int 77

B.5 Autoconf Macro Index

This is an alphabetical list of the Autoconf macros. To make the list easier to use, the macros are listed without their preceding 'AC_'.

A

ACT_IFELSE 324
AH_BOTTOM 37
AH_HEADER 34
AH_TEMPLATE 37
AH_TOP 37
AH_VERBATIM 37
AIX 305
ALLOCA 305
ARG_ARRAY 305
ARG_ENABLE 288
ARG_PROGRAM 290
ARG_VAR 116

ARG_WITH 286
AU_ALIAS 184
AU_DEFUN 184
AUTOCONF_VERSION 18

B

BEFORE 183

C

C_BACKSLASH_A 83
C_BIGENDIAN 83

C_CHAR_UNSIGNED.............................. 84
C_CONST...................................... 83
C_CROSS..................................... 305
C_FLEXIBLE_ARRAY_MEMBER...................... 85
C_INLINE..................................... 84
C_LONG_DOUBLE............................... 305
C_PROTOTYPES................................. 85
C_RESTRICT................................... 84
C_STRINGIZE.................................. 85
C_TYPEOF..................................... 85
C_VARARRAYS.................................. 85
C_VOLATILE................................... 84
CACHE_CHECK................................. 117
CACHE_LOAD.................................. 119
CACHE_SAVE.................................. 120
CACHE_VAL................................... 117
CANONICAL_BUILD............................. 282
CANONICAL_HOST.............................. 282
CANONICAL_SYSTEM............................ 306
CANONICAL_TARGET............................ 282
CHAR_UNSIGNED............................... 306
CHECK_ALIGNOF................................ 79
CHECK_DECL................................... 71
CHECK_DECLS.................................. 72
CHECK_DECLS_ONCE............................. 73
CHECK_FILE................................... 49
CHECK_FILES.................................. 49
CHECK_FUNC................................... 61
CHECK_FUNCS.................................. 61
CHECK_FUNCS_ONCE............................. 61
CHECK_HEADER................................. 70
CHECK_HEADER_STDBOOL......................... 65
CHECK_HEADERS................................ 70
CHECK_HEADERS_ONCE........................... 71
CHECK_LIB.................................... 49
CHECK_MEMBER................................. 74
CHECK_MEMBERS................................ 74
CHECK_PROG................................... 46
CHECK_PROGS.................................. 46
CHECK_SIZEOF................................. 78
CHECK_TARGET_TOOL............................ 47
CHECK_TARGET_TOOLS........................... 47
CHECK_TOOL................................... 47
CHECK_TOOLS.................................. 47
CHECK_TYPE............................... 77, 306
CHECK_TYPES.................................. 77
CHECKING.................................... 306
COMPILE_CHECK............................... 307
COMPILE_IFELSE.............................. 108
COMPUTE_INT.................................. 79
CONFIG_AUX_DIR............................... 19
CONFIG_COMMANDS.............................. 37
CONFIG_COMMANDS_POST......................... 38
CONFIG_COMMANDS_PRE.......................... 38
CONFIG_FILES................................. 23
CONFIG_HEADERS............................... 34
CONFIG_ITEMS................................. 21
CONFIG_LIBOBJ_DIR............................ 62

CONFIG_LINKS................................. 38
CONFIG_MACRO_DIR............................. 20
CONFIG_SRCDIR................................ 19
CONFIG_SUBDIRS............................... 39
CONFIG_TESTDIR.............................. 337
CONST....................................... 307
COPYRIGHT.................................... 18
CROSS_CHECK................................. 307
CYGWIN...................................... 307

D

DATAROOTDIR_CHECKED.......................... 31
DECL_SYS_SIGLIST............................ 307
DECL_YYTEXT................................. 307
DEFINE...................................... 113
DEFINE_UNQUOTED............................. 114
DEFUN....................................... 177
DEFUN_ONCE.................................. 183
DIAGNOSE.................................... 179
DIR_HEADER.................................. 307
DISABLE_OPTION_CHECKING..................... 290
DYNIX_SEQ................................... 308

E

EGREP_CPP................................... 108
EGREP_HEADER................................ 108
EMXOS2...................................... 308
ENABLE...................................... 308
ERLANG_CHECK_LIB............................. 99
ERLANG_NEED_ERL.............................. 88
ERLANG_NEED_ERLC............................. 87
ERLANG_PATH_ERL.............................. 88
ERLANG_PATH_ERLC............................. 87
ERLANG_SUBST_ERTS_VER........................ 98
ERLANG_SUBST_INSTALL_LIB_DIR........... 30, 100
ERLANG_SUBST_INSTALL_LIB_SUBDIR....... 30, 100
ERLANG_SUBST_LIB_DIR......................... 99
ERLANG_SUBST_ROOT_DIR........................ 98
ERROR....................................... 308
EXEEXT...................................... 308

F

F77_DUMMY_MAIN............................... 90
F77_FUNC..................................... 92
F77_IMPLICIT_NONE............................ 95
F77_LIBRARY_LDFLAGS.......................... 89
F77_MAIN..................................... 91
F77_WRAPPERS................................. 91
FATAL....................................... 180
FC_CHECK_BOUNDS.............................. 94
FC_DUMMY_MAIN................................ 90
FC_FIXEDFORM................................. 94
FC_FREEFORM.................................. 93
FC_FUNC...................................... 92
FC_IMPLICIT_NONE............................. 95

FC_LIBRARY_LDFLAGS 89
FC_LINE_LENGTH 94
FC_MAIN 91
FC_MODULE_EXTENSION 95
FC_MODULE_FLAG 95
FC_MODULE_OUTPUT_FLAG 96
FC_PP_DEFINE 93
FC_PP_SRCEXT 92
FC_SRCEXT 92
FC_WRAPPERS 91
FIND_X 308
FIND_XTRA 308
FOREACH 308
FUNC_ALLOCA 54
FUNC_CHECK 308
FUNC_CHOWN 55
FUNC_CLOSEDIR_VOID 55
FUNC_ERROR_AT_LINE 55
FUNC_FNMATCH 55
FUNC_FNMATCH_GNU 55
FUNC_FORK 55
FUNC_FSEEKO 56
FUNC_GETGROUPS 56
FUNC_GETLOADAVG 56
FUNC_GETMNTENT 57
FUNC_GETPGRP 57
FUNC_LSTAT 59
FUNC_LSTAT_FOLLOWS_SLASHED_SYMLINK 57
FUNC_MALLOC 57
FUNC_MBRTOWC 58
FUNC_MEMCMP 58
FUNC_MKTIME 58
FUNC_MMAP 58
FUNC_OBSTACK 58
FUNC_REALLOC 59
FUNC_SELECT_ARGTYPES 59
FUNC_SETPGRP 59
FUNC_SETVBUF_REVERSED 308
FUNC_STAT 59
FUNC_STRCOLL 59
FUNC_STRERROR_R 59
FUNC_STRFTIME 60
FUNC_STRNLEN 60
FUNC_STRTOD 60
FUNC_STRTOLD 60
FUNC_UTIME_NULL 60
FUNC_VPRINTF 60
FUNC_WAIT3 308

G

GCC_TRADITIONAL 309
GETGROUPS_T 309
GETLOADAVG 309
GNU_SOURCE 309

H

HAVE_FUNCS 309
HAVE_HEADERS 309
HAVE_LIBRARY 309
HAVE_POUNDBANG 309
HEADER_ASSERT 65
HEADER_CHECK 309
HEADER_DIRENT 65
HEADER_EGREP 309
HEADER_MAJOR 66
HEADER_RESOLV 66
HEADER_STAT 66
HEADER_STDBOOL 66
HEADER_STDC 67
HEADER_SYS_WAIT 68
HEADER_TIME 69
HEADER_TIOCGWINSZ 69
HELP_STRING 309

I

INCLUDES_DEFAULT 42
INIT 17, 309
INLINE 309
INT_16_BITS 309
IRIX_SUN 310
ISC_POSIX 310

L

LANG 101
LANG_ASSERT 102
LANG_C 310
LANG_CALL 106
LANG_CONFTEST 104
LANG_CPLUSPLUS 310
LANG_DEFINES_PROVIDED 104
LANG_FORTRAN77 310
LANG_FUNC_LINK_TRY 106
LANG_POP 102
LANG_PROGRAM 105
LANG_PUSH 102
LANG_RESTORE 310
LANG_SAVE 310
LANG_SOURCE 104
LANG_WERROR 79
LIBOBJ 62
LIBSOURCE 62
LIBSOURCES 62
LINK_FILES 310
LINK_IFELSE 109
LN_S 310
LONG_64_BITS 311
LONG_DOUBLE 311
LONG_FILE_NAMES 311

M

MAJOR_HEADER 311
MEMORY_H 311
MINGW32 311
MINIX 311
MINUS_C_MINUS_O 311
MMAP 311
MODE_T 311
MSG_CHECKING 120
MSG_ERROR 121
MSG_FAILURE 121
MSG_NOTICE 121
MSG_RESULT 121
MSG_WARN 121

O

OBJEXT 311
OBSOLETE 311
OFF_T 312
OPENMP 79
OUTPUT 20, 312
OUTPUT_COMMANDS 312

P

PACKAGE_BUGREPORT 17
PACKAGE_NAME 17
PACKAGE_STRING 17
PACKAGE_TARNAME 17
PACKAGE_URL 18
PACKAGE_VERSION 17
PATH_PROG 48
PATH_PROGS 48
PATH_PROGS_FEATURE_CHECK 48
PATH_TARGET_TOOL 48
PATH_TOOL 49
PATH_X 96
PATH_XTRA 97
PID_T 312
PREFIX 313
PREFIX_DEFAULT 39
PREFIX_PROGRAM 40
PREPROC_IFELSE 107
PREREQ 18
PRESERVE_HELP_ORDER 285
PROG_AWK 43
PROG_CC 81
PROG_CC_C_O 81
PROG_CC_C89 82
PROG_CC_C99 82
PROG_CC_STDC 82
PROG_CPP 82
PROG_CPP_WERROR 82
PROG_CXX 86
PROG_CXX_C_O 86
PROG_CXXCPP 86
PROG_EGREP 43

PROG_F77 88
PROG_F77_C_O 89
PROG_FC 88
PROG_FC_C_O 89
PROG_FGREP 43
PROG_GCC_TRADITIONAL 85
PROG_GREP 43
PROG_INSTALL 43
PROG_LEX 44
PROG_LN_S 45
PROG_MAKE_SET 20
PROG_MKDIR_P 44
PROG_OBJC 86
PROG_OBJCPP 87
PROG_OBJCXX 87
PROG_OBJCXXCPP 87
PROG_RANLIB 46
PROG_SED 46
PROG_YACC 46
PROGRAM_CHECK 313
PROGRAM_EGREP 313
PROGRAM_PATH 313
PROGRAMS_CHECK 313
PROGRAMS_PATH 313

R

REMOTE_TAPE 313
REPLACE_FNMATCH 60
REPLACE_FUNCS 63
REQUIRE 180
REQUIRE_AUX_FILE 19
REQUIRE_CPP 102
RESTARTABLE_SYSCALLS 313
RETSIGTYPE 313
REVISION 19
RSH 313
RUN_IFELSE 109

S

SCO_INTL 313
SEARCH_LIBS 50
SET_MAKE 313
SETVBUF_REVERSED 313
SIZE_T 314
SIZEOF_TYPE 313
ST_BLKSIZE 314
ST_BLOCKS 314
ST_RDEV 314
STAT_MACROS_BROKEN 314
STDC_HEADERS 314
STRCOLL 314
STRUCT_DIRENT_D_INO 73
STRUCT_DIRENT_D_TYPE 73
STRUCT_ST_BLKSIZE 314
STRUCT_ST_BLOCKS 73
STRUCT_ST_RDEV 314

STRUCT_TIMEZONE.............................. 73
STRUCT_TM.................................... 73
SUBST...................................... 115
SUBST_FILE................................. 115
SYS_INTERPRETER............................. 97
SYS_LARGEFILE............................... 97
SYS_LONG_FILE_NAMES......................... 97
SYS_POSIX_TERMIOS........................... 97
SYS_RESTARTABLE_SYSCALLS.................. 314
SYS_SIGLIST_DECLARED...................... 314

T

TEST_CPP................................... 315
TEST_PROGRAM............................... 315
TIME_WITH_SYS_TIME......................... 315
TIMEZONE................................... 315
TRY_ACT.................................... 324
TRY_COMPILE................................ 315
TRY_CPP.................................... 315
TRY_LINK................................... 315
TRY_LINK_FUNC.............................. 316
TRY_RUN.................................... 316
TYPE_GETGROUPS.............................. 75
TYPE_INT16_T................................ 75
TYPE_INT32_T................................ 75
TYPE_INT64_T................................ 75
TYPE_INT8_T................................. 75
TYPE_INTMAX_T............................... 75
TYPE_INTPTR_T............................... 75
TYPE_LONG_DOUBLE............................ 75
TYPE_LONG_DOUBLE_WIDER...................... 75
TYPE_LONG_LONG_INT.......................... 76
TYPE_MBSTATE_T.............................. 76
TYPE_MODE_T................................. 76
TYPE_OFF_T.................................. 76
TYPE_PID_T.................................. 76
TYPE_SIGNAL................................ 316
TYPE_SIZE_T................................. 76
TYPE_SSIZE_T................................ 76

TYPE_UID_T.................................. 76
TYPE_UINT16_T............................... 76
TYPE_UINT32_T............................... 76
TYPE_UINT64_T............................... 76
TYPE_UINT8_T................................ 76
TYPE_UINTMAX_T.............................. 77
TYPE_UINTPTR_T.............................. 77
TYPE_UNSIGNED_LONG_LONG_INT................. 77

U

UID_T..................................... 316
UNISTD_H.................................. 316
USE_SYSTEM_EXTENSIONS....................... 98
USG....................................... 317
UTIME_NULL................................ 317

V

VALIDATE_CACHED_SYSTEM_TUPLE.............. 317
VERBOSE................................... 317
VFORK..................................... 317
VPRINTF................................... 317

W

WAIT3..................................... 317
WARN...................................... 317
WARNING................................... 179
WITH...................................... 317
WORDS_BIGENDIAN........................... 317

X

XENIX_DIR................................. 317

Y

YYTEXT_POINTER............................ 318

B.6 M4 Macro Index

This is an alphabetical list of the M4, M4sugar, and M4sh macros. To make the list easier to use, the macros are listed without their preceding 'm4_' or 'AS_'. The prefix is 'm4_' for all-lowercase macro names and 'AS_' for all-uppercase macro names.

_

__file__................................... 138
__line__................................... 138
__oline__.................................. 138

A

append..................................... 155
append_uniq................................ 155

append_uniq_w.............................. 156
apply...................................... 151
argn....................................... 147
assert..................................... 140

B

bmatch..................................... 144
BOURNE_COMPATIBLE.......................... 173
BOX.. 167

bpatsubst 138
bpatsubsts 144
bregexp 138
builtin 137

C

car 147
case 144
CASE 167
cdr 147
changecom 137
changequote 137
chomp 156
chomp_all 156
cleardivert 143
cmp 159
combine 156
cond 144
copy 138
copy_force 138
count 151
curry 151

D

debugfile 137
debugmode 137
decr 137
default 145
default_nblank 145
default_nblank_quoted 145
default_quoted 145
define 137
define_default 146
defn 138
DIRNAME 167
divert 139
divert_once 143
divert_pop 143
divert_push 143
divert_text 143
divnum 137
dnl 138
do 151
dquote 152
dquote_elt 152
dumpdef 139
dumpdefs 139

E

echo 152
ECHO 167
ECHO_N 168
errprint 137
errprintn 140
escape 157

ESCAPE 168
esyscmd 137
esyscmd_s 139
eval 137
EXECUTABLE_P 168
exit 139
EXIT 168
expand 152

F

fatal 140
flatten 157
for 147
foreach 148
foreach_w 148
format 137

H

HELP_STRING 288

I

if 139
IF 169
ifblank 146
ifdef 137
ifnblank 146
ifndef 146
ifset 146
ifval 146
ifvaln 146
ignore 153
include 139
incr 137
index 137
indir 137
init 144
INIT 173
INIT_GENERATED 173

J

join 157
joinall 157

L

len 137
LINENO_PREPARE 174
list_cmp 159
LITERAL_IF 170
LITERAL_WORD_IF 170
location 141

M

make_list 153
maketemp 139
map 148
map_args 149
map_args_pair 149
map_args_sep 150
map_args_w 150
map_sep 148
mapall 148
mapall_sep 148
max 159
ME_PREPARE 174
MESSAGE_FD 175
MESSAGE_LOG_FD 175
min 159
MKDIR_P 169
mkstemp 139

N

n 146
newline 157
normalize 157

O

ORIGINAL_STDIN_FD 175

P

pattern_allow 164
pattern_forbid 164
popdef 140
pushdef 137

Q

quote 154

R

re_escape 157
rename 138
rename_force 138
reverse 154

S

set_add 160
set_add_all 161
SET_CATFILE 169
set_contains 161
set_contents 161
set_delete 162
set_difference 162
set_dump 161

set_empty 162
set_foreach 162
set_intersection 162
set_list 163
set_listc 163
set_map 163
set_map_sep 163
set_remove 164
set_size 164
SET_STATUS 169
set_union 162
SHELL_SANITIZE 174
shift 137
shift2 150
shift3 150
shiftn 150
sign 159
sinclude 139
split 157
stack_foreach 150
stack_foreach_lifo 150
stack_foreach_sep 151
stack_foreach_sep_lifo 151
strip 157
substr 137
syscmd 137
sysval 137

T

text_box 158
text_wrap 158
TMPDIR 174
tolower 158
toupper 158
TR_CPP 169
TR_SH 169
traceoff 137
traceon 137
translit 137

U

undefine 140
undivert 140
unquote 154
UNSET 170

V

VAR_APPEND 171
VAR_ARITH 171
VAR_COPY 171
VAR_IF 172
VAR_POPDEF 172
VAR_PUSHDEF 172
VAR_SET 173
VAR_SET_IF 173

VAR_TEST_SET 173
version_compare............................. 159
VERSION_COMPARE............................ 170
version_prereq............................. 160

W

warn 141
wrap 140
wrap_lifo.................................... 140

B.7 Autotest Macro Index

This is an alphabetical list of the Autotest macros. To make the list easier to use, the macros are listed without their preceding 'AT_'.

A

ARG_OPTION 330
ARG_OPTION_ARG 331

B

BANNER....................................... 331

C

CAPTURE_FILE................................ 332
CHECK 333
CHECK_EUNIT 334
CHECK_UNQUOTED 333
CLEANUP 332
COLOR_TESTS 331
COPYRIGHT.................................... 330

D

DATA 333

F

FAIL_IF..................................... 332

I

INIT 330

K

KEYWORDS..................................... 332

P

PACKAGE_BUGREPORT 337
PACKAGE_NAME 337
PACKAGE_STRING.............................. 337
PACKAGE_TARNAME 337
PACKAGE_URL 337
PACKAGE_VERSION............................. 337

S

SETUP 331
SKIP_IF...................................... 332

T

TESTED 331

X

XFAIL_IF..................................... 332

B.8 Program and Function Index

This is an alphabetical list of the programs and functions whose portability is discussed in this document.

!

!... 220

.

.... 220

/

/usr/bin/ksh on Solaris..................... 190

/usr/dt/bin/dtksh on Solaris 190
/usr/xpg4/bin/sh on Solaris 190

{

{...}.. 221

A

alloca....................................... 54

'alloca.h'....................................... 54
'assert.h'....................................... 65
awk 235

B

basename 237
break 221

C

case 221
cat 237
cc... 237
cd... 223
chgrp 237
chmod 237
chown 55
chown 237
closedir 55
cmp 238
cp... 238
'ctype.h'....................................... 67

D

date 239
diff 239
'dirent.h'...................................... 65
dirname 239

E

echo 223
egrep 239
error_at_line 55
eval 224
exec 224
exit 50
exit 225
export 226
expr 239, 240
expr ('|') 240

F

false 226
fgrep 241
find 241
'float.h'...................................... 67
fnmatch 55, 60
'fnmatch.h' 60
for 226
fork 55
free 51
fseeko 56
ftello 56

G

getgroups 56
getloadavg 56
getmntent 57
getpgid 57
getpgrp 57
grep 242

I

if.. 227
'inttypes.h'.............................. 63, 74
isinf 51
isnan 51

J

join 243

K

'ksh' 190
'ksh88' 190
'ksh93' 190

L

'linux/irda.h' 63
'linux/random.h'............................... 63
ln.. 243
ls.. 243
lstat....................................... 57, 59

M

make 253
malloc...................................... 51, 57
mbrtowc 58
memcmp 58
mkdir 243
mkfifo 244
mknod 244
mktemp 244
mktime 58
mmap 58
mv.. 245

N

'ndir.h' 65
'net/if.h' 63
'netinet/if_ether.h'........................... 64
'nlist.h'...................................... 56

O

od.. 245

P

'pdksh' 191
printf 228
putenv 52
pwd 228

R

read 228
realloc 52, 59
'resolv.h' 66
rm 245
rmdir 245

S

sed 245
sed ('t') 249
select 59
set 229
setpgrp 59
setvbuf 308
shift 231
sigaction 52
signal 52
'signal.h' 316
sleep 250
snprintf 52
sort 250
source 231
sprintf 52
sscanf 52
stat 59
'stdarg.h' 67
'stdbool.h' 65, 66
'stdint.h' 63, 74
'stdlib.h' 64, 67, 74
strcoll 59
strerror_r 52, 59
strftime 60
'string.h' 67
'strings.h' 67
strnlen 52, 60
strtod 60
strtold 60
'sys/dir.h' 65
'sys/ioctl.h' 69
'sys/mkdev.h' 66
'sys/mount.h' 64

'sys/ndir.h' 65
'sys/ptem.h' 64
'sys/socket.h' 64
'sys/stat.h' 66
'sys/sysmacros.h' 66
'sys/time.h' 69, 73
'sys/types.h' 74
'sys/ucred.h' 64
'sys/wait.h' 68
sysconf 53

T

tar 250
'termios.h' 69
test 231
'time.h' 69, 73
touch 250
tr 250
trap 233
true 234

U

'unistd.h' 69
unlink 53
unset 234
unsetenv 53
utime 60

V

va_copy 53
va_list 53
vfork 55
'vfork.h' 55
vprintf 60
vsnprintf 52
vsprintf 52, 60

W

wait 235
wait3 308
'wchar.h' 76

X

'X11/extensions/scrnsaver.h' 64

B.9 Concept Index

This is an alphabetical list of the files, tools, and concepts introduced in this document.

''

"$@" 202

$

$((expression)) 209

$(*commands*) 208
$<, explicit rules, and VPATH 262
${#*var*} 207
${*var*##*word*} 207
${*var*#*word*} 207
${*var*%%*word*} 207
${*var*%*word*} 207
${*var*+*value*} 203
${*var*-*value*} 203
${*var*:-*value*} 203
${*var*=*expanded-value*} 206
${*var*=*literal*} 206
${*var*=*value*} 204

@

'@%:@' 128
'@&t@' 128
'@:>@' 128
'@:}@' 128
'@<:@' 128
'@{:@' 128
'@S|@' 128

^

^ quoting 209

_

_m4_divert_diversion 321

‘

‘*commands*‘ 207

6

64-bit libraries 293

A

abs_builddir 26
abs_srcdir 27
abs_top_builddir 26
abs_top_srcdir 27
absolute file names, detect 199
ac_objext 62
ac_path_*variable* 48
ac_path_*variable*_found 48
ac_srcdir 22
ac_top_build_prefix 22
ac_top_srcdir 22
'acconfig.h' 304
'aclocal.m4' 5
Ash 190
at_arg_*option* 330, 331
at_optarg 330, 331

at_optarg_*option* 330
at_status 333
autoconf 11
Autoconf upgrading 318, 320
Autoconf version 18
autoheader 35
Autoheader macros 36
autom4te debugging tips 164
Autom4te Library 135
'autom4te.cache' 134
'autom4te.cfg' 136
Automake 3
Automatic remaking 32
automatic rule rewriting and VPATH 263
autopoint 14
autoreconf 13
autoscan 10
Autotest 327
AUTOTEST_PATH 335
autoupdate 304

B

Back trace 12, 133
balancing parentheses 129
Bash 190
Bash 2.05 and later 190
bindir 27
Bootstrap 341
BSD make and 'obj/' 261
buffer overruns 276
Build directories 31
builddir 26

C

C function portability 50
C types 74
Cache 117
Cache variable 118
Cache, enabling 299
Canonical system type 282
carriage return, deleting 250
CFLAGS 24
changequote 127
Coding style 184
Command Substitution 207
command-line, macros set on 261
Commands for configuration 37
Comments in 'Makefile' macros 260
Comments in 'Makefile' rules 259
Common autoconf behavior 41
Compilers 78
composing variable names 172
'config.h' 33
'config.h.bot' 304
'config.h.in' 34
'config.h.top' 304

config.site 292
config.status 301
config.sub 282
CONFIG_COMMANDS 303
CONFIG_FILES 303
CONFIG_HEADERS 303
CONFIG_LINKS 303
CONFIG_SHELL 302
CONFIG_STATUS 302
Configuration actions 21
Configuration commands 37
Configuration file creation 23
Configuration Header 33
Configuration Header Template 34
Configuration links 38
configure 5, 295
Configure subdirectories 38
'configure.ac' 5
'configure.in' 5
configure_input 24
Copyright Notice 18, 330
CPPFLAGS 24
Creating configuration files 23
Creating temporary files 244
Cross compilation 322
CXXFLAGS 25

D

Darwin 111
Data structure, set 160
datadir 27
datarootdir 27
'datarootdir' 30
debugging tips 164
Declaration, checking 71
Default includes 41
DEFS 25
deleting carriage return 250
Dependencies between macros 180
descriptors 175
Descriptors 193
Directories, build 31
Directories, installation 27
division, integer 276
dnl 177, 185
docdir 27
double-colon rules and VPATH 262
dvidir 27

E

ECHO_C 25
ECHO_N 25
ECHO_T 25
Endianness 83
environment, macros set from 261
Erlang 87

Erlang, Library, checking 98
ERLANG_INSTALL_LIB_DIR 30
ERLANG_INSTALL_LIB_DIR_library 30
ERLCFLAGS 25
exec_prefix 27
exiting portably 279
expanded before required 346
explicit rules, $<, and VPATH 262
External software 285

F

F77 88
FCFLAGS 25
FFLAGS 25
FHS 293
file descriptors 175
File descriptors 193
File system conventions 199
File, checking 49
Filesystem Hierarchy Standard 293
floating point 279
Forbidden patterns 164
Fortran 88
Function, checking 53

G

Gettext 14
GNU build system 3
Gnulib 3
Go 96
GOFLAGS 26

H

Header portability 63
Header templates 34
Header, checking 63
Help strings 288
Here-documents 192
History of autoconf 351
htmldir 27

I

ifnames 11
Imake 342
includedir 27
Includes, default 41
indirection, variable name 170
infodir 27
input 175
Install prefix 39
Installation directories 27
Instantiation 20
integer overflow 272, 275
Introduction 1

invoking the shell............................. 191

K

Korn shell.................................... 190
Ksh 190

L

Language...................................... 101
Large file support............................ 97
LDFLAGS 26
LFS... 97
'lib64'....................................... 293
libdir.. 27
libexecdir.................................... 27
Library, checking 49
LIBS 26
Libtool 4
License....................................... 341
Limitations of make.......................... 253
Limitations of shell builtins................ 220
Limitations of usual tools................... 235
Links... 38
Links for configuration...................... 38
Listing directories 243
localedir..................................... 28
localstatedir................................. 28
loop induction................................ 274
low-level output 175

M

M4.. 123
M4 quotation................................. 123
M4sugar 137
m4sugar debugging tips....................... 164
Macro invocation stack 12, 133
Macros, called once.......................... 183
Macros, obsoleting........................... 184
Macros, ordering 183
Macros, prerequisites 180
make -k 262
make and MAKEFLAGS 256
make and SHELL 256
'Makefile' macros and comments............. 260
'Makefile' macros and whitespace........... 261
'Makefile' rules and comments 259
'Makefile' rules and newlines............... 260
Makefile substitutions 23
MAKEFLAGS and make........................... 256
Making directories........................... 243
mandir.. 28
Messages, from autoconf 179
Messages, from configure 120
Messages, from M4sugar 140
Moving open files............................ 245

N

newline, deleting 250
Newlines in 'Makefile' rules................. 260
Notices in configure 18
null pointers................................. 276

O

'obj/', subdirectory 261
OBJCFLAGS..................................... 26
OBJCXXFLAGS 26
Obsolete constructs.......................... 303
Obsoleting macros............................ 184
obstack....................................... 58
oldincludedir 28
One-shot macros 183
Options, package 287
Options, Package 289
Ordering macros.............................. 183
Output variables...................... 23, 114
Output variables, special characters in 116
output, low-level 175
Outputting files 20
overflow, signed integer 272, 275

P

Package options 287
'package.m4'.................................. 337
Parallel make 257
parentheses, balancing....................... 129
Patterns, forbidden.......................... 164
pdfdir 28
polymorphic variable name 170
portability 271
Portability of C functions................... 50
Portability of headers 63
Portable C and C++ programming 271
Portable shell programming................... 189
positional parameters........................ 203
Posix termios headers........................ 97
Precious Variable............................ 115
prefix 28
Prefix for install........................... 39
preprocessor arithmetic...................... 276
Preprocessors................................ 78
prerequisite directories and VPATH.......... 266
Prerequisite macros.......................... 180
Program names, transforming.................. 290
Programs, checking 43
psdir 28

Q

QNX 4.25..................................... 111
quadrigraphs................................. 128
quotation 7, 123

R

Remaking automatically 32
Revision 19
Rule, Single Suffix Inference 269

S

sbindir 28
Separated Dependencies 269
set -b 230
set -e 229
set -m 230
set -n 231
Set manipulation 160
sharedstatedir 28
SHELL and make 256
Shell assignments 209
Shell builtins 220
Shell file descriptors 193
Shell Functions 218
Shell here-documents 192
shell invocation 191
Shell parentheses 210
Shell pattern matching 201
Shell slashes 210
Shell substitutions 201
Shell variables 211
Shellology 190
Signal handling in the shell 196
Signals, shells and 196
signed integer overflow 272, 275
Single Suffix Inference Rule 269
Site defaults 292
Site details 290
Special shell variables 211
srcdir 22, 26
standard input 175
Standard symbols 41
Structure, checking 73
Subdirectory configure 38
Substitutions in makefiles 23
Symbolic links 243
sysconfdir 28
System type 281, 282
Systemology 111

T

Target triplet 281
termios Posix headers 97

U

test group 327
testsuite 327, 335
timestamp resolution 238, 250, 269
tmp 22
top_build_prefix 26
top_builddir 26
top_srcdir 27
Transforming program names 290
Tru64 111
Types 74

U

unbalanced parentheses, managing 129
undefined macro 321
Unix version 7 111
Unordered set manipulation 160
Upgrading autoconf 318, 320

V

V7 111
variable name indirection 170
variable names, composing 172
Variable, Precious 115
variables and VPATH 262
Version 18
version, Autoconf 18
volatile objects 277
VPATH 262
VPATH and automatic rule rewriting 263
VPATH and double-colon rules 262
VPATH and prerequisite directories 266
VPATH and variables 262
VPATH, explicit rules, and $< 262
VPATH, resolving target pathnames 266

W

whitespace in command-line macros 261
whitespace in 'Makefile' macros 261
wraparound arithmetic 272, 275

X

X Window System 96

Z

Zsh 191